United States
Technology Export Control

United States
Technology Export Control

An Assessment

Douglas E. McDaniel

Westport, Connecticut
London

Library of Congress Cataloging-in-Publication Data

McDaniel, Douglas E.
    United States technology export control : an assessment / Douglas
E. McDaniel.
        p. cm.
    Includes bibliographical references and index.
    ISBN 0-275-94164-7 (alk. paper)
    1. Export controls—United States.   2. Technology transfer—
Government policy—United States.   3. United States—National
security.   4. Export controls—International cooperation.
5. National security—International cooperation.   6. East-West trade
(1945-) I. Title.
HF1414.5.M33   1993
382'.4562'000973—dc20   91-45608

British Library Cataloguing in Publication Data is available.

Library of Congress Catalog Card Number: 91-45608
ISBN: 0-275-94164-7

First published in 1993

Praeger Publishers, 88 Post Road West, Westport, CT 06881
An imprint of Greenwood Publishing Group, Inc.

Printed in the United States of America

The paper used in this book complies with the
Permanent Paper Standard issued by the National
Information Standards Organization (Z39.48-1984).

10 9 8 7 6 5 4 3 2 1

To my parents and Ulla and Alex

Contents

Figures

Introduction

For more than forty years, the United States and its allies in Europe and Asia engaged in a coordinated effort to restrict technology that had actual or potential military applications from being acquired by the Soviet Union and its allied states. With the disintegration of the Soviet Union and the Warsaw Pact, that Cold War strategic threat is now much reduced, if not entirely gone. But potential instability in the former U.S.S.R. and the proliferation of sophisticated conventional weapons, weapons of mass destruction, and related technology to unstable regions and hostile regimes in the Middle East and Asia suggests that export controls should remain an important part of U.S. national security policy. However, export controls have always engendered controversy. This study examines factors contributing to such controversy and assesses the costs and benefits to the United States of a policy that attempts to control the export of high technology. The study's objective is to address the question: To what degree and how have export controls affected significant U.S. economic and national security interests? This issue is assessed and evaluated through short studies of possible spillovers affecting key areas of U.S. foreign, defense, and economic policy.

Of course, no assessment of a major policy issue--whether it concerns export controls, farm subsidies, or strategic arms control--can be wholly "objective" or mathematically "precise." That is, even assuming agreement on the "facts," reasonable analysts will differ as to their meaning. What can be done, and is done here, is to clearly set forth the pertinent information and the author's assumptions, being as exact as the subject matter allows and--when possible and appropriate--cautiously employing quantitative evaluative indices. Examination, testing, and evaluation of the effectiveness of U.S. high-technology export controls in achieving their objectives, the significance of these controls for U.S. commercial interests and for North Atlantic Treaty Organization technological cooperation, and the impact of U.S. and Western European differences on the Alliance's cohesion lie at the heart of this study. High-technology export control issues have blossomed in recent years, periodically generating heated debate, domestically and among allies.[1] While there are numerous short studies and reports detailing various problems in this area, a more comprehensive treatment and synthesis of the subject is clearly in order.

No study could cover fully all aspects of the problems raised by assessment of high-technology export controls. Selected yet crucial issues are examined here. The study of these issues develops the background and context for the research and measurement of test criteria. The test criteria include economic and strategic/security evaluations, discussed in Chapters 3 and 4 and briefly previewed below.

This study begins with a brief overview of the West's multilateral strategic embargo regime--COCOM (Coordinating Committee for Multilateral Export Controls).[2] Recent developments and controversies affecting COCOM, as well as its early history, are presented and analyzed. The historical background sets the stage for the subsequent evaluative chapters.

The COCOM regime's early emphasis on total or near-total embargo was quickly abandoned as Cold War tensions eased and the allies quarreled over the scope of controls. Today, controls are pursued as a means of protecting the West's technological and qualitative superiority. But recently, the United States has faced the dilemma of sharing know-how with allies while fearing this information may get into the hands of hostile powers. Prior to the collapse of the Soviet Union, while all parties agreed in principle that certain technologies should be kept out of Soviet hands, diverging goals and interests caused disparate export control policies and practices. Radical and rapid changes in East-West relations, uncertainty over the ultimate outcome of the revolutionary developments which swept communism from power in Eastern Europe and the U.S.S.R., and growing concern over new threats to international security arising in the Middle East and Asia have reignited the debate over the future and efficacy of multilateral export controls. Owing to deep domestic divisions on this question, the U.S. government's case is viewed by European nations as poorly defined and implemented. Washington appears to have a public policy that allows grudging compromise within COCOM. But paralleling this is a tougher, less publicized, even coercive policy utilizing domestic laws and economic leverage to pressure compliance by allies and other advanced non-COCOM exporters. Such unilateral U.S. foreign policy upsets the Alliance's multilateral efforts. The intersection of domestic, foreign, and defense policy is a constant and important component of the high-technology export control issue.

Chapter 2 presents contending views and policies within the Atlantic Alliance as they pertained to both embargoing the former U.S.S.R. and its allies and trading with Moscow and Eastern Europe. The principal U.S. institutional and individual actors and their roles are discussed, as are selected contentious substantive issues.

In the United States, both within government and among the general public, there are three basic views. A small but influential group advocates an economic warfare approach similar to U.S. policy during the 1950s and most of the 1960s. Such sentiments enjoyed a renaissance within the Reagan administration. This group was highly mistrustful of Soviet intentions. It was and remains very wary of economic exchanges with the East for fear that they could strengthen military capabilities of a resurgent and possibly hostile Russia as well as those of the other former Soviet republics.

Other Americans object to the severity of existing policies and urge more East-West trade. To some degree, they reflect the earlier detente-era optimism (still the mainstream view among most Europeans) that trade can moderate Russian actions and lessen tensions. Moreover, some politicians and business interests argue that antiquated and burdensome regulations are damaging U.S. export performance. Finally, a third view generally accepts existing policy as reflecting the best balance of national interests.

Export control legislation has reflected the goal of expanded trade with the East since passage of the 1969 Export Administration Act (EAA). With the EAA, and subsequent amendments thereof, the United States tried to refine controls while balancing national security with commercial interests. The 1979 EAA and 1985 Export Administration Act amendments have continued this effort.[3] However, legislative efforts to reform export controls and ease their burden on business have been partly nullified or simply ignored by the Executive. Ambivalence and concern in Congress over the possibility of weakening national security as well as persistent bureaucratic delay in complying with legal mandates have thwarted any significant overhaul of export controls. Contributing to the debate, and significantly influencing current U.S. policy, was the 1976 Bucy Report. That report stressed the importance of controlling revolutionary rather than evolutionary technology and protecting manufacturing know-how and processes rather than end products.[4] The report's call for more decontrol of end-products together with greater restriction on "know-how" and "processes" remain a leitmotif for many analysts and policymakers. The latter recommendation was implemented in the Militarily Critical Technologies List,[5] which sparked a vigorous debate domestically and with COCOM allies.

In Europe, where trade is a much more important component of the economy, East-West trade has added significance. Chapter 2 presents the prevailing European view of trade with the East and examines independent variables that shape European attitudes and policies. Historical and geopolitical links, such as West Germany's earlier interest in maintaining strong ties with its communist East German neighbor and unified Germany's interest in stable and prosperous states in Eastern Europe, are important, but they may conflict with security interests. Domestic political and economic interests and factors of course also play a role. Add to this European fears of technological obsolescence and growing dependence on U.S. and Japanese technology. Further compounding distrust and mistrust are occasional heavy-handed U.S. rhetoric and extraterritorial measures. Mutual suspicions appear to stimulate policy divergence on both sides of the Atlantic.

One must keep in mind "deeper" interests or sources of concern stemming from historical and domestic factors. That is, no matter how heated the rhetoric, it is prudent to ask how real the intra-Alliance conflict really is. Put another way, does it not seem credible to expect some inevitable degree of acrimony when important, sometimes clashing national interests are at stake? That does not necessarily mean the sometimes tenuous Alliance consensus on export controls is crumbling. History suggests that some range of divergent opinions and policies is apparently both acceptable and sustainable. Yet periodic hand-wringing over the Alliance's political cohesion and the spillover from disagreements on export control policy are of continuing concern, since the *accumulated* strains may damage the allies' national and mutual security interests.

A final section in Chapter 2 briefly examines U.S. and European export control law and regulatory structures. By comparing and contrasting the most significant legal and administrative features, the study reveals legal barriers, loopholes, and regulations that reflect U.S. and allied policy priorities. For instance, the issue of extraterritorial applications of U.S. law is viewed as an infringement of sovereignty by the Europeans.[6] American business is also unhappy with what it regards as a burdensome U.S. regulatory environment.[7] Compounding the problem is a yawning U.S. trade deficit. Export competitiveness has become a buzz-word among U.S. policymakers with slow realization that the previously ignored foreign trade sector will increasingly be of vital importance to national economic health.

Chapters 3 and 4 assess the study's central thesis: that strategic export controls succeeded in slowing, if not altogether preventing, the U.S.S.R. and its allies from obtaining sensitive dual-use technology and that controls *per se* have not been an undue burden on U.S. exporters or a significant cause of lagging export competitiveness in high technology industries. The costs and benefits of a U.S. policy that attempts to control the export of high technology are evaluated. The relative damage to U.S. interests are first examined in a security context, then in an economic context.

Chapter 3 is an evaluative chapter that begins with an assessment of the relative success or failure of U.S. policy to deny the former Soviet bloc actual or potentially valuable military assets. The West's embargo has never been total. Soviet technological capabilities, while lagging behind the West, scored notable breakthroughs. Given the priority previously enjoyed by Soviet military research and development and its relative success, one can evaluate this variable with the goal of suggesting whether at some point the Western embargo has or will become useless. In addition, with inventive and production capabilities becoming globalized, the West's, particularly the U.S. defense industries', domination of high-technology markets will gradually lessen. At present, however, Western European and U.S. market shares remain formidable. Of even more acute concern is the growth of innovative dual-use technological development outside the defense sector. Neutral European and Asian countries which are not formally a part of the COCOM regime were and continue to be sources of dual-use high technology available to the Commonwealth republics and other states which pose a real or potential threat to national security. Foreign availability of similar technology puts added pressure on government and business to license and sell before a market is lost to the competition. This undermines traditional control mechanisms and is an outright challenge to U.S. high-technology predominance. These factors are significant because policymakers make judgments on the embargo's efficacy. If the capabilities of several of the republics which constituted the former U.S.S.R. and which retain significant military resources, continue to increase, pressure to liberalize the embargo is likely to grow. This will also be true for other potentially threatening states such as Iraq and North Korea. As with any boycott, the target nation can usually find alternative sources or develop indigenous capacity that undermines the boycott. Mutual suspicions among boycott participants can also be utilized by the target nation to play off members against each other the obtain desired goods.

Finally, Chapter 3 addresses the implications of restrictions on scientific information, communication, and exchanges. In the United States, an extensive effort aimed at plugging the loss of potentially sensitive scientific communication and technical know-how has been pursued. This raises fundamental questions of how far an open society must or should go in protecting the national security.[8] Why such restrictions are necessary and what the potential drawbacks may be in terms of, for example, threats to traditional civil liberties and raising obstacles to interchange of data and knowhow are studied. Critics contend that the distinct advantage flowing from the U.S. tradition of scientific openness is endangered. Consequently, economic competitiveness and innovation could be constrained, spilling over to affect national security since considerable research on dual-use technologies is done on campuses and in private labs. What can brief summaries of case studies, for example, the U.S. crackdown on international scientific exchanges, tell us? How can the costs/benefits of the existing U.S. policy be measured? In terms of the West's welfare and security, how much of an effect do restrictions have on the free flow of goods and knowledge?

In Chapter 4, damage to U.S. overseas business and export performance is initially assessed by examining the assertion that U.S. business has done poorly abroad because of restrictions. The study then looks at the possible loss of U.S. markets and its effect on export performance. Finally, selected defense-related industries and products are examined to determine whether controls have impeded U.S. export opportunities. Obstacles and hindrances to U.S.-European business cooperation in defense-related, high-technology industries are examined.

Chapter 5 concludes the study by exploring and addressing several basic questions: What are the options the United States might consider? Have reforms eased tensions among the allies? If not, what can be done? Should the present export control regime be retained, reformed, or abolished? What are the implications for export control policy of the sudden upheaval in Eastern Europe, the decline and end of Soviet hegemony over the region, of Gorbachev's and Yeltsin's apparently conciliatory foreign policy, and of domestic economic reform in the former Soviet Union? Possible alternative scenarios are sketched and their associated implications are discussed.

Final general conclusions and recommendations are briefly summarized here and more fully elaborated in Chapter 5. First, U.S. strategic export control policy appears to have succeeded in its basic goal of *delaying* Soviet advances in dual-use high technology. However, it is increasingly unlikely that the United States can, by itself, hope to prevent technology transfers to the Commonwealth and other unstable regions and threatening states without close cooperation by its COCOM allies. The rapid and globalized diffusion of technology and the revolutionary pace of innovation in high-technology fields challenge, and will continue to challenge, the existing COCOM regime. The United States invested considerable effort in revitalizing COCOM during the 1980s and this effort appears to have met with some success. But the relative decline in U.S. technological leadership combined with apparently drastic changes in the geopolitical and foreign policy rationales and circumstances informing export control policy imply that U.S. policy must be reevaluated as it was in the late 1970s and early 1980s. Slow adaptation to new realities could undermine COCOM's effectiveness, although COCOM is unlikely to dissolve despite periodic warnings of its demise, given general agreement that some strategic controls are necessary. As COCOM's driving force, the United States must not permit rapid decontrol of technologies or a loosening of enforcement until such time as technology espionage and residual threat to U.S. and other Western states' interests finally evaporate. However, the United States must be careful not to overlook or be perceived to block the allies' security and economic interest in a stable Eastern Europe and Commonwealth of Independent States, a condition which for them is achievable through expanding trade ties. Specific recommendations for improving U.S. COCOM policy are detailed in Chapter 5.

The study concludes that, based on admittedly sketchy macroeconomic and microeconomic data, high-technology trade and market share data, and government data on licensing patterns and the regulatory process, the economic cost of controls is not excessive. Much contrary anecdotal evidence is available from the private sector concerning the damage controls cause U.S. high-technology producers. However, unless concrete and quantifiable data showing an exclusive and causal link between controls and lost sales over a sustained period is publicly released by exporters, their claims remain suspect. The study recommends that exporters undertake such studies and release their findings for independent evaluation. If, as seems apparent from the available evidence and interviews, slow improvement in the regulatory process is gradually easing constraints on exporters, this is no reason for government or private watchdogs to lessen their scrutiny. Recommendations for more regular and in-depth reporting on agency efficiency and compliance with the law are made. Combined with better privately generated data, more informed judgments concerning the efficacy and costs of controls might be possible.

While the reforms undertaken by Presidents Gorbachev and Yeltsin could eventually enhance Russian military capabilities, and therefore there continues to be a rationale for maintaining relatively tougher controls on Commonwealth trade, the case for decontrolling trade with Eastern Europe is compelling. If properly safeguarded, high technology could help cement lasting political ties among Eastern Europe, Western Europe, and the United States. In addition, given the facts that controls *per se* have apparently been a relatively minimal burden on exporters, that the Commonwealth is actively seeking high technology to further its modernization efforts, and given past evidence of poor Soviet absorption and adaptation of technology, which is in any case increasingly difficult to reverse-engineer, the United States can be flexible in its evolving policy. That is, assuming that strategic risks have been weighed, the longer the presumed material and welfare benefits accrue to the Commonwealth's population from East-West trade, the more the prospects of the republics risking those ties decreases. It is even arguable that an infusion of Western aid could be decisive in preventing looming economic and social chaos. Thus, it is in the Western interest to prevent an already serious problem from deteriorating further with the attendant prospects of growing suffering in the Commonwealth and/or the possible reemergence of hostile anti-Western leaders. Yet should U.S.-Soviet relations again worsen, as the historical pattern would suggest is at least possible, increased restrictions on technology transfers to the Commonwealth in coordination with the allies would have little negative impact on U.S. exporters. Furthermore, besides the possibility of enhancing the prospects for Soviet reform and overcoming historic Russian and/or Soviet animosity toward the West, trade could also be strategically beneficial to the United States. by helping secure steady flows of critical strategic minerals and energy supplies from the Commonwealth while exploi ng an underdeveloped and potentially vast market for U.S. high-technology exports facing increasing global competition.

Strategic export control policy has been a sometimes hot, sometimes lukewarm topic since 1945, both domestically and within the Alliance. The issue has received scholarly attention but requires constant updating. The acute role high-technology development and trade play in the framework of U.S. national security policy will only grow in the future. Balancing the twin objectives of protecting the nation's security and promoting economic welfare and performance, conditions which assume a key role in any calculus of national power, is never easy. But when a nation risks its future security in the interests of a policy rooted in an age when global conditions and politics were much different, the policy is bankrupt and becomes a burden rather than an asset.

Support for part of the study reported in this volume was provided by a Fulbright Grant. The author gratefully acknowledges assistance provided by the Royal Institute of International Affairs.

NOTES

1. Controversy among Alliance partners over this issue has been featured during most of the postwar era. See Gunnar Adler-Karlsson, *Western Economic Warfare, 1947-1967* (Stockholm: Almqvist and Wiksell, 1968), probably the earliest comprehensive study of the West's embargo policy against the Soviet bloc.

2. COCOM is also known as simply "The Coordinating Committee" and by other variations. In this study, COCOM will refer to "Coordinating Committee for Multilateral Export Controls."

3. An overview of the 1969 EAA, subsequent amended versions, and the 1979 EAA are found in U.S. Congress, Office of Technology Assessment, *Technology and East-West Trade* (Washington, DC: United States Government Printing Office, November 1979), pp. 115-26. For the complete text of the 1979 EAA, see Public Law 92-72, 93 Stat. 503, approved 29 September 1979, as amended; rpt. in *Legislation on Foreign Relations Through 1985*, ed. U.S. Congress, Committee on Foreign Affairs and Committee on Foreign Relations (Washington, DC: United States Government Printing Office, 1986), II, pp. 398-470. On the 1985 amendments, see *Export Administration Act Amendments of 1985*, Public Law 99-64, 99 Stat. 120, approved 12 July 1985; rpt. in *Legislation of Foreign Relations Through 1985*, II, pp. 458-61.

4. U.S. Department of Defense, Office of the Director of Defense Research and Engineering, Defense Science Board Task Force on Export of U.S. Technology, *An Analysis of Export Control of U.S. Technology--A DOD Perspective* (Washington, DC: 4 February 1976).

5. U.S. Department of Defense, Office of the Under Secretary of Defense Acquisition, *The Militarily Critical Technologies List* (Washington, DC, October 1986), unclassified version.

6. European Parliament, *Resolution Adopted 21.2.86 on Technology Transfer* (PE 103.484), and Alman Metten, "Report Drawn Up on Behalf of the Committee on Energy, Research and Technology on Technology Transfer," European Parliament, *Report*, no. A2-99/85 (30 September 1985).

7. National Academy of Sciences, *Balancing the National Interest* (Washington, D.C.: National Academy Press, 1987); James K. Gordon, "Export Controls Hampering Sale of U.S. High Technology Products," *Aviation Week and Space Technology*, 15 December 1986, p. 88; and Frank E. Samuel Jr., "Ease Up on Export Controls," *Washington Post*, 17 November 1986, section A, p. 13, columns 3-5.

8. See National Academy of Sciences, *Scientific Communication and National Security: A Report Prepared by the Panel on Scientific Communication and National Security* (Washington, DC: National Academy Press, 1982); and U.S. Congress, House, Committee on Science and Technology, Subcommittees on Science, Research and Technology and on Investigations and Oversight, *Scientific Communications and National Security*, hearing, 98th Congress, 2nd session, 24 May 1984 (Washington, DC: United States Government Printing Office, 1984).

Abbreviations

AAAS	American Association for the Advancement of Science
AEN	Administrative Exception Note
CAD/CAM	computer-aided design/computer-aided manufacturing
CCL	Commodity Control List
CIA	Central Intelligence Agency
COCOM	Coordinating Committee for Multilateral Export Controls
COMECON	Council for Mutual Economic Assistance
DAA	Defense Department Authorization Act
DIA	Defense Intelligence Agency
DL	Distribution License
DOC	Department of Commerce

DOD	Department of Defense
DTI	Department of Trade and Industry
EAA	Export Administration Act
EAAA	Export Administration Amendments Act
EAR	Export Administration Regulations
E.C.	European Community
ECA	Export Control Act
EDC	European Defense Community
FW	Free World
FY	fiscal year
GAO	General Accounting Office
GNP	Gross National Product
GRU	Chief Directorate of Military Intelligence (U.S.S.R.-- Soviet Red Army military intelligence)
KGB	Committee for State Security (U.S.S.R.)
LPT	license processing time
MoD	Ministry of Defence
NAS	National Academy of Sciences
NASA	National Aeronautics and Space Administration
NATO	North Atlantic Treaty Organization
NBS	National Bureau of Standards

NICs	Newly Industrializing Countries
NMBTA	National Machine Tool Builders Association
NSA	National Security Agency
NSC	National Security Council
NSDD	National Security Decision Directive
OECD	Organization for Economic Cooperation and Development
OEE	Office of Export Enforcement
OEEC	Organization for European Economic Cooperation
OFA	Office of Foreign Availability
PC	personal computer
R+D	research and development
RWA	returned without action
SAMA	Scientific Apparatus Makers Association
SIG-TT	Senior Interagency Group on Technology Transfer
SXWP	Strategic Exports Working Party

United States
Technology Export Control

1

The West's Embargo of the Soviet Bloc: An Overview

This chapter provides a historical overview and assessment of the Western organization that coordinates strategic East-West trade controls--the Coordinating Committee for Multilateral Export Controls (COCOM). COCOM is the only Western organization in which joint policies on policing East-West technology transfer are regularly discussed.

The protection of U.S., Western European, and Japanese technological superiority, and COCOM's role in that effort, were at issue during the 1980s. There was disagreement between the United States and its European allies over the scope of controls on East-West trade, with Washington generally pressing for tighter restrictions. But illegal diversions, poor enforcement, and the global spread of technological innovation threatened COCOM's work and complicated and constrained U.S. policy. Adding to the dilemma for U.S. policymakers was the relative decline in U.S. economic and military predominance, which weakened U.S. influence over its COCOM allies. It was therefore clear that a strengthened multilateral approach was required to improve strategic trade controls.

An understanding of COCOM's past effectiveness (or lack thereof) is an essential precondition to a determination of its present and possible future role and utility.

THE CREATION OF COCOM

Export controls on vital war material were eased by Washington soon after World War II. But by late 1947, a growing Soviet threat to Western Europe led to mandatory licensing of exports to the Soviet bloc. In

September 1948, quiet negotiations were begun between the United States, the U.K., and France in an effort to coordinate controls.[1] During 1949, multilateral negotiations under the auspices of the Organization for European Economic Cooperation (OEEC) sought a common Western policy and broadened the discussions by including the neutral Swiss and Swedes. Consensus was reached on implementing improved export controls, although the embargo's scope was controversial. The Americans urged adoption of a broad, restrictive strategic list, but the U.K. and France opposed this idea. A less comprehensive Anglo-French list was circulated among OEEC members[2] and the multilateral talks progressed, culminating in the agreement to form COCOM.[3]

COCOM was born in the wake of the communist coup in Czechoslovakia and the Berlin blockade--a particularly tense period of the Cold War. Negotiations among the United States, the U.K., France, the Benelux nations, and Italy led to COCOM's founding on November 22, 1949. Formal operations began on January 1, 1950. During 1950, the rest of the North Atlantic Treaty Organization's (NATO) northern European members joined (except Iceland, which has never been a member) as well as West Germany and Canada. Portugal and Japan joined in 1952, followed by Greece and Turkey in 1953. Spain joined in 1985 and Australia became COCOM's newest member in 1989.[4]   Thus, COCOM's membership consists of all NATO members except Iceland, plus Japan and Australia.[5]

COCOM can be likened to an economic NATO.   Washington's containment strategy undergirded the policy which led to COCOM's creation. While there was no formal link, COCOM and NATO were founded nearly simultaneously and the memberships closely paralleled each other. American predominance was also evident in COCOM although allied assertiveness was soon evident. From the beginning, the United States was regarded as COCOM's "conscience" and was commonly acknowledged to have been the organization's driving force. Historically, the United States has had the strictest export control policy and it was the most "conscientious" in promoting COCOM's mandate and securing its effectiveness.[6] As such, U.S. attitudes and policies played a key role in the multilateral effort.

Out of the tense Cold War context, COCOM emerged and *initially* functioned as a collective means of waging economic warfare against the East.[7] In the early postwar years, economic warfare was regarded as an important component for containing the U.S.S.R. The military threat posed by Soviet troops in Eastern Europe, coupled with a justifiable perception of a heightened risk of conflict after war broke out in Korea, reinforced arguments for preventing strategic goods from reaching the Soviets and their allies. Later, the COCOM embargo would metamorphose as allied disagreements over foreign policy vis-a-vis the East clashed with general consensus on the need to control strategic exports for national security reasons.

While pushing a vocal anticommunist policy, the United States granted improved trade status to several Eastern European countries in order to reward "independence" from Moscow. For example, Washington liberalized trade with Yugoslavia (after 1948) and Poland (after 1957). In addition, Romania was placed in a less restrictive licensing category in 1964.[8] This impaired COCOM efforts. The allies' perceptions of U.S. intentions, in light of Washington's own differentiation among Eastern European states, were jarred by U.S. demands that East-West trade in general be brought under much tighter scrutiny whenever the political winds shifted. On the one hand, U.S. rhetoric warned of threatening, monolithic Soviet communism. On the other, there was recognition and encouragement of signs of East European polycentrism coupled with a growing acceptance of the geopolitical status quo in Europe. Incentives, including Most Favored Nation status, were offered by Washington as a means of exploiting rifts in the Soviet bloc. The policy of differentiation thus served U.S. foreign policy objectives by slowly and cautiously encouraging the erosion of Moscow's Eastern European empire, without openly revealing that intention.[9] Concurrently, more restrictive economic relations with Moscow were part of the policy of isolating the Soviets from Eastern Europe.

The allies also interpreted these differing signals in a way that could be used to justify their own deeply ingrained predisposition to promote East-West linkages while reestablishing traditional Eastern markets. From the beginning, COCOM's efforts and goals overlapped unavoidably with the foreign policy aspirations of its members. As COCOM's predominant member in these early years, the U.S. policy of differentiation among East-Bloc countries shaped evolving assumptions and expectations among the other states. This legacy reechoed in COCOM, often posing problems for the United States.

COCOM PROCEDURES

COCOM is unique in that its status is unofficial and based on a "gentlemen's agreement." Until recently, the organization's very existence was officially classified.[10] Stephen D. Bryen, Deputy Assistant Secretary of Defense in the Reagan administration, described COCOM as relying on consensus, unanimity, and "a system of compromise, exceptions, and precedent."[11] Its discussions and decisions are secret so as to avoid overly politicizing the embargo issue in the domestic European arena and to neutralize hostile propaganda by states which are embargoed.[12]

Weekly meetings are attended by mid-level officials but full attendance is rare. The senior U.S. representative--a State Department official--is formally attached to the Organization for Economic Cooperation and Development (OECD), but is supplemented, as circumstances dictate, by other senior State Department officials and technical experts. A Department of Defense (DOD) representative was permanently assigned to COCOM in 1986, suggesting the growing DOD role in U.S. technology security policy.[13] The Department of Commerce had no permanent representative, which allegedly permitted the DOD to exert undue influence on U.S. COCOM policy.[14] Other countries' representatives tended to be from ministries of trade, underscoring the differing emphasis put on COCOM's role by these allies.[15] From 1982 to 1988, the Reagan administration's Senior Interagency Group on Technology Transfer, chaired by the Under Secretary of State for Security Assistance, Science, and Technology, was the primary National Security Council-level body with responsibility for coordinating COCOM and related export control policy.[16]

Decisions to approve members' export requests or to change COCOM procedures must be made by unanimous consent. The unanimity rule has served U.S. interests by making it much harder to alter or dilute the embargo. Conversely, needed change and liberalization are undoubtedly delayed.[17]

Three "lists" of proscribed items were drawn up by COCOM to track and implement the export control regime: (1) the International Munitions List, (2) the International Atomic Energy List, and (3) the International List (which incorporated dual-use items with both civilian and actual or potential military applications). Three general groupings of items were included in the International List:

Items designed specially or used principally for development, production, or utilization of arms, ammunition, or military systems.

Items incorporating unique technological know-how, the acquisition of which might give significant direct assistance to the development and production of arms, ammunition, or military systems.

Items in which proscribed nations have a deficiency that hinders development and production of arms, ammunition, or military systems, a deficiency they are not likely to overcome within a reasonable period.[18]

List contents were secret, but since many countries patterned their national lists after COCOM's and the national lists were sometimes publicly available, one could gain a fair understanding of their scope. A "watch list" also evolved, including dual-use items considered sensitive enough to require statistical monitoring.[19] There were also several levels of COCOM review procedures, ranging from total embargo to requirements that so-called Administrative Exception Notes (A.E.N., monthly statistical reports on exports) be submitted.[20] In addition, weekly review and deliberation over so-called national exceptions were part of COCOM's clearinghouse function of reviewing and sanctioning shipments.

Items on the Munitions and Atomic Energy lists were generally agreed to have strategic military applications and were thus subject to embargo. Dual-use items on the International List were frequently much trickier to define as clearly having military usefulness.[21] Furthermore, whether the problem of foreign availability negated control, and whether an item's process technology (the know-how or "critical technology" required to produce an item) rather than the end product itself should be embargoed, were also considerations. Non-COCOM suppliers of the same or comparable technology could circumvent controls.   The question of process technology was of more recent origin. This issue rested on the following assertions: (1) it was impossible to control *every* embargoed item; (2) therefore, focus the effort on controlling "arrays of know-how" required to consistently produce large numbers of high-quality end products.

LEGISLATING EMBARGO COMPLIANCE: U.S. HEGEMONY AND EASING THE EMBARGO, 1950-1960

The United States passed legislation to implement domestic and allied compliance with the objectives of the embargo. The 1949 Export Control Act (ECA) and 1951 Battle Act illustrated the U.S. conviction that trade is a legitimate instrument of national security. Section 2 of the 1949 ECA declared that export controls would be used for domestic short supply reasons and to further U.S. foreign policy and national security interests.[22] Section 3 granted the Executive Branch broad authority in the area of export administration. The President was empowered to block exports of "any articles, materials, or supplies, including technical data, except under such rules and regulations as he shall prescribe."[23]   A blacklist of firms and countries that did not observe the embargo, as well as a Commodity Control List, was instituted by the Department of Commerce (DOC) in 1949 and they have been maintained.[24]   In addition, the government's authority to formulate and implement these provisions and regulations was insulated from extensive public participation and judicial review.[25] The Battle Act's provisions explicitly targeted the Soviet bloc and sought to marshal multilateral cooperation with Washington's embargo policy. Specifically, Section 101 of the act declared that military equipment, "implements of war," strategic items, and production resources were subject to embargo. Section 201 included language regulating exports of items not specified in Section 101--that is, commodities which were not clearly military or strategic--the justification being "to oppose and offset by nonmilitary action acts which threaten" U.S. security. Under Sections 102 and 202, the State Department's administrator charged with carrying out the act's provisions was required to negotiate with each U.S. aid recipient to create a multinational export control system and monitor implementation of the policy that aid recipients block exports of strategic and other goods which, based on the administrator's determination, should not reach the Soviet bloc.[26]

Sections 103(a) and 203 of the Battle Act explicitly threatened to cut off U.S. aid to any country ignoring the embargo of proscribed materials. Should the administrator find that an aid recipient was violating the embargo, he was required to recommend to the President that all aid be terminated. Upon final determination by the President, and *subject to specified conditions*, the recipient was subject to loss of all U.S. aid. However, section 103(b) provided a loophole and flexibility in deciding whether and when aid should be terminated. The President could waive punishment (1) "after taking into account the contribution of such country to the mutual security of the free world, the importance of such assistance to the security of the United States" and (2) "when unusual circumstances indicate that the cessation of aid would clearly be detrimental to the security of the United States."[27]

The threat of an aid cut-off was instrumental in persuading the reluctant Europeans and Japanese to join COCOM.[28] While there was no argument on embargoing sales of military goods, objections were raised against the embargo's broad scope and the consequences for Europe.[29] European critics feared that important sources of raw materials from Eastern Europe would evaporate as a result of Soviet retaliation for an embargo of Western trade with the East. The Battle Act's extraterritorial provisions were also resented, since they implied that the allies could not be trusted to comply with the embargo. Furthermore, the West Germans protested that trade restrictions were obstacles to reunification. Joining COCOM may have been seen as the best alternative, given mounting U.S. Congressional pressure to enforce the embargo.[30]

The tying of aid to trade and its use as a lever was discussed in Congress as early as 1947.[31] That the continued flow of U.S. aid dollars overrode allied East-West trade goals is suggested by the greater value of total U.S. military and economic aid compared with the value of East-West trade turnover (imports plus exports) for 1949-54. For this period, total Western European East-West trade turnover was $10,516.7 million while total U.S. military and economic aid equaled $29,110.2 million.[32] After 1954, U.S. aid dwindled and was surpassed by East-West trade turnover. The embargo's liberalization also began after 1954, suggesting the aid lever was effective up to that time.

Even the restrictive Battle Act was tempered by the realization that forcing a complete embargo could be counterproductive. For example, the *House Report* on the Battle Act acknowledged how dependent Western Europe was on imports of Eastern European raw materials. As the report made clear, the human suffering, and consequent propaganda loss resulting from a complete embargo, could undermine U.S. policy in Europe. For these reasons, the Battle Act provided for waiver of aid termination in the interest of national security.[33]

Europe was crucially dependent on U.S. aid and dollars to get back on its feet, but State Department officials realized that overt pressure on COCOM would cause allies to ignore the embargo and could even lead to the regime's dissolution.[34] Aid was never cut off. Legislated sticks were somewhat blunted by concessionary carrots. Marshall Plan aid, U.S.-mandated discrimination against U.S. exports, and priming of the European Payments Union were U.S. "compensation" to cushion the reduced share or loss of Eastern European markets.[35] After 1954, as U.S. economic aid shrank (although Mutual Security Assistance aid continued), influence over the allies was reduced and, significantly, the embargo began to loosen.

The outbreak of war in Korea had spurred U.S. efforts to strengthen COCOM. By 1952, COCOM lists had grown to include about 400 major categories.[36] But East-West tensions eased in the immediate wake of the ending of hostilities and Stalin's death in 1953. Furthermore, the proposed European Defense Community treaty, which the United States had backed as a means of facilitating West German rearmament, was defeated in the French Assembly in 1954. Washington wanted West German rearmament and NATO's military buildup to proceed, and these considerations probably influenced U.S. concessions on East-West trade as part of a quid pro quo.[37] Decontrol of COCOM's lists soon became controversial among the Atlantic partners. Major reductions were demanded by the Europeans and grudgingly accepted by Washington in 1954-55 and 1958.[38] The lists continued gradually to shrink, although U.S. vetoes prevented any further major reductions until the 1970s.[39] The reductions also implied that the embargo was no more than a "moving cloud,"[40] which only *delayed* bloc acquisition and development of high technologies. This called into question the viability of COCOM's existing lists. With the end of Marshall aid and signs that Moscow wanted relaxation of tensions in Europe, interest in Eastern European markets was renewed. The realities of European trading patterns were clearly reestablished and exports were an increasingly important component of growing European economies.[41]

Trade barriers reinforced the artificial division of Europe into Cold War blocs. American and European critics of the embargo felt that Moscow had used it as an excuse to strengthen its grip on Eastern Europe and to implement its autarchic policies in the region through integration of the Eastern European and Soviet economies. But the Western Europeans perceived that anti-Soviet attitudes and a desperate need for quality manufactured goods, which the Soviets could not supply, might threaten Soviet hegemony. Trade might therefore be a means of parting the Iron Curtain and gradually nudging the Eastern Europeans away from Moscow. Finally, it was argued that if traditional patterns of East-West trade and interaction were stimulated, mutually beneficial interdependence could be fostered. This would help lower regional tensions while lessening the threat of East-West conflict.

Moscow encouraged the growing desire for expanded East-West trade by promising large orders and signing contracts. The Soviets were therefore in a position to play COCOM countries against each other. This tactic posed an ongoing problem for COCOM's multilateral efforts.

1960s-1970s: DETENTE AND IMPLICATIONS FOR COCOM

Washington's stance softened during the Kennedy and Johnson administrations as "building bridges" to the East became the new policy theme. Throughout the 1960s, a reevaluation took place culminating in the Nixon era's flowering of detente and expanded trade and contacts with the East. In 1969, the liberal tone was suggested by passage of the Export Administration Act, which replaced the 1949 Export Control Act. Washington sought stronger trade ties at a time when Bonn's *Ostpolitik* and DeGaulle's initiatives in Eastern Europe were being cemented with lucrative trade concessions.

Some observers were concerned about detente's implications for COCOM. A 1976 General Accounting Office (GAO) study noted that many U.S. officials had little confidence in COCOM as a guardian of technology flows. The allies in COCOM were thought to have little "willingness to uphold multilateral security controls in the pursuit of trade"[42] in an atmosphere of increasing competition for eastern markets. U.S. actions were also suspect, heightening mutual suspicions in COCOM. The GAO noted many U.S. requests for exceptions on sales to the Soviet bloc while

Washington often vetoed allies' requests and opposed sales of lower-range goods. Other COCOM states charged that the United States used COCOM to promote sales (such as computers) to gain commercial advantage at their expense. The GAO concluded that Washington's COCOM policy was undermined, since "the appearance of commercial advantage reduces U.S. ability to influence export control decisions based on policy grounds."[43] However, William Root, former head of the U.S. COCOM delegation, argued that exceptions grew because of obsolete lists, including technology which had become commonly available, and because the United States was "conscientious in adhering to COCOM exceptions procedures."[44] He claimed that even at the height of detente in the early 1970s, total exceptions amounted to no more than 1 percent of exports to embargoed destinations.[45]

Contradictory actions and rhetoric appeared to devalue the U.S. position in COCOM. For example, the United States permitted total COCOM exceptions to grow over elevenfold in value from 1969 to 1977, even as Washington emphasized a relatively harder line in COCOM.[46] The GAO noted that Washington promised to merely raise pro forma objections to a sale of military items to a communist country by another member. In addition, the United States had "Systematically dismantled its overseas export control compliance capability and simultaneously failed to press for uniform, minimum multilateral compliance requirements and standards." For example, foreign holders of U.S. distribution licenses were not audited by the DOC from 1977 to 1984. The GAO concluded that these actions indicated that Washington had become less concerned with enforcing COCOM standards.[47] This apparent laxity on the part of the United States was also reflected in the size of COCOM lists, which by 1976 had shrunk by an estimated 65 percent since the early 1950s.[48]

The COCOM regime appeared to be fading, as the liberalization of the 1965-77 period implied. But by the late 1970s, while Western Europe continued to expand trade with Eastern Europe, global Soviet bloc activities, the perceived growing threat of the Soviet arms buildup, and the effects of the Jackson-Vanik and Stevenson amendments chilled U.S.-Soviet relations. Renewed superpower tensions reignited U.S. interest in technology transfer and COCOM's role.

RECENT DEVELOPMENTS IN COCOM: U.S. EFFORTS TO REVIVE THE REGIME

Human rights considerations and the Soviet invasion of Afghanistan provoked the Carter administration to utilizing the trade lever against Moscow. This policy spilled over and strained the Western consensus on export controls and COCOM's operations. Unilateral U.S. controls on oil and gas equipment exports in 1978 and in 1980, as well as cutoffs of grain and "of goods and technology for use related to the Summer Olympics in Moscow,"[49] signaled the tougher example Carter vainly hoped the COCOM allies would follow so as to project a united front. In 1980, a proposal in COCOM that vaguely defined "process technologies" for several industries be subject to tighter controls was met with demands that Washington specify the technologies in question. Bargaining narrowed agreement to curbing *any* exceptions for sales of embargoed goods to the U.S.S.R.[50] and controlling technology for production of three product groups.[51] This agreement underscored apparent allied willingness to accede to well thought-out and well-argued measures, even at the expense of commercial interests when strategic considerations were paramount.[52] No agreement was reached on a U.S. proposal to ban sales exceeding $100 million in value, which the allies regarded as an arbitrary figure with no apparent strategic rationale. Furthermore, allied disagreement over how to respond to Moscow's Afghanistan gambit was reflected in foreign firms' signing Soviet contracts and filling the gap left when U.S. sales were banned, despite public assurances by the Western Europeans that they would not do this.[53]

The Carter administration also initiated efforts to liberalize COCOM's China policy and to reform its outdated computer list. U.S. licensing requirements for China trade were eased. Simultaneously, a U.S. proposal for greater numbers of COCOM exceptions on China sales was favorably received.[54]

The computer lists were obsolete owing to explosive growth in the field. Therefore, in 1978 negotiations were initiated to update the lists. Stricter controls on newer computers, sophisticated software, and switching equipment were acceptable in principle, but allied reservations stressed the need to decontrol widely available models and noted the importance of controlling software with only military applications. They questioned where to draw the line on switching equipment, since some models were used only for civilian purposes. The talks progressed slowly, ending abruptly in 1980 when, in the wake of the invasion of Afghanistan, Washington presented a much harsher proposal that the allies found unacceptable.[55] It would be nearly four years before agreement was finally reached.

By 1981, a conservative Reagan administration specifically cited the drain of Western technology and know-how to the East as a dangerous development cutting the qualitative edge the West sought to maintain in the face of Warsaw Pact advantages in numbers of soldiers and material.[56] COCOM was deemed moribund, and administration officials and business representatives condemned blatant violations of COCOM prohibitions by the allies.[57]

A key part of the Reagan administration's policy of restricting strategic technology to the Soviet bloc included plans for improving multilateral controls. For example, it was a high-profile issue at Western summits.[58] In COCOM, major efforts were undertaken to shut off what was perceived to be a technology spigot allowing critical Western technology to fall into Soviet hands. American pressure on COCOM members and nonmembers sometimes led to acrimony, although certain improvements were agreed to after tough bargaining. But while the administration's rhetoric suggested a sustained push for tighter multilateral controls, actual accomplishments were more limited. Furthermore, several measures essentially carried initiatives begun under the Carter administration.

Beginning in 1981, the U.S. plan to deal with the problem had three key components: (1) to extend controls now limited to industries with direct military uses to those so-called "defense priority industries" whose output ultimately contributes to military production (e.g., metallurgy, machine tools, chemicals, truck production, microelectronics, etc.); (2) to push for the adoption in U.S. law and in COCOM practice of the "critical technology" approach which stems directly from the recommendations of the 1976 Bucy Report; and (3) to place strict limits on the exceptions granted by COCOM.[59]

U.S. pressure to broaden the list of controlled items was reflected in attempts to include less tangible items than "defense priority industries." For instance, "technical data, management and organizational skills, and scholarly communication among scientists were to be subjected to controls."[60]   The United States urged harmonization of diverging national export regulations.[61] In addition, proposals were floated to put COCOM on a formal treaty footing[62] and to expand its manpower and budget since routine business was hampered by antiquated facilities and procedures. The DOD complained in 1984 of COCOM's inadequate staff, accommodations of only 14,000 square feet in an annex to the U.S. embassy in Paris, and a meager $500,000 annual allotment funding COCOM.[63]   The cramped headquarters lacked a computer facility, modern photocopy machine, a telex link with Washington, and resources for simultaneous translations into French and English. The small staff was overburdened and lacked adequate intelligence support.[64] The DOD also urged a sharp upgrading of defense expertise on COCOM.[65]

DISAGREEMENTS WITH AND QUESTIONING OF U.S. COCOM POLICY

Interallied debates and intra-COCOM negotiations were heated during the 1980s. The allies pointed to the apparent inconsistency of permitting U.S. grain sales to the Soviets while U.S. pressure was mounting for added restrictions on pipeline and other technology transfers. American critics of COCOM procedures charged that policy compromises reflected the lowest common denominator of agreement. American threats to cut off high-technology trade with uncooperative allies were also resented and hindered multilateral agreement.[66]

The allies argued "that the current system of controls gives U.S. corporations a double advantage over foreign competitors--the American firms can side-step U.S. law by exporting to communist countries through overseas subsidiaries, while the U.S. government can snare European firms through the re-export licensing system."[67] But these charges were errone-ous. The U.S. government had blocked U.S. subsidiaries from exporting goods for the Yamal pipeline, indicating that U.S. corporations were not free to circumvent controls. Moreover, American overseas subsidiaries often imported U.S.-origin components. If these components were reexported to the East, they came under U.S. licensing provisions including vetting for banned technology. But if technology originating in the host country was included, and domestic licensing and controls were weak, a U.S. subsidiary was free from generally stricter U.S. oversight.

On the question of whether "intangible" goods such as technical data and scholarly communication should be restricted, as the United States proposed, the Europeans argued that these items were difficult to monitor and would generate numerous exception requests. They argued "that ideas can be carried across borders in people's minds, and blueprints can be transferred via diplomatic pouch."[68] One American familiar with the deliberations praised COCOM's effectiveness. In 1984, William Root castigated the unyielding U.S. position, which had contributed to gridlock in Paris. Conversely, he praised the allies' contributions as cogent and "better justified" than U.S. proposals.[69] Root criticized pending White House-supported legislation seeking to put COCOM on a formal treaty basis. Emphasizing the political sensitivities of COCOM allies, he noted that the extensive legislative debate such a proposal would engender in these countries would undermine the informal, confidential atmosphere that was a basis for consensus in COCOM.[70]

COCOM REFORM: A MIXED RECORD

Some progress was made in reforming and improving COCOM in spite of strong disagreement. In 1982, Under Secretary of State James L. Buckley indicated that classified Central Intelligence Agency briefings in allied capitals had focused attention on technology transfer issues and improved allied cooperation.[71] Early in 1984, the DOD praised the allies for having accepted many U.S. COCOM initiatives.[72]

The lifting of pipeline sanctions eased the way for a comprehensive 1982-84 COCOM list review and agreements on NATO and OECD studies of technology transfer.[73] In addition, some allies *did* react to U.S. pressure and growing awareness of covert Soviet activities by seeking greater input from defense ministries in licensing decisions.[74] And an effort to improve intelligence exchanges through a new COCOM subcommittee was also launched.[75]

The 1982-84 COCOM list review was moderately successful in that "military criticality" was accepted as an operative criterion in formulating lists. While the review was under way, members agreed to observe a "no exceptions" policy for the U.S.S.R. but not the P.R.C., and this continued until July 1989.[76] The review resulted in revamping lists and updating embargoed items based on U.S. suggestions. This agreement reflected partial U.S. success in implementing the "militarily critical technologies" approach (initiated under Carter) into COCOM practice in the face of allied opposition.[77] The goal was to limit Warsaw Pact access to "arrays of know-how" that facilitate research, development, and high-quality production of military technologies. Illustrative of relative U.S. success in limiting transfers of know-how was the DOD's assertion that no "turnkey factory for the production of sensitive goods" was licensed by COCOM from 1981 to 1986.[78] This concept was nevertheless difficult for the allies to agree on.

Some agreement was imperative in light of revolutionary and widespread technological innovation in the private sector. In the 1950s and 1960s, most leading-edge technology was spawned in the defense sector and thus could be regulated. But since about 1970, revolutionary advances in microelectronics have increasingly been generated by private business, making control much more difficult. Some analysts feared that common computer games, containing powerful microchip technology, could be studied and reverse-engineered to benefit the Soviet military.

The Western Europeans felt that their willingness to compromise, and the successful outcome of the 1982-84 list review, proved their sincerity. Yet they (and domestic U.S. interests)[79] charged that "critical technologies" would serve as a lever to produce even broader lists--and added controls--

when decontrol of less strategic low-technology items was desirable. The National Academy of Sciences (NAS) found that too many items taxed national capabilities to enforce COCOM rules. It would be better to concentrate limited resources on more effective control of shorter lists of very critical items.[80] Washington countered that decontrol was achieved in practice, since certain previously controlled end products could now be safely exported because the know-how required in their manufacture would remain embargoed.[81] While the list's size can only be estimated, published testimony in 1983 suggested that 150,000 to 200,000 *individual* items were included, a figure supporting arguments against broad lists.[82]

Future problems were expected from an agreement to develop a new COCOM "watchlist" covering emerging technologies with military potential, such as biotechnology. Advocates of the watchlist believed that by keeping abreast of such technology, there would be adequate controls in place before domestic pressures and national interests committed governments to greater export relaxation than was prudent.[83] But can COCOM keep adequately apprised of the latest innovations and quickly evaluate them, given the poor track record regarding list updates and the slow pace of COCOM decision making?[84] Furthermore, precipitous controls, in *any* form, early in the emergence of a new technology may cripple scientific and entrepreneurial cross-fertilization.

New computer technology proved to be an especially difficult problem carried over from the unsuccessful 1978-80 negotiations, and the U.S. position was once again damaged by inconsistencies. In 1982, the Reagan administration revived the talks, reintroducing more moderate proposals. Negotiations with the allies stalled after the DOD insisted on a much tougher stance at the last minute. Washington's policy was also hindered by DOD-DOC infighting over the best negotiating tactics, with the Department of Commerce advocating a more conciliatory tone.[85] With the inclusion of a permanent DOD representative at COCOM, future U.S. policy may be weakened should Commerce-State-Defense department rivalry flare up while negotiations are under way.[86]

An agreement resembling the Americans' moderate 1978 proposals was finally reached in July 1984.[87] The debate in COCOM had involved the question of where to draw the line on civil and military uses of computers. Western European and Japanese policy stressed, as usual, relatively less control and that embargoes only be applied to clearly strategic computer technology. Under the terms of the agreement, controls on mainframe computers were slightly relaxed while they were tightened on increasingly sophisticated personal and superminicomputers. In addition, computer software was closely examined and placed under stricter controls. Computer technology was more tightly controlled beginning in 1985. "The reason behind this," the DOD reported, was that "the technology to produce some items is more valuable to the Soviets than the item itself, and the same technology can be used to build larger, reliable computers."[88] Computer-controlled telecommunications switching equipment and related design and production technology were also placed under stricter control, and their sale was banned until at least 1988.[89]

Unfortunately, these promising steps were tarnished by allied disagreements over interpretation of the agreement's complex language.[90] Even the DOC, under pressure from domestic interests, argued that the new computer regulations were vague and subject to broad interpretation.[91] One review of the computer agreement called it "a tacit admission that the Warsaw Pact nations have either acquired sufficient numbers of modern Western computers or can now produce enough of their own equivalents" and warned of widespread European dissatisfaction with these decisions.[92]

Efforts to improve COCOM's effectiveness and performance continued after 1984. Continuous reviews replaced the previous triennial reviews permitting COCOM to respond more rapidly to technological developments by removing obsolete technology, modifying existing definitions, and adding new breakthroughs.[93] COCOM also agreed to further liberalize the "China differential" in September 1985, placing the P.R.C. in a less restrictive category than much of the Soviet bloc.[94] This gave official sanction to a situation that had existed for some time. In addition, COCOM endorsed studies of how to control disembodied technical know-how in 1985.

To strengthen performance, the organization's secretariat was bolstered and a computer system was installed to improve recordkeeping and expedite exception requests. Direct electronic links replaced couriers, thereby speeding Washington-Paris communications. Meeting facilities were upgraded, translation capabilities were improved, allied funding was increased 20 percent yearly (with the U.S. contributing $2 million in 1985), and a military advisory group was added despite initial Western European concerns that it would be dominated by hawkish Pentagon staff.[95] These accomplishments elicited mixed reactions in the United States. Former Under Secretary of State William Schneider Jr. praised allied acceptance of U.S. "dual-use" technology objectives, but Assistant Secretary Perle remained unsatisfied with COCOM's limited intelligence capabilities and the allies' inability or unwillingness to devote more resources to intelligence efforts.[96]

EXCEPTIONS AND THE NEW "CHINA DIFFERENTIAL":
THE ONGOING CONTROVERSY

Despite modest success and strengthening the regime, serious problems continued to plague COCOM. One controversy concerned COCOM's exceptions policy. Depending on one's perspective, exceptions either added flexibility to the regime and thereby helped prevent defections, or they undermined multilateral efforts. Under COCOM rules, governments were required to petition COCOM for a "national exception," whereupon shipment was permitted after a unanimous--albeit advisory--vote by the members. All members reviewed requests before casting their final vote in Paris. The United States was charged with obstruction owing to the lengthy review such requests underwent before a clear U.S. position emerged.[97]

Theoretically, exceptions were a loophole through which sensitive technology could flow, although this probably only occurred in a limited number of cases. Exceptions also lessened pressures to reduce lists or unilaterally circumvent COCOM strictures.[98] However, exceptions were an administrative nightmare because rapid technological evolution necessitated policy reevaluation and complex exceptions to exceptions that overburdened COCOM machinery and raised definitional problems.[99]

Numerous U.S. exception requests for China contrasted with the announced U.S. policy of curbing all members' exceptions.[100] This provoked unfounded suspicion of Washington's ulterior motives in opening new markets in China at the expense of the allies. In addition, there was concern over permitting easier technology flows, given the embryonic state of Chinese political and economic liberalization and potential security risks.[101] However, whether justified or not, suspicion could tempt other COCOM members to covertly exploit other risky opportunities. China's improved status reflected a trend toward a three-tiered COCOM, a development which underscored the political calculus influencing COCOM policy. Increasingly, Hungary and Romania were also accorded more liberal treatment owing to their "independent" economic and foreign policies. Poland (until 1989) and the U.S.S.R. remained subject to the strictest controls, but the remainder of Eastern Europe and communist Asia were subject to slightly fewer restrictions.[102]

NEUTRAL STATES AND WESTERN TECHNOLOGY SALES
TO THE NEWLY INDUSTRIALIZING COUNTRIES:
IMPLICATIONS FOR COCOM

The perennial problem of exports from Europe's neutral states and from industrializing states outside of COCOM threatened progress in improving trade controls, since allied willingness to observe controls was contingent on policing transfers from advanced neutrals.[103] Neutral states occasionally served as transshipment points to the East, and their delicate international status precluded overt alignment with COCOM, although they had cooperated informally.[104] In 1986, Washington placed Austria, Sweden, and Switzerland on a special list and restricted their access to U.S. high technology owing to lax enforcement and transfers and diversions of illegal exports. Exports of U.S. high-technology items to these and several other countries were subject to strict DOD review. This pressure apparently worked as all three countries tightened their export regulations. By 1989, they had all been rewarded with COCOM-like status by the United States and U.S. restrictions had been lifted. Several other countries reportedly remained on the DOD review list.[105] Some neutrals agreed to coordinated control of selected COCOM-origin items, but most domestically produced items remained unregulated.[106]

COCOM members also pursued bilateral talks with friendly Newly Industrializing Countries (NICs) that imported and could produce sophisticated technologies with military applications. The NICs' technology security and export controls were often ineffective or nonexistent, and COCOM efforts to monitor exports from and diversions through these countries were considered inadequate. Therefore, assistance was provided to strengthen the NICs' national controls and pattern them after the COCOM model.[107] These efforts were crucial. If non-COCOM states refused to regulate indigenous technology, COCOM would be forced to decontrol technology categories to reflect widespread availability of, for example, relatively powerful personal computer "clones" manufactured in the Far East. But given the uneven record on decontrols in the industrialized West, it is doubtful better success will be achieved with Far Eastern commodities.[108]

CIRCUMVENTING COCOM: SMUGGLING, BLACK
MARKETS, AND POOR ENFORCEMENT

COCOM's efforts were substantially undermined by a thriving market for smuggled technology, a cutthroat business environment, the soft Western market, clever Soviet manipulation of suppliers, and lax national export control enforcement.[109]

For example, in the U.K. and Norway, poor enforcement and antiquated export laws belied official advocacy of stricter controls.[110] Repeated or flagrant examples of poor export control sowed distrust among members who feared a loss of competitive advantage if they enforced controls while other states blithely ignored them.

Many allies had understaffed customs arms and too few licensing officials.[111] Even the tighter U.S. controls and the large budget for export regulation and inspections were inadequate.[112] Technology smuggling resembled narcotics trafficking: wealthy and sophisticated smugglers utilized numerous channels to circumvent harried government regulators. Relatively unimportant shipments were often ignored by customs agents in order to husband limited resources to apprehend more serious violators.[113]

Blatantly illegal diversions, such as the Toshiba-Kongsberg sale of milling machines and related computer equipment to the Soviets in 1982-84 (and earlier), received considerable attention in 1987. This episode highlighted the severity of the enforcement problem, COCOM's continuing deficiencies, and the frustration of U.S. policy.

There were disturbing allegations of official Japanese toleration and assistance for the sales.[114] Only after mounting evidence of malfeasance and strong U.S. pressure did Japanese officials launch an investigation.[115] Toshiba charged that French equipment was in Soviet hands well before the Japanese machines. Norwegian investigators found a fifteen-year trail of similar diversions by Western European and American companies.[116] These accusations suggested attitudes of mistrust and self-interest among COCOM members. Such attitudes were probably the inevitable result of the discretion permitted governments under COCOM rules. Pressure on decision makers to complete sales, past success in bending or circumventing COCOM rules, and differing perceptions of the necessity and efficacy of controls were contributory factors. In this sense, COCOM was like a cartel. There was incentive to cheat based on the assumptions that the payoff would be higher than complying with the cartel, that other members had cheated or were likely to, and that punishment could be avoided or would be minor. These factors suggested the countervailing forces diluting effective multilateral embargo efforts.

The response in the United States was loud and condemnatory.[117] Legislation was introduced to forbid imports from foreign firms that violated export controls.[118] These punitive measures were not well received by Toshiba or the Reagan administration. After considerable lobbying, the sanctions incorporated in 1988 omnibus trade legislation were diluted and merely banned U.S. government purchases of Toshiba and Kongsberg products.[119] Under Secretary of State Edward Derwinski cautioned that the proposed sanctions might cause COCOM's disintegration, although that appeared unlikely in the short run.[120] Instead, the corrosive effects of cumulative disagreements and suspicions posed a greater threat of serious rupture. The COCOM reforms could be effective only up to a point, and it was a measure of the organization's weakness that the Toshiba-Kongsberg matter was not settled quietly in Paris.

Some sign of willingness to address the enforcement issue and ease intra-COCOM licensing arose from a January 1988 COCOM agreement on "higher fences around fewer items." The United States agreed to expedite decontrol of lower-level technologies while the allies agreed to bolster enforcement of a shortened list of more sophisticated items.[121] Yet by 1991, in the wake of the systemic reforms in Eastern Europe, progress on streamlining had been slow. Disagreements between the United States and the Western Europeans over the size and contents of a shorter "core list" of technologies and whether enforcement efforts were as yet adequate were further complicated by growing concerns over the proliferation of nuclear, chemical, and biological weapons and related dual-use technology. In addition, the easing of controls on exports to fledgling Eastern European democracies, while the U.S.S.R. continued to be subject to tighter restrictions, sparked U.S.-allied disagreement and slowed COCOM's progress, although some compromises were gradually achieved.[122] Ultimately, because COCOM tended to act after the fact, or because of U.S. prodding, members' cynicism, laxity, and self-interest were constant dangers undermining the cooperative atmosphere basic to COCOM's efforts.

SUMMARY

COCOM was born in an era of frigid East-West relations when U.S. political and economic leadership was unchallenged. As those circumstances changed, the United States and COCOM slowly adapted to an evolving international political and economic environment. While debate in COCOM was characterized by allied resistance to the relatively more restrictive U.S. approach, there was reason to believe that COCOM achieved--if only imperfectly--its basic goal of screening and delaying Soviet bloc acquisition of strategic technology. Short of overt and aggressive economic warfare or a complete embargo, which was increasingly unacceptable after 1954, no embargo could ever be foolproof. By the 1980s, the global spread of technological innovation and production, and the difficulty of regulating dual-use technologies, threatened to undermine COCOM and complicated U.S. policy. Western consensus on the necessity of multilateral cooperation permitted COCOM to survive and allowed the United States to initiate, and COCOM to implement, needed reforms, although their impact was lessened owing to continuing controversies and poor enforcement.

The U.S. role remained critical since other members took cues on the export control issue based on Washington's attitudes and actions. But in its role as COCOM's conscience, the United States also had a special responsibility to avoid confusing and goading the allies with inconsistent policy, imperious demands, onerous threats, and sweeping, poorly defined proposals. Not doing so only delayed consensus building and undermined mutual trust within COCOM. By the same token, the other COCOM members, while grudgingly willing to strengthen the COCOM regime, also needed to foster U.S. confidence in their sustained commitment to improving controls on East-West trade.

Within the Alliance, perceptions of the wisdom and utility of trade controls were a function of a complex set of independent variables. Multilateral efforts were influenced by the political calculus and attitudes stemming from members' differing historical, domestic political, economic, and national security situations. The relative importance of East-West trade was an added consideration and together, these interests and constraints suggested that some degree of disagreement was inevitable. The next chapter outlines these variables, exploring their relative influence on members' policies.

NOTES

1. Gunnar Adler-Karlsson, *Western Economic Warfare 1947-1967* (Stockholm: Almqvist and Wiksell, 1968), p. 50.

2. U.S. Department of State, International Cooperation Administration, *The Strategic Trade Control System 1948-56* {hereafter, *1957 Battle Act Report*}, Ninth Report to Congress, Mutual Defense Assistance Control Act of 1951 (Washington, DC: United States Government Printing Office {hereafter cited as U.S. GPO}, 1957), p. 17.

3. Ibid. See also Gary K. Bertsch, "U.S. Export Controls," *Journal of World Trade Law*, vol. 15, no. 1 (1981), pp. 67-82; rpt. as a shortened version in *National Security and Technology Transfer*, eds. Gary K. Bertsch and John R. McIntyre, Westview Special Studies in National Security and Defense Policy (Boulder, CO: Westview Press, 1983), p. 127.

4. Hanns-D. Jacobsen, *Security Implications of Inner-German Economic Relations*, Working Papers No. 77, Woodrow Wilson International Center for Scholars, International Security Studies Program (Washington, DC: 27 August 1986), p. 28, footnote 25. See also U.S. Department of State, *1957 Battle Act Report*, pp. 4-5, 17-18; Chris Sherwell, "Australia is to Join CoCOM," *Financial Times* [London], no. 30,815 (11 April 1989), p. 6, columns 1-3 and "Curbs on Australia Lifted," *Financial Times* [London], no. 30,852 (25 May 1989), p. 10, columns 1-2.

5. A ministerial-level Consultative Group was also created in 1949 to set "broad policy outlines that would be implemented by the working level staff of COCOM." After 1958, however, the became moribund. It has not met since, although the first COCOM ministerial-level meeting in nearly 25 years did take place in Paris in 1982, and thereafter in 1983 and 1985. See John D. Hill, "Controlling East-West Trade: The U.S. Vs Western Europe," thesis, The American University, 1986, p. 23; and U.S. Congress, General Accounting Office, *Export Controls: Need to Clarify Policy and Simplify Administration*, Report to the Congress by the Comptroller General of the United States, ID-79-16 (1 March 1979), p. 7.

6. For example, the United States fought allied pressure to liberalize COCOM controls during the 1950s and advocated a revitalization of COCOM in the 1980s.

7. See Kate S. Tomlinson, "U.S. Legislative Framework for Commercial Relations With Eastern Europe," in U.S. Congress, Joint Economic Committee, *East European Economies: Slow Growth in the 1980s. Volume 1. Economic Performance and Policy*, 99th Congress, 1st session, 28 October 1985 (Washington, DC: U.S. GPO, 1985), p. 567.

8. Adler-Karlsson, *Western Economic Warfare*, p. 103.

9. On differentiation, see Lincoln Gordon, "Interests and Policies in Eastern Europe: The View from Washington," in *Eroding Empire*, ed. Lincoln Gordon (Washington, DC: The Brookings Institution, 1987), pp. 67-128.

10. Robert Price, "COCOM After 35 Years: Reaffirmation or Reorganization?", in *Selling the Rope to Hang Capitalism?*, eds. Charles M. Perry and Robert L. Pfaltzgraff, Jr. (London: Pergamon-Brassey's, 1987), p. 196.

11. Dr. Stephen D. Bryen, prepared statement, 11 May 1982, in U.S. Congress, Senate Committee on Governmental Affairs, Permanent Subcommittee on Investigations, *Transfer of United States High Technology to the Soviet Union and Soviet Bloc Nations*, Hearings, 97th Congress, 2nd session, 4, 5, 6, 11, 12 May 1982 (Washington, DC: U.S. GPO, 1982), p. 587.

12. Soviet denunciations of Western "economic warfare" could be dismissed as disinformation. See Sumner Benson, "United States Policy on Strategic Trade With the Soviet Bloc," in *Economic Relations With the Soviet Union*, ed. Angela E. Stent (Boulder, CO: Westview Press, 1985), p. 101.

13. U.S. Department of Defense, *The Technology Security Program, A Report to the 99th Congress, Second Session* (Washington, DC, 1986), p. 65; and John R. McIntyre and Richard T. Cupitt, "East-West Strategic Trade Control: Crumbling Consensus?", *Survey*, vol. 25, no. 2 (Spring 1980), pp. 81-108 rpt. as a revised and

shortened version in *National Security and Technology Transfer*, eds. Gary K. Bertsch and John R. McIntyre, Westview Special Studies in National Security and Defense Policy (Boulder, CO: Westview Press, 1983), p. 148.

14. Interview with John Copeland, Director, Export Administration, Motorola, Inc., Washington, DC, 25 February 1988.

15. McIntyre and Cupitt, "Multilateral Strategic Trade Controls," p. 148.

16. William Schneider, Jr., "East-West Relations and Technology Transfer," address delivered by Michael B. Marks, Senior Policy Adviser for Under Secretary for Security Assistance, Science, and Technology Schneider before the Federal Bar Association in Newton, MA, 29 March 1984; rpt. in *Department of State Bulletin*, vol. 84, no. 2089 (August 1984), p. 69; and National Academy of Sciences, *Balancing the National Interest* (Washington, DC: National Academy Press, 1987), p. 97.

17. U.S. Congress, General Accounting Office, *Export Controls*, p. 8.

18. National Academy of Sciences, *Balancing*, p. 97.

19. U.S. Department of State, *1957 Battle Act Report*, p. 18; and U.S. Department of State, *The 1958 Revision of East-West Trade Controls*, Twelfth Report to Congress, Mutual Defense Assistance Control Act of 1951 (Washington, DC: U.S. GPO, April 1959), p. 3. An additional list directed specifically against the People's Republic of China (P.R.C.), North Korea, and North Vietnam was the responsibility of CHINCOM (the China Committee, established in 1952), a COCOM-related organization designed to ensure a nearly total embargo of China and North Korea in the wake of the Korean War. As early as September 1950, a more restrictive COCOM embargo had been informally initiated against the P.R.C. CHINCOM formalized the arrangement and allowed COCOM to concentrate on East European controls. See *1957 Battle Act Report*, pp. 34-35.

20. On these procedures, see National Academy of Sciences, *Balancing*, p. 98, Table 4-1.

21. That this difficulty was clearly understood by Washington is illustrated by references in U.S. Department of State, *1957 Battle Act Report*, pp. 5, 26.

22. See U.S. Department of State, *1957 Battle Act Report*, p. 6.

23. Quoted in U.S. Congress, Office of Technology Assessment, *Technology and East-West Trade* (Washington, DC: U.S. GPO, November 1979), p. 112.

24. Ibid., p. 22.

25. National Academy of Sciences, *Balancing*, pp. 72-73.

26. The complete Battle Act is found in U.S. Department of State, *1957 Battle Act Report*, Appendix A, "Text of the Mutual Defense Assistance Control Act of 1951 {H.R. 4550}, Public Law 213, 82nd Congress, 65 Stat. 644, Approved October 26, 1951." The cited passages are from the *1957 Battle Act Report*, pp. 51-53.

27. U.S. Department of State, *1957 Battle Act Report*, pp. 52-53.

28. See "Hearings on H.R. 4293 to extend and amend the Export Control Act of 1949, Committee on Banking and Currency, 1969, p. 4," quoted in U.S. Congress, Office of Technology Assessment, *Technology*, pp. 113-14 and footnote 2, p. 114, which stressed this.

29. Adler-Karlsson, *Western Economic Warfare*, pp. 37-42.

30. U.S. Congress, Office of Technology Assessment, *Technology*, p. 113. See also the criticisms of embargo violations in *Text of House Report on H.R. 4550, Mutual Defense Assistance Control Act of 1951*, House Report 703, 82nd Congress, 1st session, 16 July 1951; rpt. in *U.S. Foreign Policy and the East-West Confrontation*, ed. U.S. Congress, House Committee on Foreign Affairs, Historical Series, Selected Executive Session Hearings of the Committee, 1951-56, Volume XIV (Washington, DC: U.S. GPO, 1980), pp. 229, 231-33, 237-38.

31. And the lever was incorporated in the Economic Cooperation and Foreign Assistance Acts of 1948, the latter act being the legislative framework for the Marshall Plan. See U.S., Congress, Office of Technology Assessment, *Technology*, p. 113.

32. See the U.S. Agency for International Development statistics reprinted in Adler-Karlsson, *Western Economic Warfare*, p. 46.

33. *Text of House Report on H.R. 4550*, pp. 233-34.

34. Michael Mastanduno, "CoCOM and the Special Responsibilities of the U.S.," Working Paper prepared for the Congressional Research Service Seminar on "U.S. Export Control Policy and Competitiveness," Washington, DC, 17 April 1987. Rpt. in *U.S. Export Control Policy and Competitiveness*, eds. John P. Hardt and Jean F. Boone, Congressional Research Service Report No. 87-388 S (Washington, DC: Congressional Research Service, 30 April 1987), p. 117.

35. Beverly Crawford and Stefanie Lenway, "Decision Modes and International Regime Change: Western Collaboration and East-West Trade," *World Politics*, vol. 37, no. 3 (April 1985), p. 388. See also U.S. Department of State, *Problems of Economic Defense*, Second Report to Congress, Administrator, Mutual Defense Assistance Control Act of 1951, (Washington, DC: U.S. GPO, January 1953), pp. 41-44.

36. J. Wilczynski, "Strategic Embargo in Perspective," *Soviet Studies*, vol. 19, no. 1 (July 1967), p. 74.

37. William A. Root, former Director, Office of East-West Trade, U.S. Department of State, argued that the importance of maintaining joint military programs with the allies invariably caused the United States to abstain from punishing allies who did not strictly observe the East-West trade embargo. By inference, this illustrated one of the dilemmas facing Washington, since the Americans wished to avoid using the threatened cutoff of military assistance as leverage over allies. Interview, Washington, DC, 8 March 1988.

38. CHINCOM was dissolved in 1957 when the "China differential" was unilaterally ended by the Europeans despite vociferous U.S. objections. One common set of COCOM lists was retained for all communist countries. Washington continued to embargo all trade with Beijing. See Adler-Karlsson, *Western Economic Warfare*, pp. 94-95. For details of the revisions, see Adler-Karlsson, *Western Economic Warfare*, pp. 93, 96-97; U.S. Department of State, *1957 Battle Act Report*, pp. 28-29; and U.S. Department of State, Foreign Operations Administration, *The Revision of Strategic Trade Controls*, Fifth Report to Congress, Mutual

Defense Control Act of 1951 (Washington, DC: U.S. GPO, 1954), pp. 13-20.

39. William A. Root, "Trade Controls That Work," *Foreign Policy*, vol. 56 (Fall 1984), pp. 72, 77.

40. David Buchan, "Western Security and Economic Strategy Towards the East," *Adelphi Papers*, No. 192 (London: International Institute for Strategic Studies, 1984), p. 24. In July 1989, the United States decontrolled certain 16-bit personal computers (PCs)--considered to incorporate mid-1980s technology. Secretary of Commerce Robert Mosbacher reported that this was done because similar PCs were widely available from non-COCOM sources. See Lionel Barber and Nancy Dunne, "US Relaxes Computer Export Curb," *Financial Times* [London], U.S. edition, no. 30,899 (20 July 1989), p. 6, column 1.

41. U.S. Department of State, *1957 Battle Act Report*, p. 24.

42. U.S. Congress, General Accounting Office, *The Government's Role In East-West Trade Problems and Issues*, Summary Statement of Report to the Congress by the Comptroller General of the United States, ID-76-13A (4 February 1976), p. 46.

43. Ibid., p. 47. See also J. Fred Bucy, "Technology Transfer and East-West Trade: A Reappraisal," *International Security*, vol. 5, no. 3 (Winter 1980), pp. 132-51; rpt. in *National Security and Technology Transfer*, eds. Gary K. Bertsch and John R. McIntyre, Westview Special Studies in National Security and Defense Policy (Boulder, CO: Westview Press, 1983), p. 205; and Dr. Goldberg, Office of Technology Assessment, testimony, 9 June 1983, in U.S. Congress, House Committee on Armed Services, Technology Transfer Panel, *Technology Transfer*, 98th Congress, 1st session, Hearings, 9, 21, 23 June, 13, 14 July 1983 (Washington, DC: U.S. GPO, 1984), p. 35.

44. Root, "COCOM: A Unified System," paper prepared for the Congressional Research Service seminar on "U.S. Export Control Policy and Competitiveness," Washington, D.C., 17 April 1987. Rpt. in *U.S. Export Control Policy and Competitiveness*, eds. John P. Hardt and Jean F. Boone, Congressional Research Service Report No. 87-388 S (Washington, DC: Congressional Research Service, 30 April 1987), pp. 98, 103-04.

45. Root, "Trade Controls," pp. 63-64.

46. See Table II Approved Exception Requests, 1967-77, rpt. in McIntyre and Cupitt, "Multilateral Strategic Trade Controls", p. 151. They give the source as "Special report on Multilateral Export Controls by the President," *Report to the Congress*, July 1978, p. 6.

47. U.S. Congress, General Accounting Office, *The Government's*, p. 47; and Henry R. Nau, "The West-West Dimensions of East-West Economic Relations," in *Selling the Rope to Hang Capitalism?*, eds. Charles M. Perry and Robert L. Pfaltzgraff (London: Pergamon-Brassey's, 1987), p. 213.

48. This figure is based on estimates cited in Gary Bertsch and John R. McIntyre, "The Western Alliance and East-West Trade: In Pursuit of an Integrated Strategy," in *The Politics of East-West Trade*, ed. Gordon B. Smith (Boulder, CO: Westview Press, 1984), p. 220. The authors cite figures from J. R. McIntyre and R. C. Cupitt, "Strategic East-West Trade Control: Crumbling Consensus?", *Survey*,

vol. 25 (Spring 1980). It unclear whether Bertsch and McIntyre are referring to the sum of items on *all* COCOM lists or whether they refer to a single list, presumably the dual-use list. The estimate is also based on the testimony of Joseph A. Gwyer in U.S. Congress, Senate Committee on the Judiciary, Subcommittee to Investigate the Administration of the Internal Security Act and Other Internal Security Laws, *Export of Strategic Materials to the U.S.S.R. and Other Soviet Bloc Countries*, 87th Congress, 1st session, part 1, 23 October 1961 (Washington, DC: U.S. GPO, 1961), p. 44; and Root, "Trade Controls."

49. Root, "Trade Controls," p. 66; and Vladimir N. Pregelj, *U.S. Commercial Relations With Communist Countries: Chronology of Significant Actions Since World War II, and Their Present Status*, Report no. 84-67 E, Congressional Research Service, U.S. Library of Congress (Washington, DC, 30 March 1984), pp. CRS-10-12.

50. Buchan, "Western Security," p. 24.

51. Root, "Trade Controls," p. 70.

52. William A. Root, prepared statement, 2 April 1984, in U.S. Congress, Senate Committee on Governmental Affairs, Subcommittee on Investigations, *Transfer of Technology*, 98th Congress, 2nd session, 2, 3, 11, 12 April 1984 (Washington, DC: U.S. GPO, 1984), p. 236.

53. On the Carter policy, see Root, "Trade Controls," pp. 69-70; and Buchan, "Western Security," p. 27.

54. Buchan, "Western Security," p. 26; Pregelj, *U.S. Commercial Relations*, p. CRS-12; and U.S. Congress, Office of Technology Assessment, *Technology*, p. 163.

55. Root, "Trade Controls," p. 68.

56. On the first Reagan administration, see Angela E. Stent, "East-West Trade and Technology Transfer: The West's Search For Consensus," *The World Today*, vol. 40, no. 11 (November 1984).

57. For a selection of views, see Talbot S. Lindstrom, "Devising Fair and Effective Technology-Export Controls," *Defense Management Journal*, vol. 21, no. 1 (First Quarter, 1985), p. 5; Bertsch and McIntyre, "The Western Alliance," p. 221; and written statement of James H. Mack, public affairs director, National Machine Tool Builders Association, in U.S. Congress, House Committee on Armed Services, Technology Transfer Panel, *Technology Transfer*, 98th Congress, 1st session, Hearings, 9, 21, 23 June, 13, 14 July 1983 (Washington, DC: U.S. GPO, 1984), pp. 226, 233-34. Similar sentiments were expressed by State Department officials in interviews; not-for-attribution interviews with officials at the Bureau of Economic and Business Affairs, U.S. Department of State, 23 February 1988.

58. Bertsch and McIntyre, "The Western Alliance," pp. 210, 223. They quote from the testimony of R. D. Hormats in U.S. Congress, House Subcommittee on Europe (Washington, DC: U.S. GPO, 12 November 1981).

59. Bertsch and McIntyre, "The Western Alliance," pp. 222-23.

60. Michael Mastanduno, "Strategies of Economic Containment: U.S. Trade Relations With the Soviet Union," *World Politics*, vol. 37, no. 4 (July 1985), p. 527. See also David Buchan, "Technology Transfer to the Soviet Bloc," *Washington Quarterly*, vol. 7, no. 4 (Fall 1984), p. 131.

61. Timothy Aeppel, "The Evolution of Multilateral Export Controls: A Critical Study of the COCOM Regime," *Fletcher Forum*, vol. 9, no. 1 (Winter 1985), p. 116.

62. William Root, testimony, 2 April 1984, in U.S. Congress, Senate Committee on Governmental Affairs, Permanent Subcommittee on Investigations, *Transfer of Technology*, Hearings, 98th Congress, 2nd session, 2, 3, 11, 12 April 1984 (Washington, DC: U.S. GPO, 1984), p. 237.

63. U.S. Department of Defense, *The Technology Transfer Control Program. A Report to the 98th Congress, Second Session* (Washington, DC: February 1984), pp. 24-25; and Aeppel, "The Evolution."

64. Testimony of Richard N. Perle and prepared statement of William Schneider, Jr., 1 March 1983, in U.S. Congress, House Committee on Foreign Affairs, *Extension and Revision of the Export Administration Act of 1979*, Hearings, 98th Congress, 1st session, 24 February, 1, 3, 8 March, 5, 12-14, 28-29 April, 2, 4-5, 18, 25-26 May 1983 (Washington, DC: U.S. GPO, 1986{?}), pp. 196, 211. Testimony of Richard N. Perle, 12 March 1987, in U.S. Congress, Senate, Committee on Banking, Housing, and Urban Affairs, Subcommittee on International Finance and Monetary Policy, *Export Controls*, Hearings, 100th Congress, 1st session, 12, 17 March 1987 (Washington, DC: U.S. GPO, 1987), p. 84. Testimony of Richard N. Perle, 23 April 1987, in U.S. Congress, House Committee on Science, Space, and Technology, *National Academy of Sciences Report on International Technology Transfer*, Hearings, 100th Congress, 1st session, 4 February, 23 April 1987 (Washington, DC: U.S. GPO, 1987), pp. 84, 99; and Richard N. Perle, "The Strategic Impact of Technology Transfers," in *Selling the Rope to Hang Capitalism?*, eds. Charles M. Perry and Robert L. Pfaltzgraff, Jr. (London: Pergamon-Brassey's, 1987), p. 8.

65. Richard N. Perle, testimony in U.S. Congress, House Committee on Armed Services, Technology Transfer Panel, *Technology Transfer*, 98th Congress, 1st session, Hearings, 9, 21, 23 June, 13, 14 July 1983 (Washington, DC: U.S. GPO, 1984), p. 95.

66. Jan Feldman, "Trade Policy and Foreign Policy," *Washington Quarterly*, vol. 8, no. 1 (Winter 1985), p. 70; Heinrich Vogel, "Western Security and the Eastern Bloc Economy," *Washington Quarterly*, vol. 7, no. 2 (Spring 1984), p. 46; Buchan, "Technology Transfer," p. 132; and Mastanduno, "Strategies," pp. 528-29.

67. Aeppel, "The Evolution," p. 120.

68. Mastanduno, "Strategies," p. 528.

69. Root, testimony in *Transfer of Technology*, p. 233.

70. Ibid., p. 237. Dr. Peter J. Sharfman, Program Manager for International Security and Commerce, Office of Technology Assessment, concurred and praised COCOM decisions as generally "correct and useful." See Dr. Peter J. Sharfman,

testimony, 9 June 1983, in U.S. Congress, House Committee on Armed Services, *Technology Transfer*, Hearings, 98th Congress, 1st session, 9, 21, 23 June and 13, 14 July 1983 (Washington, DC: U.S. GPO, 1984), p. 29.

71. James L. Buckley, testimony, 6 May 1982, in U.S. Congress, Senate Committee on Governmental Affairs, Subcommittee on Investigations, *Transfer of United States High Technology to the Soviet Union and Soviet Bloc Nations*, Hearings, 97th Congress, 2nd session, 4, 5, 6, 11, 12 May 1982 (Washington, DC: U.S. GPO, 1982), p. 161.

72. U.S. Department of Defense, *The Technology Transfer Control Program*, pp. 11-29.

73. Stent, "East-West Trade," p. 457-58.

74. Buchan, "Technology Transfer," p. 132; Bertsch and McIntyre, "The Western Alliance," pp. 222-23; National Academy of Sciences, *Balancing*, pp. 41-42; David Dickson, "Soviet High-Tech Spying Detailed in France," *Science*, vol. 228, no. 4697 (19 April 1985), p. 306; Perle, "The Strategic Impact," p. 8; and Stephen Bryen, "Technology Transfer and National Security: Finding the Proper Balance," in *Selling the Rope to Hang Capitalism?*, eds. Charles M. Perry and Robert L. Pflatzgraff, Jr. (London: Pergamon-Brassey's, 1987), p. 15.

75. See Buchan, "Technology Transfer," p. 132.

76. Bertsch and McIntyre, "The Western Alliance," p. 222-23; and Stent, "East-West Trade," p. 459. The "no exceptions" policy was lifted in 1989 after Soviet troops left Afghanistan. See President George Bush, "Proposals for a Free and Peaceful Europe," address at Rheingoldhalle, Mainz, Federal Republic of Germany, 31 May 1989; rpt. in U.S. Department of State, Bureau of Public Affairs, *Current Policy*, no. 1179, June 1989, p. 2.

77. The French and Dutch resisted what they viewed as a "more restrictive approach implicit in" this policy. See Bertsch and McIntyre, "The Western Alliance," pp. 222-23. They quote from J. P. Hardt and K. S. Tomlinson, "Economic Interchange with the U.S.S.R. in the 1980s," paper prepared for the Conference of California Seminar on International Security and Foreign Policy (15-17 April 1982), p. 31.

78. U.S. Department of Defense, *The Technology Security Program*, p. i.

79. See prepared statement of Thomas A. Campobasso, Vice President, Export Marketing, Rockwell International Corporation, in U.S. Congress, House Committee on Armed Services, Technology Transfer Panel, *Technology Transfer*, 98th Congress, 1st session, Hearings, 9, 21, 23 June, 13, 14 July 1983 (Washington, DC: U.S. GPO, 1984), pp. 185, 190.

80. National Academy of Sciences, *Balancing*, pp. 139-40.

81. Mastanduno, "CoCOM," pp. 116-17; and Lindstrom, "Devising Fair," p. 5.

82. Testimony of Lionel H. Olmer, Under Secretary for International Trade, U.S. Department of Commerce, in U.S. Congress, House Committee on Armed Services, Technology Transfer Panel, *Technology Transfer*, 98th Congress, 1st session, Hearings, 9, 21, 23 June, 13, 14 July 1983 (Washington, DC: U.S. GPO,

1984), pp. 58-59. Besides their size, the lists' complexity was disturbing. For example, over thirty pages were said to be required to define computers in technical generic terms. See Richard N. Perle, "The Strategic Implications of West-East Technology Transfer," in "The Conduct of East-West Relations in the 1980s, Part II," *Adelphi Papers*, vol. 190 (London: International Institute for Strategic Studies, Summer 1984), p. 26.

83. Root, "Trade Controls," pp. 77-78; Buchan, "Western Security," pp. 29-30; and U.S. Department of Defense, *The Technology Transfer Control Program*, pp. 23-24.

84. Sharfman, testimony, p. 34.

85. Stephen Woolcock, "Western Policies on East-West Trade and Technology," in *Technology Transfer and East-West Relations*, ed. Mark E. Schaffer (London: Croom Helm, 1985), p. 203.

86. As R. Roger Majak, representing the firm Tektroniks, points out. See R. Roger Majak, "U.S. Export Controls: The Limits of Practicality," in *Selling the Rope to Hang Capitalism?*, eds. Charles M. Perry and Robert L. Pfaltzgraff, Jr. (London: Pergamon-Brassey's, 1987), p. 175.

87. On the computer negotiations see Root, "Trade Controls," pp. 68-69 and Buchan, "Western Security", p. 28.

88. U.S. Department of Defense, *The Technology Security Program*, p. 63.

89. A limited number of sales have subsequently been licensed, particularly after the overthrow of communist regimes in Eastern Europe. Telecommunications sales remain controversial since, while a modern economy requires adequate communications infrastructure, advanced communications technology can also upgrade Soviet military command, control, and communications. Intelligence officials also argued that improved Soviet telecommunications intrastructure would make it harder to gather electronic intelligence. U.S. Department of Defense, *The Technology Transfer Control Program*, p. 22; Aeppel, "The Evolution," p. 111; Stent, "East-West Trade," pp. 457-58; Glennon J. Harrison and George Holliday, *Export Controls, 1990*, CRS Issue Brief, IB87122 (Washington, DC: Congressional Research Service, Library of Congress, 10 December 1990), p. CRS-9; and William Clements, Director, Office of Technology and Policy Analysis, Bureau of Export Administration, U.S. Department of Commerce, comments in *East-West Trade and the Congress*, Proceedings of a CRS Seminar, 90-529E, ed. Glennon J. Harrison (Washington, DC: Congressional Research Service, Library of Congress, 15 November 1990), pp. CRS-46-47.

90. Complicated definitional questions, such as whether international electronic transmittal of software and data was subject to controls, remained unresolved in the opinion of some observers. See Neville March Hunnings, "Legal Aspects of Technology Transfer to Eastern Europe and the Soviet Union," in *Technology and East-West Relations*, ed. Mark E. Schaffer (London: Croom Helm, 1985), pp. 149-50.

91. There was concern that that would hurt U.S. exporters, given strict U.S. interpretation of the new rules, whereas loose interpretations were an excuse for allies to violate COCOM dictums if they were not in a member's interest. See Paul Mann, "Commerce Dept. Will Strengthen Monitoring of Computer Exports," *Aviation Week and Space Technology*, vol. 122, no. 3 (21 January 1985), pp. 108-09; and Drammen [Norway] Police Department, *Report. Investigation of the Transfer of Technology From Kongsberg Vaapenfabrik to the Soviet Union*, 14 October 1987 {photocopy}, p. 25. The *Report* quoted a Norwegian Foreign Ministry note dated 6 July 1987.

92. There was evidence that widespread smuggling, diversions, and lax export oversight still allowed the East to get all it required. There were even indications that Paris and Bonn were seeking to circumvent the new agreement. See David Hebditch and Nick Anning, "Soviet Sting Sours," *Datamation*, vol. 31, no. 12 (15 June 1985), pp. 34, 36, 38, 42, 44; and John P. Hardt and Donna L. Gold, "Background Facts About East-West Trade," in U.S. Congress, Joint Economic Committee, *East-West Technology Transfer: A Congressional Dialog With the Reagan Administration*, 98th Congress, 2nd session, 19 December 1984 (Washington, DC: U.S. GPO, 1984), p. 77.

93. U.S. Department of Defense, *The Technology Security Program*, pp. 61-62.

94. David Marsh, "U.S. Wants Tighter CoCOM Control," *Financial Times*, 7 October 1985, p. 6, rpt. in U.S. Department of Defense, Department of the Air Force, *Current News*, special edition, Technology Transfer, no date, p. 66; Robert D. Hershey, Jr., "Technology Exports to China," *New York Times*, 17 October 1985, section D, p. 21; rpt. in U.S. Department of Defense, Department of the Air Force, *Current News*, special edition, Technology Transfer, no date, p. 31; National Academy of Sciences, *Balancing*, p. 137.

95. U.S. Department of Defense, *The Technology Security Program*, pp. 65-66; Perle, "The Strategic Impact," p. 8; Price, "COCOM After," p. 199; Buchan, "Western Security," p. 28; Stent, "East-West Trade," p. 460; and Lionel Olmer, "National Security Export Controls in the Reagan Administration," in *Selling the Rope to Hang Capitalism?*, (London: Pergamon-Brassey's, 1987), pp. 157-58.

96. William Schneider, Jr., "Technology Transfers and U.S. Foreign Policy: Challenges and Opportunities," in *Selling the Rope to Hang Capitalism?*, eds. Charles M. Perry and Robert L. Pfaltzgraff, Jr. (London: Pergamon-Brassey's, 1987), p. 86 and Perle in U.S. Congress, House Committee on Science, Space, and Technology, *National Academy of Sciences Report*, pp. 92-93, 98-99, 114. See also U.S. Department of Defense, *The Technology Transfer Control Program*, p. 11.

97. On COCOM exception policy, see National Academy of Sciences, pp. 142-43, and U.S. Congress, General Accounting Office, *Export Controls*, pp. 11, 15. On U.S. decision making for exceptions, see Bertsch, "U.S. Export Controls," p. 131; U.S., Congress, Office of Technology Assessment, *Technology*, p. 136; U.S. Congress, General Accounting Office, *Export Controls*, p. 10; and U.S. Department of Defense, *The Technology Security Program*, pp. 35, 37. The GAO estimated in 1979 that the value of exception exports was approximately $300

million, with national exceptions accounting for about two-thirds of this figure. "Administrative exceptions" accounted for the remaining one-third. In 1984, David Buchan of the *Financial Times* estimated that 3-5% of total Western exports to the bloc were of COCOM-controlled items. See U.S. Congress, General Accounting Office, *Export Controls*, p. 15; and Buchan, "Western Security," p. 25.

98. McIntyre and Cupitt, "Multilateral Strategic Trade," p. 154. A member *could* ignore a negative COCOM finding, however Under Secretary Schneider asserted that this rarely occurred. See Schneider, "East-West Relations," p. 70.

99. Root, "COCOM-," p. 100. These problems were compounded because COCOM's rules were not codified and decisions were based on "precedents, interpretive notes, and factors for exceptions." The flexibility this afforded members was offset by the lack of an institutional memory. See McIntyre and Cupitt, "Multilateral Strategic Trade," p. 141.

100. Root in U.S. Congress, Senate Committee on Governmental Affairs, *Transfer of Technology*, p. 237; James K. Gordon, "Three Agencies Will Cooperate To Cut Export License Delays," *Aviation Week and Space Technology*, vol. 122, no. 18 (6 May 1985), p. 106; and Price, "COCOM After," p. 198.

101. National Academy of Sciences, *Balancing*, p. 206. There were spurious allegations by foreign business interests that by using its veto, the United States blocked other allies from exporting to the P.R.C., thereby permitting U.S. exports to capture the market. But relaxed controls benefited *all* COCOM exporters and allowed the Europeans an equal chance to export to the P.R.C. As a State Department official noted, if the United States really wanted to limit access to Chinese markets, why did Washington take the lead in liberalizing controls? However, whether justified or not, suspicion could tempt other COCOM members to covertly exploit other risky opportunities. The same official also reported that at COCOM, a European confided that the existing rules actually benefited the Europeans because they limited the sale of highly advanced U.S. technology, which the Europeans did not manufacture, thereby constraining the potential U.S. market in the P.R.C. See also U.S. Congress, Office of Technology Assessment, pp. 168-69, and National Academy of Sciences, pp. 142, 186. The NAS could find no substantive evidence to verify charges of U.S. manipulation of COCOM; not-for-attribution interview, Bureau of Economic and Business Affairs, U.S. Department of State, 23 February 1988.

102. Buchan, "Western Security," pp. 25-26 and Price, "COCOM After," p. 198.

103. Mastanduno, "Strategies," p. 528.

104. This problem had vexed COCOM from the embargo's earliest days. See the scattered references in U.S. Congress, House Committee on Foreign Affairs, *U.S. Foreign Policy and the East-West Confrontation*, pp. 19, 23-24, 188-89, 237; Mastanduno, "Strategies," p. 528; Buchan, "Western Security," p. 24; Adler-Karlsson, pp. 75-78; and U.S. Congress, Senate Committee on Banking, Housing, and Urban Affairs, *Enforcement of the Export Control Enforcement Act*, Hearing, 98th Congress, 2nd session, 2 April 1984 (Washington, DC: U.S. GPO, 1984).

105. Finland also toughened its controls, increased penalities, and was granted COCOM-like status. Buchan, "Western Security," pp. 25-26.; Stuart Auerbach, "Sweden Approves Strict New Controls on Export of High-Tech Products," *Washington Post*, 6 March 1986, section E, p. 2, columns 4-6; U.S. Congress, General Accounting Office, *Export Licensing: Commerce-Defense Review of Applications to Certain Free World Nations*, NSIAD-86-169 (Washington, DC: U.S. GPO, September 1986), p. 10; and Jan Stankovsky and Hendrik Roodbeen, "Export Controls Outside COCOM," in *After the Revolutions: East-West Trade and Technology Transfer in the 1990s*, eds. Gary K. Bertsch, Heinrich Vogel, and Jan Zielonka (Boulder, CO: Westview Press, 1991), pp. 71-91.

106. National Academy of Sciences, *Balancing*, p. 149. See also the references in Bengt Sundelius, ed., *The Neutral Democracies and the New Cold War* (Boulder, CO: Westview Press, 1987), and in Andreas Flutsch, "Love and Kisses from a Swiss Letter Box. Our Country Serves as a Turntable in the Lucrative Business of Smuggling Western Technology to the East Block {sic}," *Die Weltwoche*, (Zurich), 8 August 1985, p. 9, rpt. in U.S. Department of Defense, Department of the Air Force, *Current News*, special edition, Technology Security, no date, pp. 63-66. "West Works to Plug Technology Leaks to USSR," *Government Computer News*, 28 October 1985, p. 59; rpt. in U.S. Department of Defense, Department of the Air Force, *Current News*, special edition, Technology Security, 22 January 1986, p. 13; Auerbach, "Sweden Approves," section E, p. 2, columns 4-6. David E. Sanger, "Envoy Says Austrians Botched Computer Case," *New York Times*, 11 October 1986, p. 40, rpt. in U.S. Department of Defense, Department of the Air Force, *Current News*, special edition, Technology Security, 11 December 1986, p. 6; Eduardo Lachica, "Austria to Tighten Customs Law to Halt Illegal Shipping of Sensitive Technology," *Wall Street Journal*, 12 November 1986, p. 37, rpt. in U.S. Department of Defense, Department of the Air Force, *Current News*, special edition, Technology Security, 11 December 1986, p. 8.

107. See the discussion in National Academy of Sciences, *Balancing*, pp. 139, 148-49, 203-20.

108. As was suggested by R. Roger Majak and the National Academy of Sciences. See Majak, "U.S. Export Controls," p. 175, and National Academy of Sciences, *Balancing*, pp. 141, 149. See also, David E. Sanger, "Computer Export Bar Is Easing," *New York Times*, 19 August 1987, section D, p. 1, rpt. in U.S. Department of Defense, Department of the Air Force, *Current News*, special edition, Technology Security, no. 1639 (1 October 1987), p. 26. Exports of technology to *less developed* Third World states and endemic trouble spots also posed problems since technology security might be lax, governments allegedly facilitated diversions to the Soviet bloc, or acquired technology might aid in development of indigenous dual-use items which could be used against Western forces and interests. See Ronald J. Ostrow, "U.S. Probing Noriega in Technology Transfer," *Washington Post*, 25 August 1987, section A, p. 10, columns 5-6; Mary Ann Weaver and Jon Connell, "Americans Woo India Through High-Tech Deal," *Sunday Times* [London], 9 June 1985, p. 21, rpt. in U.S. Department of Defense, Department of the Air

Force, *Current News*, special edition, Technology Security, no date, pp. 54-55; Richard M. Weintraub, "U.S. India Near Supercomputer Deal," *Washington Post*, 8 July 1986, section D, p. 1, columns 3-4; section D, p. 2, columns 1-3. Sheila Tefft, "Computer Sale: A Key Test of US-India Ties," *Journal of Commerce*, 8 January 1987, p. 1, rpt. in U.S. Department of Defense, Department of the Air Force, *Current News*, special edition, Technology Security, no. 1570 (16 April 1987), pp. 13-14, "U.S. Team Signs India Safeguards Agreement Allowing Sale of U.S.-Made Supercomputer," *Federal Contracts Report*, 2 February 1987, p. 215, rpt. in U.S. Department of Defense, Department of the Air Force, *Current News*, special edition, Technology Security, no. 1570 (16 April 1987), p. 39; Tim Carrington and Robert S. Greenberger, "Bureaucratic Battle, Fight Over India's Bid For Computer Shows Disarray of U.S. Policy," *Wall Street Journal*, 24 February 1987, p. 1, rpt. in U.S., Department of Defense, Department of the Air Force, *Current News*, special edition, Technology Security, no. 1570 (16 April 1987), pp. 47-48; David E. Sanger, "Computer Sale Seen to India," *New York Times*, 27 March 1987, section D, p. 1, column 2; section D, p. 2, columns 4-5; David E. Sanger, "Sale of Computers to Iran is Allowed," *New York Times*, 21 April 1987, section D, p. 1, rpt. in U.S. Department of Defense, Department of Air Force, *Current News*, Early Bird Edition, 21 April 1987, pp. 1, 3.

109. See the comments by the convicted smuggler in Hebditch and Anning, "Soviet Sting," p. 34, and Karen DeYoung, "Norway Irked by U.S. View on High-Tech Sale," *Washington Post*, 19 July 1987, section A, p. 18, column 6. On the dilemmas faced by firms trading with the East, see David Sneider, "Toshiba Sale: Only the Tip of Espionage Iceberg?" *Christian Science Monitor*, 21 July 1987, p. 1, rpt. in U.S. Department of Defense, Department of the Air Force, *Current News*, special edition, Technology Transfer, no. 1639 (1 October 1987), p. 1; Damon Darlin, "The Toshiba Case: Japanese Firms' Push to Sell to Soviets Led to Security Breaches Many Tended to Ignore Rules and the National Interest, Authorities Seemed Lax- But Attitudes Are Changing," *Wall Street Journal*, 4 August 1987; rpt. in *Congressional Record*, Senate, 6 August 1987, p. S11454{?}, rpt. in U.S. Department of Defense, Department of the Air Force, *Current News*, special edition, Technology Security, no. 1639 (1 October 1987), p. 18. Robert T. Gallagher, "Europeans Try to Trade High Tech For Soviet Natural Gas," *Electronics*, vol. 58, no. 28 (15 July 1985), p. 39. Dr. Stephen D. Bryen, testimony in U.S. Congress, Senate Committee on Banking, Housing, and Urban Affairs, *Enforcement of the Export Control Enforcement Act*, Hearing, 98th Congress, 2nd session, 2 April 1984 (Washington, DC: U.S. GPO, 1984), pp. 57-58. In COCOM, the Export Control Subcommittee coordinated administrative and enforcement activities among members.

110. Hebditch and Anning, "Soviet Sting," p. 38; Eduardo Lachica, "Norway, Japan Move to Back U.S. Effort To Curb Some Shipments to Soviet Bloc," *Wall Street Journal*, 24 June 1987, p. 22; Lothar G. A. Griessebach, "East-West Trade: A European Perspective," in *The Politics of East-West Trade*, ed. Gordon B. Smith, Westview Special Studies in International Relations (Boulder, CO: Westview Press, 1984), p. 243; and Jacobsen, p. 31. Norwegian regulations dated from the nineteen-

forties. See DeYoung, "Norway Irked," section A, p. 18, column 4. Johan Joergen Holst, "That Technology Diversion: Norway Replies," letter to the editor, *Washington Post*, 14 July 1987, section A, p. 14, column 4; Drammen (Norway) Police Department *Report*, which stressed that expiration of statutes of limitations prevented full prosecution of export violations.

111. For example, in July 1987, Japan doubled its "inspection force" to 80. By comparison, there were 620 inspectors in the United States at that time. See David E. Sanger, "A Bizarre Deal Diverts Vital Tools to Russians," *New York Times*, 12 June 1987, section D, p. 10, column 3 and Stuart Auerbach and Clay Chandler, "Japanese Assurances Satisfy Baldrige," *Washington Post*, 17 July 1987, section F, p. 2, column 1.

112. Bureaucratic infighting between the DOC and the Customs Service did not help matters. See U.S. Congress, Senate Committee on Banking, Housing, and Urban Affairs, *Enforcement of the Export Control Enforcement Act*.

113. Mary Thornton, "Customs Fights KGB On High-Tech Thefts," *Washington Post*, 5 February 1986, section A, p. 17, columns 5-6.

114. Sanger, "A Bizarre Deal," section D, p. 10, column 4.

115. Hobart Rowen, "Japan Needs Its Friends," *Washington Post*, 26 July 1987, section H, p. 1, columns 3-4. See also, Stuart Auerbach, "Japan Tries to Blunt Toshiba Scandal," *Washington Post*, 3 September 1987, section B, p. 2, column 1; and Yoichi Clark Shimatsu, "Toshiba-bashing is Defense Department Ploy," *San Jose Mercury News*, 24 August 1987, p. 7B, rpt. in U.S. Department of Defense, Department of the Air Force, *Current News*, special edition, Technology Security, no. 1639 (1 October 1987), pp. 28-29.

116. Robert A. Rosenblatt, "Toshiba: Executives Unaware of Sale to Soviets," *Washington Post*, 10 September 1987, section E, p. 1, columns 2-4; section E, p. 4, column 1; David E. Sanger, "Bigger roles for Toshiba and Kongsberg Cited," *New York Times*, 29 July 1987, section D, p. 2, rpt. in U.S. Department of Defense, Department of the Air Force, *Current News*, special edition, Technology Security, no. 1639 (1 October 1987), p. 5; and Drammen [Norway] Police Department *Report*.

117. Stuart Auerbach, "Europeans Sold Gear to Soviets," *Washington Post*, 22 October 1987, section A, p. 16, column 2. See also the comments by Senator Jake Garn on Public Broadcasting Service, *MacNeil-Lehrer Newshour*, interview with correspondent Judy Woodruff, 28 October 1987.

118. James M. Dorsey, "Pentagon Cutting Off Toshiba at the Wallet," *Washington Times*, 2 June 1987, p. 1, rpt. in U.S. Department of Defense, Department of the Air Force, *Current News*, Early Bird edition, 2 June 1987, p. 10. Stuart Auerbach, "Reagan Aides Ask U.S. Allies to Tighten Their Export Laws," *Washington Post*, 17 October 1987, section G, p. 2, columns 1-2. For a summary of proposed legislation, see Raymond Ahearn and Ronald O'Rourke, *Toshiba-Kongsberg Technology Diversion: Issues For Congress*, Issue Brief no. IB87184, Congressional Research Service, U.S. Library of Congress (Washington, DC, 9 October 1987), pp. CRS-14-15.

119. As of May 1988, when the trade bill was vetoed by President Reagan (for reasons unrelated to the sanctions), the sanctions' fate was still to be determined, although it appeared that Congress would not override the veto. However, senior staffmembers on the Senate Banking Committee asserted that similar legislation would be reintroduced in 1989 if the veto stood. Martin Gruenberg, Staff Director, Subcommittee on International Finance and Monetary Policy, Senate Banking Committee, interview, Washington, DC, 23 May 1988, and Wayne Abernathy, Economist, Senate Banking Committee, interview, Washington, DC, 27 May 1988. See also Robert A. Rosenblatt, "How 'Swat Team' of Toshiba Lobbyists Took on Congress- and Won," *Washington Post*, 1 May 1988, section H, p. 1, columns 2-6; section H, p. 3, columns 1-2.

120. DeYoung, "Norway Irked," section A, p. 18, column 2. Clay Chandler, "House Panel Is Warned on Toshiba Bills," *Washington Post*, 15 July 1987, section D, p. 3, column 1; Clay Chandler, "Japan Official Seeks to Soothe Angry Congress," *Washington Post*, 16 July 1987, section E, p. 1, column 1; section E, p. 2, columns 1-3 and David Butts, "Japan Trade Official Heads for Washington," *Washington Post*, 9 September 1987, section F, p. 3, columns 1-3.

121. Eduardo Lachica and E. S. Browning, "West Tightens Technology Export Rules But Shortens List of Controlled Products," *Wall Street Journal*, 29 January 1988; and U.S. Department of State, "Results of the Senior Political Meeting on Strengthening the Coordinating Committee on Multilateral Export Controls (COCOM)," Press Release, 29 January 1988.

122. On developments in COCOM since the autumn of 1989 see Gary K. Bertsch and Steve Elliott-Gower, "U.S. COCOM Policy: From Paranoia to Perestroika?" in *After the Revolutions: East-West Trade and Technology Transfer in the 1990s*, eds. Gary K. Bertsch, Heinrich Vogel, and Jan Zielonka (Boulder, CO: Westview Press, 1991), pp. 26-27; Jurgen Notzold and Hendrik Roodbeen, "The European Community and COCOM: The Exclusion of an Interested Party," in *After the Revolutions*, pp. 129-30; *Export Control News*, vol. 5, nos. 1-3 (25 January, 25 February, 26 March 1991); Harrison and Holliday, *Export Controls, 1990*, pp. CRS-5-7; Kevin F. F. Quigley and William J. Long, "Export Controls: Moving Beyond Economic Containment," *World Policy Journal* (Winter 1990), pp. 170-87 and Clyde H. Farnsworth, "U.S. Balks at Easing Technology-Export Curbs," *New York Times*, 1 March 1991, section C, p. 2, columns 1-4.

2

Trading with the Soviet Union and Eastern Europe: Contending Views and Policies Within the Atlantic Alliance

For all the major Western powers, East-West trade policy and controls on technology transfer to the Soviet Union and Eastern Europe were influenced by historical experience and economic and political considerations. This chapter briefly surveys and assesses the broad outlines of the independent variables--including historical factors, geopolitical interests, and domestic political conditions--undergirding U.S., West German, French, and British policy. In addition, these countries regulatory frameworks governing East-West trade are briefly examined.

If, as many analysts argue, the United States could only achieve an effective export control regime with multilateral help, it is necessary to understand how each major ally perceives export controls in the context of other domestic political and foreign policy considerations. Furthermore, export trade in general, and East-West trade in particular, has long been more significant to the Western Europeans than to the United States, and the political and economic rationale for such trade sometimes causes friction among the Western allies. When U.S. export regulations are perceived to jeopardize the allies' interests, the controls' viability was undermined and the Western Alliance was strained by transatlantic disagreement. Extraterritorial U.S. regulations are a case in point. The prospective creation of a single European Community (EC) market in 1992 also raises important questions regarding U.S. policy. It is therefore proper to consider and assess these factors since U.S. policymakers must weigh their relative importance in formulating realistic policy alternatives.

DEBATE IN THE UNITED STATES

U.S. East-West trade policy evolved out of a complex set of factors. These included past policy, consideration of the political and economic trade-offs involved, and domestic politics.[1] Neither antitrade nor pro-trade groups were capable of rallying domestic opinion behind their goals for any length of time.

The inability to marshal a consensus on trade was attributable to characteristics of American political life and culture--including deep-seated anti-communist values, growing political pluralism with competing groupings unable to agree on a common policy--and the political dynamics of superpower relations.[2] Furthermore, in the wake of the bitter Vietnam experience, a large body of public opinion and many policymakers dissented from the initial postwar consensus backing the use of military and economic might to halt communism, arbitrate global trouble spots, and restore prosperity. The COCOM system and postwar U.S. East-West trade policy were elements in an overarching containment policy that was now subject to domestic criticism and debate. There remained, however, influential advocates of the unilateral use of U.S. power to achieve national interests. They scoffed at the notion that growing global political and economic interdependence and relative loss of U.S. economic and military influence and power rendered economic containment ineffective and obsolete.

These characteristics shaped the debate in the United States and stimulated impulses to facilitate or restrict trade. For example, the strong Congressional and business interests favoring liberalized East-West trade during the 1960s and early 1970s, a policy supported by presidents Johnson and Nixon, were challenged by reinvigorated antitrade interests in the 1970s. The influential opposition of ideological conservatives, as well as ethnic and religious groups and organized labor, grew as the promise of detente faded and the "Soviet threat" blossomed anew. Latent suspicion of Soviet motives was rekindled and fanned by global Soviet activity at a time when the postwar balance between Congress and the Executive was shifting. An assertive Congress blocked presidential initiatives in East-West trade by passing the Jackson-Vanik and Stevenson amendments, partly in response to interest group pressure.[3]

Congress was by no means united on the question of export controls and disagreement was reflected in its legislative efforts. While the *general* thrust of Congressional efforts after 1969 was toward liberalization and easing the regulatory burden on business, some in Congress remained concerned lest national security be compromised. As a result, reform was watered down and other legislation passed that arguably bolstered national security controls.

Specifically, Congress did seek to reduce the size of control lists, speed up license processing, and make the Executive agencies more accountable and responsive to business concerns.[4] Despite these efforts, as William Long argues, the Executive Branch was able to deflect and slow full implementation of reforms. An important reason for this success was the Executive's ability to exploit disagreement in Congress over the wisdom of reform and Congressional reluctance to constrain the President's prerogatives in national security matters. For example, in 1975 Congress passed the Department of Defense (DOD) Appropriation Authorization Act (DAA) and the Export Administration Amendments Act (EAAA). These acts authorized the DOD to deny any export of technology development of which was funded by the DOD, and also authorized the DOD to review exports of dual-use technology to controlled countries.

A built-in institutional and procedural proclivity in Congress favoring compromise in order to achieve legislative results also hamstrung reform efforts. For example, Congressional conferees' inability to agree delayed passage of the 1985 EAA amendments (not to be confused with the 1975 EAAA) for two years. Consequently, initiatives were delayed and the reforms' intended effectiveness was diluted. They were further undercut by agencies that stalled (in the case of foreign availability determinations)[5] or reluctantly implemented legal mandates. The episodic, sometimes superficial, and diffused oversight by several Congressional committees of export controls also permitted the agencies considerable discretion in implementing the law.[6]

While it was a subject of sometimes heated debate, the actual importance to the U.S. economy of trade with Eastern Europe and the U.S.S.R. was minimal. As a percentage of U.S. world trade turnover, Eastern Europe's and the U.S.S.R's share had never been more than 2 percent at the height of detente in the mid-1970s. There had been a slow decline to well under 1 percent during 1981-87.[7] Furthermore, although exports to this area were important to certain industries, such as oil and gas and to grain farmers, the United States did not export heavily to the area as a whole. From a high of 2.5 percent of U.S. world exports in 1975, Eastern Europe's and the U.S.S.R.'s combined share had fallen to less than 1 percent by 1987 and U.S. officials saw little prospect for an increase.[8] Imports were of even less importance having fallen to about one-half of 1 percent by the mid-1980s.[9]

Despite the relative overall unimportance of this trade, it played a role in U.S. policy toward the area. For example, from 1981-1987, the U.S.S.R. accounted for about one-half of total U.S. trade with the Soviet

Bloc, a figure higher than that for the F.R.G. and comparable to that for the U.K. Furthermore, on average, approximately 17 to 20 percent of U.S. East-West trade was with Romania from 1981 to 1987, a significantly greater percentage than that of the principal COCOM allies. Romania illustrated trade's role in Washington's "differentiation" policy--encouraging independence from Moscow and erosion of Soviet-Eastern European ties through trade preferences--and this was also underscored by the relative importance of trade with Poland and Hungary. Polish and Hungarian trade shares averaged approximately 13 percent and 8 percent of total trade with the area from 1981 to 1987. By contrast, Bulgaria's, Czechoslovakia's, and the German Democratic Republic's shares remained approximately 3 to 4 percent for the same period. Finally, during the same period, the U.S. share of the total value of East-West trade among the Big Four allies averaged 12.7 percent which, while much less than the F.R.G.'s share, was larger than Britain's average.[10]

A relatively sharp polarization of views on East-West trade relations characterized the U.S. policy debate in the 1970s and 1980s, although no one perspective dominated. At one extreme were those who believed trade was a particularly useful means of *ameliorating* fundamental superpower conflicts, a popular sentiment during the 1970s. Few such advocates wanted completely decontrolled trade, but most believed trade should be unencumbered by political regulations. A second more skeptical school, which had evolved in the wake of disillusionment with detente, regarded trade as a part of overall U.S. deterrent policy and useful in *managing* the U.S.-Soviet relationship--denial of advanced technology being the chief aim. Trade policy supplemented political initiatives and a strong defense in deterring the Soviets, but trade was not singularly effective as a policy instrument. Finally, echoing the Cold War's economic warfare advocates, the more conservative view held that restricting East-West trade was instrumental in *waging* (and eventually triumphing in) the East-West war.[11]

Debate and disagreement over the utility of positive and negative linkage policy divided U.S. policymakers. At its heart, the debate revolved around the question of whether and to what degree trade sanctions or trade liberalization modified Soviet behavior and, secondarily, what the costs and benefits were for the U.S. economy. Adherents of positive and negative linkage shared views of the structural rigidity and economic underdevelopment plaguing planned economies, problems which offered the United States opportunities to nudge communist systems toward evolutionary change.[12] For example, the positive linkage undergirding the Nixon-Kissinger effort to build a "web of constructive relationships," drawing the Soviet leadership into greater interdependence in exchange for valued Western technology, was expected to tame Soviet adventurism.[13] Over the longer term, more trade would promote U.S. interests by encouraging domestic Soviet prosperity and opening up the communist system.[14] Business people argued that a potentially vast market of disgruntled Soviet consumers eagerly anticipated a higher standard of living provided by increased trade. To continue to restrict U.S. trade merely allowed foreign competitors to fill the vacuum.[15] Trade fostered human understanding and encouraged a vested interest among important managerial groups in the U.S.S.R. who "recognize[d] the economic interdependence of today's world."[16] Because of their desire to succeed, these managers' role as promoters of civilian production would be influential in drawing off resources and talent that might otherwise be channeled into the Soviet military.[17] A materially rich and content U.S.S.R. also was likely to be more open to new influences and domestic political reforms, less fearful of external threats, and more cooperative on a host of bilateral issues.[18] It was therefore wise to pursue positive linkage, free of unrealistic political and foreign policy considerations, to reward acceptable Soviet behavior.[19]

Policymakers advocating negative linkage generally held a more skeptical view of the utility of East-West trade to encourage a more benign Soviet foreign policy. The trade "stick" became a favored tool of U.S. administrations during the late 1970s and early 1980s as the Soviet bloc became more active globally and impinged upon U.S. interests. Unacceptable Soviet domestic and foreign policy behavior was punished by selective tightening and loosening of trade in commodities for which the U.S.S.R. was thought uniquely dependent on U.S. supplies.[20]

However, in the wake of the disappointments with detente and inconclusive--and for some economic sectors injurious--consequences of the Carter administration's sanctions policy, branded as "lightswitch diplomacy" by Reagan's Secretary of State George Schultz,[21] U.S. East-West trade policy was the subject of considerable disagreement during the Reagan administration. Under Reagan, moderate proponents of a managed, gradual, and steady U.S.-Soviet relationship--where trade figured as a key adjunct in a broader range of deterrent policies[22]--vied with conservatives echoing economic warfare principles popular in the 1950s.[23]

Moderate East-West trade policy was generally advocated by the State and Commerce Departments, some National Security Council staff,[24] and the business community. Skepticism and hostility to expanded trade flows were centered in the Defense Department and the intelligence community. A latent but deep-rooted distrust of Soviet motives in the American polity and among elements of the foreign policy establishment blossomed in the wake of the perceived failure of detente and was vocally represented by advocates of a harder line toward the Soviet bloc both within and outside the Reagan administration.

Drawing upon historical precedent, an axiom of antitraders was that Western trade and credits, far from tempering Czarist and Soviet behavior, had been a critical factor in modernizing their economic and military might, thereby facilitating inherently expansionist Czarist and communist policies.[25] Detente, growing contacts, and trade flows were regarded as fatally naive policies lacking any realistic assessment of the security implications or of how the Soviet bloc had exploited Western technology and military secrets.[26] This "giveaway" had meant much larger outlays for weapons modernization as the United States sought to maintain its strategic and conventional edge in the face of rapidly improving Soviet capabilities augmented by acquired Western technology.[27] Even more damning, the allies, whose security depended on U.S. military power, blithely sold ostensibly nonmilitary advanced dual-use technology which was incorporated in Soviet weapons[28] or civilian industry, which permitted reallocation of more resources to the military by modernizing the bloc's anemic economies.

Instead of trade encouraging domestic Soviet liberalization and integration into the global community, conservatives cited Western vulnerabilities and resource dependencies which the Soviets exploited. For example, the Soviets understood that Western democracies could be pressured by myopic domestic trade interests to dismantle multilateral controls and subsidize unprofitable[29] trade with the Soviet bloc at bargain rates. Playing Western businesses and countries against each other had the added benefit of promoting discord between the United States and its NATO allies, as the 1982 pipeline crisis demonstrated.[30] Some foresaw a future "Finlandized" Western Europe so dependent on Soviet trade and resources that the threat of a cutoff might force a choice between Soviet demands and Alliance solidarity.[31]

The economic warfare camp held sway within the Reagan administration during its first term, but by about 1985, a gradual thaw in U.S.-Soviet relations began. A complex set of factors, including the ascension of a vigorous and apparently reformist Soviet leader actively seeking more U.S. imports,[32] and movement on arms control and on regional issues, contributed a more charitable view of the Kremlin in Washington. The resignation of several top conservative policymakers from key posts in the U.S. administration bolstered the influence of more pragmatic advisors who were relatively less skeptical of the benefits of U.S.-Soviet trade and deemphasized political constraints on trade.[33] A new cycle of active trade relations appeared to gain momentum in tandem with the congenial political atmosphere and, in this respect, the late 1980s resembled the 1965-1975 period.[34] U.S. business interests, long unhappy with the scope of export controls, lobbied a sympathetic Congress--concerned by ballooning trade deficits--and achieved a series of reforms designed to ease regulatory burdens and liberalize trade. Their success also resembled trade reform efforts and achievements two decades earlier, which culminated in the 1969 EAA. This trend was not without its critics[35] and, as events in the late 1970s and early 1980s showed, deteriorating relations could reignite public distrust of the Soviet bloc and strengthen the hand of antitraders.

U.S. policy remains "a combination of restrictive and facilitative impulses reflecting the complex forces in the domestic and international environment."[36] Absent a clear and present danger to national security, resulting from a drastic deterioration in superpower relations, pro and antitrade forces remain in disagreement. Public opinion, while never free of some distrust of Soviet motives and intentions, is subject to fluctuating shifts between supporting trade and restrictions. These shifts are partly a function of the political dynamics of superpower relations just as economic relations are closely interlinked with the status of numerous bilateral issues ranging from arms control to human rights. As long as this agenda remains manageable, in an atmosphere of mutual trust, U.S. policy on trade might slowly evolve toward greater liberalization.

THE EUROPEAN VIEW OF EAST-WEST TRADE: THE F.R.G., FRANCE, AND THE U.K.

Consensus on East-West trade relations is widely shared in Europe, in comparison with the debate in the United States. The predominant paradigms among European leaders and business are rooted in the view that trade relations could contribute to resolving or attenuating East-West conflict and regional problems arising from the Soviet Union's disintegration. During the Cold War, those who urged caution or even advocated trade policies designed to *weaken* Soviet power were in the minority.[37] This remains so in the wake of the Soviet breakup.

Geopolitical reality and historical and economic factors shaped European views. First, the proximity of the Soviet Union and Eastern Europe, bordering or within a few hundred kilometers of most Western European states and capitals meant preoccupation with Eastern Europe. Historically, Western Europe had long recognized the Russian Empire as a major power-- sometime ally and sometime potential threat. Ancient trade ties between East and West developed into significant commercial relations and the complementary economic pattern developed with Eastern Europe and Russia exporting primary goods to the West. During the nineteenth and early twentieth centuries, European powers scrambled for investments in the Russian Empire and introduced modern infrastructure and know-how to tap vast resources. For example, Russo-German trade accounted for 44 percent of total Russian imports and nearly 25 percent of total Russian exports from 1868 to 1872. By 1914, the figures were 47 percent of total imports and 29 percent of total exports. Foreign investments were important for the development of the Baku oil fields, mineral deposits, and the transcontinental telegraph system. Strategic interests were also served since France, for example, believed that a modern industrialized Czarist Russian ally could be a counterweight to Germany. By the mid-1980s, the basic economic complementarity held: the U.S.S.R. offered its raw material wealth in exchange for high-quality finished goods and turnkey plants from resource-poor and trade-dependent Western Europe.[38] Moscow and the Eastern Europeans scrambled to obtain vital Western investment and technology to revive crumbling economies and ease their populations' material deprivations.[39]

Perceptions of the superpower rivalry also shape the political relationship of the West Europeans with their Soviet neighbors, and this relationship naturally spills over into the realm of East-West trade policies. The United States is a superpower with global responsibilities and interests and, especially during the Reagan presidency, perceived a seamless web of global zero-sum competition with Soviet interests. In contrast, the Europeans fear being dragged into a superpower conflict arising outside of Europe and generally seek a regional structure of peace free of global superpower entanglements.[40] Political and economic detente are very important foundations for regional security policy. East-West trade is a component of the "dialogue" engaged in with the Soviet Union and Eastern Europe to secure regional stability, complement NATO's military deterrent, and encourage evolutionary reform in Eastern Europe.[41] In believing that East-West relations are not always conflictual, the Europeans perceive an added benefit derived from the dialogue: the hoped-for establishment and reinforcement of mutual trust and interdependence perceived as crucial to European efforts at reducing East-West tensions.[42] Furthermore, this dialogue has official sanction arising out of the dual-track strategy of defense and detente, incorporated in the 1967 Harmel Report, which all NATO members had endorsed and which the West Germans in particular support. Dialogues continued relatively unabated despite Soviet bloc actions, in Europe and elsewhere--including pressure on Poland, activities in Ethiopia and southern Africa, and the invasion of Afghanistan--which Americans argued were highly threatening and demanded a forceful and united Western response.[43] When the allies disagreed with or were openly hostile to U.S. efforts to retaliate against Moscow, U.S. irritation was clearly evident.

Adding to intra-Alliance tensions was ongoing U.S. dissatisfaction with Europe's share of the defense burden. That issue embroiled the Alliance at a time when Europe was also an economic competitor forging, through the European Community (EC), a rival economic bloc that frequently squabbled with Washington over trade matters. For many U.S. policymakers, Europe's military "free ride" was made even more intolerable when the allies were perceived to benefit economically. But Washington's efforts to drum up support for sanctions against the East were greeted with skepticism when U.S. rhetoric did not match actions when American interests--such as grain sales--were endangered.[44] Furthermore, sanctions were generally thought to be ineffective in modifying another state's behavior. The Europeans decried U.S. charges and stressed the many tangible and intangible ways in which they shouldered the NATO burden. The always politically difficult trade-off between larger defense expenditures and less funding for other programs is part of the calculus that influences European policy. Communication with the East, rather than a larger and expensive deterrent, is presumably cheaper and appears to pay dividends. The economic dividend--including export-generated employment during the recessionary 1970s and early 1980s--continues to be an influential factor and might well increase in importance should future prolonged recessions limit other export opportunities. Given the economic reform and modernization efforts touted and initiated by Moscow and several other Eastern European states, the late 1980s have witnessed increased demand for Western European exports to the Soviet Union and Eastern Europe from both the East and domestic interests in Western Europe. Thus, budgetary and economic considerations, the value of the East-West dialogue, and the necessity of avoiding U.S. "decoupling" from Europe partly define and constrain European options. These considerations and related disagreements are therefore an important part of the political environment in which the major European allies and the U.S. debate the wisdom and utility of East-West trade.

THE FEDERAL REPUBLIC OF GERMANY (F.R.G.)

Of the three largest European allies, East-West trade is clearly of greatest importance for Germany,[45] which has the largest trade turnover with Eastern Europe and Russia among the European COCOM countries. Bonn's dialogue with Eastern Europe depends on a solid anchorage in the

Western Alliance. But the requirements of pursuing both policies simultaneously sometimes places Bonn in a delicate position between the Western allies and Moscow. Bonn's active interest in closer ties with Moscow occasionally raises fears in Washington of German abandonment of its superpower ally. But Bonn's dependent status also provokes fear of entanglement in issues and areas that Bonn would prefer to avoid. This fear is also due to a perception of crusading American moralism--of a liberal or conservative stripe--that could damage German interests. Systemic tensions constrained Bonn's diplomatic maneuverability from the 1950s to 1980s. Thus, by the 1980s, *deutsche Ostpolitik* was evolving into *europaische Ostpolitik* as Bonn attempted to convince much of the rest of Europe to identify with the F.R.G.'s interest in European detente[46] insulated from extra-European superpower conflicts.

As Chancellor Brandt recognized when he launched *Ostpolitik*, and no German leader forgot, the road to East Berlin passed through Moscow. Trade relations were skillfully utilized to the German advantage in the highly asymmetrical bargaining with the Soviets and East Europeans. West German economic strength permitted Brandt to abandon negative for positive economic linkage to secure political goals. Moscow had never responded to earlier West German trade restrictions--given its nearly autarchic economy--but the Soviets sought German credits and technology. Furthermore, Soviet political bargaining power *was* salient vis-a-vis both the F.R.G. and Moscow's Eastern European satellites. Brandt recognized this and turned positive economic linkage to his advantage. The resulting quid pro quo brought tangible results ending the vestiges of the F.R.G.'s political and economic embargo of the bloc and resolving lingering postwar disagreements among Bonn, Moscow, and the other Eastern European capitals. This then opened the way for expanding political and economic ties.

Ostpolitik and *Deutschlandpolitik* are clearly acceptable to the majority of West Germans.[47] West German policy relies on positive linkage between economic relations and political concessions to a much greater degree than do the United States, France, or the U.K.[48] A key premise of the *Ostpolitik* guiding Bonn's East-West trade policy is that economic ties produce desirable political dividends. During the 1960s, 1970s, and 1980s, fundamental West German goals included expanding intra-German relations and trade, securing the emigration of remaining ethnic Germans in Eastern Europe, and resolving and guaranteeing the status of Berlin.[49] There was also strong sentiment for close trade ties with East Germany (G.D.R.) to speed eventual reunification, thereby resolving a major postwar East-West conflict.[50] The upheaval in East Germany that began in the autumn of

1989 rekindled long-suppressed hopes for a reunited Germany, the pace of reunification accelerated during 1990, and a united Germany was a reality by the year's end. Bonn could also point to the positive influence West German contacts had on the G.D.R. and other Warsaw Pact countries that lowered regional tensions and alleviated popular dissatisfaction in Eastern Europe, which might otherwise have boiled over and precipitated East-West confrontation. For example, the F.R.G. subsidized the G.D.R.'s chronic trade deficit with the Federal Republic, trade which provided the G.D.R. with an export market and the East German population with a relatively high standard of living. Bonn thereby plays a role in the Alliance's political burdensharing--a role which the West Germans regarded as as important as its military role, if not more so.[51]

Economic ties are maintained, even when Bonn's political relations with the Commonwealth and Eastern Europe are strained, because they are an open channel of cooperation helping to guarantee Bonn's basic goals. Furthermore, ties with Eastern Europe are predicated on a presumption of linkage between trade and restrained Russian behavior, and this presumption is reinforced by a shrinking fear of the Russian threat among the West German public. By encouraging Gorbachev's economic modernization goals and improving economic conditions via trade and technology transfer, German policymakers assume that the resulting interdependence will mellow Russian aggressiveness, permitting and encouraging the Eastern Europeans to pursue gradual domestic liberalization,[52] and strengthening European security.

German governments consider economic health and stability a linchpin of West German security and this concern also conditions Bonn's outlook and policy. Eastern European trade increased steadily during the 1970s and early 1980s. While remaining an insignificant portion of Gross National Product (GNP), the Federal Republic had by far the largest share of East-West trade among the Big Four COCOM allies. Although Eastern Europe and the U.S.S.R. suffered economic stagnation during the 1980s, the area (excluding Yugoslavia) accounted for an average of about 6 percent of Bonn's world trade during most of the period. From 1981 to 1987, Eastern Europe's (excluding the U.S.S.R. and Yugoslavia) share of total West German exports and imports, while not large, remained fairly constant at 3.4 percent and 3.6 percent respectively. If the U.S.S.R. is included, the figures were 5.4 percent of total world exports and 6.2 percent of total world imports. The U.S.S.R. and G.D.R. accounted for the lion's share of West German trade with Eastern Europe. Of total West German trade turnover with Eastern Europe and the U.S.S.R. from 1981 to 1987, the U.S.S.R.'s average share of exports and imports averaged about 36 percent and 40.5 percent, respectively, while the G.D.R.'s share averaged 33.7 percent and 33.3 percent. In other words, nearly 70 percent of West German exports to the area went to the U.S.S.R. and G.D.R. while nearly three-quarters of imports from the area were from these two countries. Czechoslovakia, Hungary, and Poland each accounted for about 7.5 to 10 percent of total trade turnover on average during the 1981-1987 period.[53] However, total global exports made up a relatively large share of GNP and exports to the East were particularly important for certain firms and sectors in the West German economy. For example, this trade accounted for substantial employment and exports in the steel, steel pipe, and machine tool industries and a semiofficial lobby, sponsored by the Federation of German Industry, had represented East European business interests since 1952.[54]

More than any other U.S. ally, the F.R.G. was particularly sensitive to the ramifications for *Ostpolitik* and *Deutschlandpolitik* of chills in U.S.-Soviet relations because of its stakes in maintaining a relationship with the G.D.R. and Eastern Europe. Confrontation--including limiting East-West economic ties as Washington periodically advocated--reduced Bonn's diplomatic latitude between West and East. Vital national interests--emigration of ethnic Germans or Berlin's status--might be threatened. During the 1960s to 1980s, ties with the G.D.R. raised the specter among both the Americans and the rest of Western Europe that Bonn would be vulnerable to Moscow's enticements to pry the F.R.G. away from the Western Alliance.[55] Furthermore, as Europe's largest economic power having extensive political and trade ties with the Soviet Union and Eastern Europe, Germany's Eastern European policies are influential among the other West European capitals.

London and Paris also compete for Eastern European markets frequently dominated by German firms. An added complication is the latent fear, however unlikely, of a prosperous and united Germany, having established dominance in an Eastern European economic sphere, gradually becoming less and less anxious to cooperate with British and French interests owing to overriding interests in Eastern Europe. This is related to the historic dilemma stemming from fears of a Germany that is too strong or a weak Germany vulnerable to Soviet pressure. To an extent, then, London and Paris are influenced by, even if they did not always applaud, German initiatives toward Eastern Europe and the Commonwealth. This situation therefore gives Bonn an opportunity to transform *deutsche Ostpolitik* into *europaische Ostpolitik*.

While *Westpolitik*, *Ostpolitik*, and *Deutschlandpolitik* were and are vital complements to each other, frictions with Washington over East-West relations and over the role and utility of East-West trade are evident when

Bonn feels compelled by the U.S. to make undesirable trade-offs between vital interests. Prior to the upheavals in Eastern Europe which began in 1989, Bonn adhered to a policy of noninterference, accepted Eastern Europe's political and territorial status quo, and avoided criticizing domestic conditions in Eastern Europe since such attacks might retard the evolutionary liberalization process and endanger *Ostpolitik*. A carefully nurtured policy of "synchronized" relations avoided the appearance of attempting to split Eastern Europe from the U.S.S.R., which might freeze the detente process.[56] Bonn remains hesitant to mimic the U.S. practice of differentiation through trade concessions and different sets of export licensing requirements, and encourages signs of East-West rapprochement since a calm systemic condition is essential for the furtherance of *Ostpolitik*. And this was also the case with the earlier *Deutschlandpolitik*. Foreign Minister Genscher's call for an easing of East-West trade restrictions in the wake of the 1987 U.S.-Soviet agreement eliminating medium-range missiles[57] fit this pattern but provoked allies' suspicions of Bonn's motives. The allies perceived that this proposal revealed Western disunity during a complicated phase of the slowly evolving East-West relationship. Bonn seemed to be more interested in trade while disregarding the strategic consequences. This proposal illustrated the important foreign policy interests and crucial perceptual differences which at times place Bonn in the position of appearing reluctant to follow the U.S. lead on East-West trade and technology transfer.

FRANCE

A reluctance to overly politicize East-West trade also characterizes French attitudes. The American practice of linking trade concessions with Soviet foreign policy and domestic political behavior is generally regarded as short-sighted and impractical in Paris. In spite of this skepticism, French policy evolved, in some respects, along the lines of the American pattern, but also resembled West German policy during the 1970s and 1980s.

DeGaulle's legacy stressed that France must strive for maximum flexibility and independence between the hegemonic superpowers--a concept rooted in the much older French practice of seeking alliances with neighbors against a common potential enemy--influenced France's East-West trade relations through the 1970s.[58] President Giscard expanded DeGaulle's trade initiatives and advocated the benefits to be derived from detente, trade, and dialogue with the Soviets despite foreign and domestic Soviet policies that drew increasing criticism from Mitterrand's Socialists and French intellectuals disillusioned by the excesses of the Soviet regime.[59] Like the

F.R.G., France considers fostering economic security to be essential and Eastern European trade furthers that goal. It was to ensure economic health and national security that Paris imported Soviet gas, thereby diversifying supplies. Benefits also accrued to agriculture and to shaky French industries--such as steel--which relied on the Eastern European export market. This was particularly true during the 1970s and early 1980s, when economic conditions in the West were poor.[60]

Overall, however, the Eastern European and Commonwealth market represents only a small portion of total French trade. By 1987, it amounted to less than 2.5 percent of total global exports and imports, having declined steadily over the last decade. In 1975, the area's share had been 4 percent of total trade. Despite the decline, the Eastern European-Soviet market--as a percentage of France's global trade turnover--was the second largest among the Big Four allies, although about one-half the West German figure. The distribution of French trade was heavily weighted in favor of the U.S.S.R. during the 1980s, suggesting the slow but growing importance of Soviet energy supplies. Trade with the U.S.S.R. accounted for an average of nearly 63 percent of all French trade with the area from 1981 to 1987, its share having grown nearly 20 percent since 1975. Romania (7.6%), Poland (8.9%), and the G.D.R. (8.7%) accounted for the bulk of the rest of France's Eastern European trade, Poland's share having slipped considerably since 1975, when it was 22.7 percent.[61] In general, the predominance of capital goods and nationalized or quasinationalized corporations in French exports to the East created political pressure for maintaining this trade.[62]

This moderate but significant trade continued despite the rather abrupt chill in Franco-Soviet relations and Eastern Europe's economic downturn during the Mitterrand presidency.[63] There was no enthusiasm for U.S. calls for economic sanctions to punish the Soviet and Polish governments for the occupation of Afghanistan and the crackdown on domestic Polish opposition. To participate would have implied a constraint on France's independent foreign policy and freedom of action,[64] and Mitterrand felt such actions were ineffective and counterproductive. Important French interests--such as the Yamal pipeline investments--would also be threatened.

Dialogue with Russia and the other republics matters, even when East-West relations are strained, partly because it shows that France's policy is free of Washington's dictates. Franco-Soviet dialogue also was a means of engaging the Kremlin at a time of leadership transition (in the early 1980s), to prevent the regeneration of monolithic blocs that might reemerge as U.S.-Soviet relations deteriorated, and to finally end the Yalta legacy of a divided Europe. Rapid social, political, and economic changes and associated domestic difficulties could engulf Eastern Europe. Such conditions might result in the Kremlin's perceiving a threat to Russian security interests and undermine Yeltsin's leadership. A spasmodic crackdown in Eastern Europe or the former Soviet republics is a possibility, and must be avoided as must external pressures that slow what Mitterrand perceives as communism's internal weakening and evolution. Furthermore, DeGaulle had pursued an independent course vis-a-vis the Soviet bloc safe in the knowledge of a superior U.S. nuclear deterrent. But by the early 1980s, Paris expressed concern over the relative weakening of this deterrent. The evolving strategic situation therefore influenced Mitterrand's general sympathy with U.S.-led efforts to strengthen the Western Alliance, including initiatives in the trade area. There was also an element of the French desire to project an image as Europe's leader, further motivated by concern that deteriorating superpower relations narrowed Europe's options and excited neutralist sentiments in the F.R.G., the Benelux area, and in Scandinavia. Yet Mitterrand's denunciations of Soviet policy reflected growing French disillusionment with the limited success of detente and the benefits of trading with the U.S.S.R.[65]

By the late 1980s, French attitudes on East-West trade relations resembled the mainstream American view that trade was one element of East-West conflict management. It was a lever that complemented a range of options making up the Alliance's deterrent policy but which by itself was unlikely to be decisive.[66] Political and economic considerations still play a role when France's interests are involved.[67] Paris remains wary of Bonn's relatively close ties with the East. This concern stems, to a lesser degree, from commercial rivalry. Of greater concern is the latent fear that Germany might eventually drift away from the Western Alliance, enticed by the promise and the prospect of lucrative ties with the East.[68] These concerns, along with the continuing emphasis on France's freedom of action between the blocs, means that France tends to "talk like the Americans but act like the Germans,"[69] distancing itself from policy that might identify Paris as Washington's handmaiden. At times, French policy therefore clashed with Washington's initiatives, causing friction and occasionally strident criticism of what were perceived as heavy-handed American actions--as was the case with the Polish sanctions during the early 1980s. When important geopolitical and economic interests were at stake, Mitterrand cast aside the "politics of indignation," softening harsh lectures against Soviet-style regimes. An apparently resurgent U.S.-led Western Alliance, and an economically sclerotic and troubled Soviet Union and Eastern Europe, permitted the French leader to pursue closer ties with the East.[70]

THE UNITED KINGDOM

Much the same could be said about the U.K.'s policy on East-West trade relations under the Thatcher government. Trade-dependent Britain historically kept trade and politics separate,[71] although trade remained a marginally useful instrument of policy in encouraging signs of independence from Moscow among the Eastern Europeans.[72] There is a predisposition to encourage exports wherever opportunities arise, but because there are no ethnic or other traditional ties to Eastern Europe, as is the case with the F.R.G. and France, the U.K. sees little benefit from an activist policy in the area.[73]

Until the mid-1960s, Britain had been a Western leader in Soviet trade. According to OECD data, in 1965 the U.K.'s share of total OECD countries' trade turnover (exports and imports) with the U.S.S.R. was 14.4 percent compared with the F.R.G. (11.0%), France (6.8%), and the U.S. (2.8%). At that time, both Washington and Bonn still restricted East-West trade--the 1949 Export Control Act governed U.S. trade relations and Bonn maintained a negative linkage policy to wrest political concessions from Moscow. However, by the late 1960s, serious domestic economic problems and the entry of commercial rivals into Eastern Europe cut British market share, an especially worrisome trend during a recessionary period.[74] A few sectors depended on Eastern sales and London's financial lobby was heavily engaged in underwriting Eastern European debt obligations and therefore advocated economic links.[75] But the U.K.'s economic ties with the area were limited. Of the West's Big Four allies, the U.K.'s Eastern European and Soviet trade, as a percentage of total world exports and imports, averaged about 1.7 percent, during the 1980s compared with 0.9 percent for the U.S., 6 percent for the F.R.G., and 3.2 percent for France. The U.K. also ranked second to last in exports to and imports from the area and had the lowest average trade turnover of the four allies during the 1980s. Besides the unsurprising predominance of Soviet trade (about 48% of total trade with, the area), the U.K.'s other major Eastern European trading partner was Poland, where the U.K. engaged in a significantly larger portion of its East-West trade than the other three allies during the 1980s. From 1981 to 1987, Poland's share averaged 16.4 percent while the figures for the other allies were U.S.(13%), F.R.G.(9.4%), and France (9%).[76] In contrast with France and West Germany, the U.K. was self-sufficient in energy and did not have to weigh Soviet gas in policy calculations.

London also retained its "special relationship" with the United States. However, after joining the EC, the British did pay more attention to the insecurities of the West Germans while growing more conscious of the potential dangers facing Europe when superpower relations grew cozy or deteriorated. Furthermore, London and Washington had disagreed--sharply at times--over COCOM and East-West trade policy. The British were therefore disinclined to permit the "special relationship" to color East-West trade policy.[77]

While there was a relative distancing of British policy from traditionally very close Anglo-American ties after 1973, Conservative Prime Minister Thatcher's good relationship with the Reagan administration meant general agreement on policy toward Eastern Europe. The Thatcher government's skepticism over the benefits of detente and her periodic criticism of Moscow's adventurism echoed the view in Washington in the early 1980s. London even joined U.S.-led economic sanctions in the wake of the Afghanistan and Poland crises, although British sanctions were more limited in scope. This was a shift away from earlier pro-trade Labour policies. By the mid-1980s, British policymakers, while unequivocally agreeing on the utility of maintaining limited economic ties with the Soviet Bloc, were less inclined to see political benefits deriving from trade.[78] The realities of the previous decade's growing East-West tensions meant that firm deterrence policy dictated a realistic appraisal of East-West trade relations as but one element in Anglo-Soviet relations, not *the* key to regional harmony. It remained to be seen whether a new cycle of warmer East-West relations would change British policy.

Reforms of the COCOM and national export control systems, and moderation on both sides of the Atlantic, have lowered the salience of the technology transfer issue within the Alliance. But the United States continues to assert a broad right to control technology extraterritorially. U.S. policymakers claim that this practice offers the best guarantee against diversions. But when vital interests are perceived to be jeopardized by U.S. regulations, allied governments quickly condemn what they regard as an unwarranted exercise of U.S. leverage. Since this policy continues to be controversial--albeit removed from everyday publicity--its background and ramifications warrant discussion.

EXTRATERRITORIALITY AND EXPORT CONTROLS: CONTENDING U.S. AND EUROPEAN VIEWS

One of the most contentious issues dividing the United States and Europe is the question of the extraterritorial extension of U.S. export control law and regulations. These require that foreign subsidiaries of U.S. companies, and U.S.-origin goods and technology incorporated in foreign manufactures, are subject to U.S. reexport review and licensing. Allied governments protest that this violates national sovereignty.

Controversy over the extraterritorial extension of U.S. antitrust law in Europe increased during the 1950s and 1960s, although as an issue within the West's multilateral export control regime, extraterritoriality was of relatively minor consequence until the 1965 *Fruehauf* case pitting Washington against the French government.[79] By the late 1970s, anger over U.S. legal practices had grown to such a degree that several European countries enacted so-called blocking legislation--such as the U.K.'s Protection of Trading Interests Act--specifically designed to bar extraterritorial enforcement. This act was invoked in 1982 during the Yamal pipeline crisis.[80]

Complicated issues of international legal jurisdiction are embedded in the extraterritoriality debate. The so-called territoriality and nationality principles and the effects doctrine of international law are particularly salient. Under the territoriality principle, all states have the right to exercise "'supreme authority'"[81] over individuals, things, and acts located and taking place within the state's territory. Only the state itself can impose limits within its territorial jurisdiction and no foreign state may limit another state's territorial supremacy. Virtually all the COCOM allies subscribe to the territoriality principle. However, under the exception known as the nationality principle, any state may also enforce its laws on its citizens outside state borders, that is, within the territory of another state.[82] This principle, linked with the effects doctrine, is at the heart of U.S. policy.[83]

International law also recognizes claims of jurisdiction based on the "effects doctrine." Under the effects doctrine, extraterritorial jurisdiction is permitted if some action outside a state's territory causes undesirable effects within the territory of the state. The European Community and the Arrondissementbank court of The Hague (in *Compagnie Europeenne des Petroles S.A. v. Sensor Nederland B.V.*), dismissed the effects doctrine as it related to the Yamal pipeline controversy arguing that European exports to the U.S.S.R. could have no "direct" or "substantial" effect in the U.S.[84] This view is debatable since the illegal export of a supercomputer, for example, *could* have a very deleterious effect on all the allies, or be of very little consequence, depending on the degree of perceived threat its actual or potential end use posed to the Alliance.

The "nationality" principle is one of the key issues sparking controversy within the Alliance. Under Section 5 of the 1979 EAA, "the President, may, in accordance with the provisions of this section, prohibit or curtail the export of any goods or technology subject to the jurisdiction of the United States or exported by any person subject to the jurisdiction of the United States." Furthermore, Section 16 defines "United States person" as "any

United States resident or national any domestic concern (including any permanent domestic establishment or any foreign concern) and any foreign subsidiary or affiliate (including any permanent foreign establishment) of any domestic concern which is controlled in fact by such domestic concern, as determined under regulations of the President."[85]   This wording represents a significant change and expansion of the power to control U.S. exports from that found in the 1969 EAA.   In the 1969 version, the President was merely authorized to restrict "'exportation from the United States,'"[86] whereas the 1979 EAA authorizes restrictions on exports by any person subject to U.S. jurisdiction *and* by foreign subsidiaries of U.S. companies which are "controlled in fact" by the U.S. parent.   Although partly revised after foreign protests, U.S. licensing rules, based on the 1979 EAA's "controlled in fact" clause in Section 5, hold that overseas companies are subject to U.S. jurisdiction if, for example, as little as 25 percent of the firm's stockholders are U.S. citizens with a controlling interest.[87]

In authorizing the President to restrict "exportations of property subject to the jurisdiction of the United States,"[88] Section 5 is also grounds for asserting that U.S.-origin technology does not lose U.S. "nationality" and is therefore continuously subject to U.S. law--even after passing through several overseas transactions and modifications--until it reaches the final end user.

Despite gradual regulatory liberalization--permitting unlicensed intra-COCOM exports containing up to 25 percent U.S.-origin components, and the prospective decontrol of most intra-COCOM trade mandated by the 1988 Omnibus Trade Act--the scope of U.S. requirements is unique among the Western allies.[89]   For example, a European firm that purchases controlled U.S.-origin components to be included as part of machinery destined for Eastern Europe could be required under U.S. regulations to apply for a U.S. reexport license even after the firm's government has licensed the transaction.   Under the system used by most of the allies, the end user's government is responsible for preventing diversions and not the nation that initially obtained and retransferred the technology.[90]   The U.S. view is that U.S.-origin technology does not lose its "nationality" and that a paper trail is necessary to prevent diversion after numerous transactions.[91]

Experts argue that legislative history clearly revealed Congressional intent to broaden Executive authority to use extraterritorial powers to further *foreign policy* objectives.[92]   However, Section 5 of the 1979 EAA covers *national security controls*.   The act's wording and its interpretation--as reflected in regulatory language and actions by the government--suggests a very broad assertion of extraterritorial rights.   The apparent overlapping of national security language and the intent of foreign policy controls compound distrust of U.S. motives among allies. Memories of the 1982 Yamal pipeline sanctions, and the acrimony U.S. actions caused within the Alliance, linger. Moreover, despite Congressional efforts to rein in Executive authority under the 1985 EAA amendments--such as protecting contract sanctity--the Executive retains much of its traditional discretionary power.[93] Given this discretion, the ill-defined language found in the EAA, and diverging U.S. and European policies toward the Commonwealth and Eastern Europe, extraterritoriality remains a serious issue.

Because of the extra time and cost stemming from the licensing process, allegedly intrusive U.S. audits of license holders, and U.S. regulations governing use or domestic resale--implying that the United States does not trust the applicant's national export control authorities--foreign companies are wary of contracting with U.S. firms for fear of sudden U.S. export prohibitions and import sanctions.[94] Western European firms are discouraged from business dealings with Eastern Europe for similar reasons.[95] Contracts with Eastern Europe might have to be breached owing to U.S. rulings, with resulting heavy legal fines and loss of sales and business reputation.[96] Furthermore, a European company can be fined and blacklisted by the United States for reexport violations of foreign laws that are committed overseas.[97] U.S. officials made contradictory claims about the sanctions' effectiveness and the relative degree of compliance with regulations.[98]

Bilateral negotiations and a more accommodating U.S. attitude lowered tensions, but *any* extraterritorial claims continue to cause anti-American resentment in Europe.[99] Suspicion of U.S. motives fuels dubious conspiracy theories, further fertilized by revelations of what could be interpreted as politically or commercially motivated U.S. policies and activities that take advantage of proprietary information in license applications.[100] Plausible critics asserted that U.S. practice was in conflict with recognized standards of international law and accepted principles of national sovereignty.[101]

In response to U.S. assertions of jurisdiction over foreign subsidiaries, the EC noted the commonly held practice of determining a firm's nationality based on its place of incorporation. Therefore, a U.S. corporate, personal, or any other link is invalid as grounds for U.S. jurisdiction. Ultimate jurisdiction rests with the state where incorporation took place consistent with the territoriality principle. U.S. legal opinion distinguishes between foreign branches and subsidiaries, the former having the nationality of the parent and therefore subject to the same laws as the parent. But the *Fruehauf* and Yamal cases suggested that a host government could easily overturn this argument, utilizing national legal standards such as the French *abus de droit* principle and blocking legislation.[102] Citing the 1976

Timberland decision by the U.S. 9th Circuit Court as precedent, Douglas Rosenthal, former senior Justice Department official and Chairman of the Committee on the Extraterritorial Application of United States Law of the American Bar Association's International Law Section, held that it is therefore advisable to exercise extraterritorial jurisdiction with due regard for principles of international comity, "reasonableness," and careful balancing of the affected nations' sovereign interests.[103]

The EC rejected the assertion that technology retained its original nationality after export from its "birthplace." The technology's origins did not determine jurisdiction and U.S. law was not applicable.[104] Legal experts, including Patrizio Merciai of the University of Geneva, Ann Zeigler, Executive Editor, *Houston Journal of International Law*, and Robert Y. Stebbings, senior partner, Stebbings & Skydell, P.C., of New York City agreed that the EC's arguments were supported by international and past U.S. legal precedent.[105] However, since national security is recognized by U.S. courts as an area where the Executive Branch enjoys wide discretion, it is doubtful prevailing U.S. legal opinion would swing against existing extraterritorial laws.[106] In addition, contractual agreements, including provisions requiring a foreign contractee to observe U.S. laws, are a complicating factor.

Submission clauses contractually agreed to by European companies, in which the latter voluntarily agreed to comply with U.S. export regulations prior to export, are denied any basis under international legal practice. First, as the British argued: "It is not possible for a private person in the United Kingdom to enter into an agreement with an authority of another State which has the effect of undermining a jurisdiction properly exercisable by the United Kingdom and thereby prejudicing the sovereignty of the United Kingdom."[107] The contract cannot be expected to cause the British government (for example) to force compliance with the contract's terms on the part of a British firm if the contract's submission clause--which can be said to be reflective of U.S. jurisdictional and policy objectives--restricts British jurisdiction. In other words, if the contract's terms are in conflict with a sovereign state's policy, under the territoriality principle the contractee's sovereign state--where the contractee resides--is the final judge of whether the contractual obligations are legal and are to be fulfilled and enforced.[108] Yet the legal dilemma U.S. allies face--owing to heavy reliance on U.S.-origin technology--suggests the practical limits to principled opposition to such clauses, at least in the short term. Voluntary acceptance by foreign firms of U.S.-mandated restrictions and audits is sometimes necessary to forgo the loss of critical U.S. sources and markets and resultant business losses.[109] Legal opinion in the United States is, predictably, more supportive of the view that contractual obligations are binding on foreign subsidiaries.[110]

Beyond asserting that accepted standards of international law are violated by U.S. extraterritoriality rules, the allies also question whether such rules are compatible with the Treaty of Rome. For example, U.S. reexport regulations are perceived as hampering the free flow between EC states of goods containing U.S.-origin technology. U.S. regulations therefore constitute a barrier to free trade within the EC, the elimination of such barriers being a key goal of the Rome Treaty.[111] Under strict interpretation, these licensing requirements represent U.S. interference in EC members' commercial policies. Furthermore, any company holding a coveted U.S. Distribution License also is believed to have a commercial advantage that might engender litigation in European courts on the basis of anti-discrimination law.[112]

Adding to this conflict is the issue of how the planned elimination of all EC internal trade barriers in 1992 would affect U.S. and COCOM control efforts. Several European states reportedly argued they would be obligated to dismantle their controls to comply with the Single European Act.[113] The act was interpreted to require elimination of all barriers to trade within the EC, including export controls and end-use verification. However, the national security provisions of the Rome Treaty (articles 36 and 223)[114] do give EC members the right to exercise regulations in the interest of national security even if they are contrary to the goals of free trade among members. Furthermore, some accommodation would be required for Ireland, a neutral EC member (but not a member of COCOM), or EC and COCOM policies would possibly be jeopardized. In January 1988, a COCOM agreement to decontrol lower-level technologies for COCOM destinations, in exchange for better residual enforcement, followed by subsequent agreements at meetings in 1989-90, were efforts to address the 1992 changes in the EC and suggested that all parties were anxious to reach an accord.[115] However, the possibility of diversions worried U.S. officials and some Europeans.[116]

COMPARING U.S-EUROPEAN EXPORT CONTROL LAW, LICENSING, AND REGULATIONS: A BRIEF EXAMINATION

The legal and administrative frameworks governing export controls in the principal COCOM countries reflect differing policy priorities. They also reflect institutional barriers and loopholes that must be accounted for when considering the domestic factors influencing East-West trade and export control policy.

In general, laws and bureaucratic practices tend to encourage exporters in Europe whereas there appears to be a relatively stronger legal and regulatory bias in the United States that discourages U.S. exporters. Furthermore, in contrast to the widely diffused character of export control authority in the United States, where numerous executive agencies and Congressional committees have responsibility for regulation, rule and lawmaking authority is, generally speaking, more concentrated within European governments.

Authority for U.S. national security export controls derives from the 1979 Export Administration Act, as amended (1979 EAA),[117] which embodies several significant themes. Under it, national security and foreign policy controls are separated and procedures for their application are explicitly delineated. The act encompasses a set of contradictory and ambivalent policy goals. In Section 3(1), U.S. policy is declared to be one of minimizing "uncertainties in export control policy and to encourage trade with all countries with which the United States has diplomatic and trading relations." This is followed by Section 3(2), which authorizes national security controls on exports that endanger national security by making a "significant contribution to the military potential" of an adversary or adversaries. Finally, echoing the 1949 Export Control Act, Section 3(4) declares that U.S. "economic resources" are to be used to further both economic well-being and national security and foreign policy objectives.[118] This language reveals contradictory policy goals that simultaneously mandate expansion and restriction of exports as means of promoting national welfare *and* security. The contradictions are magnified given ambiguous and vague Congressional language, a reluctant Executive, and a markedly discretionary bureaucratic mind-set.[119] Under Section 5, national security controls are to be carried out in furtherance of policy set forth in part 3(2)(A), the "Declaration of Policy." In it, the President is authorized to impose national security controls on goods and technology that "would make a significant contribution to the military potential of any other country or combination of countries which would prove detrimental to the national security of the United States." Ambiguous language contributes to neutralizing Congressional intent by permitting substantial bureaucratic leeway in interpreting the law. Agencies therefore differ over, for example, what constitutes a "significant contribution" (Section 3(2)), since Congress leaves it up to the Executive agencies to implement the EAA. Blurred lines of authority and limited accountability mean that policy easily becomes politicized and consistent policy decisions succumb to bureaucratic dynamics. Although the EAA does designate the DOC as the lead agency in export administration, in practice the diffusion of authority and responsibility among numerous agencies with distinct--often opposing--perspectives and values further muddies consistent interpretation. The inevitable compromises and trade-offs among agencies add to the pressures neutralizing the legislative intent.

As noted above, the U.S. Executive Branch has usually been able to water down or circumvent Congressional reform efforts. Such was the case with the 1979 EAA, as amended, and the 1988 Omnibus Trade Act. The EAA reflects Congressional and public dissatisfaction with previous foreign policy export controls as delineated in procedural limitations on the Executive's power to impose such controls, although these restrictions are nonbinding. Many of these provisions have indeed been ignored by the Executive. By contrast, relatively fewer restrictions hampered Executive discretion in the area of national security controls in the 1979 EAA. Stress was laid on accelerating foreign availability determinations in order to facilitate pruning control lists. Furthermore, the 1988 Omnibus Trade Act mandated decontrol of most (but not all) exports to COCOM countries subject to a determination by the Secretary of Commerce that the other members had adequate controls. However, Executive Branch resistance to these reforms continued, as evidenced by the exceedingly slow pace of foreign availability determinations and the delay in implementing the COCOM decontrol provision.[120]

In Sections 2(3) and 3(10) of the EAA, Congress asserts the importance for the U.S. national interest "that both the private sector and the Federal Government *place a high priority on exports*," and that it is U.S. policy "that export trade by United States citizens be *given a high priority* [emphasis added]." This language does not suggest the bestowal of a right to export,[121] but instead reflects the continuing attitude that exporting is a privilege, not a right.

This should be contrasted with the basic thrust of West Germany's 1961 Statute on Foreign Commerce (*Aussenwirtschaftgesetz*) which--together with a foreign economic decree governs export controls on goods and technical data--guarantees the right of citizens to export, although there are certain applicable national security and foreign policy restrictions.[122]

Prior to political and economic unification, a 1949 allied military statute incorporated into West German law covered trade with the G.D.R. Under the statute, *all* inner-German trade required either a general or validated license. This echoed the more restrictive U.S. approach while deemphasizing the right to export incorporated in the *Aussenwirtschaftgesetz*. As a result, inner-German trade was--in legal terms--much more regulated than trade with other states. However, a CIA analyst disputed this claim and a West German Foreign Ministry official admitted that a huge trade volume and limited resources taxed authorities. Berlin was also a vulnerable diversion point.[123]

The relative discretion enjoyed by the U.S. agencies is also reinforced in the regulatory framework governing current administration of U.S. export controls (and hereunder, national security controls)--the Export Administration Regulations (EAR).[124] An applicant for any export license consults the EAR, has to be familiar with periodic revisions published in the *Federal Register*,[125] and negotiates a complicated bureaucratic maze. Only limited judicial review of export regulations and licensing decisions is permitted and very little public participation in the creation of administrative and regulatory standards is allowed. In this regard, existing regulations and procedures favor exporters in Germany and the U.K.

German law assures the exporter greater freedom and leeway than comparable U.S. law. For example, a license can only be denied if there is clear proof that the export damages economic or political security. Furthermore, the Bundestag can override trade restrictions within four months, a license denial is subject to judicial review, and an exporter can petition for compensation due for the loss of a license.[126] British exporters also have the right to appeal a license denial. It was unclear whether new regulations introduced in 1989 would substantially hamper German exporters. There was concern that German law was not an adequate deterrent and hindered enforcement. But tighter regulations suggested that Bonn recognized the problem.[127]

The bureaucratic structure administering export controls is similar in these four COCOM countries. The three lead agencies in each country include the trade, foreign affairs, and defense ministries. But whereas licensing and policymaking remains fairly centralized in the European countries, among a few ministries and a relative handful of decision makers, a large and varying number of additional bureaucratic interests can participate in and influence U.S. decisions. For example, while the DOC has responsibility for day-to-day evaluation and licensing of most commercial high technology and data, the Department of Defense, the Department of Energy, and the Central Intelligence Agency advise the DOC regarding commercial exports. Overall policy and bureaucratic coordination in the Reagan White House was the responsibility of the Senior Interagency Group on Technology Transfer (SIG-TT).[128] Up to eighteen agencies or organizations with an interest in technology transfer participate in the SIG-TT. In France, by contrast, no more than twenty individuals determine export control policymaking.[129]

Adding to the political cross-pressures and tending to politicize and publicize export control issues in the United States is the significant oversight role played by Congress. Diffusion of this responsibility among several committees further complicates the legislative picture. The principal committees with jurisdiction over export controls are the Subcommittee on International Economic Policy and Trade of the House Foreign Affairs Committee and the Senate Banking, Housing, and Urban Affairs Committee's Subcommittee on International Finance and Monetary Policy. Occasionally, the House Armed Services and Energy and Commerce committees and the Senate Foreign Relations and Governmental Affairs committees also hold hearings on technology transfer and export control-related issues. In addition, the General Accounting Office undertakes investigations as directed by Congress.

In Europe, the statist tradition and administrative practice allow parliaments a relatively smaller voice in day-to-day foreign policy and national security issues. While debates on export control policy do occasionally take place in the House of Commons and the Bundestag, in-depth oversight apparently is the exception.[130]

Another significant feature relates to the degree to which U.S. business interests lobby Congress (with varied success) to seek regulatory reform and relief from controls. This stems in part from the characteristically adversarial business-government relationship found in the United States, whereas European ministries consult closely with exporters in order to facilitate sales.[131] Adding to European business confidence in the ministries is the latters discreetness, a relative lack of bureaucratic dissonance, and general agreement over the broad lines of policy among the major players. Contrast this consensus with frequently open and public sniping and bureaucratic turf battles that often infuse U.S. export control debates and policy and licensing decisions.

In the United States, the DOD's relatively prominent and controversial role reflects the importance security considerations play in the administrative process. While security concerns are not ignored in allied countries, the relative importance of trade for economic, foreign policy, and national security reasons meant that commercial considerations frequently tended to be given greater weight, at least until the 1980s. At that time, growing disillusionment with detente and concern over covert Soviet activities apparently influenced the French and British governments' decision to bolster defense and security agencies' input.

As noted, in the mid-1970s the DOD was granted authority to deny some licenses. Under Section 10(g) of the 1979 EAA, the DOD also gained an explicit and controversial role in the review of license applications for exports to *any* country subject to national security export controls.[132] This grant in effect gives the DOD a veto over exports deemed injurious to national security, although in practice the DOD's review jurisdiction is limited to the Soviet Union, Eastern Europe, and a few selected noncommunist countries. The DOD is also able to exercise influence in interagency meetings called to resolve disagreements over particularly controversial licensing recommendations.[133]   Defense ministries have also gained a larger role in France and the U.K.

France's export control effort was reorganized in 1981 along with implementation of a new regulation governing dual-use technology. A classified list of particularly critical core technologies was also drawn up. During the 1970s, permissive export control policies earned France a reputation for disregarding COCOM rules and capturing sales at allies' expense. Evidence suggests that the 1981 reorganization occurred in the wake of revelations of Soviet spying against French high-technology industries, which stunned Mitterrand and the few administrators responsible for export controls. Under the 1981 reorganization, particularly critical technologies are reviewed by the senior-level interministerial Surveillance Committee chaired by a member of the Prime Minister's office. Reportedly, the committee includes the ministries of Industry, Foreign Affairs, Finance, and Defense, giving Defense a voice in control decisions for the first time and somewhat balancing pro-trade biases.[134]   A similar interministerial body operates in the U.K. The Ministry of Defence (MoD) chairs the Strategic Exports Working Party (SXWP)--an interdepartmental group created in 1983 which reports to the Cabinet Office--where the Department of Trade and Industry (DTI) is balanced by the other generally more control-oriented members, including MoD, the intelligence services, and Customs. The SXWP decides sensitive and contentious cases, coordinates enforcement activities, and reportedly could veto any proposal--presumably including exception requests--the U.K. puts to COCOM. This is a further check on DTI's role as the principal licensing ministry.[135]   The situation is less clear in Germany. Although the ministries of Foreign Affairs and Defense are asked to judge items eligible for COCOM consideration and can veto an export, they rarely do so.[136]

Heightened concern over technology losses also prompted the Thatcher government to give enforcement higher priority with the creation of a Cabinet Committee on Enforcement and an allegedly successful upgrading of Customs and Excise efforts to curb smuggling.[137]   This resembled similar efforts in the United States in the wake of criticism of the DOC's enforcement record. Created in 1982, the DOC's Office of Export Enforcement (OEE) was given increased status with the appointment of a Deputy Assistant Secretary for Export Enforcement. The Customs Service was also assigned an expanded role under the Reagan administration in 1981, and it launched Operation Exodus, a publicized and controversial effort to prevent contraband from leaving the United States.[138]

In France, however, despite the cooling in Franco-Soviet relations during the 1980s, the hierarchical and centralized character of the French licensing system implies that a change in political climate and leadership might mean a return to more permissive policies. Clearly, the lack of a business anticontrol lobby confirms that consensual government-business collaboration smooths exporting in contrast with the adversarial relationship characterizing the U.S. system. In addition, no blacklist is maintained and as of 1986-87, there had been only one known prosecution for export control violations. Together with claims that the French exercised broad discretion in interpreting COCOM rules and favored many administrative exceptions, the legacy of permissiveness and the substantial employment generated by East-West trade suggested evidence of institutional bias and domestic economic conditions favoring exporters.[139]

SUMMARY

East-West trade is of minor economic importance to all the major Western allies' economies, although imports of Soviet energy and raw materials are likely to grow in importance for Western Europe, given long-term trends. However, the political rationale for such trade is significant, especially for Germany. Furthermore, foreign policy and domestic economic considerations play a role in determining East-West trade policy, although the relatively limited trade with the East suggests that pure economic interest is not overriding despite apparent European regulatory and institutional bias favoring exports. The U.S. traditionally perceives that fewer foreign and national security benefits derive from trading with the Soviet Union and Eastern Europe, and used trade sanctions expressly to punish Soviet transgressions. Despite improved relations with Moscow after 1985, U.S. consensus over a clear and consistent policy remains elusive. The Europeans are reluctant to mix trade and politics so overtly. They believe trade fosters interdependence, moderates Soviet behavior, and improves material conditions in Eastern Europe. This supposedly nurtures regional detente and it is hoped eases domestic restrictions within the Commonwealth and Eastern Europe. Gradual domestic Eastern European reform--accompanied by prosperity--and a less threatening perception of Western intentions thereby reduces Commonwealth security worries. Economic ties are, therefore, important given the apparent end of Moscow's domination of Eastern Europe. In addition, gradually and peacefully reducing Russia's grip on Eastern Europe and its military threat to the West is preferable to what is perceived to be the confrontational and unpredictable approach characteristic of U.S. policy. These contending perceptual and policy differences are inflamed when Washington insists on imposing--in the allies' view--a U.S. extraterritorial *diktat* over what can or cannot be traded.

Publicly, the extraterritoriality issue *did* subside as a cause of intra-Alliance disagreement by the late 1980s. East-West and U.S.-Soviet relations improved in tandem with the emergence of relatively moderate leaderships in Washington (during Reagan's second term and continued under George Bush) and apparently in Moscow as well. Thus, the political atmosphere was less charged than in the late 1970s and early 1980s, when detente floundered and Soviet adventurism spawned concerns over East-West trade and technology transfer. After 1986, Washington expressed a desire for improved trade ties at a time when Moscow actively courted Western know-how. Furthermore, the bitter legacy of the Yamal sanctions and the deep rift they caused in the Alliance, together with a highly orchestrated U.S. effort to improve allied export controls and licensing, were also influential. Neither side wanted to repeat the Yamal imbroglio and the allies' steps to improve licensing procedures, the limited success of detente during the 1970s (at least for France, Britain, and the F.R.G.), and alacrity over technology diversions reflected sensitivity to U.S. concerns. This coincided with the approaching birth of the single European Community market and domestic business and Congressional pressure to liberalize U.S. regulations in part owing to evidence that reexport controls were ineffective and frequently ignored. In early 1988, agreement in COCOM to reduce intra-COCOM controls while bolstering enforcement was a step toward recognizing the reality of 1992. The 1988 Omnibus Trade Act also mandated a license-free COCOM while bilateral negotiations diffused other instances of disagreement over extraterritoriality and sovereignty.

The fact remains that U.S. legislation, regulations, and policy continue to imply a uniquely broad assertion of extraterritorial jurisdiction. Despite apparent congruence of U.S. and European attitudes and policies toward the Commonwealth and Eastern Europe, this harmony is contingent on the manageability of East-West relations. In the context of East-West relations, as long as there is a lack of serious allied disagreement over security, economic, and geopolitical issues involving vital national interests, the harmony should continue. But despite the lower salience of the issue, U.S. extraterritoriality, combined with a legitimate perception of unpredictability and arrogance vis-a-vis the allies, continues to trouble European policymakers and business people since licensing and trade sanctions could be used at any time in the future.

The United States justifies this practice on national security grounds claiming that only by such means can U.S.-origin technology be safeguarded, although the claim is open to question. This policy irritates allied governments and discourages foreign companies. U.S. export control regulations and procedures also *allegedly* damage the nation's economic competitiveness and defense-related industries. Consequently, there are serious implications for national security. The next two chapters evaluate these claims and briefly analyze whether export controls effectively hamper Russian military capabilities.

NOTES

1. Gary K. Bertsch, "U.S. Policy Governing Economic and Technological Relations With the USSR," in *Gorbachev's Economic Plans*, ed. U.S. Congress, Joint Economic Committee, Study Papers, 100th Congress, 1st session, 23 November 1987 (Washington, D.C.: US GPO, 1987) vol. II, p. 433 and John P. Hardt, Associate Director for Senior Specialists, Congressional Research Service, Library of Congress, testimony in U.S. Congress, House Committee on Energy and Commerce, Subcommittee on Commerce, Transportation, and Tourism, *U.S. Trade Relations With the Soviet Union*, Hearing, 99th Congress, 2nd session, 25 June 1986 (Washington, DC: U.S. GPO, 1986), pp. 88-96.

2. Bertsch, "U.S. Policy," p. 436; Gary K. Bertsch, "American Politics and Trade With the USSR," in *Trade, Technology, and Soviet-American Relations*, ed. Bruce Parrott (Bloomington, IN: Indiana University Press, 1985), pp. 243-82; Joan Edelman Spero, *The Politics of International Economic Relations*, 2nd ed. (New York: St. Martin's Press, 1981), pp. 317-18; and Arnaud de Borchgrave and Michael Ledeen, "Selling Russia the Rope," *The New Republic*, 13 December 1980, pp. 13-16.

3. The Jackson-Vanik Amendment to the 1974 Trade Act prohibited the Soviet Union and Eastern European countries from being granted Most Favored Nation status unless emigration policies (especially for Jews) were liberalized. The Stevenson Amendment to the 1974 Export-Import Bank Act put a ceiling on Eximbank credits to the U.S.S.R. and was linked to Jackson-Vanik in the Trade Act. By mid-1989, the Bush administration was considering a temporary waiver of Jackson-Vanik as it applied to the U.S.S.R. given relaxed Soviet emigration policies. See Francis T. Miko, "U.S. Interests, Issues, and Policies in Eastern Europe," in *East European Economies: Slow Growth in the 1980s. Volume 1. Economic Performance and Policy*, ed. U.S. Congress, Joint Economic Committee, 99th Congress, 1st session, 28 October 1985 (Washington, DC: U.S. GPO, 1985), pp. 552-53; Kate S. Tomlinson, "U.S. Legislative Framework For Commercial Relations With Eastern Europe," in *East European Economies: Slow Growth in the 1980s. Volume 1. Economic Performance and Policy*, ed. U.S. Congress, Joint Economic Committee, 99th Congress, 1st session, 28 October 1985 (Washington, DC: U.S. GPO, 1985),

p. 573; President George Bush, "Change in the Soviet Union," address at Texas A&M University, 12 May 1989, rpt. in U.S Department of State, Bureau of Public Affairs, *Current Policy*, no. 1175 (May 1989); Henry Trewhitt et al., "Bush's Bold Bid to Rescue NATO," *U.S. News and World Report*, vol. 106, no. 23 (12 June 1989), p. 28; Spero, *The Politics*, pp. 317-18; and John P. Hardt and Jean F. Boone, *U.S.-U.S.S.R. Commercial Relations: Issues in East-West Trade*, Issue Brief no. IB86020, Congressional Research Service, U.S. Library of Congress (Washington, DC: U.S. GPO, 24 March 1987), pp. CRS-12-13. See also Angela E. Stent, "East-West Economic Relations and the Western Alliance," in *Trade, Technology, and Soviet-American Relations*, ed. Bruce Parrott (Bloomington, IN: Indiana University Press, 1985), p. 288.

4. For example, the 1969 EAA and 1977 amendments to the EAA mandated that foreign availability be considered in order to reduce the control list's size. A 90-day license processing deadline was mandated in 1974 amendments with an additional requirement that a written explanation for any breech of the deadline be provided along with an estimate of when the review would be completed. By 1985, the deadline was reduced to 15 working days (increased to 30 days upon agency request). In addition, the 1972 Equal Export Opportunity Act directed the Department of Commerce to create Technical Advisory Committees where industry and government representatives reviewed export control policy for various commodities.

5. William J. Long, "The Executive, Congress, and Interest Groups in U.S. Export Control Policy: The National Organization of Power," in *Controlling East-West Trade and Technology Transfer: Power, Politics, and Policies*, ed. Gary K. Bertsch (Durham, NC: Duke University Press, 1988), p. 57; and Harold Paul Luks, "U.S. National Security Export Controls: Legislative and Regulatory Proposals," in *Balancing the National Interest*, Working Papers, ed. National Academy of Sciences (Washington, DC: National Academy Press, 1987), p. 91.

6. Long, "The Executive," pp. 39-40.

7. Calculated from data in Lincoln Gordon (ed.), *Eroding Empire* (Washington, DC: The Brookings Institution, 1987), Tables A-5, A-6, A-7, A-8, pp. 335-38; International Monetary Fund, *Direction of Trade Statistics Yearbook 1987* (Washington, DC: International Monetary Fund, 1987) and International Monetary Fund, *Direction of Trade Statistics*, March-December 1987, February-June 1988.

8. The critical nature of the Soviet market for the oil and gas industry was stressed by Arden Judd, representative for Dresser Industries, interview, Washington, DC, 27 April 1988. For sources giving Eastern Europe's share of U.S. global exports, see Lincoln Gordon (ed.), *Eroding Empire* (Washington, DC: The Brookings Institution, 1987), Tables A-5, A-6, A-7, A-8, pp. 335-38; International Monetary Fund, *Direction of Trade Statistics Yearbook 1987* (Washington, DC: International Monetary Fund, 1987) and International Monetary Fund, *Direction of Trade Statistics*, March-December 1987, February-June 1988. Assistant Secretary of Commerce Paul Freedenberg predicted that there would be no "boom" in U.S.-Soviet joint ventures, despite Soviet overtures, because of the poor economic

prospects for business in the U.S.S.R.--a sentiment echoed by some business representatives. Paul Freedenberg, comments at a National Issues Forum on *U.S. Export Control Policy: Balancing National Security Issues and Global Competitiveness*, held at The Brookings Institution, Washington, D.C., 9 June 1988 and interview, John Copeland, Director, Export Administration, Motorola, Inc., Washington, DC, 25 February 1988.

9. See Lincoln Gordon (ed.), *Eroding Empire* (Washington, DC: The Brookings Institution, 1987), Tables A-5, A-6, A-7, A-8, pp. 335-38; International Monetary Fund, *Direction of Trade Statistics Yearbook 1987* (Washington, DC: International Monetary Fund, 1987) and International Monetary Fund, *Direction of Trade Statistics*, March-December 1987, February-June 1988.

10. Ibid.

11. This typology is drawn from Dr. Henry Nau's work. See Henry R. Nau, "The West-West Dimensions of East-West Economic Relations," in *Selling the Rope to Hang Capitalism?*, eds. Charles M. Perry and Robert L. Pfaltzgraff, Jr. (London: Pergamon-Brassey's, 1987), pp. 205-206, 208.

12. U.S. Congress, Office of Technology Assessment, *Technology and East-West Trade* (Washington, DC: U.S. GPO, November 1979), pp. 71-72.

13. See Gary K. Bertsch, "U.S.-Soviet Trade: The Question of Leverage," *Survey*, vol. 25, no. 2 (Spring 1980), rpt. in *National Security and Technology Transfer*, eds. Gary K. Bertsch and John R. McIntyre, Westview Special Studies in National Security and Defense Policy (Boulder, CO: Westview Press, 1983), pp. 67-69.

14. Commerce Secretary Verity explicitly promoted the view that trade helped resolve East-West tensions: "I favor helping Gorbachev. If he can get more attention paid to consumer products, he will be forced to put more emphasis on the domestic side of the economy instead of the military. It will also get the Soviets to be a less closed, more open society and instill more of a market system in their country. It could lead to their entering the world the way the world is now instead of trying to change it to fit their philosophy." Quoted in Elizabeth Tucker and Stuart Auerbach, "U.S. Businesses, Soviets Increasing Joint Ventures," *Washington Post*, 22 November 1987, section K, p. 9, columns 2-3. On Verity's views, see Stuart Auerbach and Lou Cannon, "President Nominates Verity As Secretary of Commerce," *Washington Post*, 11 August 1987, section A, p. 1, columns 1-2 and section A, p. 10, columns 1-5; Stuart Auerbach, "Commerce Nominee Calls On Chairman of Key Senate Panel," *Washington Post*, 12 August 1987, section F, p. 1, columns 5-6 and section F, p. 4, column 3; Anne Swardson, "Verity Cool To Law On Trade," *Washington Post*, 9 November 1987, section D, p. 1, column 5 and section D, p. 2, columns 3-6; Stuart Auerbach, "Senate Confirms Verity As Commerce Secretary," *Washington Post*, 14 October 1987, section F, p. 1, columns 4-5 and section F, p. 4, column 1 and the comments in Bertsch, "U.S.-Soviet Trade," p. 70.

15. See Bertsch, "U.S.-Soviet Trade," pp. 69-70; testimony in U.S. Congress, House Committee on Foreign Affairs, Subcommittee on International Economic Policy and Trade, *Omnibus Trade Legislation (Vol. II)*, Hearings, 99th Congress, 2nd session, 10, 17 April 1986 (Washington, DC: U.S. GPO, 1987), and in U.S. Congress, Senate Committee on Banking, Housing, and Urban Affairs, Subcommittee on International Finance and Monetary Policy, *Export Controls*, Hearings, 100th Congress, 1st session, 12, 17 March 1987 (Washington, DC: U.S. GPO, 1987), and the comments by the president of an engineering firm in Tucker and Auerbach, "U.S. Businesses," section K, p. 9, columns 2-3.

16. Kempton B. Jenkins, vice-president, ARMCO steel and the U.S.-U.S.S.R. Trade and Economic Council, prepared statement, 14 December 1982, in U.S. Congress, Senate Committee on Foreign Relations and Library of Congress, Congressional Research Service, *The Premises of East-West Commercial Relations*, Workshop, 97th Congress, 2nd session, 14-15 December 1982 (Washington, DC: U.S. GPO, 1983), p. 123.

17. Ibid., pp. 123-24.

18. Donald M. Kendall, testimony in U.S. Congress, Joint Economic Committee, Subcommittee on Trade, Productivity, and Economic Growth, *Prospects For Improved American Soviet Trade*, Hearing, 99th Congress, 1st session, 9 October 1985 (Washington, DC: U.S. GPO, 1986), p. 84. See also Gordon B. Smith, "The Politics of East-West Trade," in *The Politics of East-West Trade*, ed. Gordon B. Smith, Westview Special Studies in International Relations (Boulder, CO: Westview Press, 1984), pp. 25-26.

19. Smith, "The Politics," pp. 25-26.

20. Samuel P. Huntington, "Trade, Technology, and Leverage: Economic Diplomacy," *Foreign Policy*, vol. 32 (Fall 1978), pp. 66, 70-71, 76; Smith, p. 13; and Robert E. Klitgaard, "Sending Signals," *Foreign Policy*, vol. 32 (Fall 1978), pp. 103-06.

21. William B. McIlvaine, Jr., "Reaction of the Private Sector to U.S. Foreign Trade Policies Towards the Soviet Union and Eastern Europe," in The *Politics of East-West Trade*, ed. Gordon B. Smith, Westview Special Studies in International Relations (Boulder, CO: Westview Press, 1984), p. 207.

22. Henry R. Nau, "Trade and Deterrence," *The National Interest*, vol. 7 (Spring 1987), p. 51; and Nau, "The West-West," p. 209. Ambassador Allan Wendt, the State Department's Senior Representative for Strategic Technology Policy expressed a moderate view: "U.S. economic policy toward the Soviet Union *is but one component* of our bilateral relationship and our global stance and it is well founded in history. The promotion of U.S.-Soviet economic relations in the early 1970s outpaced other areas of the relationship. This resulted in feelings of frustration and failure" [emphasis added]. Ambassador Allan Wendt, "U.S. Stance Toward the Soviet Union on Trade and Technology," address before the Houston Club, Houston, TX, 27 October 1988; rpt. in U.S. Department of State, *Current Policy*, no. 1128, November 1988, pp. 2-3.

23. The economic warfare view is outlined in U.S. Congress, Office of Technology Assessment, *Technology*, p. 72.

24. Such as Dr. Henry Nau who served on the NSC during Reagan's first term.

25. Carl Gershman, "Selling Them the Rope: Business and the Soviets," *Commentary*, April 1979, pp. 36-38; and Miles M. Costick, "Soviet Military Posture and Strategic Trade," in *From Weakness to Strength*, ed. W. Scott Thompson (San Francisco, CA: Institute for Contemporary Studies, 1980), p. 194. Empirical studies have attempted to evaluate the contributions of Western trade and technology. See Antony C. Sutton, *Western Technology and Soviet Economic Development*, 3 volumes (Stanford, CA: Hoover Institution Press, 1968, 1971, 1973); and Mark E. Miller, "The Role of Western Technology in Soviet Strategy," *Orbis*, vol. 22, no. 3 (Fall 1978), pp. 539-68. More anecdotal and polemical accounts are found in Antony C. Sutton, *National Suicide: Military Aid to the Soviet Union* (New Rochelle, NY: Arlington House, 1973); and Louis J. Walinsky, "Coherent Defense Strategy: The Case For Economic Denial," *Foreign Affairs*, vol. 61, no. 2 (Winter 1982-83), pp. 271-92.

26. Senator Henry M. Jackson, "Technology Transfer Policy--The High Stakes," *Congressional Record*, vol. 128, no. 12 (11 February 1982), p. S769, column 3 and p. S771, column 3; Costick, "Soviet Military," p. 211.

27. Tucker and Auerbach, "U.S. Businesses," section K, p. 8, column 2 and section K, p. 9, column 1; De Borchgrave and Ledeen, "Selling Russia," p. 14; Costick, "Soviet Military," pp. 203-04, 209; Richard N. Perle, statement in U.S. Congress, House Committee on Armed Services, Technology Transfer Panel, *Technology Transfer*, Hearings, 98th Congress, 1st session, 9, 21, 23 June, 13, 14, July 1983 (Washington, DC: U.S. GPO, 1984), p. 70.

28. Richard N. Perle, testimony in U.S. Congress, House Committee on Armed Services, Technology Transfer Panel, *Technology Transfer*, Hearings, 98th Congress, 1st session, 9, 21, 23 June, 13, 14 July 1983 (Washington, DC: U.S. GPO, 1984), p. 86. See also the comments by Senators Jake Garn and Richard Shelby in U.S. Congress, Senate Committee on Banking, Housing, and Urban Affairs, Subcommittee on International Finance and Monetary Policy, *Toshiba-Kongsberg Diversion Case*, Hearing, 100th Congress, 1st session, 17 June 1987 (Washington, DC: U.S. GPO, 1987).

29. Gershman, "Selling Them," p. 40.

30. In another example, the Soviets approached U.S. firms to acquire sensitive computer chip-manufacturing technology but warned that they would seek partners in Western Europe if U.S. businesses were not forthcoming. See Louise Kehoe and David Thomas, "Soviet Union Seeks Computer Trade With US," *Financial Times* [London], 24 October 1988, p. 28, columns 1-5.

31. Paige Bryon, Scott Sullivan, and Steve Pastore, "Capitalists and Commissars," *Policy Review*, vol. 22 (Fall 1982), pp. 23, 34, 45-47, 50-52; De Borchgrave and Ledeen, "Selling Russia," pp. 16-17; Jackson, "Technology Transfer," p. S771, column 2; and Charles Wolf, Jr., Dean, Rand Corporation Graduate School, prepared statement, 15 December 1982, in U.S. Congress, Senate Committee on

Foreign Relations and Library of Congress, Congressional Research Service, *The Premises of East-West Commercial Relations*, Workshop, 97th Congress, 2nd session, 14, 15 December 1982 (Washington, DC: U.S. GPO, 1983), p. 150.

32. At the December 1987 summit in Washington, Mikhail Gorbachev urged U.S. business to help expand U.S.-Soviet trade. The joint communique included a passage stating both leaders' "strong support for the expansion of mutually beneficial trade and economic relations" and specifically mentioned the desirability of joint ventures in this context. See Elizabeth Tucker and Stuart Auerbach, "Rush for Freer Trade, Business Leaders Urged," *Washington Post*, 11 December 1987, section A, p. 31, columns 5-6; and "Joint Statement By Reagan, Gorbachev," *Washington Post*, 11 December 1987, section A, p. 34, column 4.

33. Commerce Secretary Verity was quoted as having "'reservations'" about the Jackson-Vanik amendment. See Anne Swardson, "Verity Cool to Law on Trade," *Washington Post*, 11 September 1987, section D, p. 1, column 5; and Stuart Auerbach, "Senate Confirms Verity As Commerce Secretary," *Washington Post*, 14 October 1987, section F, p. 4, column 1.

34. At the 1988 Moscow summit, spokesman Marlin Fitzwater was quoted as saying that President Reagan would urge the Soviets that "'we would like to cooperate in any way possible to increase trade opportunities in the Soviet Union,'" See Jim Hoagland, "The Fat Russians," *Washington Post*, 1 June 1988, section A, p. 2, column 5.

35. Fred Hiatt, "Carlucci Cautions the West To Stay Vigilant on Moscow," *Washington Post*, 7 June 1988, section A, p. 1, columns 1-2 and section A, p. 17, columns 1-2; Rowland Evans and Robert Novak, "Soviet Talk on Trade With Moscow," *Washington Post*, 7 March 1988, section A, p. 13, columns 1-3; and Rowland Evans and Robert Novak, "The Rush to Trade With the Soviets," *Washington Post*, 18 April 1988, section A, p. 15, columns 1-5. The State Department's Allan Wendt saw no evidence of a slackening in Soviet acquisition efforts and feared that an East-West thaw might be exploited by the Soviets; comments at a National Issues Forum on *U.S. Export Control Policy: Balancing National Security Issues and Global Competitiveness* held at The Brookings Institution, Washington, DC, 9 June 1988. A similar argument was made at this forum by Stephen D. Bryen, Director, Defense Technology Security Administration, and Deputy Under Secretary of Defense for Technology Security Policy.

36. Bertsch, "U.S. Policy," p. 446.

37. Nau, "The West-West Dimensions," pp. 205, 208. A few skeptics cautioned European leaders against infatuation with signs of conciliatory Soviet policy perceiving that this was merely a ploy. See Leopold Labedz, "A Stubborn Refusal to Learn From History," *The Independent* [London], 26 November 1988, p. 17, columns 4-5.

38. "By 1900, foreign companies owned over 70% of the capital invested in Russian mining, metallurgy, and machine-building." Quoted from R. J. Carrick, *East-West Technology Transfer in Perspective*, Policy Papers in International Affairs, no. 9 (Berkeley, CA: Institute of International Studies, University of California,

1978), p. 4. Carrick cites D. W. Green and H. Levine, "Implications of Technology Transfer for the USSR," in *East-West Technological Cooperation* (no publisher, no date), p. 44. The figures for Russo-German trade during 1868-72 and 1914 are drawn from Juergen Kuczynski and Grete Wittkowski, *Die deutsch-russischen Handelsbeziehungen in den letzten 150 Jahren* (Berlin: no publisher, 1947), pp. 24-25, rpt. in U.S. Congress, Office of Technology Assessment, *Technology*, p. 173, Table 28. President Gorbachev's efforts to improve material conditions also led to Moscow offering Europe expanded markets for food and consumer exports. See David Buchan, "Moscow Faces Up to a Hesitant Community," *Financial Times* [London], 3 November 1988, p. 4, columns 4-8; and Marsha Taylor, "Russians Open the Door For Business," *The Sunday Times* [London], 13 November 1988, section D, p. 12, columns 1-4.

39. The growing seriousness of Hungary's economic and social crisis was described by George Schopflen of the London School of Economics. He cited an announcement by the Chairman of Hungary's State Planning Office that consumption had fallen by 3% in 1987 and that 700,000 people were living below the poverty line. Schopflen privately estimated that the percentage of Hungary's population living at or below the poverty line had risen from 25-30% in the 1970s to 30-35% by the 1980s. George Schopflen, "Hungary's Crisis: Change, Collapse or Reform?", address given at The Royal Institute of International Affairs, London, 15 February 1989, mimeograph, p. 2, citing Budapest Radio, 17 November 1988 and *Magyar Lirlap*, 25 November 1988. See also Jackson Diehl, "East Europeans Scramble To Catch Up With West," first part of a three-part series entitled "Eastern Europe: The High-Stakes Quest For High Tech," *Washington Post*, 19 October 1986, section A, p. 1, columns 4-5 and section A, p. 48, columns 3-6; Myra MacPherson, "The Hybridization of Hungary," *Washington Post*, 4 November 1986, section D, p. 1, columns 1-3 and section D, p. 10, columns 1-4; Jackson Diehl, "East Bloc Ventures Face Uncertainties," *Washington Post*, 1 March 1987, section H, p. 3, columns 4-5; and Jackson Diehl, "Eastern Europeans Turn to West in Effort To End Technology Gap," *Washington Post*, 28 February 1988, section H, p. 1, columns 1-2 and section H, p. 18, columns 1-3.

40. Pierre Hassner, "Recurrent Stresses, Resilient Structures," in *The Atlantic Alliance and Its Critics*, eds. Robert W. Tucker and Linda Wrigley (New York: Praeger, 1983), p 67; and Stanley R. Sloan, *NATO's Future* (Washington, DC: National Defense University Press, 1985), p. 88.

41. Pierre Lellouche, "Does NATO Have a Future?" in *The Atlantic Alliance and Its Critics*, eds. Robert W. Tucker and Linda Wrigley (New York: Praeger, 1983), pp. 144-45. One British observer illustrated the two-pronged approach, arguing that increased trade with Moscow not only eased the material poverty of Soviet consumers, thereby strengthening the hand of Soviet reformers for whom world revolution was not a primary goal, but also would bring about a "happier and less threatening society" more quickly than the interminable East-West strategic and conventional arms negotiations. That the West was also enriched by this strategy was an added benefit; Nicholas Ashford, "Can We Help the Russians to Enjoy a

Richer Menu?" *The Independent* [London], no. 653 (12 November 1988), p. 10, columns 7-8. Britain's former Ambassador to Moscow, Bryan Cartledge, expressed a similar view, although he felt there should be no radical easing of COCOM prohibitions. See Bryan Cartledge, "Russia Stumbles Into a Social Contract," *The Independent* [London], 26 November 1988, p. 17, columns 6-7. The Conservative Chairman of the Commons Select Committee on Defence also felt that trade encouraged reform: "We must not allow COCOM to become a device to block trade between East and West, not only for our economic benefit but also because if we can show the citizens of the Soviet bloc the wonders produced by capitalism, they will be encouraged to back Mr. Gorbachev's reforms." A West German Foreign Ministry official echoed this view arguing that "making capitalist society in Eastern Europe" ensured systemic change and encouraged moderation as the population learned of the positive aspects of life in the capitalist world; Michael Mates, letter to the author, 10 February 1989 and not-for-attribution interview, Ministry of Foreign Affairs, Bonn, 3 March 1989.

42. There was a marked tendency among some British businessmen to perceive trade as a force moderating Soviet behavior. Some argued that "it [trade] creates friends on the other side" and that since domestic factors and needs ruled Soviet external behavior, the moderating influence of trade would dampen aggressive Soviet policy by breaking down mutual suspicions; Hugh Malim, Assistant Director, Barclays Bank, PLC, interview, London, 26 October 1988 and not-for-attribution interviews with British businessmen, 17 October and 11 November 1988.

43. Lellouche, "Does NATO," pp. 139, 144; and Pieter Dankert, "Europe Together, America Apart," *Foreign Policy*, vol. 53 (Winter 1983-84), p. 22.

44. Sloan, *NATO's Future*, p. 89. The shifting and inconsistent nature of U.S. policy on East-West trade--stressing liberalization in the early 1970s and advocating economic warfare in the 1980s--continued to perplex and concern West German officials and business people; not-for-attribution interviews, London, Bonn, Cologne, January and March 1989.

In June 1988, the EC and COMECON announced mutual diplomatic recognition, a move which some U.S. officials feared might eventually lead to COMECON's driving a wedge between the United States and Western Europe. See Robert J. McCartney, "Comecon, EC End Hostilities," *Washington Post*, 26 June 1988, section A, p. 22, column 1 and section A, p. 27, column 3.

45. Stent, "East-West Economic," p. 290.

46. Lellouche, "Does NATO," pp. 146-47. The concept of abandonment is found in Gregory F. Treverton, "West Germany and the Soviet Union," in *Western Approaches to the Soviet Union*, ed. Michael Mandelbaum (New York: Council on Foreign Relations, 1988), pp. 2-3.

47. These policies "gave the Federal Republic a distinctive foreign policy identity that reflects its history and geopolitical situation and provides a channel for practical activities serving West German interests"; Jonathan Dean, "How to Lose Germany," *Foreign Policy*, vol. 55 (Summer 1984), p. 58. Dr. Angela Stent has stressed the asymmetrical bargaining between Bonn and Moscow; see Stent, "East-

West Economic," pp. 152-53, 178, 241, 249.

48. Stent, p. 294. In interviews, West German officials stressed the continuing importance of this linkage for *Ostpolitik*; not-for-attribution interviews, London, 31 January 1989, Bundeshaus and Foreign Ministry, Bonn, 2-3 March 1989.

49. Stent, "East-West Economic," p. 295; Angela Stent, *From Embargo to Ostpolitik* (Cambridge, UK: Cambridge University Press, 1981), pp. 3, 7. In 1987, there were approximately 12 million inner-German visits. By late 1988, record numbers of ethnic Germans were flooding in to the F.R.G.; see Secretary of State George Shultz, "Vienna Meeting: Commitment, Cooperation, and the Challenge of Compliance," address at the closing session of the Conference on Security and Cooperation in Europe (CSCE), Vienna, 17 January 1989, rpt. in U.S. Department of State, *Current Policy*, no. 1145, January 1989, p. 2; and Niels Norlund, "Pladsen i herberget [A Place in the Shelter]," *Berlingske Tidende* [Copenhagen], 240th year, no. 353 (24 December 1988), section 1, p. 14, columns 1-3.

50. Nau, "The West.-West Dimensions," p. 206.

51. On the F.R.G.'s subsidy of the G.D.R.'s trade deficit, see Robert J. McCartney, "West German Aid Helps East Germany Avoid Crisis," *Washington Post*, 8 August 1989, section A, p. 14, columns 3-6. An advisor on security affairs for the Social Democratic Party forcefully argued that the reforming and moderate policies being launched in the Eastern Bloc during the 1980s were the fruits of Bonn's sustained *Ostpolitik* begun in the 1960s. He said that "on the whole, the approach has justified itself" and discounted arguments made by some American conservatives that the West was being fooled by signs of Soviet moderation--as had allegedly occurred in the 1960s and early 1970s. Instead, the failures of expansionist Soviet policies forced Moscow to renew and expand the links carefully established through years of *Ostpolitik* dialogue; not-for-attribution interview, Bundeshaus, Bonn, 2 March 1989; Dean, "How to Lose," pp. 61, 70-71; Walther Leisler Kiep, "The New Deutschlandpolitik," *Foreign Affairs*, vol. 63, no. 2 (Winter 1984-85), p. 318; and Arthur A. Stahnke, "The Economic Dimensions and Political Context of FRG-GDR Trade," in *East European Economic Assessment: Part I- Country Studies, 1980*, ed. U.S. Congress, Joint Economic Committee, 97th Congress, 1st session, 27 February 1981 (Washington, DC: U.S. GPO, 1981), p. 375.

52. Treverton notes the lessened threat perception, p. 10. He cites Hans Rattinger, "The Federal Republic of Germany: Much Ado About (Almost) Nothing," in Gregory Flynn and Hans Rattinger, eds., *The Public and Atlantic Defense* (Paris: Atlantic Institute for International Affairs, [nd]), p. 19. See also Hanns-D. Jacobsen, "The Special Case of Inter-German Relations," in *Economic Warfare or Detente?*, eds. Reinhard Rode and Hanns D. Jacobsen, International Perspectives on Security Series, No. 1 (Boulder, CO: Westview Press, 1985), p. 124; and Josef Joffe, "The View From Bonn: The Tacit Alliance," in *Eroding Empire*, ed. Lincoln Gordon (Washington, DC: The Brookings Institution, 1987), pp. 158-59.

It was reported in May 1988 that several West German banks had agreed to grant Moscow a $2.1 billion credit line. Foreign Minister Genscher, speaking in support of assisting Gorbachev's reforms, said: "We don't want to divide Europe and the world economically and technologically, but to link it through cooperation. We don't want to use our economic power to weaken our neighbors in the East; instead, we see opportunity for us." As Moscow continued its policy of economic reforms, West German businessmen and officials expressed the desirability of bolstering Gorbachev's efforts in light of the formidable domestic political and structural hurdles he needed to overcome. More trade providing Soviets consumer goods gave Gorbachev time to succeed and "something visible" to show for his initiatives while helping to silence domestic critics and opponents. The security benefits of stronger East-West contacts were stressed by government and opposition representatives in interviews. Genscher quoted in Robert J. McCartney, "Soviets Get W. German Credit Line," *Washington Post*, 10 May 1988, section A, p. 1, column 2 and section A, p. 16, column 1. See also the comments by Foreign Minister Genscher in Hans-Dietrich Genscher, "Toward an Overall Western Strategy for Peace, Freedom, and Progress," *Foreign Affairs* (Fall 1982), p. 43, rpt. in Gebhard Schweigler, "The Domestic Setting of West German Foreign Policy," in Uwe Nerlich and James A. Thomson, eds., *The Soviet Problem in American-German Relations* (New York: Crane Russak, 1985), p. 40; not-for-attribution interviews, F.R.G. government official, London, 31 January 1989, an advisor on security affairs for the Social Democratic Party, Bundeshaus, Bonn, 2 March 1989; David Marsh, "Profitting From Perestroika," *Financial Times* [London], no. 30,787, 7 March 1989, p. 18, columns 3-7, quoting Eberhard von Koerber, Chairman, West German subsidiary of Asea Brown Boveri and Hans-Gerd Neglein, Siemens; Heinrich Vogel, Bundesinstitut fur ostwissenschaftliche und internationale Studien, Cologne, "The Gorbachev Challenge: To Help or Not to Help?", revised version of a paper presented to the conference on "The Western Community and the Gorbachev Challenge," Luxembourg, 19-21 December 1988, pp. 7, 9 (photocopied); and not-for-attribution interviews, Ministry of Economics, Bonn, 1 March 1989 and Ost-Ausschuss der Deutschen Wirtschaft [Eastern Committee], Cologne, 6 March 1989.

53. For the sources for these figures, see Lincoln Gordon (ed.), *Eroding Empire* (Washington, DC: The Brookings Institution, 1987), Tables A-5, A-6, A-7, A-8, pp. 335-38; International Monetary Fund, *Direction of Trade Statistics Yearbook 1987* (Washington, D.C.: International Monetary Fund, 1987); International Monetary Fund, *Direction of Trade Statistics*, March-December 1987, February-June 1988; Bundesrepublik Deutschland, Statistisches Bundesamt, *Warenverkehr mit der Deutschen Demokratischen Republik und Berlin (Ost)*, Fachserie 6, Reihe 6 (Jahreshefte und Monatsheft Dezember 1987) (Wiesbaden, Federal Republic of Germany: Statistisches Bundesamt, 1988(?)) and *Berechnungen des DIW*. The importance to Bonn of maintaining a strong economy is noted in Sloan, *NATO's Future*, p. 87.

54. See Jean-Marie Guillaume, "A European View of East-West Trade in the 1980s," in *Economic Relations with the USSR*, ed. Abraham S. Becker (Lexington, MA: D.C. Heath and Company, 1983), pp. 137-38; and Angela Stent Yergin, "East-West Technology Transfer: European Perspectives," *Washington Papers*, vol. 8, no. 75 (1980), pp. 17-19, 21. One 1982 estimate put the number of West German

workers dependent on East-West trade at 275,000. See Gary Bertsch and John R. McIntyre, "The Western Alliance and East-West Trade: In Pursuit of an Integrated Strategy," in *The Politics of East-West Trade*, ed. Gordon B. Smith (Boulder, CO: Westview Press, 1984), p. 215. The authors cite Heinrich Vogel, "East-West Relations: A German View," paper presented at the Kennan Institute for Advanced Russian Studies, Washington, DC, 11 March 1982.

55. Kiep, "The New," p. 324 and Hassner, "Recurrent Stresses," pp. 73, 85-86. Britain's former Defense Minister, Michael Hesseltine (Conservative), warned that Soviet calls for greater East-West cooperation on ecological issues were a veiled attempt to stir up anti-NATO sentiment among leftist, neutralist, and antinuclear Green Party partisans and sympathizers. This might ultimately result in pressures on the West German and other Western governments to scrap NATO nuclear force modernization and permit the export of sophisticated technology, ostensibly for use in Soviet anti-pollution projects, but which also could be used by the Soviet military. His assessment reflected the F.R.G.'s allies' concern over the unique pressures that could be brought to bear on Bonn by a sophisticated Soviet leadership; Michael Hesseltine, "A Strategy For Europe," speech given at the Royal Institute of International Affairs, London, 23 November 1988.

56. Joffe, "The View," pp. 150-51, 153, 162-64, 183-84.

57. Reported in a not-for-attribution interview, Bureau of Economic and Business Affairs, U.S. Department of State, 23 February 1988. Genscher's position was supported by the West German opposition Social Democrats (SPD). A Commerce Department official reported that Genscher's call for relaxation of COCOM controls was soundly rebuffed at COCOM's high-level meeting in January 1988. Not-for-attribution interview, Bundeshaus, Bonn, 2 March 1989; and interview, Anstruther Davidson, Director, Office of Export Enforcement, International Trade Administration, U.S. Department of Commerce, Washington, D.C., 24 February 1988. Domestic business interests were also quick to respond to and exploit any sign of an easing of tensions reflected in COCOM liberalization. When restrictions on China trade were eased, while Soviet bloc controls remained relatively unchanged, West German business complained that this handicapped them since the bloc was an important West German market while the United States gained expanded trade with the P.R.C. To the extent these interests had any influence, Bonn also took into account the domestic political and business ramifications of *Ostpolitik*. See Peter Montagnon, "A Challenge for High-tech Censors," *Financial Times* [London], 19 October 1988, p. 3, columns 1-4; David Marsh, "W Germans Sign Nuclear Reactor Deal With Moscow," *Financial Times* [London], 25 October 1988, p. 9, columns 1-3; and Peter Montagnon, "Export Controls: Key Questions Raised," *Financial Times* [London], no. 30,718 (13 December 1988), p. 38, columns 1-4.

58. See Stanley Hoffmann, "Gaullism By Any Other Name," *Foreign Policy*, vol. 57 (Winter 1984-85); and Pierre Hassner, "The View From Paris," in *Eroding Empire*, ed. Lincoln Gordon (Washington, DC: The Brookings Institution, 1987), p. 191.

59. See F. Roy Willis, *The French Paradox* (Stanford, CA: Hoover Institution Press, 1982), pp. 82-83, 88; Dominique Moisi, "Mitterrand's Foreign Policy: The Limits of Continuity," *Foreign Affairs*, vol. 60, no. 2 (Winter 1981-82), p. 349; Ambassador Robert Luc, "The Foreign Policies of Francois Mitterrand," speech given at the University of California at Santa Barbara, Santa Barbara, CA, 8 February 1983; Michael M. Harrison, *The Reluctant Ally*, (Baltimore, MD: The Johns Hopkins Press, 1981), p. 230; and Hoffmann, "Gaullism."

60. Hassner, "The View," p. 205; Renata Fritsch-Bournazel, "France," in *Economic Warfare or Detente?*, eds. Reinhard Rode and Hanns-D. Jacobsen, International Perspectives on Security Series, No. 1 (Boulder, CO: Westview Press, 1985), pp. 130-32; and Stent, "East-West Economic," pp. 296-97. One 1982 estimate put the number of French workers dependent on East-West trade at nearly 1% of the active population. See Bertsch and McIntyre, "The Western Alliance," p. 215.

61. For the sources on France's Eastern European trade, see the data in Lincoln Gordon (ed.), *Eroding Empire* (Washington, DC: The Brookings Institution, 1987), Tables A-5, A-6, A-7, A-8, pp. 335-38; International Monetary Fund, *Direction of Trade Statistics Yearbook 1987* (Washington, DC: International Monetary Fund, 1987); and International Monetary Fund, *Direction of Trade Statistics*, March-December 1987, February-June 1988.

62. According to French and U.S. Commerce Department officials, the relative concentration of decision making on East-West trade among a few officials in European governments, and the intimate government-business "interface" among officials and business people, well acquainted through previous service in government, offered unique opportunities for lobbying. In addition, a small handful of nationalized or quasipublic French corporations were frequently involved in East-West trade which helped expedite trade as the distinctions between national and business interests blurred; Jean-Marie Guillaume, "A European View of East-West Trade in the 1980s," in *Economic Relations With the USSR*, ed. Abraham S. Becker (Lexington, MA: D.C. Heath and Company, 1983), p. 138; and not-for-attribution interview, U.S. Department of Commerce, 2 February 1988, Washington, DC.

63. Hassner, "The View," p. 205.

64. See Lord Saint Brides, "Foreign Policy of Socialist France," *Orbis*, vol. 26, no. 1 (Spring 1982); and Yves Guihannec, "Washington Isn't France's Capital," *New York Times*, 4 January 1983, p. 25, column 3.

65. In general, see Moisi, "Mitterrand's,"; Luc, "The Foreign Policies,"; Lord Saint Brides, "Foreign Policy," p. 43; Stent, "East-West Economic," pp. 296, 298; and Hoffmann, "Gaullism," pp. 47-48, 52.

66. Nau, "The West-West Dimensions," p. 208.

67. Signs of independence among Moscow's satellites were encouraged--utilizing trade carrots--without provoking the U.S.S.R.; Hassner, "The View...," pp. 214, 227. The widening trade deficit with the U.S.S.R. worried Paris, which agreed to a $2 billion credit package for Moscow in November 1988. The French Foreign Minister noted, however, that the credits were contingent on progress at the

conventional arms reduction talks. See Paul Betts, "France Draws up $2bn Package of Credit for Soviet Union," *Financial Times* [London], no. 30,703 (25 November 1988), p. 16, columns 2-4.

68. Fritsch-Bournazel, "France," pp. 133, 135.

69. Hassner, "The View," p. 216.

70. Ibid.

71. U.S. Congress, Office of Technology Assessment, *Technology*, p. 189.

72. Stent, "East-West Economic," p. 298.

73. Edwina Moreton, "The View From London," in *Eroding Empire*, ed. Lincoln Gordon (Washington, D.C.: The Brookings Institution, 1987), pp. 243, 257, 266; and Stent, "East-West Economic," p. 298.

74. The OECD data are from Gary K. Bertsch and Steven Elliott, "Controlling East-West Trade in Britain: Power, Politics, and Policy," in *Controlling East-West Trade and Technology Transfer: Power, Politics, and Policies*, ed. Gary K. Bertsch (Durham, NC: Duke University Press, 1988), p. 212, Table 7.2, citing OECD Monthly Statistics of Foreign Trade (Series A) and OECD Historical Statistics of Foreign Trade (Series A). On British trade performance after the mid-1960s, see Stephen Woolcock, "Great Britain," in *Economic Warfare or Detente?*, eds. Reinhard Rode and Hanns-D. Jacobsen, International Perspectives on Security Series, No. 1 (Boulder, CO: Westview Press, 1985), pp. 142, 145-46. The Commons Industry and Trade Committee noted the poor British performance in a report issued in early 1989; see U.K. House of Commons, Trade and Industry Committee, *Trade With Eastern Europe*, Second Report, Session 1988-89, Report together with the Proceedings of the Committee; Minutes of Evidence taken in Sessions 1987-88 and 1988-89; and Appendices (London: Her Majesty's Stationary Office [hereafter HMSO], 26 January 1989).

75. Stent, "East-West Economic," p. 299, and Woolcock, pp. 146-47. The East European Trade Council, a quasi-public British lobby group, argued that despite reported difficulties, the Soviet economy "is a good deal more robust than it has been fashionable to report" offering business "fresh fields to conquer as disenchantment with some other world markets increases." Another businessman remarked on the huge potential of a market with 400 million consumers. Other businessmen were less sanguine over the prospects for expanding trade, even in the wake of liberalizations encouraging joint ventures, given the problems and rigidities of centrally planned economies. East European Trade Council, "The Problems Involved in Trading With the Soviet Union," in U.K. House of Commons, Foreign Affairs Committee, *UK-Soviet Relations*, Session 1984-85, Minutes of Evidence, 8 May 1985, rpt. in U.K. House of Commons, Foreign Affairs Committee, *UK-Soviet Relations*, Second Report, Vol. II, Session 1985-86, Minutes of Evidence and Appendices (London: HMSO, 26 March 1986), p. 3; representative for a British trade lobby, not-for-attribution interview, 17 October 1988 and Anthony Bruce, John Brown Plc, Ralph Land, Rank Xerox, and R.A. Fletcher, BP International Limited, testimony, 29 June 1988 in U.K. House of Commons, Trade and Industry Committee, *Trade With Eastern Europe*, p. 63.

76. For the sources from which these figures are derived, see Lincoln Gordon ed., *Eroding Empire* (Washington, DC: The Brookings Institution, 1987), Tables A-5, A-6, A-7, A-8, pp. 335-38; International Monetary Fund, *Direction of Trade Statistics Yearbook 1987* (Washington, DC: International Monetary Fund, 1987); and International Monetary Fund, *Direction of Trade Statistics*, March-December 1987, February-June 1988. Complete statistics comparing total trade turnover among the U.K., U.S., F.R.G., and France from 1980 to 1985 are found in Gordon, *Eroding Empire*, pp. 335-38.

77. Moreton, "The View," pp. 255-56. During the 1950s and 1960s, London had led allied demands for trade liberalization. In 1962, the U.K. refused to go along with the U.S.-inspired NATO boycott of oil-pipe sales for the Soviet "Friendship" pipeline. The U.S. Ambassador to NATO, Thomas Finletter, expressed exasperation with British intransigence. In 1989, the U.K. urged the new Bush administration to lift COCOM's "no exceptions" rule for exports to the U.S.S.R. in the wake of the Soviet withdrawal from Afghanistan. There was also bipartisan support for relaxation in Parliament; see Alan P. Dobson, "The Kennedy Administration and Economic Warfare Against Communism," *International Affairs* [London], vol. 64, no. 4 (Autumn 1988), p. 608. Dobson cites a letter in the Kennedy Library archives: Kennedy Library, NSF, box 171-3, folder: UK General 2/12/63-3/5/63, Finletter to Rusk, 12 Feb. 1963; Lionel Barber, "UK in Drive to Lift CoCOM Bans," *Financial Times* [London], no. 30,764 (8 February 1989), p. 6, columns 5-7; John Bullock, "US and Britain Want NATO Summit in May," *The Independent* [London], no. 731 (13 February 1989), p. 8, column 2; and U.K. House of Commons, Trade and Industry Committee, *Trade With Eastern Europe*.

78. Stent, "East-West Economic," pp. 298, 300, and Woolcock, "Great Britain," pp. 142, 144, 147-48, 150.

79. Particularly sharp allied disagreements over U.S. anti-trust prosecutions revealed extraterritoriality as an issue where fundamentally contradictory views separated the allies. Important investigations and cases included *In re Investigations of World Arrangements with Relation to the Production, Transportation, Refining and Distribution of Petroleum*, 13 F.R.D. 280 (1952), *International Law Reports*, vol. 19, p. 197; *Mountship Lines Limited, et al., v. Federal Maritime Board*, 295 F. 2d 147 (1961); and *United States v. The Watchmakers of Switzerland Information Center, Inc.*, 1963 Trade Cases [paragraph] 70,600 (S.D.N.Y. 1962), *order modified*, 1965 Trade Cases [paragraph] 70,352 (S.D.N.Y. 1965). These examples are cited in A. V. Lowe, *Extraterritorial Jurisdiction: An Annotated Collection of Legal Materials* (Cambridge, UK: Grotius Publications Limited, 1983), pp. xxii, 22. See also Ann Zeigler, "The Siberian Pipeline Dispute and the Export Administration Act: What's Left of Extraterritorial Limits and the Act of State Doctrine?" *Houston Journal of International Law*, vol. 6, no. 1 (Autumn 1983), pp. 72-73. The landmark case was *United States v. Aluminum Company of America*, 148 F. 2d 416 (2d Cir. 1945). The U.S. effort to prevent the sale of U.S. truck parts by Fruehauf's French subsidiary, for eventual export to the People's Republic of China, was rebuffed by a French court and the contract was completed. *Fruehauf* set an

important precedent in that the French court's ruling rejected U.S. claims of jurisdiction based on the U.S. citizenship of the subsidiary's majority of directors. On *Fruehauf*, see Patrizio Merciai, "The Euro-Siberian Gas Pipeline Dispute- A Compelling Case For the Adaption of Jurisdictional Codes of Conduct," *Maryland Journal of International Law and Trade*, vol. 8, no. 1 (Spring-Summer 1984), pp. 30-31.

80. For the text of the Protection of Trading Interests Act and an example of British "blocking," see "United Kingdom: Protection of Trading Interests Act 1980, and the Protection of Trading Interests (U.S. Reexport Control) Order, 1982," rpt. in *Extraterritorial Jurisdiction: An Annotated Collection of Legal Materials*, ed. A. V. Lowe (Cambridge, UK: Grotius Publications Limited, 1983), pp. 186-93. France also had a "blocking" statute and both the British and French laws were enacted *prior* to the 1982 pipeline controversy; see Zeigler, "The Siberian Pipeline," p. 74.

81. Joseph E. Pattison, "Extraterritorial Enforcement of the Export Administration Act," in *Export Controls*, ed. Michael R. Czinkota (New York: Praeger, 1984), p. 94. Pattison cites Juan L. Oppenheim, *International Law*, 8th ed. (1955), p. 286.

82. Pattison, "Extraterritorial Enforcement," p. 94.

83. For a discussion of these principles, see Douglas E. Rosenthal and William M. Knighton, *National Laws and International Commerce: The Problem of Extraterritoriality* (London: Routledge and Kegan Paul, 1982), Chatham House Papers, No. 17, pp. 3, 10, 56; and Stanley D. Nollen, "The Case of John Brown Engineering and the Soviet Gas Pipeline," in *Export Controls*, ed. Michael R. Czinkota (New York: Praeger, 1984), p. 138.

84. Commission of the European Community, *Note and Comments of the European Community on the Amendments of 22 June 1982 to the Export Administration Act, Presented to the United States Department of State on 12 August 1982* rpt. in *Extraterritorial Jurisdiction: An Annotated Collection of Legal Materials*, ed. A. V. Lowe (Cambridge, UK: Grotius Publications Limited, 1983), p. 205. Other legal experts, including Patrizio Merciai of the University of Geneva's Graduate Institute of European Studies, Daniel Marcus, partner, Wilmer, Cutler & Pickering, expressed similar views. See Merciai, "The Euro-Siberian," pp. 26-27; Daniel Marcus, "Soviet Pipeline Sanctions: The President's Authority to Impose Extraterritorial Controls," *Law and Policy in International Business*, vol. 15, no. 4 (1983), p. 1166; and Geric Lebedoff and Caroline Raievski, "A French Perspective on the United States Ban on the Soviet Gas Pipeline Equipment," *Texas International Law Journal*, vol. 18, no. 3 (Summer 1983), p. 497, footnote 89.

85. *Legislation on Foreign Relations Through 1985* [hereafter, *Legislation on Foreign Relations*], ed. U.S. Congress, Committee on Foreign Affairs and Committee on Foreign Relations (Washington, DC: U.S. GPO, 1986), II, pp. 404, 454.

86. Cited in Robert Y. Stebbings, "Export Controls: Extraterritorial Conflict-- The Dilemma of the Host Country Employee," *Case Western Reserve Journal of International Law*, vol. 19 (1987), p. 305.

87. See William A. Root, "COCOM: An Appraisal of Objectives and Needed Reforms," in *Controlling East-West Trade and Technology Transfer: Power, Politics, and Policies*, ed. Gary K. Bertsch (Durham, NC: Duke University Press, 1988), p. 437.

88. Stebbings, "Export Controls," p. 305.

89. Reexports of goods containing more than $10,000 worth of U.S.-origin technology and destined for the bloc still required a U.S. license. See U.S. Department of Commerce, Bureau of Export Administration, *Export Administration Annual Report FY 1987* (Washington, DC: U.S. GPO, November 1988), p. 19. See also National Academy of Sciences, *Balancing*, pp. 99, 140, 145-46; Kenneth W. Abbot, "Defining the Extraterritorial Reach of American Export Controls: Congress as Catalyst," *Cornell International Law Journal*, vol. 17, no. 1 (Winter 1984), p. 155; Allan I. Mendelowitz, General Accounting Office, response to written questions of Senator Heinz, in U.S. Congress, Senate Committee on Banking, Housing, and Urban Affairs, Subcommittee on International Finance and Monetary Policy, *Export Controls*, Hearings, 12, 17 March 1987, 100th Congress, 1st session (Washington, DC: U.S. GPO, 1987), pp. 205-06; interviews with Eric Hirschhorn, attorney, executive secretary for the Industry Coalition on Technology Transfer, and former DOC official, Washington, DC, 18 April 1988, and John Copeland, Director, Export Administration, Motorola, Inc., Washington, D.C., 25 February 1988. In March 1987, before the Senate Subcommittee on International Finance and Monetary Policy, Paul Freedenberg, Assistant Secretary for Trade Administration, testified that the *de minimus* level then in place was 10% U.S content, above which a reexport license was required. Interviews with business people nearly a year later revealed that the informal level was now up to 25%, indicating that the United States was grudgingly liberalizing its regulations. The Omnibus Trade and Competitiveness Act did mandate decontrol of all intra-COCOM trade, subject to determination by the DOC that allies' export controls were adequate. This determination had not been made by 1991, although substantial elimination of most intra-COCOM controls had been ordered by President Bush; see Paul Freedenberg, testimony, 12 March 1987, in U.S. Congress, Senate Committee on Banking, Housing, and Urban Affairs, Subcommittee on International Finance and Monetary Policy, *Export Controls*, p. 32; "Commerce Formally Delays Decision on License-Free High Technology Sales," *Inside U.S. Trade*, 2 December 1988, pp. 7-9; Clyde H. Farnsworth, "U.S. Balks at Easing Technology-Export Curbs," *New York Times*, 1 March 1991, section C, p. 2, columns 1-4; Glennon J. Harrison and George Holiday, *Export Controls, 1990*, CRS Issue Brief, IB87122 (Washington, DC: Congressional Research Service, Library of Congress, 10 December 1990), pp. CRS-4, 7-8; and Kevin F. F. Quigley and William J. Long, "Export Controls: Moving Beyond Economic Containment," *World Policy Journal* (Winter 1990), pp. 181-82. The allies also practiced extraterritorial licensing, albeit on a much smaller scale and without fanfare according to former National Security Council member Henry R. Nau; see Henry R. Nau, "Export Controls and Free Trade: Squaring the Circle in COCOM," in *Controlling East-West Trade and Technology Transfer: Power, Politics, and*

Policies, ed. Gary K. Bertsch (Durham, NC: Duke University Press, 1988), p. 409.

90. National Academy of Sciences, *Balancing*, p. 99, and Malcolm R. Hill, "East-West Technology Transfer: The British Experience," *Review of Socialist Law*, no. 4 (1988), p. 356. For a schematic comparison of licensing procedures and related import, consignee, and other governmental assurances required by the U.K., France, and the F.R.G., see Root et al., "A Study," Appendix A: Comparison of Export Control Countries, pp. 236-42.

91. Richard N. Perle, statement, 23 April 1987, U.S., Congress, House Committee on Science, Space, and Technology, *National Academy of Sciences Report on International Technology Transfer*, Hearing, 2 February, 23 April 1987, 100th Congress, 1st session (Washington, DC: U.S. GPO, 1987), p. 90. Cases that appeared to justify U.S. concerns regarding the need for reexport licenses occasionally appeared in the newspapers; see Steven Greenhouse, "French Linked to Soviet Sale," *New York Times*, 17 Oct. 1987.

92. This assertion is made by Stebbings, "Export Controls," p. 305.

93. Long, "The Executive," p. 56. Legal experts were skeptical of the Executive's broad assertion of extraterritoriality, said to be implicit in the 1979 EAA, and did not feel that legislative history or Congressional intent supported this assertion. See prepared statements of Stanley J. Marcuss, Esq., Partner, Milbank, Tweed, Hadley and McCloy, and of Douglas E. Rosenthal, Esq., attorney, Southerland, Asbill, and Brennan in U.S. Congress, Senate Committee on Foreign Relations, Subcommittee on International Economic Policy, *Soviet-European Gas Pipeline*, hearing, 97th Congress, 2nd session, 3 March 1982 (Washington, DC: U.S. GPO, 1982), pp. 37, 44.

94. Many British political and business leaders objected to U.S. requirements that U.S. Commerce Department inspectors be permitted to audit British companies in exchange for receiving a bulk shipment license, which obviated the need for applying separately for individual shipments. This was not binding under British law and some MPs alleged that the United States was "spying" on British companies. However, an uneasy U.S.-U.K. compromise permitted companies to be audited voluntarily without revealing customers. This suggested that the United States retained some leverage and that Britain was still dependant on U.S. supplies so that it would be too risky to completely forbid audits. In the F.R.G., government officials and business people admitted that the large U.S. market--and fear of losing access to it--gave the U.S. leverage. A voluntary program of business compliance with U.S. auditing rules was also instituted, although West German Customs representatives were assigned to accompany U.S. auditors. Given the rancor audits produced, and the pressure to seek non-U.S. sources of supply, as the National Academy of Sciences reported, it was unclear how long allies would tolerate this and similar U.S. policies. France also instituted its own version of internal auditing, reportedly to forgo auditing by U.S. inspectors. A Commerce Department official denied there was any improper use of proprietary business information, noting that all such information is protected under Section 12(C) of the 1979 EAA. See Bertsch and Elliott, "Controlling East-West," pp. 233-34; Christopher Joyce, "Technology

Transfer Through the Iron Curtain," *New Scientist*, vol. 111, no. 1521 (14 August 1986), p. 42, column 1; A. H. Hermann, "Export Controls and U.S. Pressure," *Financial Times*, 13 June 1985, p. 33; rpt. in U.S., Department of Defense, Department of the Air Force, *Current News*, special edition, Technology Security, no date; "High-tech Trade Caught in Red Tape," *New Scientist*, vol. 111, no. 1518 (24 July 1986), p. 21; and not-for-attribution interview, Ost-Ausschuss der Deutschen Wirtschaft [Eastern Committee], Cologne, 6 March 1989.

U.S. regulations even required licenses or restricted selling or moving some products *within* an allied country, which also upset the British. In another case, there were problems with U.S. restrictions on the movement of computers between British army bases in the U.K. and the F.R.G.; see Calman J. Colman, Vice President, Emergency Committee for American Trade, testimony, 17 March 1987, in U.S. Congress, Senate Committee on Banking, Housing, and Urban Affairs, Subcommittee on International Finance and Monetary Policy, *Export Controls*, Hearings, 12, 17 March, 100th Congress, 1st session (Washington, DC: U.S. GPO, 1987), p. 126; John Lamb, "US and Britain tangle over supercomputers," *New Scientist*, vol. 110, no. 1510 (29 May 1986), p. 18; Alex McLoughlin, Head, Trade Relations, International Computers Limited, untitled address given at a conference on *Strategic Trade Controls*, the Royal Institute of International Affairs, London, 19 November 1987, rpt. in *Conference Proceedings* (available from RIIA), p. 64; Marie-Helene Labbe, "Controlling East-West Trade in France," in *Controlling East-West Trade and Technology Transfer: Power, Politics, and Policies*, ed. Gary K. Bertsch (Durham, NC: Duke University Press, 1988), pp. 191, 201-02 and not-for-attribution interview, U.S. Department of Commerce, Washington, DC, 9 March 1988. Additional problems were raised when U.S. regulations conflicted with national laws governing business activities. In one example, the DOC denied a license to I.B.M.-Germany to sell a computer to a Soviet-controlled company in Hamburg. I.B.M. feared that it would be prosecuted for violating West German laws prohibiting customer discrimination. A West German official complained that: "It amounted to the United States telling one German company, IBM Germany, that it could not sell to another German company, Transnautic. German export control law does not have any prohibition on sales to a Soviet-controlled company in a third country. It is the eternal problem of the United States trying to apply extraterritorial controls"; quoted in Susan F. Rasky and David E. Sanger, "U.S. Split Over Computer Sale To a Soviet-Owned Company," *New York Times*. 29 September 1987, section A, p. 1, section D, p. 6.

95. The Dutch firm Philips was reportedly avoiding sales of sensitive goods to Eastern Europe owing to concern that access to its important American market might be closed if it violated U.S. regulations. Furthermore, the United States discouraged European use of Soviet rockets for orbiting satellites because the latter contained sensitive U.S. components. Testifying in late 1988, senior representatives for a British trade lobby observed that U.S. extraterritorial claims over U.S.-origin technology continued to be a "significant barrier" to British trade with Eastern Europe. Potential Eastern European customers avoided importing items containing

U.S.-origin technology fearing the supply might be embargoed in the future; see Alman Metten, "Report Drawn Up on Behalf of the Committee on Energy, Research and Technology," European Parliament, *Reports*, PE DOC A 2-99/85 (Luxembourg: Office for Official Publications of the European Communities, 30 September 1985), p. 17; Edward Cody, "Soviets Use Paris Air Show to Pitch for Western Satellite Launch Contracts," *Washington Post*, 18 June 1987, section A, p. 34, columns 2-3; Kathy Sawyer, "Soviets Move Aggressively In Marketing Space Services," *Washington Post*, 13 January 1988, section A, p. 12, column 1 and Dr. Norman Wooding, Deputy Chairman, and Mr. James McNeish, Director, East European Trade Council, testimony, 2 November 1988, in U.K. House of Commons, Trade and Industry Committee, *Trade With Eastern Europe*, p. 105. It was common practice to include a 90-day clause in contracts between Western companies and Eastern European trade organizations. Under this clause, the company had a maximum of 90 days to secure all required licenses or lose the contract. One British businessman complained that it often took longer than 90 days just to obtain approval from the exporter's national government--besides the time required to get COCOM permission. The Eastern Europeans then simply went to another supplier promising quicker results; J. Beran, Managing Director, Berox Machine Tool company, Inc., interview, London, 8 November 1988.

96. Mr. L. Friedman, Chairman, T.A.C. Ltd, testified before the House of Commons Foreign Affairs Committee that just the prospect of U.S. reexport controls and blacklisting caused companies to forego even applying for a license: "Very often it does not even go to the stage where one has an official application for export licence. Many companies just look over their shoulders because they look at business in the United States and say 'We would rather not touch it. What will the US customer say?"; testimony in U.K. House of Commons, Foreign Affairs Committee, *UK-Soviet Relations*, Session 1984-85, Minutes of Evidence, 8 May 1985, rpt. in U.K. House of Commons, Foreign Affairs Committee, *UK-Soviet Relations*, Second Report, Vol. II, Session 1985-86, Minutes of Evidence and Appendices (London: HMSO, 26 March 1986), p. 37.

97. Such a provision was incorporated in the U.S. Trade Act passed in the autumn of 1988. The EC and the individual allies formally protested this provision. As one EC official put it, it "would increase the extraterritorial aspects of the U.S. exports controls legislation"; Auke Haagsma, First Secretary, Legal Affairs, EC Commission Delegation, Washington, DC, "Export Controls and the Single European Market," *Europe*, no. 274 (March 1988), p. 17; and not-for-attribution interview, Foreign and Commonwealth Office, London, 3 November 1988.

98. Root, "COCOM," p. 438, and Freedenberg, comments. For example, Assistant Secretary of Commerce for Trade Administration Paul Freedenberg testified that no more than 10% of all reexport requests were from the largest European companies. It was small European exporters, who did not apply, which were the chief reexport violators; see Paul Freedenberg, testimony, 12 March 1987, in U.S. Congress, Senate Committee on Banking, Housing, and Urban Affairs, Subcommittee on International Finance and Monetary Policy, *Export Controls*,

Hearings, 12, 17 March 1987, 100th Congress, 1st session (Washington, DC: U.S. GPO, 1987), p. 27. The Director of the DOC's Office of Export Enforcement echoed this view, noting that compliance went down for foreign companies which had limited or infrequent business with U.S.-origin technology; interview, Davidson.

99. For example, a U.S.-U.K. agreement on an acceptable security plan governing use of U.S.-origin supercomputers located in the U.K. took two years to negotiate. The United States had previously required that a U.S. plan be implemented, which aroused strong opposition from British academics. The United States finally accepted that a British security plan would govern use while a U.S. license was still required. Potential end users were to be warned by the U.K. that any violation of the security plan would also violate the terms of the U.S. license; not-for-attribution interview with a British businessman at a U.S. subsidiary, London, 29 November 1988. Sir Brian Tovey, Defense and Political Adviser, Plessey Electronic Systems Ltd. and former Director-General of the U.K.'s Government Communications Headquarters, noted the more accommodating U.S. stance but cautioned that reexport controls continued to be a political football for MPs and others seeking to distance the U.K. from the U.S.; Sir Brian Tovey, "COCOM Restrictions, Extraterritoriality Claims and Their Impact on the Information Technology Industry," unpublished speech and Sir Brian Tovey, interview, London, 15 December 1988.

100. One conspiracy theory was promulgated in Kevin Cahill, *Trade Wars: The High-Technology Scandal of the 1980s* (London: W. H. Allen, 1986). Cahill, a journalist, had also served as an aide to Paddy Ashdown, leader of the Democrats in the House of Commons and one of the most outspoken critics of U.S. extraterritorial controls and the Thatcher government's response to them. Suspicions persisted in the mass media and among many business people. The attitude of European officials was that an orchestrated U.S. conspiracy was a fiction or, that there was no evidence to support the charges, and that those who made them were misinformed about the workings of COCOM. Americans who worked closely with officials and businesses on both sides of the Atlantic also heard claims of U.S. duplicity but correctly pointed out the virtual impossibility of orchestrating such a vast conspiracy given the internecine turf-wars, jealousies, and press leaks that are the reality of Washington politics. However, there were instances where U.S. actions had been tainted by outcomes that implied a certain degree of manipulation, technological protectionism, or even espionage against allies utilizing confidential information. In particular, the liberalization of controls on COCOM exports to the P.R.C. was said to have been carried out by Washington after warning interested U.S. companies. The impression was that they were therefore well positioned--owing to inside information--to take advantage of the liberalization. Furthermore, it was alleged that U.S. intelligence had drawn up a list of all nuclear sites in the West, based on information gathered from license applications submitted by the British government, and supplied this information to businesses. Significantly, while there were many allegations, when asked if *they* had suffered commercially owing to manipulation or cheating by the U.S. or other allies, business people and government officials

admitted they had no hard evidence or acknowledged that U.S. businesses suffered more from restrictive U.S. policies. A Rank Xerox (U.K.) executive noted that as a U.S. subsidiary, Rank Xerox (U.K.) was doubly penalized since it had to comply with both U.S. and U.K. licensing rules; not-for-attribution interviews, Ministry of Defence, Foreign and Commonwealth Office, and Department of Trade and Industry, London, 31 October, and 9 November 1988; not-for-attribution interviews, F.R.G. government official, London, 31 January 1989, Foreign, Defense, and Economics ministries, Bonn and Ost-Ausschuss der Deutschen Wirtschaft [Eastern Committee], Cologne, 1-3, 6 March 1989, foreign policy expert at an official think-tank, Cologne, 8 March 1989; Terence Roche Murphy, Partner, Murphy and Malone, Washington, D.C., "The High-Tech Balancing Act," speech given at a conference on *Strategic Export Controls*, the Royal Institute of International Affairs, London, 19 November 1987, rpt. in *Conference Proceedings* (available from RIIA), pp. 15-17; not-for-attribution interviews with a businessman and Foreign and Commonwealth Office official, London, 17 October and 3 November 1988; Mr. R. R. Land, General Manager, East European Operations, Rank Xerox Ltd, J. N. Cooper, Chairman, and F. P. Korn, Deputy Chairman, M. Golodetz (Overseas) Ltd, testimony, in U.K. House of Commons, Foreign Affairs Committee, *UK-Soviet Relations*, Session 1984-85, Minutes of Evidence, 8 May 1985, rpt. in U.K. House of Commons, Foreign Affairs Committee, *UK-Soviet Relations*, Second Report, Vol. II, Session 1985-86, Minutes of Evidence and Appendices (London: HMSO, 26 March 1986), pp. 16, 40-41; Ralph Land, Rank Xerox, testimony, 29 June 1988 in U.K. House of Commons, Trade and Industry Committee, *Trade With Eastern Europe*, pp. 67-69; and Paul Brown, "US Halts Spy 'Trick' on British Hi-tech," *The Guardian* [Manchester], 2 November 1988, p. 4, columns 1-3.

101. In interviews, the author found agreement among British government officials and business people in opposing the extraterritorial nature of U.S. reexport licensing. One argued that the issue was so basic that Britain had fought wars to stop similar violations of national sovereignty; Hugh Malim, Assistant Director, Barclays Bank, PLC, interview, London, 26 October 1988. Also, not-for-attribution interviews, Ministry of Defence and Foreign and Commonwealth Office, 31 October and 3 November 1988, and Stewart Nunn, Director (Policy Unit) Export Controls, Nick Cooper, North American Trade Policy Section, Peter Goate, Economist, and Michael Franklin, all with the Department of Trade and Industry, interview, London, 9 November 1988.

102. American Bar Association, *Report to the House of Delegates Section of International Law and Practice*; rpt. in U.S. Congress, House Committee on Foreign Affairs, Subcommittee on International Economic Policy and Trade, *Extension and Revision of the Export Administration Act of 1979*, Hearings, 24 February, 1, 3, 8 March, 5, 12-14, 28, 29 April, 2, 4, 5, 18, 25, 26 May 1983, 98th Congress, 1st session (Washington, DC: U.S. GPO, 1985), p. 848. The ABA cited *Restatement (Revised) of the Foreign Relations Law of the United States*, [paragraph] 216 (Tentative Draft No. 2, 27 March 1981). On *abus de droit*, see Lebedoff and Raievski, "A French Perspective," p. 499. In the *Sensor* case, the Hague court

specifically cited the place-of-incorporation argument and the 1956 U.S.A.-Netherlands Treaty of Friendship, Commerce and Navigation as grounds for ordering a Dutch subsidiary of a U.S. company to ship embargoed gas pipeline equipment to a French firm; see Confederation of British Industry, letter to Sen. Jake Garn, 19 April 1983, rpt. in U.S. Congress, Senate Committee on Banking, Housing, and Urban Affairs, Subcommittee on International Finance and Monetary Policy, *Reauthorization of the Export Administration Act*, hearings, 98th Congress, 1st session, 2, 16 March and 14 April 1983 (Washington, DC: U.S. GPO, 1983), p. 1190.

103. Reasonableness was determined by considering such factors as: "conflict with the laws of the foreign country" and "when the interests of the state attempting to assert extraterritorial jurisdiction outweigh the competing jurisdictional claims of another state"; see American Bar Association, *Report*, pp. 849-50 citing *Restatement (Revised)...*, [paragraph] 403 and accompanying Comments and Reporter's Notes; Rosenthal, prepared statement, p. 44, footnote 7 citing *Timberlane Lumber Co. v. The Bank of America*, 549 F. 2d 597.

104. Commission, *Note and Comments*, pp. 198-211.

105. On the territoriality principle and legal precedents suggesting that U.S. claims are invalid, see *Barcelona Traction and Power Company* (Second Phase) (*Belgium v. Spain*), International Court of Justice (Judgement of 5 February 1970), p. 3, and *Compagnie Europeane des Petroles S.A. v. Sensor Nederland B.V.*, Number 82/716 (District Court) The Hague, 17 September 1982. The U.S. Supreme Court affirmed this principle in *American Banana Company v. United Fruit Company*, 213 U.S. 347, 356 (1909) and in *Banco Nacional de Cuba v. Sabbatino*, 376 U.S. 398, 428 (1964). These examples are cited in Merciai, "The Euro-Siberian," p. 27 (*Barcelona Traction*), Pattison, "Extraterritorial Enforcement," p. 95 (*Sensor*), and Zeigler, "The Siberian," pp. 76-77 (*American Banana, Sabbatino*). See also Stebbings, "Export Controls," pp. 305, 307. In the EC case against technology retaining nationality, the EC cited *American President Lines v. China Mutual Trading Company*, 1953 A.M.C. 1510, 1526 (Hong Kong Supreme Court) and *Moens v. Ahlers North German Lloyd*, 30 R.W. 360 (Tribunal of Commerce, Antwerp (1966)). See Commission, *Note and Comments*, p. 203, footnote 2.

106. Perhaps the signal case in this respect was *United States v. Curtiss-Wright Export Corporation* (1936) where the U.S. Supreme Court affirmed the wide scope of Executive Branch discretion in foreign affairs and national security. See Stebbings, "Export Controls," p. 339, and Zeigler, "The Siberian," p. 74. There was some pressure to alter U.S. legal practice. For example, in 1986, the American Law Institute (ALI) urged a "balancing test" to determine whether courts should rule on issues of extraterritoriality. The ALI also rejected "'unreasonable'" extraterritorial jurisdiction. Terence Roche Murphy, Partner, Murphy and Malone, Washington, DC, "The High-Tech Balancing Act," speech given at a conference on *Strategic Export Controls*, the Royal Institute of International Affairs, London, 19 November 1987, rpt. in *Conference Proceedings* (available from RIIA), pp. 22-23. He cited American Law Institute, *Restatement of the Foreign Relations Law of the United*

States (Revised) (1986), Section 403(1).

107. United Kingdom, Foreign and Commonwealth Office, "Note No. 174, of 4 September 1981," rpt. in *Extraterritorial Jurisdiction: An Annotated Collection of Legal Materials*, ed. A.V. Lowe (Cambridge, U.K.: Grotius Publications Limited, 1983), p. 155.

108. See the arguments in Professor Luzius Wildhaber, "The Continental Experience," in *Extra-territorial Application of Laws and Responses Thereto*, ed. Professor Cecil J. Olmstead (Oxford: International Law Association and ESC Publishing Limited, 1984), p. 66; Neville March Hunnings, "Legal Aspects of Technology Transfer to Eastern Europe and the Soviet Union," in *Technology Transfer and East-West Relations*, ed. Mark E. Schaffer (London: Croom Helm, 1985), p. 163; and Stebbings, "Export Controls," p. 306.

109. The Minister for Information Technology, Geoffrey Pattie, expressed the nub of the dilemma in House of Commons debate when he noted that British blocking legislation should not be invoked irresponsibly. Even though it would overturn U.S. extraterritorial actions, such legislation "could jeopardise British companies dependent on continued access to United States goods and technology," owing to blacklisting and denying U.S. technology, which would put companies out of business. This admission was, predictably, not well received by the Opposition; see U.K., Hansard, *Parliamentary Debates*, House of Commons, vol. 101, no. 149, 15 July 1986, (London: HMSO, nd), pp. 879-81. Leverage could also be had through issuing coveted U.S. "gold card" bulk distribution licenses to companies which complied with auditing and internal requirements. A "gold card" holder who depended on U.S.-origin components thereby avoided delays arising from having to apply for individual U.S. licenses; see Hill, "East-West," p. 358.

110. Homer E. Moyer, Jr., Attorney, Miller and Chevalier, Chairman, American Bar Association Subcommittee on the Extraterritorial Application of the Export Administration Act, testimony, 13 April 1983, in U.S. Congress, House Committee on Foreign Affairs, Subcommittee on International Economic Policy and Trade, *Extension and Revision of the Export Administration Act of 1979*, Hearings, 24 February, 1, 3, 8 March, 5, 12-14, 28, 29 April, 2, 4, 5, 18, 25, 26 May 1983, 98th Congress, 1st session (Washington, DC: U.S. GPO, 1985), pp. 855-56. A final controversy concerned the so-called protective principle of international law. Under this principle, a state could exercise jurisdiction extraterritorially if threatened by acts that seriously endangered the state's national security, government, and political independence. On this point--which resembled the effects doctrine--there appeared to be tentative agreement among legal experts that, subject to principles of international comity, national security controls could be based on the protective principle. But since there had been no test case, such assertions were speculative and based on the general COCOM consensus regarding the need and utility of national security controls. However, should there be disagreement over whether national security or foreign policy motives were grounds for jurisdiction, the protective principle might lose its force. It was, after all, common for the allies to disagree over what constituted strict national security and foreign policy goals; see

Abbott, "Defining," pp. 154-55; Commission, *Note and Comments*, p. 203, footnote 2; Wildhaber, "The Continental Experience," p. 67; and American Bar Association, *Report*, p. 854.

111. For example, the Rome Treaty's Article 34 prohibited "'quantitative restrictions on exports and all measures having equivalent effect'"; Hunnings, "Legal Aspects," p. 157. See also Root, "COCOM," p. 438.

While the official number of items unilaterally controlled by the United States held relatively steady at around 30, there was increasing concern on both sides of the Atlantic about the trend of increasing numbers of dual-use goods assigned to the U.S. Munitions List. The State Department's Office of Munitions Control had primary licensing responsibility for these items, assisted by the DOD. However, Commodity Control List items could be reclassified under the Munitions List, in effect putting them under unilateral control since the Munitions List was not based on the lists drawn up under COCOM reviews; Dr. Friedrich Futschik, Defence Affairs, Philips International B.V., "Export Controls in Practice," speech given at a conference on *Strategic Export Controls*, the Royal Institute of International Affairs, London, 19 November 1987, rpt. in *Conference Proceedings* (available from RIIA), p. 81; and not-for-attribution interview with a businessman, London, 11 November 1988. There was also some question whether the EC's common external trade policy, provided for under the Rome Treaty's Article 113, might also come into conflict with individual members' control policies. This was possible should EC authority eventually preempt the members' powers in this realm. Furthermore, U.S. reexport control licenses were required for any state exporting U.S. technology to Cuba and the Southeast Asian communist area, a situation which might eventually be at odds with common EC export policy; see Hunnings, "Legal Aspects," p. 158; and Root, "COCOM," p. 438. The EC repeatedly complained of the extraterritorial nature of U.S. law and the European Parliament passed a resolution urging all members to adopt legislation similar to the British Protection of Trading Interests Act. See the diplomatic notes from the Delegation of the Commission of the European Communities to the Department of State 19 September 1986 and 29 January 1987, rpt. in American Electronics Association, *Case Study Report American Electronics Association Export Control Task Force* (12 March 1987), pp. 48-50, and *A Resolution of the European Parliament Concerning Technology Transfer*, Document # A2-99/85, adopted February(?) 1986, an incomplete translation is found in American Electronics Association, *Case Study*, pp. 38-40. The resolution was also reprinted in U.S. Congress, Senate Committee on Banking, Housing, and Urban Affairs, Subcommittee on International Finance and Monetary Policy, *Export Controls*, pp. 226-27.

112. Alex McLoughlin, Head of Trade Relations, ICL (UK), Ltd., comments at the *Strategic Export Controls Conference*, the Royal Institute of International Affairs (RIIA), London, 19 November 1987, rpt. in *Conference Proceedings* (available from RIIA), p. 120.

113. Interview, William Root, former Director, Bureau of East-West Trade, U.S. Department of State, Washington, DC, 8 March 1988.

114. Under article 223 (paragraph 1(b)), "Any member State may take such measures as it considers necessary for the protection of the essential interests of its security which are connected with the production or trade in arms, munitions and war material; such measures shall not adversely affect the conditions of competition in the Common Market regarding products which are not intended for specifically military purposes." The EC Council is also required to draw up a list of products coming under the provisions in paragraph 1. While never published, the list is available to EC nationals from their government; Hunnings, "Legal Aspects," p. 157.

115. Jurgen Notzold and Hendrik Roodbeen, "The European Community and COCOM: The Exclusion of an Interested Party," in *After the Revolutions: East-West Trade and Technology Transfer in the 1990s*, eds. Gary K. Bertsch, Heinrich Vogel, and Jan Zielonka (Boulder, CO: Westview Press, 1991), pp. 127-31.

116. See National Academy of Sciences, *Balancing*, p. 195. One solution was to create a license-free zone in the COCOM area. Language ending most reexport controls between the U.S. and the COCOM allies was included in the 1988 Omnibus Trade Act but implementation was slow. As the deadline approached, various opinions were voiced regarding the impact of 1992. Allen Wendt of the State Department worried whether the effectiveness of controls would be undermined. Pentagon officials warned of leakages after 1992 since U.S.-origin goods could theoretically be reshipped from fairly secure countries, such as the U.K, to less reliable Greece or Portugal. One European's response was that any high-technology shipments from these areas "'would have to stick out like a sore thumb'" and therefore regulation would be easy, although a former senior British intelligence official was much less sanguine. A Commerce Department official foresaw the end of COCOM and the possibility of some alternative including non-COCOM countries such as Ireland. A State Department official reported that COCOM had held discussions on the 1992 question, but later that year there were reports that decontrol efforts in COCOM were progressing very slowly with only seven of 127 categories scrapped after nine months. Some European business people were adamant in insisting on the elimination of *all* barriers and one representative of an important British high- technology company warned that unless U.S. licensing within the EC was rescinded, by 1992 companies would bring the U.S. before the European Court to seek redress. Government officials foresaw fewer problems. One British Department of Trade and Industry official noted that intra-COCOM trade was being liberalized by the United States and that after 1992, EC governments would continue to determine their own control policy. There was also speculation that the Rome Treaty permitted border controls on strategic goods, although this view conflicted with free-trade advocates. Another proposal called for creation of an EC body to take over vetting of sensitive exports--something Washington was unlikely to favor. West German government representatives--while stressing that much more work remained before these issues were resolved--thought that some kind of common customs enforcement would be maintained on EC borders with non-EC states. They noted that intra-EC enforcement might be achieved through a Community Federal

Bureau of Investigation proposed by Chancellor Kohl and through mutual efforts to bolster export control security in the southern European member states. It was unclear how enthusiastic EC capitals were for supranational curbing of sovereignty in such a delicate policy area. See Eduardo Lachica and E. S. Browning, "West Tightens Technology-Export Rules But Shortens List of Controlled Products," *Wall Street Journal*, 29 January 1988; U.S. Department of State, "Results of the Senior Political Meeting on Strengthening the Coordinating Committee on Multilateral Export Controls (COCOM)," Press Release, 29 January 1988; Wendt, comments; Tovey, interview; not-for-attribution interview, U.S. Department of Commerce, 14 March 1988; not-for-attribution interview, Bureau of Economic and Business Affairs, U.S. Department of State, 23 February 1988; "COCOM to Lessen Curbs," *Financial Times* [London], 28 October 1988, p. 5, column 2; not-for-attribution interview, Ministry of Defence, London, 31 October 1988; not-for-attribution interview with a British businessman, London, 11 November 1988; Alex McLoughlin, Head of Trade Relations, ICL (UK), Ltd., address given at the conference on *Strategic Export Controls*, the Royal Institute of International Affairs (RIIA), London, 19 November 1987, rpt. in *Conference Proceedings* (available from RIIA), pp. 60-75; Dr. Friedrich Futschik, Defence Affairs, Philips International B.V., "Export Controls in Practice," address given at the conference on *Strategic Export Controls*, the Royal Institute of International Affairs (RIIA), London, 19 November 1987, rpt. in *Conference Proceedings* (available from RIIA), pp. 76-84; not-for-attribution interviews, Department of Trade and Industry, Foreign and Commonwealth Office, and Ministry of Defence, London, 31 October and 3, 9 November 1988; not-for-attribution interviews with West German government officials, London, 31 January 1989, Ministries of Foreign Affairs and Economics, Bonn, 1, 3 March 1989; David Buchan, "European Community Seeks Warmer Relations With Moscow," *Financial Times* [London], 19 August 1988; Robert Fisk, "US Fears 1992 May Boost Technology Flow to Soviet Bloc," *The Times* [London], 17 October 1988; and Peter Montagnon, "A Challenge For High-tech Censors," *Financial Times* [London], 19 October 1988, p. 3, columns 1-4.

117. 50 United States Code, App. 2401 *et seq.*, Public Law 96-72, 96th Congress, 29 September 1979. Amendments were made in 1981 and 1985 under Public Laws 97-145, 97th Congress, 29 December 1981, and 99-64, 99th Congress, 12 July 1985. It expired on 30 September 1990. President Bush subsequently invoked the International Emergency Economic Powers Act (50 U.S.C. 1702), which continued export controls provided for in the 1979 EAA. Legislation amending and reauthorizing the 1979 EAA was pocket-vetoed in November 1990 and further Congressional efforts to pass a new EAA in the 102nd Congress were anticipated. See Harrison and Holliday, *Export Controls, 1990*, pp. CRS-1-2, 9-13. The 1979 EAA, as amended, is reprinted in Evan R. Berlack, Cecil Hunt, and Terence Roche Murphy, *Coping With U.S. Export Controls 1986* (Practising Law Institute, 1986), pp. 471-510. Military goods, defense services, and related data are controlled under the 1976 Arms Export Control Act, as amended.

118. *Legislation on Foreign Relations*, p. 400.

119. John R. McIntyre, "The Distribution of Power and the Interagency Politics of Licensing East-West High Technology Trade," in *Controlling East-West Technology Trade: Power, Politics, and Policies*, ed. Gary K. Bertsch (Durham, NC: Duke University Press, 1988), pp. 99-101.

120. Public Law 92-72, 93 Stat. 503, approved 29 September 1979, as amended; rpt. in *Legislation on Foreign Relations*, p. 400; Long, "The Executive," pp. 48-51, 56-57; and U.S. Congress, Acts and Bills, *Omnibus Trade and Competitiveness Act of 1988* (Washington, DC: U.S. GPO, 1988), pp. 102 Stat. 1348-49.

121. *Legislation on Foreign Relations*, pp. 399, 401; Harold L. Marquis, "Export of Technology," *California Western Law Review*, vol. 20, no. 3 (Spring 1984), p. 393, footnote 18; and National Academy of Sciences, *Balancing the National Interest* (Washington, DC: National Academy Press, 1987), pp. 72-73.

122. A Foreign Ministry official emphasized that, in contrast with U.S. practice--where nothing may be exported unless specifically licensed--in the F.R.G., any item could be exported unless specifically forbidden; not-for-attribution interview, Foreign Ministry, Bonn, 3 March 1989; Lothar G. A. Griessebach, "East-West Trade: A European Perspective," in *The Politics of East-West Trade*, ed. Gordon B. Smith, Westview Special Studies in International Relations (Boulder, CO: Westview Press, 1984), p. 243; and Hanns-Dieter Jacobsen, "East-West Trade and Export Controls: The West German Perspective," in *Controlling East-West Trade and Technology Transfer: Power, Politics, and Policies*, ed. Gary K. Bertsch (Durham, NC: Duke University Press, 1988), p. 164.

123. Hanns-D. Jacobsen, *Security Implications of Inner-German Economic Relations*, Working Papers No. 77, Woodrow Wilson International Center for Scholars, International Security Studies Program (Washington, DC: 27 August 1986), pp. 32-33, footnotes 37, 39; and Jacobsen, "East-West Trade," pp. 166-67. Jacobsen also asserted that while the allies avoided formal Customs inspections at Berlin checkpoints, to deemphasize any hint that Berlin was a divided city, leakages were not a problem. However, a CIA analyst indicated that the F.R.G. (including Berlin) was one of the worst areas for technology leaks in COCOM. West German officials strongly denied that there was any significant leakage across the G.D.R. border. However, one official with expertise on COCOM matters acknowledged that with 15 million export cases yearly (not including goods carried by travellers and in-transit goods) the authorities were stretched thin. Conversation with CIA official, 9 June 1988, Washington, DC, and not-for-attribution interviews, London, 31 January 1989 and Foreign Ministry, Bonn, 3 March 1989.

124. *Code of Federal Regulations*, vol. 15, pp. 368-99.

125. National Academy of Sciences, *Balancing*, pp. 80-81.

126. William A. Root, Solveig B. Spielmann, and Felice A. Kaden, "A Study of Foreign Export Control Systems," in National Academy of Sciences, *Balancing the National Interest*, Working Papers (Washington, DC: National Academy Press, 1987), p. 219; and Werner Hein, "Economic Embargoes and Individual Rights Under German Law," *Law and Policy in International Business*, vol. 15, no. 2

(1983). Hein noted that the government-backed Hermes insurance company provided embargo risk insurance which was apparently available to companies trading with COCOM-controlled states; see Hein, pp. 421-22, footnote 120.

127. For example, prior to 1989 the burden of proof needed to obtain a conviction for licensing violations rested on the difficult task of proving that a company had intentionally sought to by-pass the law. Furthermore, it was left up to individual companies to determine whether a license was required, there was no monitoring of end users, and border inspections were rare. Revelations of illegal sales of German weapons technology to Libya and Iraq resulted in passage of stiffer criminal penalties and an increase in licensing and enforcement personnel. These efforts earned praise from U.S. officials but other observers, such as Richard Perle, remained skeptical. See Eduardo Lachica, "Norway, Japan Move to Back U.S. Effort To Curb Some Shipments to Soviet Bloc," *Wall Street Journal*, 24 June 1987, p. 22; Marsh, "W Germany to Tighten," columns 4-8; David Goodhart, "Bonn to Tighten Rules for Sensitive Exports," *Financial Times* [London], no. 30,740 (11 January 1989), p. 2, columns 1-5; David Goodhart, "W Germany Tightens Rein on its Exporters," *Financial Times* [London], no. 30,770 (15 February 1988), p. 3, columns 1-5; David Goodhart, "W Germans Raise Weapons Export Penalty," *Financial Times* [London], no. 30,771 (16 February 1989), p. 32, columns 1-4; Nancy Najarian, "Germany Tightens Export Curbs," *Export Control News*, vol. 5, no. 2 (25 February 1991), pp. 14-15; "Interview: Richard Perle," *Export Control News*, vol. 5, no. 2 (25 February 1991), p. 18; and National Academy of Sciences, *Finding Common Ground: U.S. Export Controls in a Changed Global Environment* (Washington, DC: National Academy Press, 1991), pp. 277-79.

128. William Schneider, Jr., Under Secretary of State, prepared statement, in U.S. Congress, Senate Committee on Governmental Affairs, Permanent Subcommittee on Investigations, *Transfer of Technology*, Hearings 98th Congress, 2nd session, 2, 3, 11, 12 April 1984 (Washington, DC: U.S. GPO, 1984), p. 267.

129. Labbe, "Controlling," p. 198.

130. In recent times, the expansion of the British committee system's oversight activities a la the U.S. model is reflected in hearings held by the Commons Trade and Industry and Foreign Affairs committees, which occasionally review export control issues.

131. The British occasionally lobbied within COCOM to secure a ruling favorable to British interests--as did all the members, presumably. DTI admitted to *bilateral* representations to other COCOM members to speed decisions and London used its veto owing to commercial considerations very infrequently. Bilateral lobbying is not unknown in any organization but this admission implied that informal "deals" were struck among COCOM members, distrust of which possibly heightened mutual suspicions. The scope for interpretation of COCOM rulings was illustrated by DTI's reporting that exports of certain items placed on the COCOM lists after the 1984 list review would be permitted until such time as British law was changed to conform with the new restrictions. This decision cushioned the rulings' impact on exporters. See Department of Trade and Industry, "The Strategic Embargo

(SOV/73)," memorandum in U.K. House of Commons, Foreign Affairs Committee, *UK-Soviet Relations*, Session 1984-85, Minutes of Evidence, 27 November 1985, rpt. in U.K. House of Commons, Foreign Affairs Committee, *UK-Soviet Relations*, Second Report, Vol. II, Session 1985-86, Minutes of Evidence and Appendices (London: HMSO, 26 March 1986), p. 247; and not-for-attribution interview, Foreign and Commonwealth Office official, London, 3 November 1988.

132. *Legislation on Foreign Relations*, pp. 438-39. The DOD's authority under Section 10(g) remained controversial with disagreements over Congressional intent, legislative history, and interpretation of actual wording. For example, William Root argued that 10(g) gave the DOD far too much say in licensing decisions. He believed that no President would publicly overrule his Secretary of Defense on a licensing decision--as the act permitted--since that would make it appear as if he did not control his Cabinet. See William A. Root, "COCOM: An Appraisal of Objectives and Needed Reforms," in *Controlling East-West Trade and Technology Transfer: Power, Politics, and Policies*, ed. Gary K. Bertsch (Durham, NC: Duke University Press, 1988), pp. 435-36. See also the exchange over interpreting 10(g) between Democrat Don Bonker, Republican Toby Roth, and Deputy Under Secretary of Defense Stephen D. Bryen, in U.S. Congress, House Committee on Foreign Affairs, Subcommittee on International Economic Policy and Trade, *Implementation of the Export Administration Amendment Act of 1985*, hearings, 99th Congress, 1st session, 10 October and 6 November 1985 (Washington, DC: U.S. GPO, 1988), pp. 98, 100.

133. Formal consultations began at weekly meetings of the Operating Committee of the Advisory Committee on Economic Policy, including senior-level staff, and chaired by a DOC official. The bulk of decisions were reached through unanimity and compromise at this level. Unresolved disputes over licenses were discussed at progressively higher levels up to the Cabinet-level Export Administration Review Board including the DOC (the chair), DOD, State Department, and the Energy Secretary. Under President Reagan, there was a relative deemphasis of the EARB in favor of the Technology Transfer Steering Group, a National Security Council-level body chaired by the Deputy Assistant National Security Advisor and including the DOD, DOC, and State Department (which held non-voting status). On the interagency process, see U.S. Congress, Office of Technology Assessment, *Technology*, pp. 134-36; National Academy of Sciences, *Balancing*, pp. 78-79, Figure 4-2, "U.S. government IVL review flowchart"; Eduardo Lachica, "Agency Seeks Reactivated Panel to Settle Disputed Over Exports of Strategic Goods," *Wall Street Journal*, 21 January 1987, p. 6, rpt. in U.S. Department of Defense, Department of the Air Force, *Current News*, special edition, Technology Security, 16 April 1987, no. 1570, p. 18; U.S. Congress, Joint Economic Committee, *East-West Technology Transfer: A Congressional Dialogue With the Reagan Administration*, 98th Congress, 2nd session, 19 December 1984 (Washington, DC: U.S. GPO, 1984), pp. 37, 39-40; Harold Relyea, "U.S. Government Organization For Technology Transfer Control," in U.S. Congress, Joint Economic Committee, *East-West Technology Transfer: A Congressional Dialogue With the Reagan Administra-*

tion, 98th Congress, 2nd session, 19 December 1984 (Washington, DC: U.S. GPO, 1984), p. 132; James K. Gordon, "Three Agencies Will Cooperate To Cut Export License Delays," *Aviation Week and Space Technology*, vol. 122, no. 118 (6 May 1985), p. 104; Arthur F. Van Cook, "Checks on Technology Transfer: The Defense Stakes Are High," *Defense Management Journal*, vol. 21, no. 1 (Fall Quarter 1985), p. 15; and McIntyre, "The Distribution," pp. 123-24.

134. On France, see Root et al., "A Study," pp. 215-18; Lebedoff and Raievski, "A French," p. 490; U.S. Congress, Office of Technology Assessment, *Technology*, pp. 187-88; National Academy of Sciences, *Balancing*, p. 196; David Buchan, "Western Security and Economic Strategy Towards the East," *Adelphi Papers*, no. 192 (London: International Institute for Strategic Studies, 1984), p. 21; and Labbe, "Controlling," pp. 190-95, 199-200.

135. On the U.K. in general, see Root et al., "A Study," pp. 211-13; Buchan, "Western Security," p. 22; U.S. Congress, Office of Technology Assessment, *Technology*, p. 191; Bertsch and Elliott, "Controlling," pp. 215-20; East European Trade Council, "The Problems Involved in Trading With the Soviet Union, in U.K. House of Commons, Foreign Affairs Committee, *UK-Soviet Relations*, Session 1984-85, Minutes of Evidence, 8 May 1985, rpt. in U.K. House of Commons, Foreign Affairs Committee, *UK-Soviet Relations*, Second Report, Vol. II, Session 1985-86, Minutes of Evidence and Appendices (London: HMSO, 26 March 1986), p. 5; R. R. Land, General Manager, East European Operations, Rank Xerox Ltd, testimony, 8 May 1985, rpt. in UK House of Commons, Foreign Affairs Committee, *UK-Soviet Relations*, Session 1984-85, Minutes of Evidence, 8 May 1985, rpt. in U.K. House of Commons, Foreign Affairs Committee, *UK-Soviet Relations*, Second Report, Vol. II, Session 1985-86, Minutes of Evidence and Appendices (London: HMSO, 26 March 1986), p. 16; United Kingdom, Department of Trade and Industry, "The Strategic Embargo (SOV/73)," p. 249; D. J. Hall, Grade 5, Overseas Trade Division 2 (COCOM), Department of Trade and Industry/British Overseas Trade Board, testimony, 27 November 1985, rpt. in U.K. House of Commons, Foreign Affairs Committee, *UK-Soviet Relations*, Session 1984-85, Minutes of Evidence, 8 May 1985, rpt. in U.K. House of Commons, Foreign Affairs Committee, *UK-Soviet Relations*, Second Report, Vol. II, Session 1985-86, Minutes of Evidence and Appendices (London: HMSO, 26 March 1986), p. 265 and Confederation of British Industry [CBI], "UK-Soviet Trade Relations (SOV/49)," memorandum submitted by the CBI as Appendix 17 in U.K. House of Commons, Foreign Affairs Committee, *UK-Soviet Relations*, Session 1984-85, Minutes of Evidence, 8 May 1985, rpt. in U.K. House of Commons, Foreign Affairs Committee, *UK-Soviet Relations*, Second Report, Vol. II, Session 1985-86, Minutes of Evidence and Appendices (London: HMSO, 26 March 1986), p. 363.   The problems and delays reported in 1985 testimony apparently continued as government officials and businessmen noted that U.K. licensing and Customs officials were overburdened with a large volume of highly technical and often indecipherable applications. License processing continued to be unacceptably slow resulting in lost sales. But by 1988, businessmen suggested that licensing had improved, although expertise and resources were still lacking; not-

for-attribution interviews, Ministry of Defence and Foreign and Commonwealth Office, London, 31 October and 3 November 1988, with a representative of a British trade organization, London, 17 October 1988, and testimony in U.K. House of Commons, Trade and Industry Committee, *Trade With Eastern Europe*.

136. Root et al., "A Study, p. 219; U.S. Congress, Office of Technology Assessment, *Technology*, p. 182; and Jacobsen, "East-West Trade," pp. 164-65. There was a lack of adequate numbers of qualified personnel to check export license applications at a time when the license-processing burden could be expected to grow owing to more restrictive legislation. The U.S. Commerce Department had similar problems. See David Marsh, "W Germany to Tighten Export Control Laws," *Financial Times* [London], no. 30,731 (30 December 1988), p. 2, columns 7-8.

137. This positive conclusion was expressed by a British scholar. See Hill, "East-West," pp. 354-55.

138. On enforcement, see U.S. Department of Commerce, International Trade Administration, *Commerce Enforcement of U.S. Export Controls: The Challenge and the Response*, revised edition, September 1986, p. 5; "Responsibilities of Commerce and Customs under the EAA," *Federal Register*, vol. 50 (11 October 1985), p. 41545, rpt. in Berlack et al., pp. 767-71; U.S., Congress, General Accounting Office, *Export Control Regulations Could be Reduced Without Affecting National Security*, Report by the Comptroller General of the United States, ID-82-14 (26 May 1982), pp. 25-26, 46; and William Schneider, Jr., Under Secretary of State For Security Assistance, Science, and Technology, prepared statement, 1 March 1983 in U.S. Congress, House Committee on Foreign Affairs, Subcommittee on International Economic Policy and Trade, *Extension and Revision of the Export Administration Act of 1979*, Hearings, 98th Congress, 1st session, 24 February, 1, 3, 8 March, 5, 12-14, 28-29 April, 2, 4-5, 18, 25, 26 May 1983 (Washington, DC: U.S. GPO, 1985), p. 221.

139. These charges sometimes were leveled by European business rivals, although government officials also raised questions. See R. Berger, Consultant, The 48 Group of British Traders with China, testimony in U.K. House of Commons, Trade and Industry Committee, *Trade With China*, Session 1984-85, Minutes of Evidence, 5 June 1985, rpt. in U.K. House of Commons, Trade and Industry Committee, *Trade With China*, Third Special Report, Vol. II, Session 1984-85, Minutes of Evidence and Appendices (London: HMSO, 11 July 1985), p. 61; and J. Beran, Managing Director, Berox Machine Tool Company, Inc., interview, London, 8 November 1988. An example of policy that might appear to undermine COCOM efforts was the signing of telecommunications contracts with Soviet bloc countries (for delivery after 1988) after the 1984 COCOM agreement to block all such sales until 1988. A Foreign and Commonwealth Office official noted that France left it up to individual businesses to decide whether to export items coming under the Administrative Exception Note controls. Given the disagreement and differing interpretations of COCOM rules practiced by all the allies, France's policy could be viewed as permitting too much discretion for items which--in certain contexts--might be militarily sensitive. American and British rules required similar

items to be licensed and scrutinized--however superficially--by the authorities. A representative for a West German lobby said that both French and British licensing officials granted licenses more quickly than did authorities in the F.R.G.; not-for-attribution interviews, Foreign and Commonwealth Office, London, 3 November 1988 and Ost-Ausschuss der Deutschen Wirtschaft [Eastern Committee], Cologne, 6 March 1989. For evidence suggesting continuing problems with the French system, see Steven Greenhouse, "French Linked to Soviet Sale," *New York Times*, 17 October 1987; Joseph Fitchett, "French Investigate Executive in Technology Leak to Russia," *International Herald Tribune*, 15 March 1989, p. 2, columns 1-6; Labbe, "Controlling," pp. 185-87, 191, 195, 198-99, 200-01. 203 and Root, et al., "A Study," pp. 216, 218.

3

A Strategic Evaluation of U.S. High-Technology Export Control Policy

The principal goal of strategic export control policy is to deny critical high technology from use by the Russian military and by the remnants of the former Red Army which now constitute the core of the military forces in several of the newly independent former Soviet republics. Export controls assist U.S. and NATO efforts in maintaining a qualitative lead in weaponry, command, control, and communications--an important advantage, given the Warsaw Pact's quantitative preponderance in men and material during most of the postwar era. During the 1970s and 1980s, growing concern over accelerated advances in Soviet weapons design and an apparent narrowing of the technological gap between East and West called into question the effectiveness of enforcement of U.S. denial policy. Critics warn that Western technology is directly and indirectly subsidizing improvements in sophisticated Russian weapons, improvements which threaten to erode NATO's technological edge. Such warnings are fodder for advocates of maintaining or enhancing strategic export controls, even as social and political changes and economic crises in the U.S.S.R. and Eastern Europe suggest that vestiges of the Cold War circumstances from which strategic denial policy emerged seem to be disappearing. While none of the COCOM allies advocate completely lifting strategic controls, ongoing disagreement between Washington and the allies over the scope of controls is exacerbated given changes in Eastern Europe, Russia, and the other former Soviet republics, and improving prospects for closer East-West political and economic relations.

This chapter evaluates the strategic implications of U.S. strategic export control policy. Utilizing DOD, intelligence community, and scholarly studies of Soviet dual-use capabilities, this chapter assesses whether strategic denial is effective.

TECHNOLOGY DENIAL AND THE SOVIET MILITARY

There is considerable, even conclusive, evidence that Soviet and other Warsaw Pact military forces have benefited from acquisition of advanced U.S. and Western technology. Yet, while improvements in the sophistication of Russian military systems have serious implications for the West, the case for the effectiveness of technology denial by means of export controls on broad ranges of end products remains controversial.

The U.S. intelligence community has determined that there are four principal means by which the Russians acquire Western technology: espionage, open-source information, illegal trade diversions and smuggling, and legal trade. Espionage, open-source collection of technology data and information, and illicit trade are cited by informed professionals such as Admiral Bobby R. Inman, former Deputy Director of the CIA; and William Root, former Director of the State Department's Bureau of East-West Trade, as the most damaging practices.[1] Two widely circulated U.S. intelligence community studies, *Soviet Acquisition of Western Technology* (1982) and *Soviet Acquisition of Militarily Significant Western Technology: An Update* (1985), revealed the central roles of the Soviet KGB and GRU (Soviet military intelligence) in this effort. The former study stated that "the overwhelming majority of what the United States considers to be militarily significant technology acquired by and for the Soviets was obtained by the Soviet intelligence services and East European intelligence services."[2] The 1985 *Update* listed thirtythree examples of Western documents, hardware, and dual-use products that the Soviets had acquired. Of these examples, over 80 percent had been collected by the KGB, the GRU, or by both services. Reports and interviews, including the National Academy of Sciences' (NAS) 1991 study *Finding Common Ground*, confirm that such covert activities have not slackened and may actually be increasing. Yet, export controls have little impact on such covert operations. This suggests that better counterintelligence and enforcement efforts are needed, since the success of the U.S.-led effort to limit legal high-technology trade flows has forced the Soviets to rely on covert means of acquisition and "techno-bandits."[3]

Soviet technology acquisition efforts have a long history. Numerous specific examples of legal and covert Soviet acquisitions from the 1940s to the 1970s that enhanced military systems or manufacturing capabilities have been cited by Arnaud de Borchgrave, Michael Ledeen, Richard Perle, and Miles Costick as examples of the acquisition policy's success.[4] In the 1980s, the Reagan administration cited improved Soviet look-down/shoot-down radar, a new air-to-air missile, and the MiG-29, Su-27, and Su-25 fighters--among others--as systems that benefited directly from free world technology and know-how. Such improvements were thought to necessitate greater Western defense and research and development (R&D) expenditures to counter the increased threat and to maintain U.S. qualitative superiority.[5] The seriousness of what has been termed a technology "hemorrhage" was emphasized in the 1986 edition of *Soviet Military Power* by Secretary of Defense Weinberger. He asserted that during the late 1970s and early 1980s, "virtually every" Soviet military project had benefited from acquired Western hardware and documentation, and this was so pervasive that the West was subsidizing the Soviet buildup.[6] Such subsidies are believed to enhance the performance of Soviet military R&D and production, perhaps the most "efficient" sector of the otherwise anemic Soviet economy.

While there is convincing evidence of a systematic Soviet effort to acquire militarily critical Western technology, there is some question about its overall effectiveness and impact on the East-West military balance and U.S. security posture. Partly, this is due to the limited amount and classified nature of intelligence gathered by the West on Soviet acquisition efforts. The National Academy of Science's Panel on the Impact of National Security Controls on International Technology Transfer--whose membership included former U.S. Air Force Chief of Staff Lew Allen, Jr.; former Secretary of Defense Melvin R. Laird, and Admiral Inman--after studying highly classified reports, termed such intelligence "incomplete and fragmentary" and often dated by the time it is assessed by policymakers (although an important exception was the so-called Farewell papers discussed below). For example, an intelligence community consensus eventually emerged that imported U.S. grinders (machines capable of producing delicate bearings used in guidance systems) contributed little to improving Soviet missile accuracy.[7] Besides spying, diversions, and legal channels the Russians can also obtain valuable information from captured arms or purchases of Western military systems on the international arms market.[8] The NAS panel concluded that "it is only in rare occasions--for instance, when isolated examples of specific Western components, or copies of them, appear in Soviet military equipment--that the Intelligence Community can declare without reservation that the application of Western technology has contributed substantially to Soviet military developments." Having a few discrete components makes little difference overall.[9] Of much greater consequence for the Soviets, the NAS panel acknowledged, is acquisition of even limited numbers of certain "process and manufacturing hardware" capable of producing large numbers of high-quality end products such as semiconductors.   This conclusion echoed the Bucy Report's findings. Even in this instance, however, the best conclusions are not always irrefutable.   The grinder case suggests this, as does the controversy surrounding quieting of Soviet submarines, a trend attributable to other factors besides quieter propellers produced on illegally acquired machining centers.   Clearly, as the Office of Technology Assessment concluded, the Russians are capable of developing virtually any capability given adequate resources and time.[10]   Slowing and crippling indigenous developments is an important goal of export controls and suggests why the Soviets rely so heavily on espionage.

In 1981, French intelligence obtained one of the few pieces of hard evidence of the effectiveness of Soviet acquisition strategy, the so-called Farewell papers. Covering 1976-1980, these Soviet documents describe the actual structure of the Soviet acquisition effort, specify technology samples and documentation targeted for acquisition, and evaluate the effectiveness of the program.   They were extensively referred to in U.S. government publications and testimony after their existence was revealed in 1983 and the NAS panel specifically cited the importance of this intelligence.[11]

A careful evaluation of a portion of the papers by Philip Hanson throws light on the scope and effectiveness of Soviet acquisition. Affirming their authenticity, Hanson concluded that 44 percent of the thousands of samples collected by the KGB in 1980 went to the Soviet defense sector and the remainder divided evenly between civilian industry and the KGB.[12] Presumably, the KGB attempts to derive valuable intelligence by examining samples for the same reasons U.S. intelligence services examine advanced Soviet technology.   Hanson also concluded that the pattern of acquisition suggested that samples and documents were channeled into preexisting indigenous military R&D programs.   Acquisitions are used as building blocks or as a means of comparing Soviet with state-of-the-art Western designs--a practice also found in capitalist economies among competing firms.[13]   This reflects an ingrained Soviet caution in designing new systems, and a fear of dependence on controlled and unreliable Western supplies, and is corroborated by studies of the utilization of Western technology by Soviet military design bureaus. These bureaus may gain an initial learning boost from the Western technology. Quickly, however, Russian designers attempt to adapt the new knowledge to Russian needs and standards, often producing a substantially altered product and sometimes advancing development and introduction of new systems more rapidly than anticipated by the West.[14]   An additional benefit comes from cost saving arising from avoiding R&D deadends, which speeds the procurement process.   But while Russian ability to design and introduce advanced systems relatively quickly compares favorably with the troubled U.S. procurement process, this is probably due more to inefficient U.S. procurement than to the singular contribution of free world technology to Soviet efforts--as the Packard Commission and Defense Science Board found.   In addition, determining the performance characteristics of U.S. technologies also assists in developing countermeasures to defeat them. However, the magnitude of these savings, while substantial, is debatable.[15] There are also costs incurred from running a massive acquisition effort as well as paying high prices for targeted examples.[16]

Some technology nuggets may have been acquired by the Soviets.   The Farewell   intelligence   survey   also   documents   the   emphasis,   relative sensitivity of acquisitions, and effectiveness of the overall effort.   According to the National Academy of Sciences, the Soviets estimated that about 70 percent of the items acquired are subject to Western national security controls. Given the acknowledged scope of covert Soviet acquisition efforts, this suggests that export controls are effective since such a large percentage of controlled technology was acquired by covert means.   Electronics-based technologies were the most sought after in terms of samples and technical documents acquired each year.   Electronics acquisitions were also the most useful in terms of stimulating new R&D and shortening development times.[17]   However, the Farewell documents emphasize that while hardware samples are generally useful, most of the acquired documents are not, although Soviet agents reportedly spent a great deal of time collecting publicly available information.[18]   Over 80 percent of acquired documents were unclassified, including business brochures, congressional hearings, and academic papers, and fewer than 50 percent were deemed useful.   It is generally   agreed   that   "document   trolling"   (widespread   and   systematic collection of open-source documents) as a means of acquisition is relatively ineffective. The difficulty and inefficiency of covert acquisition is suggested by the fact that most priority targets were either not obtained or were acquired only after many years.[19]   This also suggests that strategic controls have been relatively effective.

Overt and legal attempts to acquire Western technology were also listed in the Farewell documents.   Although a precise breakdown is unavailable, the large *covert* effort suggests that legal channels are of relatively small importance. However, technology transfer hawks, taking a maximalist line, plausibly argue that *any* leakage or series of occasional small leaks has a serious cumulative effect on the East-West military balance. Furthermore, a key axiom of this argument is that reverse-engineering of militarily critical dual-use technology permits the Russians to discover the secrets of the most sophisticated Western technology, sometimes incorporated in seemingly innocuous products. This argument buttresses and underlies justifications for tighter control of dual-use end products.[20]

On balance, circumstantial evidence, unclassified studies, and the increasing complexity of leading-edge technology undermine the maximalist position without entirely discounting the threat posed by technology leaks. First, Russian acquisition and technological development does not take place in a vacuum. Western technical progress is also ongoing and dynamic. It is generally agreed that it has accelerated since 1945 and that, since the 1970s, development in--for instance--the information, microelectronics, and biotechnology fields has been revolutionary. Russian acquisitions can be viewed as an effort to withdraw examples from the ongoing "flow" of Western technological development. But these examples may rapidly become obsolete because innovations improve upon existing technology and the Russians cannot guarantee acquisition of the most up-to-date models. This means they will lag behind Western developments. Clearly, some acquisitions are at or close to the leading edge of Western developments-- including so-called revolutionary technologies--which could give a signifi- cant technological boost to military production and supplement demonstrable indigenous capabilities.[21] The fact that the Russians continue to target 1960s technology strongly implies that controls are effective and that Russian technology is lagging significantly behind--at least in some areas-- even though the military and defense industries enjoy top priority in obtaining the best design and production talent and materials. Indeed, some acquisitions from the "flow" will always be older, even outdated technology. Piecemeal acquisition of increasingly complex components or manufacturing systems (e.g., microelectronics production) may therefore not result in con- structing the most modern facilities since some subcomponents are dated.[22] Given the scope and pace of global technological development, Russian specialists cannot expect to immediately identify all developments nor can they expect to judge each breakthrough's significance or applicability since this may not even be evident to Western scientists and engineers for some time after a discovery is made, a process is perfected, and it is incorporated into a Western system.

A second hurdle the Russians face is the prospect of ongoing dependence on basic Western *designs* as a basis for improving and producing indigenous technology. Such dependence implies that Russian designs remain at least one (or more) generations behind the state of the art. A 1981 CIA study found indirect confirmation of Soviet dependence. Admiral Inman testified that expected Soviet R&D investment in developing indigenous technology had not materialized and that Western technology was utilized instead.[23] Reliance on U.S. and Western designs may also be growing in the case of personal computers (PCs), owing to increasing availability of inexpensive PC-clones from non-COCOM sources.[24] Seymour Goodman has found that initially impressive Soviet strides in computers and microelectronics were followed by stagnation in the 1960s and a *widening* performance gap between U.S. and Soviet computers.[25] This is reflected in the Soviet decision to base the indigenous RYAD computer series on 1960s-era IBM *architecture*.[26] While IBM was and is an acknowledged world leader, computer technology has advanced several generations since then. Thus, in 1985, the DOD asserted that Soviet dependency had grown in tandem with the computer's growing complexity.[27] However, the RYAD series--based on 1960s architecture--remained important through the early 1980s. The centralized and hierarchical structure of Soviet R&D and economic planning, and the substantial investments required to develop the RYAD standard, meant that the Soviets were committed to a specific design type and standard which became outdated.

A danger with this approach--which is relevant to other dual-use areas-- is the uncertainty attached to identifying, choosing, and investing in high-technology "winners" to be the basis for systems with diverse military applications. The wrong choice could have serious consequences including wasting finite resources, introducing systems that are less capable than those they are designed to attack or defend against, and delays while design flaws or poor performance parameters are rectified.[28] It is likely that the difficulty in implementing new designs, and resulting waste owing to pushing the frontiers of technology--problems which plague U.S. weapons R&D--has also been the Soviet experience.

Waste arising from structural problems in Russian industry and R&D is magnified by the increasing difficulty of reverse-engineering highly complex technology. While disagreement continues over the ease and effectiveness of reverse-engineering, various experts discount the danger. Among these are the NAS panel, Goodman, and David A. Wellman. The NAS panel called such attempts "unproductive" in many instances.[29] In their studies of the Soviet computer and microelectronics fields, Goodman and Wellman note the rapidly growing complexity of microelectronic and computer chip designs--necessitating design environments that themselves utilize highly sophisticated computer-aided design tools and test instruments--where billions of circuits are packed onto ever smaller chips. Replicating such environments with embargoed tools and analyzing and producing extremely complex circuit or chip designs--assuming an adequate design environment and production infrastructure is available--is a daunting task.[30]

Even if a truly capable, sufficiently high-quality Russian computer design is produced, sectoral weaknesses plaguing the Russian industrial and technological infrastructure (and aggravated by export controls) limit full utilization of the computer's potential. For example, the notoriously poor Russian telecommunications net restricts widespread computer networking. Near total reliance on Western software, limited stocks of high-quality spare parts for Western designs, and poorly trained maintenance technicians unfamiliar with documentation on the latest advances (because it is controlled) handicap users.[31] It is therefore plausible that controls on civilian dual-use technology do hamper Russian military R&D, given the primacy accorded defense industries in obtaining and utilizing any advanced technology acquisitions. But Russian ability to reverse-engineer remains controversial with observers such as Sir Brian Tovey, former Director-General of the U.K.'s Government Communications Headquarters. He argues that it is possible given sufficient time and resources.[32]

Extrapolating from the Soviet experience in the microelectronics field to other militarily critical dual-use technologies is an uncertain exercise given the paucity of hard evidence. However, CIA analysts stated in 1987 that the dual-use gap with the West had grown, that Soviet lags were worsening, and that this trend would continue. Furthermore, it is unlikely that the Russians could surprise the West by deploying a new breakthrough weapon based on Western technology. Weapons development is predictable and is based on an accumulation of years of basic research that both sides are familiar with. Although relatively dynamic, according to the CIA, the Russian defense sector is not particularly innovative, particularly in small-scale cumulative advances that have an impact on low-priority programs.

This suggests a critical structural and/or institutional factor and fundamental weakness afflicting the Russian acquisition effort.[33] Because microelectronics is a key component in modern industrial and military systems, perhaps *the* key component, any difficulties and lags in Russian performance, coupled with the dynamism of Western R&D, imply strongly that the West, at minimum, will continue to maintain its lead in this field.

Some indication of the relative U.S. and Soviet standing in several critical technologies can also be gleaned from Figure 1. Based on DOD studies, Figure 1 indicates that the U.S. lead over the U.S.S.R. in computer and microelectronics technology--and other technologies utilizing such components, including automated production and manufacturing technology-- was being maintained. Only in optics and directed energy did the trend favor the U.S.S.R. But the *decided* Soviet lead over the United States in

Figure 1
Relative U.S. versus U.S.S.R. Standing in 21 Militarily Related Technology Areas, 1980-1987

BASIC TECH.	1980[A]			1984[B]		
	>U.S.	=	>U.S.S.R.	>U.S.	=	>U.S.S.R.
1.		X		X		
2.	X			X		
3.			X->		X	
4.	<-X			X		
5.	X			X		
6.		X				X
7.	X->			X->		
8.	X->			X->		
9.	X->			X->		
10.	<-X			X		
11.		X				X
12.	X->					X
13.			X->			X
14.	X->			X		
15.		X		X->		
16.	X			X		
17.		X		X->		
18.	X			X		
19.				X		
20.				X		
21.				X		

Sources:

[A] U.S. Department of Defense, Deputy Under Secretary of Defense, Research, and Engineering, Program for Development, Research and Acquisition [?], *USDDR&E Estimate of the Relative Standing of the U.S. and U.S.S.R. in the Twenty Most Important Areas of Basic Technology Affecting Military Forces*, rpt. in Anthony H. Cordesman, *East-West Trade: Analyzing* Technology Transfer From a New Perspective, The Wilson Center, International Security Studies Program, *Working Papers*, no. 24, revised 14 July 1981; rpt. in U.S. Congress, Senate Committee on Banking, Housing, and Urban Affairs, *Proposed Trans-Siberian Natural Gas Pipeline*, hearing, 97th Congress, 1st session, 12 November 1981 (Washington, DC: U.S. GPO, 1982), p. 75.

[B] U.S. Department of Defense, Secretary of Defense, *The Technology Transfer Control Program*, A Report to the 98th Congress, 2nd session, February 1984, p. 4, Figure 1.

[C] U.S. Department of Defense, Under Secretary of Defense for Policy, *Assessing the Effect of Technology Transfer on U.S./Western Security*, February 1985, p. E-4, Figure E-3.

Figure 1 (continued)

1985[C]			1986[D]			1987[E]		
>U.S.	=	>U.S.S.R.	>U.S.	=	>U.S.S.R.	>U.S.	=	>U.S.S.R.
				X		X		
<-X			X			X->		
				X			X->	
X->			<-X			X		
				X			X->	
<-X			X			X->		
				X		X		
			X->			X->		
X->			X			X		
				X			X	
			X->				X->	
				X			X	
			X->			X->		
<-X			X			X->		
				X		X		
			X->			X->		
<-X			X			X		
X			X			X->		
			X			X		
			X			X->		

[D] U.S. Department of Defense, Under Secretary of Defense, Research, and Engineering, "The FY 1987 DoD Program for Research and Development (Statement by the Under Secretary to the 99th Congress, 2nd session, 1986)," rpt. in National Academy of Sciences, *Balancing the National Interest* (Washington, DC: National Academy Press, 1987), p. 48, Table 2-1.

[E] Thomas P. Christie, Deputy Assistant Secretary of Defense for Plans and Resources, attachment to a letter to Sen. William Proxmire dated 19 November 1987 labeled "Table 1," titled "Relative U.S./U.S.S.R. Standings in the 20 Most Important Basic Technology Areas," current as of 17 November 1987, rpt. in U.S. Congress, Joint Economic Committee, Subcommittee on National Security Economics, *Allocation of Resources in the Soviet Union and China- 1986*, hearings, 100th Congress, 1st session, 19 March, 3 August 1987 (Washington, DC: U.S. GPO, 1988), p. 159.

Notes:
  Basic Tech. = Basic Technologies
  ">" = U.S./U.S.S.R. superior
  "=" = U.S./U.S.R.R. equal
  "<-/->" = Overall trend, e.g., "<-U.S." means U.S. lead is increasing relative to U.S.S.R.

Figure 1 (continued)

Types of basic technologies:
1. = Aerodynamics/fluid dynamics
2. = Automated production/control/manufacturing
3. = Conventional warhead (including chemical explosives)
4. = Computers (computer technology)
5. = Software
6. = Directed energy (laser)
7. = Electro-optical sensor (including infrared)
8. = Guidance and navigation
9. = Hydro-acoustic/nonacoustic (including submarine detection/silencing)
10. = Microelectronic materials and integrated circuit manufacture
11. = Nuclear warhead
12. = Optics
13. = Power sources/generation, weapon (mobile, including energy storage)
14. = Propulsion (aerospace/ground vehicles)
15. = Radar sensor/sensor technology
16. = Signal processing
17. = Structural materials (lightweight, high-strength, armor/ceramic
    coatings)
18. = Telecommunications
19. = Life sciences (human factors/genetic engineering/bacteriological/chemical
    warfare
20. = Robotics and machine intelligence
21. = Signature reduction (Stealth)

conventional warheads and power sources and generation has vanished since 1980 (Figure 2) and the U.S.S.R. did not lead any category as of 1987. Furthermore, in selected newly emerging fields such as robotics and machine intelligence, the United States was superior, although recent analysis suggests that this outright lead may be eroding in the new field of life sciences (i.e., biotechnology).

Figures 1 and 2 support opposing views in the debate over the strategic consequences of East-West technology transfer and the effectiveness of technology denial. Advocates of strong export controls can argue that tighter U.S. regulations and a revamped COCOM have been effective in reestablishing and maintaining U.S. technological superiority.[34] That recent trends appear to show that relative erosion of the U.S. lead, particularly in emerging fields, is all the more reason to stay vigilant and review licensing and enforcement procedures. Conversely, critics of the conservative view--and those who question the maximalist ideal of a leakproof denial

Figure 2
Overall Trend for 1980-1987 Compared with Trend in 1980

BASIC TECH.	STATUS 1980	OVERALL TREND 1980-87	OVERALL TREND COMPARED WITH 1980
1.	U.S. = U.S.S.R.	<-U.S. = U.S.S.R.	BETTER FOR U.S.
2.	>U.S.	>U.S.	SAME
3.	U.S.S.R.->	U.S. = U.S.S.R.->	BETTER FOR U.S.
4.	<-U.S.	>U.S.	SAME
5.	>U.S.	>U.S.*	SAME
6.	U.S. = U.S.S.R.	U.S. = U.S.S.R.->	SLIGHTLY WORSE FOR U.S.
7.	U.S.->	U.S.->	SAME
8.	U.S.->	U.S.->	SAME
9.	U.S.->	U.S.->	SAME
10.	<-U.S.	>U.S.	SLIGHTLY WORSE FOR U.S.
11.	U.S. = U.S.S.R.	U.S. = U.S.S.R.	SAME
12.	U.S.->	U.S.= U.S.S.R.->	SLIGHTLY WORSE FOR U.S.
13.	U.S.S.R.->	<-U.S. = U.S.S.R.	MUCH BETTER FOR U.S.
14.	U.S.->	U.S.->	SAME
15.	U.S. = U.S.S.R.	>U.S.->	BETTER FOR U.S.
16.	>U.S.	>U.S.	SAME
17.	U.S. = U.S.S.R.	U.S.->	BETTER FOR U.S.

Notes:
* = Information available for 1980 and 1984 only.
** = OVERALL TREND 1984-87

For other symbols, see Figure 1, 1980-1987.

Figure 2 (continued)

BASIC TECH.	STATUS 1980	OVERALL TREND 1980-87	OVERALL TREND CO-MPARED WITH 1980
18.	>U.S.	>U.S.	SAME
19.	NA	U.S.->**	NA
20.	NA	>U.S.**	NA
21.	NA	U.S.->**	NA

policy--could argue that tighter controls probably make little or no difference. Overall, relative U.S. superiority has been maintained and remains virtually the same as in 1980, before the Reagan administration's policy of stricter licensing and enforcement was fully implemented. In addition, during specific periods and for specific technologies, trends have suggested relative enhancement or erosion of the U.S. or Soviet position. But there is no clear or continuous pattern of improvement in Soviet capabilities or erosion of U.S. superiority that justifies stricter controls.[35] Focusing on specific instances of relative U.S. loss or Soviet advance is risky, since the process may be quickly reversed owing to indigenous breakthroughs and other unforeseen factors. In response to assertions that apparent erosion of the U.S. lead in emerging technologies necessitates tighter controls, critics can argue that *existing* overly restrictive practices are the chief culprits, not lax licensing and enforcement. Restrictions on newly emerging technologies may be stifling the fields' development.

If the standings in Figure 1, the estimated lead times in Figure 3, and the conclusions in Goodman's and Wellman's studies are weighed, it appears that technology denial has been effective in *delaying* Soviet advances.[36] Some of this is due to the cumulative effect and to the uncertainty controls introduce into an inherently rigid, inefficient, and technologically handi-capped Soviet design and production process.[37] Thus, the lag in acquisition, analysis, adaptation, and introduction into a Soviet military system is compounded when other critical analytical, design, test, and production tools and processes are also denied. Furthermore, imperfect "translation" from an original Western sample to a mass-produced Soviet clone may mean qualitatively inferior systems that cannot perform as well as the originals under extremely hostile conditions.[38] Finally, while delays accumulate at each point in the Soviet R&D and production process, the more efficient Western high-technology industries and R&D efforts do not stand still.

It is possible, however, that Gorbachev's and Yeltsin's modernization

Figure 3
Selected Advanced Manufacturing Technologies: The United States versus the U.S.S.R.

	Approximate Length of U.S. Lead in Years			
	6	8	10	12
Microprocessors		XXXXX		
Computer-operated machine tools		XXXXXXXXXXXXXXXXXX		
Minicomputers		XXXXXXXX		
Mainframes		XXXXXXXXXXXXXXXXX		
Supercomputers			XXXXXXXXXX	
Software	XXXXXXXXXXXXXXXXXX			
Flexible manufacturing systems	XXXXXXXXXXXX			

Source: Based on Douglas MacEachin and Rear Adm. Robert Schmitt, "Gorbachev's Modernization Program: A Status Report," a paper presented by the Central Intelligence Agency and the Defense Intelligence Agency for submission to the Subcommittee on National Security Economics of the Joint Economic Committee, Congress of the United States, 19 March 1987, in U.S. Congress, Joint Economic Committee, Subcommittee on National Security Economics, *Allocation of Resources in the Soviet Union and China- 1986*, hearings, 100th Congress, 1st session, 19 March and 3 August 1987 (Washington, DC: U.S. GPO, 1988), p. 17.

Note: U.S. lead is based on projections of length of time required for Soviets to achieve series production of levels of each technology similar to those in U.S. series production today.

policy--seeking to improve material conditions in Commonwealth by utilizing Western technology and stressing high-technology industries and existing defense-sector management practices--could reinvigorate indigenous Russian civilian R&D and encourage civil-military cross-fertilization. This also assumes that East-West trade and COCOM controls will be liberalized, as happened in the 1970s. Their stress on expanded East-West trade could result in sophisticated dual-use technology being utilized for military purposes and improving design environments that ultimately translate into improved innovative capabilities.[39]   More generally and controversially, over the *long* term, expanded civilian trade could improve the Russia's defense industrial base--improving the efficiency of strategic resource extraction, for example--and defense infrastructure[40] with an added benefit of freeing capital for investment in defense programs.   Alternatively, these savings might be reinvested in an expansion of production to satisfy pent-up consumer demand and improve the citizenry's welfare.   Trade with the Commonwealth would also enrich Western firms supplying technology, know-how, and consumer goods, profits which might be reinvested in advanced dual-use technologies.   This advantage must be weighed against the potentially negative consequences of the leadership's modernization policy.

While the strategic implications of technology transfer and the effectiveness of strategic denial continue to be debated, the next issue concerns the immediate and long-term implications of the effects of export control on basic scientific research and scientific communication.

NATIONAL SECURITY EXPORT CONTROLS AND SCIENTIFIC COMMUNICATION

Increased U.S. government efforts to tighten and limit legal and covert technology transfer to the Soviet Union and Eastern Europe also have implications for scientific communication and research conducted on university campuses and in private laboratories.   Beginning in the Carter administration and culminating in 1985, a spate of controversial episodes highlighted government concern over technology losses via scientists. Officials including Adm. Inman and the DOD's Frank Carlucci warned of actual and potential losses of sophisticated technology and know-how from academic institutions, scientific conferences, and publications.   They advocated improved security over information dissemination and greater caution in the scientific community.   Data bases were also deemed vulnerable, as suggested by an (ultimately unsuccessful) 1986 government plan to create a new category of sensitive but unclassified information in automated information systems.[41]

These warnings and efforts were met by skepticism from many scientists, engineers, and other academics who decried what they felt were the disturbing implications of government initiatives.   Opponents and skeptics such as Edward C. Bertnolli of the Institute of Electrical and Electronic Engineers, the NAS's Corson Panel, and F. Karl Willenbrach of Southern

Methodist University argued that undue restrictions on the unique American tradition of free and unhindered scientific communication might be undermined. Given that the tradition of openness in science was deemed by many to be a distinct U.S. advantage that further unfettered and pioneered basic and applied research and technological progress, any constraints were undesirable. Critics felt that constraints could not only adversely affect economic competitiveness by strangling innovations but also endanger national security, since important research on dual-use technologies (e.g., biotechnology and Very High Speed Integrated Circuits) was undertaken on campuses and in private labs. Contributing to the quality of that research and related engineering studies were the stimulation and enrichment that came from awareness of and exposure to the work of the international scientific community. Because the United States was no longer preeminent in many scientific fields, continuing intellectual cross-fertilization was an absolute necessity if U.S. science was to remain vigorous and maintain its reputation.[42]

Although there is some clearcut evidence of Soviet acquisition, its significance is certainly less than the impact of espionage against defense-related firms or diversions of controlled goods. Furthermore, in contrast with the vocal criticism leveled against export control regulations and administration by business, and the drawn-out effort to streamline export controls, the academic community has reached an accommodation with regulators, at least for the time being.

Deteriorating East-West relations caused the Carter administration to sharply limit scientific exchanges with the U.S.S.R. and Eastern Europe. In accordance with the Reagan administration's generally tougher line on East-West trade and technology flows, officials warned of Soviet targeting of specific top U.S. research institutions and open scientific literature and conferences. The DOD required several scientific conference organizers to withdraw papers on sensitive subjects and to limit access for certain presentations to U.S. citizens and suitably cleared foreigners.[43]

The traditionally open academic environment is considered a particularly effective means of technology transfer. Teaching, technical exchange with ongoing contact, and training in high-technology areas effectively transfer the "detail of how to do things." This is at the core of technology transfer issues.[44] Furthermore, universities and academic researchers are increasingly involved in applied as well as fundamental research, and the gap between them is narrowing and increasingly unclear, at least in some areas such as biotechnology.[45] Concern has grown over Soviet tapping of applied research, in particular, since this involves utilization of engineering processes and know-how in a variety of high-technology areas. Finally, there is concern that the vast body of open scientific literature and data bases will individually yield harmless, discrete insights and principles from which a "mosaic" emerges, which then leads to discovery of otherwise classified militarily critical technology.[46]

The actual significance and impact of technology transfer via universities, scientific exchanges, and academic meetings is slight according to studies by the NAS's Corson Panel and prestigious analysts. Government watchdogs appear to have belatedly determined that this channel is marginal, although they continue to assume that a significant loss or losses *could* occur, or that fundamental and applied research might yield a discovery with significant military applications.[47]

There was considerable controversy and disagreement between academia and government over the question of scientific freedom and national security. Several panels and forums were established--such as the Corson Panel and the DOD-University Forum--to discuss the matter. Initially, the government's trend was toward broadening the scope of what could be classified and subject to export control, including the products and public dissemination of on-campus scientific work. Controversy flared over the implications of President Reagan's Executive Order 12356 (EO 12356), issued in 1982. EO 12356 broke with the long postwar trend of shrinking the scope of what may be permissibly classified.[48]

Some members of Congress and the academic community sharply criticized EO 12356. Universities and scientific associations generally warned that restrictions would only hurt U.S. scientific achievement, were unnecessary given a lack of substantive evidence of damage to national security, and would jeopardize the uniquely open tradition of U.S. science. Overt classification or voluntary self-censorship would limit the peer-review process and dismantle the networks of scientists whose informal and unhindered links with colleagues ensured creative interaction and rapid communication about fast-breaking developments in the field. There was also concern that large numbers of foreign researchers and graduate students--an increasingly important part of the U.S. scientific establishment-- would be kept away from certain research and training at U.S. universities by pervasive restrictions on what and where they could study and what U.S. professors could present in the open classroom. Any barriers to technical diffusion between scientists and engineers could rebound to hurt the application of developments in basic science to defense technology by blocking interchanges. Given the traditionally dominant role of federal, and particularly DOD, funding in U.S. national and campus-based research and development, it was feared that a restrictive DOD approach would guide emerging policy.[49]

Since 1985, federal policy has moved away from the approach of EO 12356. In September 1985, National Security Decision Directive 189 (NSDD 189) proclaimed that the principal means of controlling the products of fundamental research at universities would be classification. Thereafter, in practice, researchers receiving federal funds were advised of the likelihood of their results being classified during contract negotiations; terms to that effect are included in the final contract. This policy was hailed by critics, although a significant clause in NSDD 189 provides a possible loophole around the classification criteria.[50] Specifically, the directive states that "No restrictions may be placed upon the conduct or reporting of federally-funded fundamental research that has not received national security classification, *except as provided in applicable U.S. statutes*" (emphasis added). Among these statutes are the Export Administration and the 1984 Defense Authorization acts.

While some skepticism remained, DOD Directive 2040.2 eased concerns over undue classification. First, the directive automatically exempted from classification, or restrictions on dissemination, a large portion of DOD-funded fundamental research done on campuses. The largest share of DOD funding to university labs goes to fundamental research. Second, the directive assigned chairmanship of the DOD panel responsible for controls on scientific communication to the Deputy Undersecretary for Research and Advanced Technology. Previously, the more control-oriented Undersecretary for Policy had lead authority.[51]

The reaffirmation of openness was also given a boost by the 1985 Export Administration Amendments Act (EAAA).[52] In Section 3(12), Congress strongly supported unfettered scientific communication and a minimum of controls on the dissemination of research: "It is the policy of the United States to sustain vigorous scientific enterprise. To do so involves sustaining the ability of scientists and other scholars freely to communicate by means of publication, teaching, conferences, and other forms of scholarly exchange." However, the Conference Committee did sanction classification if scientific information came under strictures in EO 12356 or if limited by "'contract controls or proprietary or trade restrictions.'" The committee also cited DOD for having intruded excessively into scholarly exchanges.[53] Regulatory language in the Export Administration Regulations (EAR) retained the spirit, thrust, and language of the EAAA's Section 3(12) and NSDD 189. The EAR also eased potential problems associated with technology transfer to foreign scientists employed at U.S. universities and private labs, and to overseas labs affiliated with or owned by U.S. multinationals.[54]

Several actual and potential areas of controversy remain. Although the emphasis on classification and a contractual basis for restricting research eased some of the science community's concerns, the 1984 Defense Department Authorization Act (1984 DAA) authorizes the DOD to restrict dissemination of unclassified data under its control which would otherwise be freely exported. Only qualified U.S. and foreign firms are permitted access to data restricted under the 1984 DAA.[55] Finally, in 1984, National Security Decision Directive 145 (NSDD 145) announced a comprehensive policy for telecommunications and automated information systems, including government scientific data bases, and brought civilian data bases under National Security Agency (NSA) oversight.[56] An initial attempt to create a new category of sensitive but unclassified information in government telecommunications and automated information systems was cancelled in 1987 after loud protests. Subsequent legislation reassigned responsibility for oversight of civilian data bases to the National Bureau of Standards, a move which pleased the academic community.[57]

The implications of the 1984 DAA and the other DOD initiatives bothered the NAS. It criticized the imposition of a de facto and unnecessary category of unclassified but restricted information, and warned of the chilling effects it had on professional societies. Some papers have had to be withdrawn and closed sessions have been held at scientific conferences, actions justified by the DOD on the basis of the 1984 DAA. Irritation over restrictions on foreign scientists' access to and participation in conferences has also been voiced. Defenders of the DOD's policy argue that the 1984 DAA actually promotes dissemination of information since classification is replaced by export control regulations. Conference participants--including non-U.S. citizens--must pledge not to disseminate presentations without DOD approval.[58] Since the 1984 DAA authorized restrictions on DOD-*controlled* data, some presumably derives from DOD-sponsored research on campuses or in off-campus laboratories affiliated with academic institutions. Contracts should therefore indicate the possibility of restrictions--including restrictions on open presentations--and scientists presumably acknowledge this when they agree to the contract's terms. It is, in any case, reasonable to expect the DOD to control dissemination of information on research that is *clearly* weapons related. Furthermore, a study by the American Association for the Advancement of Science (AAAS) suggests that the chilling effect has been minimal and this reflects resistance to closed meetings by prominent scientific societies, however informal restricted sessions are still held.[59] Despite this, in interviews, several analysts stressed that there have been fewer episodes of presentations being cancelled and that the issue's salience has diminished.[60]

Whether individual researchers can exert counterleverage against the funding enticements and accompanying contractual obligations of federal sponsors remains unclear. Several leading universities prohibit classified research on campus but do have off-campus labs--Berkeley's Livermore lab, for example--where classified research is conducted. But interviewees noted that researchers at several reputable "second-rank" universities had been willing to accept on-campus restrictions.[61] Furthermore, restrictions are quite common in contracts between federal agencies (DOD or NASA, for example) and the private sector. It is possible that a private company--contractually obligated to observe export control restrictions--may subcontract with a university passing on restrictions into the university's contract.[62] This poses a dilemma for the scientist, given growing private sector-campus cooperation, and may have negative consequences for the nation's R&D and scientific competitiveness.

The scientist and university can reject any terms presented by the federal sponsor that they feel are unreasonable or in violation of the professional tradition of openness. But this may mean forgoing substantial funding for highly prestigious projects at the boundaries of scientific knowledge, which others may be clamoring to study. Conversely, if the federal sponsor is not able to contract with the best researchers, there is also a risk that research will not be of as high a quality or that potentially important national security projects will be delayed or possibly cancelled. Federal agencies do have an interest in flexibility and can compromise when faced with opposition to unacceptable contractual terms.[63]

While potential abuses and disincentives are evident (overclassification, for example[64]), the contract-based approach puts the burden of classification on the sponsoring agency and gives the researcher the choice of accepting or rejecting the contract's terms.[65] This is, arguably, a reasonable compromise between the extreme of completely unfettered and open scientific communication--with the attendant, if slight, chance of losing critical know-how--and the prospect of comprehensive prior restraint on communication among researchers and self-censorship. There is little evidence that the threat of technology loss justifies the latter approach. More restrictions would raise constitutional questions,[66] be unenforceable, and be contrary to established scientific practices.

SUMMARY

The Russians have sought to acquire advanced dual-use Western technology for incorporation into military systems. As long as Russia and the other former Soviet republics and allies constitute a threat to the West, it is advisable to deny them clear military-related technology. The denial policy has been effective, as is suggested by substantial Soviet reliance on espionage, illegal diversions, and publicly available scientific literature in order to acquire technology and know-how. Indeed, it is likely that the enhanced effectiveness of controls has forced the Soviets to rely increasingly on surreptitious means of acquiring dual-use technology. This evidence, and the increasing difficulty of reverse-engineering rapidly emerging generations of extremely complex microelectronics-based technologies, suggests that more encompassing controls are not warranted at this time. This conclusion is supported by studies and comparisons of the relative U.S.-Soviet standing in key dual-use technologies, which indicate that the East-West technology gap may be accelerating. Furthermore, as the Corson Panel and others concluded, the small amount of applied technology lost via academic sources does not warrant stifling open scientific communication. Excessive controls on scientific communication could jeopardize proven advantages accruing from unhindered scientific cross-fertilization. In this instance, a satisfactory balance was found between the interests of federal agencies and scientists.

There is a case for a policy of technology denial--particularly applied technology--to thwart pervasive Russian efforts to acquire militarily critical dual-use technology. But the debate over acceptable and sustainable economic costs associated with strategic export controls generates intense controversy. The next chapter examines whether exporters of dual-use high technology are penalized excessively by the export administration process and U.S. government restrictions.

NOTES

1. Admiral Inman estimated that espionage accounted for "about" 70% of acquisitions. William Root noted that much Soviet semiconductor manufacturing equipment was obtained from illegal diversions during the 1970s and not through legal trade; Admiral Bobby R. Inman, prepared statement, 11 May 1982, in U.S. Congress, Senate Committee on Governmental Affairs, Permanent Subcommittee on Investigations, *Transfer of United States High Technology to the Soviet Union and Soviet Bloc Nations*, hearings, 97th Congress, 2nd session, 4-6, 11-12 May 1982 (Washington, DC: U.S. GPO, 1982), p. 577; and William A. Root, "COCOM: An Appraisal of Objectives and Needed Reforms," in *Controlling East-West Trade and Technology Transfer: Power, Politics, and Policies*, ed. Gary K. Bertsch (Durham, NC: Duke University Press, 1988), pp. 423-24.

2. U.S. Central Intelligence Agency, *Soviet Acquisition of Western Technology*, photocopy (no publisher, April 1982), p. 3. The CIA is not listed as the principal author, however, since this was an interagency effort and the Director of

Central Intelligence coordinates all U.S. intelligence activities, one can assume CIA authorship. The document is also reprinted in U.S. Congress, Senate, *Transfer of United States High Technology*, pp. 7-23.

3.   Ministry of Foreign Trade, U.S.S.R. Chamber of Commerce and Industry, and Soviet Academy of Sciences representatives also are active in *overt* acquisition efforts, although to a much smaller degree. See U.S. Department of Defense, *Soviet Acquisition of Militarily Significant Western Technology: An Update* (Intelligence Community White Paper, September 1985), Table 2, pp. 9-10 and pp. 20-21. See also, U.S. Department of State, *Intelligence Collection in the USSR Chambers of Commerce and Industry* (no publisher, no date), based on information available as of 2 January 1987.

Espionage, as well as recruiting alleged agents, and using legal and bogus "front" companies and "techno-bandits" are frequently reported. Then CIA Deputy Director Robert M. Gates warned of the continuing espionage effort and public statements, and interviews by and with Americans and Britons revealed similar concerns. See Walter S. Mossberg, "U.S. Diplomat, Suspected of Being Spy For Soviets, Had Technology-Policy Role," *Wall Street Journal*, 24 July 1989, section A, p. 16, columns 2-3; Carl Hartman, "5 Charged With Attempting Illegal Exports to Soviets," *Washington Post*, 19 August 1989, section D, p. 11, columns 3-6; Joe Pichirallo, "Bloch Played Major Role in Technology Export Issue in Austria," *Washington Post*, 27 August 1989, section A, p. 23, columns 1-6, section A, p. 24, columns 3-4; Robert J. McCartney, "Two Germanys Remain Crossroads of East-West Espionage," *Washington Post*, 28 August 1989, section A, p. 15, columns 1-3, section A, p. 17, columns 4-6; Mary Thornton, "Customs Fights KGB On High-Tech Thefts," *Washington Post*, 5 February 1986, section A, p. 17, columns 4-6; Susan F. Rasky and David E. Sanger, "U.S. Split Over Computer Sale to a Soviet-Owned Company," *New York Times*, 29 September 1987, section A, p. 1, section D, p. 6; Kathryn Jones, "CIA Official Expects Soviets to Step Up Industrial Spying," *Dallas Morning News*, 12 February 1988, p. D1, rpt. in U.S. Department of Defense, Department of the Air Force, *Current News*, special edition, *Technology Security*, no. 1703 (22 March 1988), p. 30; Allen Wendt, Senior Representative for Strategic Technology Policy, U.S. State Department and Allen Mendelowitz, Senior Associate Director for Trade, Energy and Finance, U.S. General Accounting Office, comments at a National Issues Forum on *U.S. Export Control Policy: Balancing National Security Issues and Global Competitiveness* held at the Brookings Institution, Washington, D.C., 9 June 1988; not-for-attribution interview, U.S. Department of State, Bureau of Economic and Business Affairs, Washington, D.C., 23 February 1988; not-for-attribution interview, Ministry of Defence, London, 31 October 1988; and National Academy of Sciences, *Finding Common Ground: U.S. Export Controls in a Changed Global Environment* (Washington, DC: National Academy Press, 1991), pp. 28-32.

4.   Examples from the 1940s, early 1950s, and 1970s include basing the first generation Soviet heavy bomber on the design of a U.S. B-29 Superfortress forced to land in the U.S.S.R., utilizing stolen U.S. atomic secrets to further the Soviet

nuclear weapons program, improved ICBM accuracy owing to *legally* exported U.S. bearing grinders, and airplane and missile designs derived from U.S. designs. These examples are discussed in Arnaud de Borchgrave and Michael Ledeen, "Selling Russia the Rope," *The New Republic*, 13 December 1980, pp. 13-16; Richard N. Perle, Assistant Secretary for International Security Policy, Department of Defense, written statement, in U.S. Congress, House Committee on Armed Services, Technology Transfer Panel, *Technology Transfer*, hearings, 98th Congress, 1st session, 9, 21, 29 June and 13-14 July 1983 (Washington, DC: U.S. GPO, 1984), pp. 79-83; Miles M. Costick, "Soviet Military Posture and Strategic Trade," in *From Weakness to Strength*, ed. W. Scott Thompson (San Francisco: Institute for Contemporary Studies, 1980), pp. 189-213; and Julian Cooper, "Western Technology and the Soviet Defense Industry," in *Trade, Technology, and Soviet-American Relations*, ed. Bruce Parrott (Bloomington, IN: Indiana University Press, 1985), pp. 169-202.

5.   These examples are cited by several key Reagan administration technology security policymakers, including Richard N. Perle, "The Strategic Impact of Technology Transfers," Stephen Bryen, "Technology Transfer and National Security: Finding the Proper Balance," and Jack Vorona, "Technology Transfer and Soviet Military R&D," in *Selling the Rope to Hang Capitalism?*, eds. Charles M. Perry and Robert L. Pfaltzgraff, Jr. (London: Pergamon-Brassey's, 1987), pp. 3-22. The increased defense expenditure burden is noted by David G. Wigg, Deputy Assistant Secretary of Defense, Policy Analysis, prepared statement, 22 September 1987, in U.S. Congress, House Committee on Foreign Affairs, Subcommittees on Europe and the Middle East and on International Economic Policy and Trade, *United States-Soviet Trade Relations*, hearings, 100th Congress, 1st session, 14 July and 22 September 1987 (Washington, DC: U.S. GPO, 1988), p. 162.

6.   U.S. Department of Defense, *Soviet Military Power 1986*, 5th ed. (Washington, DC: U.S. GPO, March 1986), p. 5.

7.   There was also disagreement over the impact of the Toshiba-Kongsberg diversion on Soviet improvements in submarine propeller technology--and resulting significant quieting. U.S. intelligence estimated that the Soviets saved 7 to 10 years in development time and billions of dollars. But private analysts disputed this claim and Admiral Sir James Eberle, Director of the Royal Institute of International Affairs, noted that many other improvements in submarine design could have contributed to quieter Soviet subs. See Gordon B. Smith, "Controlling East-West Trade in Japan," in *Controlling East-West Trade and Technology Transfer: Power, Politics, and Policies*, ed. Gary K. Bertsch (Durham, NC: Duke University Press, 1988), p. 151, citing *Christian Science Monitor*, 20 July 1987, p. 13; Admiral Sir James Eberle, comments at a conference for major corporate funders of the institute on *The Future of East-West Relations*, the Royal Institute of International Affairs, London, 17 April 1989; and Thane Gustafson, *Selling the Russians the Rope? Soviet Technology Policy and U.S. Export Controls*, prepared for the Defense Advanced Research Projects Agency (Santa Monica, CA: RAND Corp., April 1981), p. 10.

8. For example, large U.S. weapons stocks, fighters, and equipment were captured when the U.S.-backed South Vietnamese government fell in 1975. The sale of highly sophisticated U.S. and other Western systems to countries in volatile areas increases the probability that Soviet-backed regimes will permit access to captured hardware. Friendly allies receiving U.S. technology may be vulnerable to Russian or other hostile espionage or may ship weapons based on U.S. designs to other vulnerable countries or unstable areas. The thriving international arms market also provides a source for acquisitions as it has for the Pentagon. See U.S. Central Intelligence Agency, *Soviet Acquisition of Western*, p. 7; Tom Raum, "NSC Approves Sale to Iran of U.S. Computer System," *Washington Post*, 22 April 1987, section F, p. 4, columns 1-2; Patrick E. Tyler, "Pentagon Agrees to Let Egypt Produce M1 Tank," *Washington Post*, 29 June 1987, section A, p. 1, columns 5-6; section A, p. 16, columns 1-4; Richard M. Weintraub, "U.S., India Near Supercomputer Deal," *Washington Post*, 8 July 1986, section D, p. 1, columns 3-4; section D, p. 4, columns 1-3; David E. Sanger, "Computer Sale Seen to India," *New York Times*, 27 March 1987, section D, p. 1, column 2; section D, p. 2, columns 4-5; David B. Ottaway, "Israelis Aided China on Missiles," *Washington Post*, 23 May 1988, section A, p. 1, column 4; section A, p. 17, columns 1-5; and Molly Moore, "Psst, You Wanna Buy a Used MiG Real Cheap?", *Washington Post National Weekly Edition*, vol. 6, no. 15 (13-19 February 1989), p. 33, columns 1-4.

9. National Academy of Sciences, *Balancing the National Interest* (Washington, DC: National Academy Press, 1987), pp. 4-5.

10. U.S. Congress, Office of Technology Assessment, *Technology and East-West Trade: An Update*, (Washington, DC: U.S. GPO, 1983), p. 76.

11. National Academy of Sciences, *Balancing, p. 5.*

12. Industrial espionage is not uncommon within the West, although the close linkage between Soviet defense and civilian industry makes it hard to distinguish between the two. However, given Gorbachev's emphasis on economic reform, including having relatively more efficient defense industries assist in improving overall economic competitiveness, such information could possibly be channeled to civilian industry in the future; Philip Hanson, *Soviet Industrial Espionage: Some New Information*, RIIA Discussion Papers, No. 1 (London: Royal Institute of International Affairs, 1987), pp. 10-11.

13. Ibid., pp. 18-19.

14. Cooper, "Western Technology," p. 192.

15. For example, the NAS discounted claims of Soviet savings in the DOD's study *Assessing the Effect of Technology Transfer of U.S./Western Security*. See National Academy of Sciences, *Balancing*, pp. 46, 110.

The Packard Commission's conclusion, in *A Quest for Excellence: Final Report to the President*, is noted in National Academy of Sciences, *Balancing the National Interest*. In 1987, the Defense Science Board determined that technology was not rapidly introduced into systems and that this inefficiency "'is a primary contributor to the growing crises in military competition as Soviet weapons system performance approaches, and, in some cases exceeds, that of the U.S.'" Charles H. Ferguson of

MIT notes that one reason for the lag in incorporating state-of-the-art technology in U.S. weapons is the practice of continually purchasing low volumes of obsolete components for 10 to 25-year-old systems with long life cycles that require considerable maintenance. This policy creates "technological drag" and illustrates why new weapons incorporate electronic components 5 to 8 years behind commercial state of the art. He bases the 5 to 8 year gap on interviews with DOD employees and semiconductor and defense industry executives. See National Academy of Sciences, *Balancing*, p. 6; Defense Science Board, "Report of the Defense Science Board 1987 Summer Study on Technology Base Management," prepared for the Office of the Under Secretary of Defense for Acquisition, December 1987, p. E-2; quoted in U.S. Congress, Office of Technology assessment, *Holding the Edge: Maintaining the Defense Technology Base*, OTA-ISC-420 (Washington, DC: U.S. GPO, April 1989), p. 129, footnote 2 and ff; and Charles H. Ferguson, "High Technology Life Cycles, Export Controls, and International Markets," in *Balancing the National Interest*, Working Papers, ed. National Academy of Sciences (Washington, DC: National Academy Press, 1987), pp. 70-71.

16. Philip Hanson, *Western Economic Statecraft in East-West Relations*, Chatham House Papers, No. 40 (London: Routledge and Kegan Paul, 1988), p. 36.

17. Electronics-based technologies accounted for 31 and 23% of acquisition tasks during 1979 and 1980, respectively; Hanson, *Soviet Industrial Espionage*, Tables 1-2, pp. 30-31; and National Academy of Sciences, *Balancing*, p. 5.

18. Phillip A. Parker, former Deputy Assistant Director, Intelligence Division, Federal Bureau of Investigation, "The Challenge of Industrial Espionage," in *Selling the Rope to Hang Capitalism?*, eds. Charles M. Perry and Robert L. Pfaltzgraff, Jr. (London: Pergamon-Brassey's, 1987), p. 180.

19. In some instances, up to 20 years passed before an item was finally acquired. Hanson, *Soviet Industrial Espionage*, pp. 14, 20-21; and Richard N. Perle, Assistant Secretary of Defense of International Security Policy, Department of Defense, testimony, 23 April 1987, in U.S. Congress, House Committee on Science, Space, and Technology, *National Academy of Sciences Report on International Technology Transfer*, hearings, 100th Congress, 1st session, 4 February, 23 April 1987 (Washington, DC: U.S. GPO, 1987), p. 105.

20. See U.S., Department of Defense, *Soviet Acquisition...An Update*, p. 11.

21. Examples of Soviet achievements include Sputnik (admittedly given an assist by captured German expertise), the general Soviet space effort, and world leadership in certain materials, manufacturing, and propulsion processes. World-class Soviet-developed exports include electro-magnetic casting equipment, large-diameter gas pipe welding, ion gun hardening for industrial cutting tools, and biotechnology products such as hepatitis B vaccine, single-cell proteins, and interleukin-2. See U.S. Department of Defense, *Soviet Military Power 1986*, pp. 106-07; and Carol Rae Hansen, International Affairs Fellow, The Council on Foreign Relations Fellow, Johns Hopkins Foreign Policy Institute, testimony, 13 April 1988, in U.S. Congress, House Committee on Foreign Affairs, Subcommittee on Europe and the Middle East, *United States-Soviet Relations: 1988 (Volume II)*,

hearings, 100th Congress, 2nd session, 2, 8, 25 February, 17, 28 March, 13, 20, 27 April 1988 (Washington, DC: U.S. GPO, 1988), p. 435.

22. This is, probably unwittingly, implied by the DOD's Stephen Bryen, Under Secretary of Defense for Trade and Security Policy, who warned that one illegal sale could be used to improve Soviet computer hardware "over the next 20 years." While Soviet systems might be improved, two-decade-old technology was not likely to be as threatening in the early 21st century. Bryen quoted in Steven Greenhouse, "French Linked to Soviet Sale," *New York Times*, 17 October 1987.

23. Admiral Bobby R. Inman, testimony, 11 May 1982, in U.S. Congress, Senate Committee on Governmental Affairs, Permanent Subcommittee on Investigations, *Transfer of United States High Technology*, pp. 238, 243.

24. In July 1989, the DOC justified decontrolling certain desktop PC models, representing mid-1980s technology, owing to foreign availability from Brazil, Taiwan, Singapore, and India; Lionel Barber and Nancy Dunne, "US Relaxes Computer Export Curb," *Financial Times*, [U.S. edition], no. 30,899 (20 July 1989), p. 6, column 1.

25. Seymour E. Goodman, "Technology Transfer and the Development of the Soviet Computer Industry," in *Trade, Technology, and Soviet-American Relations*, ed. Bruce Parrott (Bloomington, IN: Indiana University Press, 1985), pp. 117-40.

26. A distinction should be made between copying a design outright and copying computer architecture argues Hugh Donaghue, Senior Vice President, Government Programs and International Trade Relations, Control Data Corporation. The RYAD was based on IBM architecture--that is, it is IBM-compatible, and it is not a direct copy as DOD officials suggest. Newer-generation Soviet high-speed computers are now patterned after 1970s-era Burroughs architecture, but there are estimated to be no more than 50 installed in the U.S.S.R. See Hugh Donaghue, "A Business Perspective on Export Controls," in *Selling the Rope to Hang Capitalism?*, eds. Charles M. Perry and Robert L. Pfaltzgraff, Jr. (London: Pergamon-Brassey's, 1987), p. 189. See also Seymour E. Goodman, "Soviet Computing and Technology Transfer: An Overview," *World Politics*, vol. 31, no. 4 (July 1979), p. 556, quoted in Gustafson, p. 25; and Peter Wolcoft and Seymour E. Goodman, "High-Speed Computers of the Soviet Union," *Computer*, September 1988, p. 34.

27. U.S., Department of Defense, Office of the Under Secretary of Defense for Policy, *Assessing the Effect of Technology Transfer on U.S./Western Security* (no publisher, February 1985), pp. 3-10.

28. Other anecdotal information tends to confirm this. For example, the Soviets took 13 years to develop an analytic centrifuge based on a relatively unsophisticated model acquired from the West. But by the time the Soviet version was complete, it was obsolete. R.J. Carrick, *East-West Technology Transfer in Perspective*, Policy Papers in International Affairs, no. 9 (Berkeley, CA: Institute of International Studies, 1978), p. 44, citing Z. Medvedev, *The Medvedev Papers* (London, 1971).

29. This echoed the 1976, Bucy Report which concluded that reverse-engineering "is rarely an effective technique for discovering current design and manufacturing technology." An official with the DOC's Export Administration Program Review Staff reported that "The possibility of reverse-engineering has been discounted by many exporters who claim that their manufacturing techniques cannot be derived by examining the finished products." See National Academy of Sciences, *Balancing*, pp. 5, 47; U.S. Department of Defense, Director of Defense Research and Engineering, *An Analysis of Export Control of U.S. Technology- A DOD Perspective*, A Report of the Defense Science Board Task Force on Export of U.S. Technology (no publisher, 4 February 1976), P. 5; and U.S. Congress, Office of Technology Assessment, *Science, Technology, and the First Amendment*, OTA-CIT-369 (Washington, DC: U.S. GPO, January 1988), p. 51, footnote 73, citing "Direct communication to OTA project staff, June 19, 1987."

30. The intelligence community concurs, at least regarding integrated circuits. Reverse-engineering or chips can also be thwarted by manufacturers designing chips to self-destruct if tampered with, according to Harold Relyea of the Congressional Research Service; interview, Washington, D.C., 24 June 1988. See also U.S. Department of Defense, *Soviet Acquisition...An Update*, p. 12; Goodman, "Technology Transfer," pp. 126-27; and David A. Wellman, *A Chip in the Curtain* (Washington, DC: National Defense University Press, 1989), pp. 80-81.

Presently, the Soviets are thought to be lagging behind the West by 5 to 9 years in semiconductor manufacturing technology and chip capacity. In addition, experience and insight that engineers gain from independent R&D is not acquired from simply copying another's product. Learning-by-doing is retarded. Furthermore, experience with legal technology transfer to U.S. subsidiaries overseas suggests that even when adequate tools and training are provided, there is a time lag before quality standards are met. This lag is probably compounded in the Soviet case given technology denial barriers and suggests a reason for the size, scope, and increasing emphasis on illegal Soviet acquisition efforts. The DOD acknowledged the success of tighter controls on East-West trade and resulting increase in covert efforts and diversions. The figures for Soviet semiconductor manufacturing technology and chip capacity are from Wellman, *A Chip*, p. 83, citing Norman R. Augustine, Semiconductor Task Force, Defense Science Board, News Briefing, 12 February 1987; and from Douglas MacEachin and Rear Adm. Robert Schmitt, "Gorbachev's Modernization Program: A Status Report," paper presented by the CIA and Defense Intelligence Agency for submission to the Subcommittee on National Security Economics of the Joint Economic Committee, Congress of the United States, rpt. in U.S. Congress, Joint Economic Committee, Subcommittee on National Security Economics, *Allocation of Resources in the Soviet Union and China- 1986*, hearings, 100th Congress, 1st session, 19 March and 3 August 1987 (Washington, DC: U.S. GPO, 1988), Figure 3, p. 17. See also Wellman, *A Chip*, p. 95; National Academy of Sciences, *Balancing*, p. 47; Dr. Lew Allen, Jr., Director, Jet Propulsion Laboratory, Pasadena, CA, testimony, 4 February 1987, in U.S. Congress, House Committee on Science, Space, and Technology, *National Academy of Sciences Report on International Technology Transfer*, hearing, 100th Congress, 1st session, 4 February, 23 April 1987 (Washington, DC: U.S. GPO 1987), pp. 69-70; U.S., Department of Defense, Secretary of Defense, *The Technology Transfer Control Program*, A Report to the 98th Congress, 2nd session, February 1984, p. 54; U.S. Department of Defense, Secretary of Defense, *The Technology Security Program*, A Report to the 99th Congress, 2nd session, 1986, pp. iv, 1, 12, 16; and Michael Lorenzo, Deputy Under Secretary of Defense Research and Engineering (International Programs and Technology), "Military Technology Transfer," address delivered to the American Society for Engineering Management at George Washington University, 11 March 1982, rpt. in U.S. Congress, Senate Committee on Governmental Affairs, Permanent Subcommittee on Investigations, *Transfer of United States High Technology*, p. 569.

    31. These and related handicaps are discussed in Wolcoft and Goodman, pp. 33, 35; and Judith A. Thornton, *A New Export Regime For Information Technologies*, Foreign Policy Briefs, no. 19, Foreign Policy Institute, Johns Hopkins University (Washington, DC: Johns Hopkins Foreign Policy Institute, November 1988). Analysts believe that the relative backwardness of civilian industry in the U.S.S.R. is a significant constraint on attempts to modernize Soviet military technology since the military relies on civilian industry for many of its inputs. See Herbert S. Levine, Professor of Economics, Codirector, Lauder Institute of Management and International Studies, University of Pennsylvania, prepared statement, 27 April 1988, in U.S. Congress, House Committee on Foreign Affairs, Subcommittee on Europe and the Middle East, *United States-Soviet Relations: 1988 (Volume I)*, hearings, 100th Congress, 2nd session, 2, 8, 25 February, 17, 28 March, 13, 20, 27 April 1988 (Washington, DC: U.S. GPO, 1988), p. 563.

    32. Sir Brian Tovey, interview, London, 15 December 1988.

    33. Douglas MacEachin, Director, Soviet Analysis and Mr. Whitehouse, Chief, Economic Performance Division, Central Intelligence Agency, testimony, 19 March 1987, in U.S. Congress, Joint Economic Committee, Subcommittee on National Security Economics, *Allocation of Resources in the Soviet Union and China-1986*, hearings, 19 March and 3 August 1987 (Washington, DC: U.S. GPO, 1988), pp. 86-87; Gustafson, *Selling the Russians*, p. 6; and Paul Cocks, Office of Soviet Analysis, CIA, "Soviet Science and Technology Strategy: Borrowing From the Defense Sector," in U.S. Congress, Joint Economic Committee, *Gorbachev's Economic Plans*, Volume 2, Study Papers, 100th Congress, 1st session (Washington, DC: U.S. GPO, November 1987), p. 160. John Kiser, president of Kiser Research, Inc., argues that the Soviet defense industry is one of the most innovative sectors having produced numerous civilian spinoffs and manufacturing a significant portion of consumer durables. See John W. Kiser, "How the Arms Race Really Helps Moscow," *Foreign Policy*, vol. 60 (Fall 1985), pp. 44-45.

    34. Richard Perle, Assistant Secretary of Defense for International Security Policy, "Response to Written Questions of Senator Garn From Richard Perle," in U.S. Congress, Senate Committee on Banking, Housing, and Urban Affairs, Subcommittee on International Finance and Monetary Policy, *Export Controls*,

hearings, 100th Congress, 1st session, 12, 17 March 1987 (Washington, DC: U.S. GPO, 1987), p. 178.

35. A 1990 comparison of U.S.-Soviet standing in 20 militarily related technologies published by the NAS does not suggest any reason to revise these conclusions. National Academy of Sciences, *Finding Common Ground*, p. 35, Table 4-2.

36. Public admissions to this effect by the Soviet military are naturally, unheard of. But complaints by the Eastern European civilian sector over restrictions caused by COCOM are growing. U.K. Parliament, House of Commons, Trade and Industry Committee, Report, in *Trade with Eastern Europe*, Second Report, Session 1988-89 (London: HMSO, 26 January 1989), p. xviii.

37. Delaying Soviet progress is stressed by many analysts as the only practical and realistically achievable goal of technology denial policy. For example, the former Assistant Secretary of the Air Force for Research and Development, Dr. Alexander Flax, argued that "it's the time delay that's important" and felt that controls are effective because "lead time delay is considerable." The DOC's Director of the Office of Export Enforcement made a similar argument and, reportedly, so did Robert Dean, responsible for technology transfer issues at the Reagan National Security Council. See Dr. Alexander Flax, "Policies for Control of the Export of Technology: Do They Benefit American Security Interests?", address at the American University, Washington, DC, 10 November 1987; Anstruther Davidson, interview, Department of Commerce, Washington, DC, 24 February 1988; and John Copeland, Director, Export Administration, Motorola, Inc., interview, quoting Robert Dean, Washington, DC, 25 February 1988.

38. This is implied in the 1986 edition of *Soviet Military Power*. See U.S. Department of Defense, *Soviet Military Power 1986*, p. 108. The poor performance of Soviet weapons in combat conditions--in the Middle East, for example--suggests that the benefits of Western technology is not always that decisive. Commerce Undersecretary Paul Freedenberg noted that Soviet-built jets had fared quite poorly against Israeli fighters in dogfights over Lebanon. Comments at a National Issues Forum on *U.S. Export Control Policy: Balancing National Security Issues and Global Competitiveness*, held at The Brookings Institution, Washington, DC, 9 June 1988.

39. Secretary of Defense Carlucci warned of these consequences in the wake of the June 1988 U.S.-Soviet summit. See Fred Hiatt, "Carlucci Cautions the West to Stay Vigilant on Moscow," *Washington Post*, 7 June 1988, section A, p. 1, columns 1-2; section A, p. 17, columns 1-2. See also "Supplemental Questions Submitted by the Subcommittee on Europe and Middle East to the Department of Defense and Responses Thereto," in U.S. Congress, House Committee on Foreign Affairs, Subcommittee on Europe and the Middle East, *United States-Soviet Relations: 1988 (Volume II)*, hearings, 100th Congress, 2nd session, 5, 11-12 May, 27, 29 June, and 12, 14 July 1988 (Washington, DC: U.S. GPO, 1988), p. 525; and Richard F. Kaufman, "Industrial Modernization and Defense in the Soviet Union," in *The Soviet Economy: A New Course?*, ed. Reiner Weichhardt, NATO Colloquium, 1-3 April

1987 (Brussels: North Atlantic Treaty Organization, 1988), pp. 247-61.

40. For example, aluminum and titanium production are closely integrated with weapons industries including aviation and submarine plants. See U.S. Department of Defense, *Soviet Military Power 1986*, p. 114; and Charles M. Perry and Robert L. Pfaltzgraff, Jr., "West-East Technology Transfer: Implications for U.S. Policy," in *Selling the Rope to Hang Capitalism?*, eds. Charles M. Perry and Robert L. Pfaltzgraff, Jr. (London: Pergamon-Brassey's 1987), pp. 224, 226-29.

41. Adm. Inman's views are described in Harold C. Relyea, *National Security Controls and Scientific Information*, Issue Brief, no. IB82083, U.S. Library of Congress, Congressional Research Service, 17 June 1986, p. CRS-2. See also Frank Carlucci, Deputy Secretary of Defense, letter to William D. Carey, Executive Officer and Publisher, *Science*, rpt. in "Scientific Exchanges and U.S. National Security," *Science*, vol. 215 (8th January 1982), pp. 140-41; and Systems Security Steering Group, "National Policy on Protection of Sensitive, But Unclassified Information in Federal Government Telecommunications and Automated Information Systems," 29 October 1986.

42. Edward C. Bertnolli, Vice President, Professional Activities, U.S. Activities Board, Institute of Electrical and Electronic Engineers, letter to Sen. Patrick Leahy, Chairman, Senate Subcommittee on Technology and the Law, dated 18 April 1988 (photocopied); National Academy of Sciences, *Scientific Communication and National Security* (National Academy Press, 1982); and F. Karl Willenbrach, Ceil H. Green, Professor of Engineering, Southern Methodist University, "Role of Professional Communications in U.S. Technological Progress," address at the AAAS/IEEE Congressional Seminar "Information Controls and Technological Competitiveness," 30 January 1986 (photocopied).

43. Institutions were asked to restrict and monitor the activities of Soviet, Eastern European, and Chinese academics and students. Dale R. Corson, "Scientific Communication and National Security," edited version of a paper presented 30 January 1986 at a Congressional seminar on "Information Controls and Technological Competitiveness," Washington, DC; rpt. in *National Security Controls and University Research: Selected Readings*, ed. David A. Wilson, prepared by the Association of American Universities for the Department of Defense-University Forum (Washington, DC: the Association of American Universities, 1987), p. 10; and Janice R. Long, "Scientific Freedom: Focus of National Security Controls Shifting," *Chemical and Engineering News*, vol. 63, no. 26 (1 July 1985), pp. 7-11. Pages 8-9 list 17 scientific conferences in which restrictions on attendees or presentations were implemented, or papers were withdrawn.

Early in 1982, Admiral Inman called for a peer review system--patterned after an existing panel which reviews cryptology papers--that would consider "potential harm to the nation" *prior* to initiating research or publishing findings. The alternative might mean draconian restrictions on scientific freedoms, he warned. Given counterintelligence success in limiting covert Soviet efforts to acquire dual-use technology and know-how, the university community remained vulnerable to increased Soviet efforts. This theme was later underlined in the DOD's 1985 report

Soviet Acquisition of Militarily Significant Technology: An Update. See Ruth Greenstein, "National Security Controls on Scientific Information," *Jurimetrics Journal*, vol. 23, no. 1 (Fall 1982), pp. 50-51, footnote 5; Robert Kuttner, "Spooks and Science: An American Dilemma," *Washington Post*, 20 August 1989, section B, p. 20, columns 2-4; and U.S. Department of Defense, *Soviet Acquisition...An Update*, pp. 21-24.

44. The FBI warns that a Soviet student, given sufficient training and education, can interpret and elicit information more effectively from U.S. scientists than what can be gleaned from perusing open literature. See Parker, "The Challenge," p. 181; U.S. Department of Defense, Office of the Director of Defense Research and Engineering, *An Analysis...A DOD Perspective*, pp. 3, 6; and Lewis Branscomb, former chief scientist, IBM, quoted in Stephen B. Gould, Director, Project on Access to Scientific and Technical Information, Committee on Scientific Freedom and Responsibility, American Association for the Advancement of Science, "National Security Controls on Technology Information: In Search of a Consensus," in *U.S. Export Control Policy and Competitiveness*, eds. John P. Hardt and Jean F. Boone, U.S. Library of Congress, Congressional Research Service, no. 87-388S, 30 April 1987, p. 131. Filipp Staros and Iosef Berg, two U.S.-educated electrical engineers, are credited with establishing the first Soviet design bureau to produce PCs and to pioneer microelectronics in the U.S.S.R. Staros apparently defected to Czechoslovakia in 1950 after he was implicated in the Rosenberg espionage case, and was invited to the U.S.S.R. in the mid-1950s. This episode illustrates the effectiveness of technology transfer via trained individuals, although it appears to be a unique case. Mark Kuchment, "Active Technology Transfer and the Development of Soviet Microelectronics," in *Selling the Rope to Hang Capitalism?*, eds. Charles M. Perry and Robert L. Pfaltzgraff, Jr. (London: Pergamon-Brassey's, 1987), pp. 60-69.

45. This is typically the case in Very Large Scale Integrated Circuit and biotechnology research. Researchers must often "develop a series of practical steps to apply a scientific principle to manufacture a produce." This "recipe" is essential since the underlying scientific principle is useless without it. See Margaret J. Lam, "Restrictions on Technology Transfer Among Academic Researchers: Will Recent Changes in the Export Control System Make a Difference?" *Journal of College and University Law*, vol. 13, no. 3 (Winter 1986), p. 317, footnote 54. Deborah Runkle of the American Association for the Advancement of Science noted that the traditional categories of what is basic versus applied research are increasingly fuzzy as researchers frequently jump back and forth between both activities; interview, 13 July 1988; and Mitchel B. Wallerstein, Associate Executive Director, Office of International Affairs, National Research Council, interview, Washington, DC, 22 July 1988.

46. John Shattuck and Muriel Morisey Spence, *Government Information Controls: Implications for Scholarship, Science and Technology* (Washington, DC: Association of American Universities, March 1988), p. 10. The FBI reportedly checks the identities of technical and scientific library patrons since Soviet envoys comb U.S. libraries for open sources. Protests forced the FBI to restrict the

program in 1988. Soviet scientists acknowledge that they tap data bases via modems and global computer networks to receive information on current scientific developments and software. KGB "hackers" have also been discovered. The United States has studied the national security implications but both U.S. and foreign analysts are unsure how to stop illegal access without unnecessarily hindering legitimate users. It is unclear whether data on *basic* scientific principles gathered this way can be *applied* to produce weapons and weapon-related technology. The growing ease and sophistication of data transmission is a challenge to existing export control efforts and in 1988, the National Security Agency was reportedly engaged in tapping such overseas data transmissions in an effort to determine whether substantial losses are incurred. See Bill McAllister, "Librarians Want FBI to Shelve Request About Foreign Readers," *Washington Post*, 27 March 1988, section A, p. 3, columns 1-6; Nat Hentoff, "The FBI In the Library," *Washington Post*, 23 July 1988, section A, p. 23, column 6; "The FBI Shelves Its Program Targeting New York Library Users," *Washington Post National Weekly Edition*, vol. 6, no. 3 (21-27 November 1988), p. 39, columns 1-2; Michael Schrage, "U.S. Seeking to Limit Access of Soviets to Computer Data," *Washington Post*, 27 May 1986, section A, p. 1, columns 1-3; section A, p. 18, columns 1-3; Michael Schrage, "U.S. Limits Access to Information Related to National Security," *Washington Post*, 13 November 1986, section A, p. 1, columns 1-5; section A, p. 29, columns 1-4; David Marsh, "W Germany Uncovers Spy Ring," *Financial Times* [London], no. 30,784 (3 March 1989), p. 20, columns 2-5; Relyea, interview; and not-for-attribution interview, Ministry of Defence, London, 31 October 1988.

47. In 1982 Congressional testimony, Admiral Inman noted that "technical exchanges conducted by scientists and students" were the source of only a small percentage of losses. By 1984, the intelligence community had still not been able to document an instance where transfer from the U.S. scientific community had clearly damaged national security. Another 1984 DOD study found that less than 5% of a sample of university-generated DOD research reports were either classified or subject to limited distribution. A senior DOD official responsible for reviewing selected papers to be presented at professional meetings has admitted that on average only 3% should be restricted. See Inman, p. 578; Mitchel B. Wallerstein, "Scientific Communication and National Security in 1984," *Science*, vol. 224, no. 4648 (4 May 1984), pp. 462-63 and footnote 6; Mitchel B. Wallerstein and Lawrence E. McCray, "Scientific Communication and National Security: Issues in 1984," *NAS News Report* (Washington, DC: National Academy of Sciences, April 1984), cited in U.S. Congress, Office of Technology Assessment, *Science, Technology*, pp. 42-43; and Gould, "National Security Controls," p. 130.

In 1982, a prestigious NAS panel chaired by Dale R. Corson, president emeritus of Cornell University, released a report that concluded that "universities and open scientific communication have been the source of very little of this technology transfer problem." The Corson Panel concluded that, restricting hands-on research rather than restricting dissemination of scientific papers was the best means of preventing leaks. Furthermore, both a State Department representative and the NAS president testified that reviews had determined that U.S.-Soviet exchanges have not been a channel for acquiring military technology. Finally, even as it warned of targeted U.S. universities, the DOD concluded--based on the Farewell evidence--that only "about" 5% of the most significant technology the Soviets had acquired during the late 1970s and early 1980s had come from this source. The DOD also found little evidence of Soviet scientists being assigned to acquire technology useful for Soviet military development. Relyea, "National Security," p. CRS-9; Wallerstein, "Scientific," p. 461; Frank Press, President, National Academy of Sciences, prepared statement, 13 April 1988, in U.S. Congress, House Committee on Foreign Affairs, Subcommittee on Europe and the Middle East, *United States-Soviet Relations: 1988 (Volume I)*, hearings, 100th Congress, 2nd session, 2, 8, 25 February, 17, 28 March, 13, 20, 27 April 1988 (Washington, DC: U.S. GPO, 1988), p. 398; Department of State, responses to additional questions posed by Sen. Jake Garn, letter dated 28 May 1982, in U.S. Congress, Senate Committee on Banking, Housing, and Urban Affairs, Subcommittee on International Finance and Monetary Policy, *East-West Trade and Technology Transfer*, hearing, 97th Congress, 2nd session, 14 April 1982 (Washington, DC: U.S. GPO, 1982), p. 118; and U.S. Department of Defense, *Soviet Acquisition...An Update*, pp. 21, 23.

48. The order expanded the scope of classification to include any information "'owned by, produced by, produced for, *or...under the control of* the United States Government'" (emphasis added). Additional language (in section 1.6(b)) gives agencies discretion in classifying nongovernmentally sponsored research--i.e., privately developed scientific information. This was not authorized under the previous order. Information may also be reclassified if "'the information requires protection in the interest of national security and [if] the information may reasonably be recovered'." See Shattuck and Spence, pp. 12-14, and footnote 34 quoting from EO12356, Sec. 1.6(c). See also U.S., Office of Technology Assessment, *Science, Technology*, p. 44, quoting *Code of Federal Regulations*, vol. 47, p. 14,847, Section 6.1(b); and Ruth L. Greenstein, "Federal Contractors and Grantees: What Are Your First Amendment Rights?, *Jurimetrics Journal*, vol. 24, no. 3 (Spring 1984), revised version of remarks prepared for delivery at the 1983 annual meeting of the Law and Society Association, rpt. in *National Security Controls and University Research: Selected Readings*, ed. David A. Wilson, prepared by the Association of American Universities for the Department of Defense-University Forum (Washington, DC: Association of American Universities, 1987), p. 76.

49. Hindering exchanges could weaken international scientific cooperation forcing economic competitors to pursue expensive multinational high-technology efforts absent U.S. participation. Ultimately, that would mean larger U.S. R&D expenditures. Given the steep costs of important scientific projects (e.g., space exploration and fusion research), scientific advances outside the United States, and budgetary constraints, international cooperation and sharing of the financial burden among several countries' research establishments is increasingly necessary. However, if controls isolate the United States from such cooperation, U.S. R&D expenditures might ultimately have to grow as the United States single-handedly

pursued "big science" projects. Furthermore, since the innovation process relies heavily on the gathering of discrete packages of information and repackaging information into new patterns of knowledge, disruptions in the information flow between scientists and engineers might unknowingly retard innovation. Corson, "Scientific Communication," p. 11; U.S. Congress, Office of Technology Assessment, *Holding the Edge*, p. 138; Greenstein, "Federal Contrators," pp. 73-84 and David A. Wilson, "Federal Control of Information in Academic Science," *Jurimetrics Journal*, vol. 27, no. 3 (Spring 1987), rpt. in *National Security Controls and University Research: Selected Readings*, ed. David A. Wilson, prepared by the Association of American Universities for the Department of Defense-University Forum (Washington, DC: Association of American Universities, 1987), pp. 105-16.

The linkage between information-gathering and innovation is discussed in Stuart Macdonald, "Hemorrhage and Tourniquet: U.S. Export Controls and Industrial Espionage in High Technology," paper presented to the Ninth taInternational Economic History Congress, Berne, August 1986, p. 9; and Stuart Macdonald, "United States Export Controls and High Technology Information," paper presented at the Royal Institute of International Affairs, London, 6 February 1987. In 1987, government funding accounted for nearly one-half of the $123 billion annual expenditure on pure and applied research. See Malcolm Gladwell, "A National Interest in Global Markets," *Insight*, 29 June 1987, supplement to *Washington Times*, p. 13. The importance of DOD involvement in spurring early university and private sector research and development in computing, superconductivity, and other dual-use technologies is described in Kenneth Flamm and Thomas L. McNaugher, "Rationalizing Technology Investments," in *Restructuring American Foreign Policy*, ed. John D. Steinbruner (Washington, DC: The Brookings Institution, 1989), pp. 119-57.

50. Administration officials reaffirmed the thrust of NSDD 189 on several occasions. See Wilson, "Federal Control," pp. 105-16 and p. 114, footnotes, 54, 55. See also Leo Young, "Commentary: The Control of Government-Sponsored Technical Information," *Science, Technology, and Human Values*, vol. 10, no. 2 (Spring 1985), pp. 84-85; Robert L. Park, Professor of Physics, University of Maryland, Executive Director, Office of Public Affairs, American Physical Society, "Comments Prepared for the Export Control Policy Forum on Technical Data Export Controls," 11 February 1988, photocopied, p. 1; and Donald L. Langenberg, Chancellor, University of Illinois, Chicago, "Secret Knowledge and Open Inquiry," *Society*, vol. 23, no. 5 (July-August 1986), p. 11.

51. David A. Wilson, "National Security Control of Technological Information," *Jurimetrics Journal*, vol. 25, no. 2 (Winter 1985), rpt. in *National Security Controls and University Research: Selected Readings*, ed. David A. Wilson, prepared by the Association of American Universities for the Department of Defense-University Forum (Washington, DC: Association of American Universities, 1987), pp. 98, 100.

52. The International Traffic in Arms Regulations (ITAR) also regulate exports of scientific data related to munitions and clearly military related technology. This discussion will only focus on the EAAA and questions pertaining to civilian dual-use

export controls.

53. Export Administration Amendments Act of 1985 [Public Law 99-64; 99 Stat. 120], rpt. in U.S. Congress, House and Senate Committees on Foreign Affairs and Foreign Relations, *Legislation on Foreign Relations Through 1985*, Volume II (Washington, DC: U.S. GPO, June 1986), p. 402 and Lam, "Restrictions," p. 324, footnote 101, citing Rep. Roth, statement, *Congressional Record*, vol. 131 (1985), p. H2006.

54. Under the EAR, fundamental research is defined exactly as in NSDD 189, all university research is normally considered fundamental and open, and the products of such research only require a self-issued general license and may be exported to all destinations unless contractual terms restrict dissemination. Otherwise, a validated license is required for national security-related data. Wilson, "Federal Control," pp. 110-11, 113; National Academy of Sciences, *Balancing*, pp. 87, 90; and Stephen B. Gould, "The Role of Foreign Nationals in U.S. Science and Engineering," in *Balancing the National Interest*, Working Papers, ed. National Academy of Sciences (Washington, DC: National Academy Press, 1987), pp. 19-20.

55. Furthermore, DOD identifies such data when they fall in a category in the Militarily Critical Technologies List (MCTL), a vast compendium of definitions that is a virtual catalog of high technology. The DOD also initiated creation of a subset of dual-use technologies and associated data, drawn from the MCTL, to be subject to validated licensing to Western destinations. This would apply regardless of the technology's and data's origin--i.e., including academic research. See National Academy of Sciences, *Balancing*, pp. 21, and Shattuck and Spence, *Government Information*, pp. 57-58.

56. Echoing the mosaic theory, NSDD 145 asserted that "'information, even if unclassified in isolation, often can reveal sensitive information when taken in aggregate'"; Shattuck and Spence, *Government Information*, pp. 25-26.

57. Mitchel B. Wallerstein and Stephen B. Gould, "A Delicate Balance: Scientific Communication vs. National Security," *Issues in Science and Technology*, vol. 4, no. 1 (Fall 1987), p. 43; Shattuck and Spence, *Government Information*, p. 25; Daniel J. Marcus, "Senate OKs Computer Security Bill; Commerce Will Set Guidelines," *Defense News*, 4 January 1988, p. 7, rpt. in U.S. Department of Defense, Department of the Air Force, *Current News*, special edition, *Technology Security*, no. 1683 (26 January 1988), p. 33; and Office of Technology Assessment, *Science, Technology*, pp. 62-64.

58. NAS study missions in Europe and Japan reported such complaints. These episodes do nothing to alleviate existing mistrust over U.S. motives with critics insinuating that the United States is becoming a technological isolationist for competitive reasons. However far-fetched such mistrust is, it deters the smooth operation of multilateral controls and potentially invites retaliation against U.S. scientists. See National Academy of Sciences, *Balancing*, pp. 21, 185, 210; Manfred von Nordheim, "Technology Transfer and Alliance Relations: A West German Perspective," in *Selling the Rope to Hang Capitalism?*, eds. Charles M. Perry and Robert L. Pfaltzgraff, Jr. (London: Pergamon-Brassey's, 1987), p. 202;

Ora E. Smith, Director, External Technology Development, Rockwell International Corporation, statement, in U.S. Congress, House Committee on Science, Space, and Technology, Subcommittee on International Scientific Cooperation, *Sharing Foreign Technology: Should We Pick Their Brains?*, hearing, 100th Congress, 2nd session, 27 April 1988 (Washington, DC: U.S. GPO, 1989), pp. 50-51; Jean-Claude Derian, counsellor for science and technology, French embassy, Washington, DC, "France," in "A Delicate Balance: Scientific Communication vs. National Security," eds. Mitchel B. Wallerstein and Stephen B. Gould, *Issues in Science and Technology*, vol. 4, no. 1 (Fall 1987), p. 48; Alman Metten, "Report Drawn Up on Behalf of the Committee on Energy, Research and Technology on Technology Transfer," European Parliament, *Report*, no. A 2-99/85 (30 September 1985), p. 23; and Sumner Benson, Deputy Director for Technology Cooperation and Security, Office of the Secretary of Defense, "Overcoming Complacency," *Society*, vol. 23, no. 5 (July/August 1986), p. 15.

59. The AAAS found that restricted conferences are very much the exception with numerous professional societies prohibiting closed or restricted sessions. In September 1985, 12 professional scientific societies informed Secretary of Defense Weinberger that they would no longer hold "export controlled" sessions at conferences they sponsored; letter to Secretary of Defense Caspar Weinberger from the presidents of 12 professional scientific societies, dated 17 September 1985, photocopy. See also Michael Schrage, "Scientists Defy Pentagon on Research Restrictions," *Washington Post*, 21 September 1985, p. 11; "U.S. Views Supercomputer Visa Limits," *Advanced Military Computing*, 7 October 1985, p. 4; Shattuck and Spence, p. 21, citing "Access to Scientific and Technical Information," American Association of Science Bulletin, Summer 1986; and U.S. Congress, Office of Technology Assessment, *Science, Technology*, p. 58.

60. Wallerstein, interview; Park, interview, Washington, DC, 28 June 1988; Relyea, interview; Runkle; interview and Tom Suttle, Institute For Electrical and Electronic Engineers, Inc., interview, Washington, DC, 6 July 1988.

61. One such institution is the University of Dayton according to Robert Park; Park, interview; Wallerstein and Runkle, interviews.

62. David A. Wilson, Co-Chairman of the DOD-University Forum Working Group on Export Controls, makes this point; Wilson, "Federal Control," p. 116, footnote 52.

63. This is the opinion of the Association of American Universities in a handbook for university administrators; Association of American Universities, *National Security Controls and University Research: Information for Investigators and Administrators*, prepared by the Association of American Universities for the Department of Defense-University Forum (Washington, DC: Association of American Universities, June 1987), p. 10.

64. Given the DOD's primacy in the classification of scientific work and inherent bureaucratic bias in favor of classification when there is any doubt, consistency is jeopardized according to Stephen B. Gould of the AAAS; Gould, "National Security," pp. 129-30.

65. Analysts believe that the "eyes open" approach is practical and justified. If the DOD funds research it has a right to dictate such terms to protect national security; interviews, Relyea, Department of State, and Department of Commerce.

66. David A. Wilson, "National Security Control," p. 91, footnote 15, citing Funk, "National Security Controls on the Dissemination of Privately Generated Scientific Information," *UCLA Law Review*, vol. 30, pp. 405-54; Theodore B. Olson, Assistant Attorney General, to Henry B. Mitman, Capital Goods Production Division, Department of Commerce, Memorandum on EAR (28 July 1981); and David A. Dorinson, Associate Counsel, University of California, to David A. Wilson, Executive Assistant to the President, University of California, *Constitutionality of the International Traffic in Arms Regulations and the Export Administration Regulations with Respect to Export of Technical Data in the Academic Setting* (26 August 1981).

4

Economic Evaluation of
U.S. High-Technology
Export Control Policy

Export controls impose a cost on economic performance. For example, some high-technology industries whose exports are heavily licensed must cope with administrative paperwork, bureaucratic red tape, and competition from foreign firms that may be free of such regulatory constraints. Many analysts, Congressional critics, and high-technology exporters believe that the burden on exporters is unsustainable. Strategic export controls were singled out by the President's Commission on Industrial Competitiveness and the National Academy of Sciences as contributing to declining U.S. technological leadership with potentially serious implications for domestic welfare and national security. These studies highlighted a crisis of confidence in relative U.S. economic and military strength, which is increasingly reliant on leading-edge technologies. As we have seen, the target of controls, principally Russia, other former Soviet republics now in the Commonwealth of Independent States, and the few remaining communist states of the former Soviet bloc, also sustain costs in terms of lagging behind the United States in key areas of dual-use high technology such as microprocessors and computers. The Russians must allocate additional scarce resources to overcome these lags, resources which could be used more productively in other sectors of the economy or to improve military capabilities. Limiting such options is one argument put forward in the United States for bearing the burden of controls. Utilizing Commerce Department data, General Accounting Office studies, and Congressional testimony, this chapter evaluates the economic implications for the United States of strategic export control policy and assesses whether the economic costs are acceptable.

EVALUATION

In theory, any export control regulation imposes some cost on the economy and individual businesses. There is general agreement on the necessity of export controls to protect national security. In essence, disagreement over the scope of controls and their effect on economic performance revolves around what constitutes an acceptable, supposedly zero-sum trade-off between more (or less) security and less (or more) economic welfare. If dynamic sectors of the economy are hard hit by controls, the macroeconomic implications are believed to have a far-reaching effect, at least in the longer term. For high-technology industries, because they are considered essential for future national prosperity and are a key element of the defense-industrial base, the impact of export controls is of particular concern.

Until quite recently, with government implementation of certain reforms and signs that these initiatives are having some positive effect, dissatisfaction with Washington's policy had been widespread in the business community. But even with an apparent easing of the regulatory burden, many business people remain dissatisfied. The litany of business' complaints is long, often-repeated, and frequently anecdotal.[1] They include the following.

First, a broad policy guideline for export controls, weaving together foreign policy, national security, and economic interests in the context of evolving global international political and economic evolution, is lacking. Although recent regulatory changes suggest dawning recognition of changed international political and economic realities, the underlying rationale for technology denial policy remains rooted in Cold War ideology and outdated bipolar concepts. Foreign economic policymaking has been slow to account for global structural changes and relatively diminished U.S. economic and technological leadership. Second, although the principal line agencies with responsibility for export controls incorporate their unique views in policy formulation and implementation, imbalance in the interagency process complicates licensing and slows needed liberalization and streamlining. The dominance of the DOD and the relative paucity of expertise and resources at the Commerce and State departments exacerbates an already lengthy, costly, and complicated licensing process. Control lists and regulations are too long and complicated. Reforms, including the foreign availability provision in the EAA (which mandates decontrol of a technology if similar technology is available from a non-U.S. source and if the President cannot negotiate an agreement with the non-U.S. supplier to control its export), have been blocked by bureaucratic inertia and in-fighting. Actual licensing reviews are often unnecessary and/or perfunctory since many licensed exports are destined for COCOM allies and are not militarily critical, and agency evaluators have little time to cope with large numbers of applications.

For individual firms, licensing delays and uncertainties impose a variety of costs that, while incurred by all licensees, are particularly burdensome for medium and small businesses.[2]   Serious sales losses have continued allegedly because U.S. exporters are put at a competitive disadvantage by controls that are much tougher than those enforced by COCOM allies and non-COCOM exporters of high technology. Lost sales may grow if foreign customers refuse to contract with U.S. firms owing to auditing requirements and the uncertainties associated with U.S. reexport regulations. U.S. firms are, so the argument goes, perceived by foreign clients as unreliable suppliers with the result that distribution networks erode and future add-on and spare parts sales are lost as foreign companies de-Americanize their products and seek non-U.S. suppliers. Large investments are then required to attempt to reestablish markets once buying preferences change.[3]

Vocal complaints by businesses of lost sales and declining competitiveness owing to national security controls are generally not backed by publicly available microeconomic studies by the affected companies and industries. This lack of evidence undermines industry's case. A systematic examination of Congressional hearings since 1975 yielded no documented studies of costs submitted for the record by the American Electronics Association, the Electronics Industry Association, Dresser Industries, the Computer and Business Equipment Manufacturer's Association, the Scientific Apparatus Makers Association, the National Machine Tool Builders Association, the National Association of Manufacturers, and Rockwell International.[4] These industry groups and companies represent a broad cross section of electronics, computer, and other high-technology industries that consistently complain of the adverse affect controls have on exports. While some industry representatives did acknowledge that in-house studies had been undertaken that prove there are significant losses, they argued that these studies contain proprietary information that precludes their public release. Other interviewees cited the difficulty of identifying lost sales because the members of an industry-wide association did not keep such records. They describe a reluctance among companies to dwell on lost sales, and companies find it very difficult to isolate a lost sale due exclusively to U.S. controls and regulations. Many representatives cited the 1987 NAS study *Balancing the National Interest* as the best available estimate of losses.[5]

An example of the incompleteness of documented industry studies claiming to show losses is suggested by statistics supplied by the National Machine Tool Builders Association (NMTBA). For example, NMTBA figures show that U.S. machine tool exports to the U.S.S.R. rose from $6.2 million in 1970 to a high of $89.1 million in 1975. Thereafter, yearly U.S. exports generally declined so that by 1988, the United States exported $1.3 million to the U.S.S.R. Furthermore, NMTBA figures show that in 1988, European (particularly West German and Swiss) and Japanese suppliers accounted for the bulk of machine tools exported by the West to the Soviet and Eastern European market. Given the close ties between Council for Mutual Economic Assistance (COMECON) economies, generally less sophisticated machine tools were also imported in significant numbers from, for example, East Germany. The NMTBA argues that the decline in U.S. exports is due to narrow interpretation of COCOM rules by U.S. authorities while other COCOM countries are much more flexible in their rule interpretations. This assertion is questionable, at least for the period before the general tightening of controls in 1979. Other explanations include the increasing competitiveness of other countries' machine tool exporters (Japan's in particular) coupled with a relative deterioration in the U.S. machine tool industry, the cyclical nature of the machine tool market, and possibly the developing economic troubles in the Soviet bloc which reached crisis proportions by the late 1980s. Former Commerce official Clyde Prestowitz points out that tight controls imposed on U.S. machine tool exports during the Cold War, when U.S. industry leadership was unchallenged, also fostered development of efficient foreign competitors who wanted machine tool supplies free of U.S.-imposed regulations. The NMTBA also alleges outright cheating by COCOM allies. In light of the Toshiba-Kongsberg case and evidence compiled by Norwegian investigators, there is some data supporting the NMTBA's contention. NMTBA statistics include suggestive data showing U.S. exports to the P.R.C. *rising* from $1.5 million in 1981 to nearly $41 million in 1989. This rise is attributable to the liberalization of controls on trade with China and by implication suggests that similar liberalization could be expected to increase exports to the U.S.S.R. and Eastern Europe. Unfortunately, no definite or verifiable empirical connection between lost sales and national security export controls is established. Instead, allegations are presented backed by discrete examples and other anecdotal evidence.[6]

Any attempt to quantify the economic costs of controls is fraught with uncertainty. Identifying controls as *the* specific cause of a decline in exports is difficult given the complex interaction and impact of other factors, including exchange rates, non tariff barriers, and unfair trade practices.[7] However, as debate over the impact of controls has grown, several studies have attempted to quantify the costs of controls. Unfortunately, the wide variation in estimates suggests the difficulty of such measurements.[8] The only microeconomic study (not done by industry) that an industry association representative did cite as accurate is a study of controls' impact on analytic instruments done by the National Academy of Sciences.

Perhaps the most widely quoted analysis in recent years was the 1987 NAS study *Balancing the National Interest* (Allen Report), which influenced passage of the 1988 Omnibus Trade Act's decontrol provisions.[9] Because it criticized the existing export control framework and its conclusions were favorable to business, exporters and Congressional critics generally hailed it. But as with all such studies, detractors question the report's bias, methodology, and conclusions.[10] While the NAS study's attempt to formulate and apply a methodological model is an important step, the difficulty in disaggregating the effect of controls from other factors suggests a need for a judicious weighing of its conclusions.

A representative of the Scientific Apparatus Makers Association (SAMA), while noting that SAMA had not been able to identify costs in its own studies, did praise the NAS's microeconomic study of analytic instruments included in the Allen Report arguing that the NAS finding was consistent with industry experience.[11] Analytic instruments can have dual-use applications and also contained certain embedded microprocessors that were themselves subject to U.S. and COCOM controls during the mid-1980s. The NAS found that the value of exports of analytic instruments rose 7 percent over projected levels, after U.S. controls were eased in early 1984, compared to the level expected if there had been no change in controls. When this relaxation was rescinded in late 1984, exports fell 12 percent (by value) below projected levels (through the third quarter of 1985).[12] From 1980 to 1987 (inclusive), the value of *worldwide* U.S. exports of "professional and scientific instruments" (a broad category of exports which most closely resembles the tariff classification for analytic instruments) rose an *average* of 3.1 percent yearly.[13] In 1983, exports of "professional and scientific instruments" were valued at $6,867 million.[14] Assuming that the projected rise in the value of this category of exports would be 3.1 percent (with controls unchanged), this is equivalent to a rise to approximately $7,080 million for 1984. However, the 7 percent rise in exports owing to the removal of controls is equivalent to projected 1984 exports of $7,576 million. Thus, one estimate of losses owing to controls would be $496 million. This is the difference between the projected value of exports had there been no change in controls, and the projected value of exports after controls were removed in 1984. Furthermore, as noted, exports of analytic instruments fell 12 percent below projected levels in 1985. Utilizing the average growth rate of exports (by value) from 1980 to 1987 (3.1%), the *projected* value of exports in 1985 (assuming no change in controls) would have been nearly $7,300 million. However, with the reimposition of controls, the 12 percent decline was equivalent to a decline to $6,424 million. Thus, the estimated loss owing to reimposition of controls was about $876 million. In total, estimated export losses for 1984-85 were therefore about $1,372 million, representing about 9.5 percent of the projected value of global exports of professional and scientific instruments for 1984-1985.

It should be borne in mind that numerous exogenous factors could have influenced export levels including fluctuating exchange rates and cyclical swings in demand. Table 22 (see Appendix) also shows that the value of U.S. exports to Western Europe of "Measuring, checking, etc. instruments" (presumably including analytic instruments) *grew* over 43 percent in 1983-84 and that the *average* growth in the value of this category of exports from 1980 to 1987 was almost 38 percent per year. The sharp increase in 1983-84 could be expected to have resulted in a relative slump in demand in succeeding years as importers presumably would have fulfilled requirements. This cyclical falloff in demand may have contributed to declines in exports attributed to controls in 1984-85. In addition, the 38 percent growth rate tends to weaken the argument that controls are *consistently* depressing exports, at least to Western Europe. While the NAS's microeconomic study is suggestive, the absence of similar publicly available studies of the analytic instruments industry covering a longer time, or of studies of other individual commodities, or broader ranges of commodity categories, tends to undermine industry claims.

Although empirical data are sketchy, government data on export controls, testimony by officials, and data on high-technology exports *suggest* the *relative* impact that controls have on exports. While inconclusive, data principally from annual DOC export administration reports, DOC studies of the U.S. market share in certain high technologies, annual export figures, GAO studies of the administrative process, and testimony suggest that:

* The licensing system is less of a burden on exporters than claimed.
* License processing times are slowly improving and recent liberalization efforts may be benefiting technology exports.
* The overall impact on the high-technology sector is less than feared.

(Fuller textual elaboration describing and documenting the basis for these observations follows in the remainder of the chapter.) In fact, rapid sales growth in some high technologies (e.g., automatic data processing equipment, CAD/CAM, and robots) and dominant U.S. market shares belie the alleged negative impact of controls. There are some costs and hindrances imposed by the licensing process that may have a long-term negative cumulative impact for both large and small exporters. In the short term, however, small exporters apparently do bear a greater burden of these costs than do larger firms having more experience with controls. However, interviews suggest that regulatory liberalization and streamlining are easing some of the uncertainty and delay associated with licensing.

Based on government statistics, license processing does not appear to be unduly restrictive. Tables 1-6 (see Appendix) show the number of licenses denied or returned without action (RWA)[15] for applicants wishing to export to the West, the P.R.C., and to certain neutral communist countries. (These destinations are collectively termed by the government as Free World, FW, a euphemism identifying a specific category of country in such government publications as the Department of Commerce's *Export Administration Annual Report*). These tables also give similar figures for exports to the U.S.S.R. and allies. While the DOC statistics do not disaggregate licenses denied solely for national security reasons from licenses denied because of foreign policy, nuclear proliferation, or short supply reasons, a substantial proportion are for dual-use goods. This is an important qualification since including denials and RWAs for other than national security reasons tends to skew the figures.

Tables 1-6 show that the number of applications have more than doubled for exports to the Free World since the mid-1970s.[16] From 1980 to 1987, the number of applications to the U.S.S.R. and allies increased over 46 percent (Tables 1 and 3). The FW increase was partly due to liberalized trade with the P.R.C. (curtailed in 1989) and government emphasis on--and business awareness of--controls because of growing concerns over losses of sophisticated U.S. technology. Wider awareness also suggests that compliance has improved and that businesses--while perhaps unhappy with the additional regulatory burden--are not necessarily forgoing exports because of allegedly tighter licensing procedures. Significantly, neither denial or RWA rates for Free World and Soviet and allied destinations appear to be consistently or excessively high. For the period surveyed, the denial rate for Free World exports has consistently remained below 1 percent (Tables 2 and 4). Reexport licenses also had a low denial rate.[17] The apparent increase in RWAs is expected given the increase in applications and, consequently, larger numbers of inexperienced applicants who are unfamiliar with the licensing process.

Low denial rates do not by themselves prove that exporters are not unduly burdened. As suggested by Tables 9-11, during the 1970s and 1980s lengthy license processing delays may well have disadvantaged exporters even though a license was eventually granted. For example, if a foreign competitor was granted a license more quickly, a U.S. sale could be lost. Further elaboration on license processing times appears below.

Applications for exports to the U.S.S.R. and allies average about 9.1 percent of *total* processed applications to both FW and U.S.S.R. and allied destinations. While the DOD is authorized by law to review all exports to the *U.S.S.R. and allies*, in practice the DOD only reviews about one-third of licenses to these destinations (see Table 4). This amounted to approximately 3.1 percent of *all* applications to the FW, U.S.S.R., and its allies from 1979 to 1987. Responsibility for the rest is delegated to the DOC. As expected, both denials and RWAs are higher for licenses to the U.S.S.R. and allies, although foreign policy controls inflated the figure during the early 1980s.

When FW and U.S.S.R. and allied denials and RWAs are viewed as a percentage of combined, processed FW and U.S.S.R. and allied applications, the figures are lower with U.S.S.R. and allied denials remaining under 1 percent. As a historical comparison, in 1967 about 2 percent of exports to Eastern Europe were denied. Average denial and RWA rates for the FW and the U.S.S.R. and allies are about 0.3 and 0.4 percent, respectively (Table 5). Overall, as Table 6 shows, combined denials and RWAs averaged about 12.4 percent from 1978 to 1987.

Of particular concern to business is the effect of licensing on exports to major trading partners. While hard evidence is lacking, Table 7 and DOC data on reexport applications are suggestive. Table 7 indicates that for licenses for exports to COCOM and allied countries, presumably including both exports which will remain in the importing country and goods which will be reexported from these destinations, denials are negligible. Since many U.S. exporters also ship subcomponents to foreign manufacturers and subsidiaries to be incorporated into other commodities and reshipped to third countries, reexport licensing is also an important factor in business planning. Data from the DOC indicate that in 1985 only 0.08 percent (11) applications for reexports to COCOM from the United States were denied and 0.43 percent (61) of applications from COCOM (i.e., from the U.S. and other COCOM states) to non-COCOM destinations were denied.[18] Table 8 also suggests that reviews of many licenses for exports to Europe and Asia are unnecessary given the relatively small percentage of exports to these areas controlled for national security reasons. Furthermore, Table 1 shows that since 1986, the number of processed applications to FW destinations has declined, suggesting that decontrol and liberalization efforts principally directed to reducing West-West licensing are having some effect. Greater efficiency, more rapid automated license processing, and improved responsiveness to license inquiries on the part of the DOC is acknowledged by business people and Congressional analysts, including Motorola's John Copeland, Jim LeMunyon of the American Electronics Association, London-based representatives of major U.S. computer and office equipment firms, and Eric Hirschhorn, representing the Industry Coalition on Technology Transfer.[19]   These measures have greatly improved U.S. licensing, according to some exporters. Foreign observers expressed envy over the resources and efficiency of the U.S. system.[20] When the provision of the 1988 Omnibus Trade Act, which in effect mandates creation of a license-free zone in Europe among qualified countries, is fully implemented, this liberalization should be reflected in a further decline in the number of applications. Liberalization should also end criticism that most West-West licensing is an unnecessary paper exercise since the vast majority of licenses are approved, as was the case during the early 1980s.[21]

According to some exporters, added costs and delays are incurred owing to unnecessary applications for exports to the COCOM area. A sale may hinge on which firm can promise quickest delivery and a U.S. exporter is at a disadvantage if its license is delayed. Tables 9, 10, and 11 suggest that license processing time has been relatively lengthy and, although processing time has improved and appears to meet statutory deadlines, the U.S. continues to take longer than several of the COCOM allies to process applications to several non-COCOM areas. Although a potential disadvantage, interviewees stated that an experienced exporter, aware of the licensing process, factors the expected processing time into the calculations for fulfilling a delivery.[22] Furthermore, a U.S. supplier may offer certain advantages (e.g., better price, servicing, or the best product), which outweigh the license problem in the foreign customer's view. As for exports to COCOM, the data suggest that exporters' criticism is overstated. As Table 11 indicates, the decline in U.S. processing time is bringing the United States close to the times of its export competitors--at least for exports to the COCOM area. Because of differing and imprecise definitions, exact comparisons are difficult. However, for exports to its most important markets, the COCOM area and the wider Free World, speeded-up processing appears to have narrowed the gap. This is significant given the size of these markets and past complaints that slow processing hurts U.S. export competitiveness, and causes foreign customers to seek alternative non-U.S. sources who can supply similar technology in less time without having to go through a lengthy licensing process. There is some justification for charges that licenses to COCOM are merely a paper exercise, as Table 7 suggests. However, given the rise in the total number of processed licenses and the fall in license processing time for exports to COCOM (Table 10), the United States does appear to have improved its licensing efficiency.

Comparison of license processing times at different periods during the 1970s and 1980s reveals a drop in the percentage of licenses processed in less than thirty days between the mid-1970s and early 1980s. By 1981, over 70 percent of licenses to all destinations were taking the DOC longer than thirty days to process (Table 9). In part, this is explained by the increase in applications submitted, the increased use of foreign policy sanctions necessitating tighter license reviews, and a relative lack of resources at the DOC to cope with the expanded workload. Tables 9, 10, and 12 also show that the DOC's processing efficiency increased by 1987 in tandem with a growth in the DOC's export administration budget and staffing. Backlogs were reduced, claimed overall average license processing time (i.e., West-West and West-East) was down to fourteen days, and 80 percent of all licenses to all destinations were processed within fifteen days. Furthermore, for the critical area of licenses to COCOM destinations (excluding the U.S.S.R. and Eastern Europe), claimed DOC processing time was down to five days in 1988, well within the fifteen-day statutory deadline for COCOM destinations mandated by the 1985 EAAA.[23] These apparent improvements should be compared with the NAS study's findings that actual processing time for *all* destinations was double the DOC's claim of twentyseven days in 1986. Electronic issuance of licenses will presumably reduce processing time considerably, at least for some exporters.[24]

License processing times for exports to the U.S.S.R. and Eastern Europe have also fallen. Both the DOC and the DOD have significantly reduced average processing times since the mid-1980s (Table 10). Furthermore, as noted in Table 5, while applications for exports to this area annually make up less than 10 percent of total processed applications, denials and RWAs have also fallen during the 1980s. Faster licensing and fewer denials suggest that technology transfer may be increasing. However, just as total U.S. trade with the U.S.S.R. and Eastern Europe has declined to well under 1 percent of world trade turnover during the 1980s, U.S. high-technology exports to the area have also remained negligible. From 1980 to 1987, U.S. high-technology exports to the U.S.S.R. and Eastern Europe averaged about 0.2 percent of total exports (by value). In comparison, the COCOM area received an average of slightly over 51 percent of total U.S. exports of high technology, and by 1987 its share had increased by nearly 5.5 percent over 1980. The Soviet and Eastern European share remained virtually unchanged over the same period.[25]

In the important category of Distribution Licenses (DL), processing time has also dropped from 200 to about seventyfive days (Table 13). The DL is particularly important for multinationals making numerous bulk shipments overseas to subsidiaries and foreign distributors, since the DL eliminates individual validated licenses for each transaction. Concurrent with the drop in processing time, more stringent auditing is now required. This raises companies' administrative costs,[26] angers foreign firms, and provokes extraterritoriality issues.

While the number of active and new DLs has fallen, the apparent damage to larger U.S. exporters appears to be minimal, at least in the short term. This is so for several reasons. First, the DL had been abused prior to reintroduction of auditing, thus a trade-off between some losses incurred by exporters and enhanced national security appears reasonable. Second, major COCOM allies, including the U.K., Germany, and France, have compromised on auditing, which has eased tensions somewhat while the United States has also liberalized West-West licensing rules. Third, over 75 percent of audits have been of domestic U.S. firms and their subsidiaries. Finally, there has also been an increase in the numbers of general licenses and firms have developed alternative arrangements that make up for some of the decline in active DLs. At least some foreign-based U.S. subsidiaries and European firms have not found auditing requirements too burdensome or have decided that continued access to the U.S. market outweighs trade with the U.S.S.R. and Eastern Europe or other potentially suspicious end users. Deep interdependence between U.S. and foreign business further enhances U.S. leverage in this regard. They therefore grudgingly accept U.S. requirements, particularly after their governments worked out compromises on inspections.[27]

Larger U.S. firms can better afford to pursue lengthy licensing decisions and the costs of internal auditing than can smaller firms. The DL does benefit larger firms for which exports are a major ongoing interest. Smaller firms, as the NAS found, are generally less experienced with complex licensing procedures and more likely to be denied a license. Because overseas markets are generally less important for them, they are less likely to use a DL and therefore they rely relatively more on the individual validated license, which must be documented and tracked each time an application and export is made. It appears, therefore, that there is unintended regulatory discrimination against smaller firms.[28] Compounding export delays are the DOD's allegedly obstructionist role and activities.

The Defense Department is frequently blamed for delays in licensing and decontrolling widely available technology. The Allen Report cautioned against DOD dominance of the interagency process and consequent overemphasis on military and/or technical security to the detriment of economic and other policy considerations.[29] While these charges were valid in the recent past, the relatively small number of licenses (as a percentage of *total* applications) the DOD reviews suggests that its overall effect may be overstated. Furthermore, the DOC does not always defer to the DOD. As outlined below, studies suggest that some of the DOD's activities are duplicative and unnecessary but that the DOD's expertise is not being fully consulted. However, poor cooperation between the DOC and DOD and the DOC's slow implementation of the foreign availability provisions mandated by Congress also contribute to slowing the decontrol effort.

Processing of licenses by the DOD has slowly improved since the early 1980s, after efficiency fell considerably from the levels claimed in the mid-1970s (see Table 14). Given the relative sensitivity of cases, DOD examines (cases also examined by the DOC), longer processing times are to be expected. The Defense Department reviews only selected cases for export to the U.S.S.R. and Eastern Europe or to several Free World countries, and exports of certain particularly sensitive equipment, including nuclear-related technology and supercomputers. Based on statistics in Tables 3 and 5, for *1979-1985*, DOD reviews of exports to the U.S.S.R. and Eastern Europe were never more than 3.5 percent of yearly processed applications to *all* destinations (i.e., FW and U.S.S.R. and allies). From 1979 to 1987, the average was 3.1 percent. By 1985, when the DOD was authorized to review licenses for reexports to fifteen Free World countries in eight product categories, the additional cases did boost the percentage of licenses the DOD reviewed, although it remained under 10 percent according to the GAO and fell after 1986 along with a 47 percent decline in the total number of applications reviewed by the DOD during fiscal years (FY) 1986-1988.[30]

Although it is possible that the added DOD authority may slow overall licensing, given the shrinking number of Free World exports the DOD reviews, relatively improved DOD processing time, and the relative unimportance--for U.S. exports--of the Free World countries for which the DOD reviews licenses, significant added delays are unlikely.[31] Furthermore, the General Accounting Office found that the DOC tends to ignore DOD recommendations on West-West licensing and that it adds little to the licensing process. As illustrated in Table 15, of 611 applications which the DOD recommended for approval, the DOC actually approved only 78 percent and denied or returned over 20 percent. Of the sixty applications the DOD recommended for denial, 65 percent were approved by the DOC and only 5 percent were denied outright. A larger sample covering June 1987 to June 1988 did indicate that the DOC generally agreed with the DOD recommendations for approval, although the DOC concurred in only 13 percent of the cases where the DOD recommended denial. A breakdown of West-West and West-East cases shows that DOD recommendations had a definite impact on DOC decisions in 44 percent of the West-East cases sampled, but the DOD had an impact in only 6 percent of the DOC's West-West licensing decisions. These results also suggest that DOD influence on overall West-West license processing is marginal and that it contributes little to the review process.[32]   Yet the DOD's bureaucratic clout remains controversial.

Interagency conflict between the DOC and DOD, and tardy DOC implementation of legislation did significantly slow decontrol efforts based on foreign availability determinations prior to 1986. But according to the DOC's *Annual Report* for FY 1987 and GAO studies,[33] the foreign availability program has decontrolled more items. Furthermore, unilateral controls--which critics charge impose a competitive disadvantage on U.S. exporters if there are foreign sources for unilaterally controlled items--have also declined since the early 1970s. These trends suggest a relative easing of the burden of controls--at least for some exporters--although efforts to reduce the overall number of controlled items should continue.

Under the EAA, the President is directed to consider foreign availability as a reason for authorizing decontrols, unless he determines that controls are required for reasons of national security. Beginning with the 1977 EAA, Congress directed the DOC to consider foreign availability during list reviews. However, the foreign availability effort was hampered by poor coordination among different agencies and poor utilization of available information. In 1983, the DOC formally instituted a foreign availability program to coordinate the overall effort. After further delay, the 1985 EAA required the DOC to establish an Office of Foreign Availability (OFA).[34] Besides inertia in instituting the program, the DOC has been criticized for ignoring recommendations of technical advisory committees--which include industry representatives and which recommend products for decontrol--and for delaying until 1986 before issuing the first decontrol order based on a positive finding of foreign availability.

The DOC is required to solicit and examine claims of foreign availability submitted by industry. However, business representatives generally have a low opinion of technical advisory bodies, which include company representatives, whose task it is to assist with the foreign availability effort. The perception is that more often than not, the advisory bodies' recommendations are ignored. Moreover, the highly technical nature of the work and the difficulty of gathering comprehensive data from around the world exacerbate delays. Adding to industry frustration is a provision in the EAA that allows the President to delay a foreign availability decontrol action for up to eighteen months while negotiations are undertaken to eliminate foreign availability.[35]

The GAO also criticized the DOC's lengthy foreign availability determination studies for exceeding statutory deadlines. For example, while the 1985 EAAA stipulates a ninety-day deadline for the DOC to make a foreign availability determination once foreign availability is certified by a technical advisory committee, in 1987 the GAO found that the DOC had taken six to twentyeight months to assess several foreign availability claims. The GAO also suggested that the DOC was reluctant to finalize a determination in the face of DOD opposition, although DOD concurrence is not required. Furthermore, the GAO and DOC officials charge that often the DOD has been unwilling to share some relevant information and expertise pertinent to making determinations. The DOD's evidence against decontrol was sometimes deemed inconclusive, while often the DOC did not adequately share its information or contact relevant agencies to gather intelligence.[36]

The 1985 EAA specifies that the DOC must only consult with the DOD and is not bound by DOD recommendations. But lack of DOC assertiveness and adroit DOD maneuvering often permit the latter to block decontrol decisions at the National Security Council (NSC) level. The DOC's vacillation and/or timidity may also be a function of the conflicting personalities of agency officials.[37]

A small sign of Congressional efforts to redress the balance is a provision (Section 5(f)(7)) added to the 1988 Omnibus Trade Act. It specifies that all departments must allow OFA "access to any information from a laboratory or other facility within such department or agency."[38] This language strengthens the DOC's hand vis-a-vis the DOD by addressing charges that the DOD had not allowed the OFA adequate access to DOD scientists and analysts, who are experts on technical matters pertinent to foreign availability assessments. The provision's effectiveness is dependent on the extent to which the DOD complies with the law--which it often does not.

After considerable delay and mounting Congressional criticism the DOC appeared to be fully implementing the foreign availability program by 1987. In FY 1987, eleven items were decontrolled based on foreign availability determinations, but industry remains understandably skeptical of the still underutilized foreign availability program.[39] Despite this skepticism, the foreign availability decontrols, together with the 67 percent decrease in number of categories subject to unilateral controls from 1978 to 1987 (Table 16), are evidence that the Commodity Control List (CCL) is slowly being reduced, although it still does not conform precisely with the COCOM list, which most members pattern national lists after. While reductions may help some exporters,[40] the positive cumulative impact could be negated. If decontrol proceeds too slowly owing to deepening interagency disagreements and rivalry--although GAO studies indicate that DOC-DOD friction is overstated (see Table 15)--exporters may still be at a disadvantage. The problem may become acute given two-year cycles for the emergence of new generations of high technology.[41] Commodity decontrol policy clearly faces a formidable challenge owing to rapid technological developments and the globalization of technological capabilities.

A sharp erosion of U.S. market share in high technology or a significant and steady decline in U.S. exports of high technology could be signs that export controls are undermining U.S. competitiveness and causing U.S. technology to be designed out of foreign commodities.[42] Tables 17-25 do not suggest that this is occurring. For example, Table 17 is derived from a DOC study comparing the export shares of the United States and thirteen other Organization of Economic Cooperation and Development (OECD) countries, all producers and exporters of sophisticated dual-use high technology. In five principal high-technology commodity categories, for the period 1965-1982, the U.S. share among all fourteen countries fell 2.7 percent. It is important to note that the U.S. high-technology trade position and market share deteriorated substantially from 1982 to 1988, although much of this decline can be attributed to several factors including unfavorable exchange rates and global structural shifts unrelated to export controls.[43] However, for the period surveyed in Table 17, the United States actually increased its export share of office, computing, and accounting machines. Shares increased as well--between 1976 and 1982--in aircraft and parts and in engines, turbines, and parts. Furthermore, in the NAS study, *Balancing the National Interest*, the five categories in Table 17 are described as the most heavily affected by national security export controls on dual-use goods accounting for nearly 83 percent of U.S. high-technology exports in 1985.[44] Although the NAS based its conclusions regarding lost export sales on extrapolations from analysis of how one high-technology category--analytic instruments--was affected by controls, its estimate of total lost export sales does not suggest severe damage to U.S. exporters. For example, an export decline of 12 percent compared to expected sales was attributed to reinstatement of more restrictive controls on analytic instruments commencing in late 1984 through the third quarter of 1985. This figure was used to extrapolate estimated losses of total West-West and West-East export sales for 1985, the combined losses coming to $7.3 billion. For 1985, DOC data indicate that the total export value of the five high-technology commodity categories in Table 17 plus five additional high-technology categories was $68,425 million.[45] Based on the NAS estimate of total export sales losses for 1985, these losses amounted to about 10.6 percent of the total export value of the ten categories. This suggests that the overall impact of controls on exports is overstated.

The NAS also concluded that 40 percent of all U.S. exports of non-military manufactures in 1985 were subject to controls. About 42 percent of manufactured exports were of high-technology commodities and over 48 percent of U.S. high-technology exports consisted of goods in the aircraft and computing categories in Table 17.[46] Since these two categories consistently outperformed the overall average of nine high-technology commodities (labeled as "Ave. 1-5+Other") in each year group, this *suggests* that export controls have not been unduly harmful to aircraft, computing, and related goods. In fact, the aircraft and computing categories (categories 2 and 3) show the strongest growth rates (Table 18). Further-more, given the dual-use sensitivity and the large proportion of licenses for exports in these two categories (particularly computers), we might expect: (1) that controls disproportionately affect these exports, and (2) a significant fall in the U.S. share of exports of these commodities if controls were hindering exports. Neither trend is evident. Tables 24-25 also indicate that U.S. competitiveness and market share in certain key dual-use high-technology products remains formidable. Exports of robots and of computer aided design and manufacturing systems (CAD/CAM) grew rapidly from 1977 to 1983, with forecasts for continued growth. Surveys of U.S. CAD-/CAM markets in Europe indicate that U.S. sales doubled each year during the 1980s and that market share ranged from 70 percent in the Federal Republic of Germany to 90 percent in Sweden.[47] Based on this assessment of critical dual-use commodities--believed to be increasingly essential for Soviet military modernization--it appears that, at most, strategic export controls have a minor impact on exports and competitiveness.

A similar conclusion can be drawn from Tables 18-23. Although Table 19 indicates that the rate of average increase in value of selected high-technology exports slowed from 1977 to 1987, it is difficult to isolate export controls as the chief cause of this slowdown. For example, unfavorable exchange rates and a slump in demand also depressed sales. Furthermore, Tables 20-23 indicate that the value of high-technology exports globally and to important trading partners showed an overall increase from 1980 to 1987. Although there have been fluctuations from year to year, there appears to be no pattern of steady decline. In addition, in selected years, growth has been quite strong. In the case of the P.R.C.--a country subject to U.S. controls stricter than West-West controls--export growth was strong relative to growth globally, in developed countries, and in the E.C. area (Table 20).

Another indication that controls appear to have a minimal impact comes from categories 2-5 in Tables 21 and 22. These categories include computer and sophisticated exports incorporating microelectronic components. Each category had particularly high average growth rates for exports globally and to Western Europe from 1980 to 1987.

Overall costs to the economy in terms of associated GNP losses also appear to be minimal. Table 26 projects the value of U.S. high-technology exports from 1978 to 1987 assuming that there were no controls on exports. The projection is derived from the estimate of total lost West-West and West-East export sales for 1985 reported in the NAS study *Balancing the National Interest*. The NAS estimated that there was a $7.3 billion export sales loss in 1985 owing to national security controls, representing about 10.6 percent of the total value of ten categories of high-technology exports in 1985. The ten categories together constitute the bulk of total U.S. high-technology exports by value and come under the Commerce Department's "DOC-3" definition.[48] In Table 26, the following is assumed. First, the NAS estimate is assumed to be approximately correct; no other adequately documented estimate based on econometric studies appears in the literature. Second, to account for exogenous variables that may have caused higher losses in specific years, it is assumed that the NAS estimate was 50 percent too low. Therefore, a figure of 15.9 percent is derived as the projected yearly loss owing to controls. The projected value of high-technology exports (assuming that exports would have been 15.9 percent higher without controls) is then calculated. By utilizing a multiplier of two (also used in the NAS study) and multiplying this with the difference between projected and actual exports, associated GNP losses are determined. As Tables 26 and 27 show, these high-technology export losses were minimal from 1978 to 1987, never amounting to more than seven-tenths of one percent of yearly GNP.

These findings suggest that strategic export controls alone have a relatively slight impact on the U.S. GNP. Export administration reforms, including higher *de-minimus* standards instituted by the DOC, appear to be having the desired effect.[49] Smaller firms and companies that are inexperienced with the export administration and licensing process are disproportionately penalized in the present regulatory environment, although gradual liberalization--particularly of West-West trade--should benefit these exporters. Overall, these data suggest that there are insufficient grounds to conclude that the reputation and performance of U.S. high-technology firms are adversely affected or that a widespread trend toward de-Americanization or designing out U.S. high-technology components is evident among foreign customers.

SUMMARY

Military and economic security pose dilemmas for policymakers in the context of the debate over strategic export controls: ehancing one may diminish the other.   Yet this chapter's economic evaluation *suggests* that while some U.S. economic interests are sacrificed because of the inevitable costs associated with controls, their impact on exporters may be overstated. Disaggregating the influence of controls per se is very difficult. However, examination of the licensing process and interviews with, among others, John Copeland of Motorola and Jim LeMunyon of the American Electronics Association, *suggest* that while U.S. exporters (particularly smaller, inexperienced firms) may be disadvantaged by a relatively cumbersome regulatory and bureaucratic process, recent streamlining, West-West liberalization, and compromises with trading partners have improved conditions.

Adding to the impression of relative health of high-technology exporters are longer-term statistics showing robust U.S. market shares and dual-use high-technology sales growth since the mid-1960s. This datum *suggests* that de-Americanization (i.e., the designing out of U.S.-origin components from foreign technology) is not a firmly established trend overseas among foreign firms located in important markets.   Specifically, while we might expect controls to affect computer and related exports in particular (since a large percentage of licensed exports are microelectronics-based technology), strong growth in this export category implies that controls have had at most a marginal impact on exports of microelectronics-based technology.

But some cause for concern is warranted particularly if progress in West-West decontrol is arrested or if the product decontrol program and license processing efforts are allowed to stagnate because of interagency inertia and disputes. Yet liberalization must not be implemented at the cost of harming national security.   In addition, the radical transformations in governments and social upheaval in Eastern Europe, a loosening of Russian military domination over the area with prospects for sharply reduced East-West tensions, and Eastern European desire for Western technology and trade raise important questions about COCOM's future and the future of strategic export controls.   These rapidly changing circumstances may well alter the entire postwar framework of assumptions upon which policymakers formulated national security policy.   And this raises the issue of the future relevance of controls, which must be weighed as the United States strives to balance conflicting national interests.

The final chapter summarizes the study's principal findings, assesses U.S. policy, and poses the question of whether the present export control regime should be retained, reformed, or abolished. Possible alternative scenarios are set forth and discussed in order to formulate some conclusions and policy prescriptions suggested by the issues raised in the study.

NOTES

1. When asked, industry representatives claim that propriety interests preclude them from releasing in-house quantitative studies that purport to show how controls damage exports.

2. These costs include warehousing and carrying costs, contract penalties if deliveries are delayed, added transportation costs to make up for delays, and lost sales. Internal administrative and documentation costs are incurred, especially owing to the auditing requirements recently imposed by the DOC for Distribution License holders. Associated costs can be substantial according to interviewees, even for larger, well-established firms that are also responsible for establishing proper control and in-house auditing procedures in overseas subsidiaries as well; Jerome Drucker, Manager, Corporate Export/Trade, Digital Equipment Corp., interview, Washington, DC, 4 May 1988.

3. Businesses and some analysts also argue that losses of sales and market share by dual-use high-technology producers will depress revenues. This will result in falling investments and a cutback in R&D. This in turn hinders innovation in fields and products that are, or could be, important for the economy and national security. If the U.S. defense-industrial base is allowed to erode owing to the effects of export controls, growing dependence on foreign sources for militarily critical high technologies will threaten national security.

4. The index examined was the Congressional Information Service, Inc., selected volumes, *Four Year Cumulative Index*, *Annual Index*, *Annual Abstracts*, *CIS/Index* (Index, Abstracts), 1975-90 (Washington, DC: Congressional Information Service, Inc.).

5. These views are drawn from in-person and telephone interviews. A partial list includes John Copeland, Director, Export Administration, Motorola, Inc. interview, Washington, DC, 25 February 1988; Drucker, interview; not-for-attribution interview, U.S. Chamber of Commerce, Washington, DC, 14 April 1988; Mike Duff, Scientific Apparatus Makers Association, Washington, DC, telephone interview, 5 April 1990; the Senior Manager, Government Relations, American Electronics Association, Washington, DC, telephone interview, 5 April 1990; Kevin Shannon, Electronic Industries Association, Washington, DC, telephone interview, 5 April 1990; and Ann Urban, Computer and Business Manufacturer's Association, Washington, DC, telephone interview, 13 April 1990.

6. U.S. and allies' export figures were supplied by Daniel L. Keen, International Economist, National Machine Tool Builders' Association (photocopied). For a sample of testimony suggesting how controls hinder U.S. machine tool exports, see James H. Mack, Public Affairs Director, NMTBA, letter to Rep. Helen D. Bentley,

21 September 1989 (photocopied); Sen. Don Riegle, Jr., et al., letter to President George Bush, 9 February 1990 (photocopied); and James A. Gray, President, NMTBA, "Machine Tools: Exporting for Survival," in *Common Sense in U.S.-Soviet Trade*, eds. Margaret Chapman and Carl Moray (Washington, DC: American Committee on East-West Accord, August 1983), pp. 133-38. See also Clyde V. Prestowitz, Jr., *Trading Places: How We Allowed Japan to Take the Lead* (New York: Basic Books, 1988), p. 220.

7. Industry representatives also acknowledge the impact of factors other than export controls. See Thomas A. Christiansen, Manager, International Trade Relations, Hewlett Packard, prepared statement on behalf of the American Electronics Association, 10 April 1986, in U.S. Congress, House Committee on Foreign Affairs, Subcommittee on International Economic Policy and Trade, *Omnibus Trade Legislation (Vol. II)*, hearings, 99th Congress, 2nd session, 10, 17 April 1986 (Washington, DC: U.S. GPO, 1987), p. 51. See also U.S. Congress, House Committee on Science, Space, and Technology, *Export Controls, Competitiveness and International Cooperation: A Critical Review*, A Summary and Analysis of Hearings on the National Academy of Sciences Report on National Security Export Controls, staff report, 101st Congress, 1st session, February 1989 (Washington, DC: U.S. GPO, 1989), p. 13.

8. A 1982 General Accounting Office report estimated that submitting license applications cost industry $6.1 million in 1981. In 1985, the President's Commission on Industrial Competitiveness found that unilateral controls resulted in a yearly loss of over $11 billion in sales. The 1987 NAS study, *Balancing the National Interest*, concluded that in 1985 controls caused a $7.3 billion loss in export sales, a $17.1 billion loss in Gross National Product, and the loss of over 188,000 jobs, principally in the high-technology sector. In addition, firms absorbed an estimated $1/2 million in administrative costs associated with controls. See U.S. Congress, General Accounting Office, *Export Control Regulation Could Be Reduced Without Affecting National Security*, GAO/ID-82-14 (Washington, DC: U.S. GPO, 26 May 1982), p. 7; President's Commission on Industrial Competitiveness, *Global Competition: The New Reality* (Washington, DC: U.S. GPO, January 1985), cited by Gary K. Bertsch, "Introduction," in *Controlling East-West Trade and Technology Transfer: Power, Politics, and Policies*, ed. Gary K. Bertsch (Durham, NC: Duke University Press, 1988), p. 14; and National Academy of Sciences, *Balancing the National Interest* (Washington, DC: National Academy Press, 1987) pp. 264, 266, Table D-3, and p. 275.

9. Rep. Don Bonker, comments at a National Issues Forum on *U.S. Export Control Policy: Balancing National Security Issues and Global Competitiveness*, held at The Brookings Institution, Washington, DC, 9 June 1988.

10. The DOD, which had originally helped fund the study, ended its support in 1986 and charged that the final report was biased owing to the presence of business people on the NAS panel. This was an unfair accusation given the long and distinguished government service of many of the panel members and because the panel specifically noted that it had not reached its conclusions *solely* on the basis of

the evaluation of economic costs. There are valid methodological criticisms, however. First, the study partly relied on a survey mailed to a sample of 170 high-technology firms to determine how they had been affected by controls. Although several follow-up interviews were conducted, the use of mailed questionnaires is considered a poor means of survey research and conclusions based on such methods are open to question. For example, respondents typically bias results by examining the entire survey before answering, thereby formulating tailored responses. Second, and more seriously, a House committee staff report has concluded that reported sales and job losses--while not negligible--were overstated. The House report estimated that if a more realistic measure of sales per employee than that in the NAS report were used, job losses would be 15 to 20% of the NAS figure. See Daniel S. Greenberg, "Pentagon Shoots Itself in the Foot," *Journal of Commerce*, 10 February 1987, p. 15, rpt. in U.S. Department of Defense, Department of the Air Force, *Current News*, special edition, *Technology Security*, no. 1570 (16 April 1987), pp. 41-42; Deborah Runkle, Committee on Scientific Freedom and Responsibility, American Association for the Advancement of Science, interview, Washington, D.C., 13 July 1988; and U.S. Congress, House Committee on Science, Space, and Technology, *Export Controls*, pp. 37-40, 43.

11. Duff, interview.

12. National Academy of Sciences, *Balancing*, pp. 248-49, 270-71.

13. The U.S. *Tariff Schedules* under tariff numbers 711-712 (encompassing a broad range of analytic instruments) were compared with the subcategories under Commodity Code 87 (labeled "Professional, Scientific and Controlling Instruments and Apparatus, N.S.P.F.") in *U.S. Exports Schedule E*. These categories were found to be nearly identical. Figures for the projected value of professional and scientific instrument exports are based on figures in *United States Trade: Performance in 1985 and Outlook* and *United States Trade Performance in 1987*. The full citations follow: U.S. International Trade Commission, *Tariff Schedules of the United States Annotated (1983)*, USITC Publication 1317, beginning p. 660; U.S. Department of Commerce, Bureau of the Census, *U.S. Exports Schedule E Commodity by Country*, FT 410/ November 1988 (Washington, DC: U.S. GPO, 1989), pp. I-8-9; U.S. Department of Commerce, International Trade Administration, *United States Trade: Performance in 1985 and Outlook* (Washington, DC: U.S. GPO, October 1986), Table 15, p. 132; and U.S. Department of Commerce, International Trade Administration, *United States Trade Performance in 1987* (Washington, DC: U.S. GPO, June 1988), Table 15, p. 110.

14. *United States Trade Performance in 1987*, Table 15, p. 110.

15. "Returned without action" typically means that the application was improperly completed or that additional information is required. An RWA does not necessarily suggest that a license would be denied, although in some cases an improperly completed application *may* be a sign of an attempt to export a banned item.

16. British Free World licensing volume is approximately the same as that of the United States. In 1986-88, the U.K.'s Department of Trade and Industry received 92,260, 101,860, and 93,970 (projected) applications. The percentage of British FW licenses averaged about 97% compared with the U.S. average of about 91% for 1985-87. See "Supplementary Note by the DTI," 2 November 1988, in U.K. Parliament, House of Commons, Trade and Industry Committee, 2nd Report, session 1988-89, *Trade With Eastern Europe*, (London, HMSO, 2 January 1989), p. 115 and Table 5, below, in the Appendix.

17. Reexport licensing applications, the bulk of which are for intra-COCOM and FW trade, also are not denied in excessive numbers. For fiscal years 1983-85, an average of 1.2% of reexport applications were denied, although the volume of reexport applications grew over 70%. These figures are based on DOC data. See National Academy of Sciences, *Balancing*, p. 245, Table C-11.

18. National Academy of Sciences, *Balancing*, p. 245, Table C-11.

19. For example, in 1988 the DOC introduced a license issued via "electronic mail." The STELA computerized license tracking and information system permits rapid access to a license's status; Stuart Auerbach, "Export License Can Be Issued Electronically," *Washington Post*, 22 January 1988, section F, p. 2, columns 3-4. The business views are from interviews in Washington, DC and London: Copeland; Eric Hirschhorn, Executive Secretary, Industry Coalition on Technology Transfer, Washington, DC, 18 April 1988; Jim LeMunyon, Senior Manager, Government Relations, American Electronics Association, Washington, DC, 11 May 1988; and not-for-attribution interviews, London, 29 November and 2 December 1988.

20. In testimony before a British parliamentary committee, one businessman observed that: "DTI is particularly underresourced in comparison with United States, in the resources they can bring to bear in analysing a particular application." [Question posed by a committee member.] "Is this in terms of numbers, or the technical expertise of their employees?" [Answer.] " Both." See Ralph Land, Rank Xerox, testimony, 29 June 1988, in U.K. Parliament, House of Commons, Trade and Industry Committee, 2nd Report, Session 1988-89, *Trade With Eastern Europe*, (London: HMSO, 26 January 1989), p. 68. See also Michael Bonsignore, President, Honeywell International, "Balancing Competitiveness and National Security Issues: A View From American Business," address at a National Issues Forum on *U.S. Export Control Policy: Balancing National Security Issues and Global Competitiveness*, held at The Brookings Institution, Washington, DC, 9 June 1988; not-for-attribution interview, electronics association representative, Washington, DC, 24 June 1988; John Walsh, minority staff economist, Senate Committee on Banking, Housing, and Urban Affairs, Subcommittee on International Finance and Monetary Policy, interview, Washington, DC, 7 June 1988; LeMunyon, interview; Tovey, interview; not-for-attribution interview, representative of a major U.S. multinational computer firm, London, 29 November 1988; Stewart Nunn, Director, Security Export Controls (Policy Unit), Branch 3, Overseas Trade Division 2, Department of Trade and Industry, interview, London, 9 November 1988; and not-for-attribution interview, Ministry of Defence, London, 31 October 1988.

21. However, the low denial rate also suggests that applications may not be getting adequate review in part because the DOC is overburdened and has too little expertise. Export licensing staff and budgets have grown significantly since the early 1980s, and most analysts believe technology leaks are due to espionage and illegal diversions via third countries. Poor enforcement may therefore be a weak link and the United States has stressed improved enforcement to COCOM allies. Inadequate resources and poor reviews apparently are not a major problem in the United States; U.S. Congress, House Committee on Science, Space, and Technology, *Export Controls, Competitiveness*, p. 15.

22. Business representatives stressed the wisdom of factoring license processing and potential delays into an exporter's plans, something the small or inexperienced exporter may not be cognizant of; Copeland, interview; not-for-attribution interview with a representative of a U.S. electronics firm, Arlington, VA, 17 March 1988.

23. U.S. Department of Commerce, *Export Administration Act Annual Report FY 1985* (Washington, DC: U.S. GPO, November 1986), p. 9.

24. The NAS, utilizing a more realistic--from the exporter's point of view-- definition of processing time, counted the period from the actual date an application is mailed until a DOC notice of action is received by the applicant. Whereas DOC claimed a 27-day average in 1986, under the NAS definition, processing time averaged 54 days; National Academy of Sciences, *Balancing*, p. 236.

25. These figures are derived from U.S. Department of Commerce, International Trade Administration, *United States Trade: Performance in 1985 and Outlook* (Washington, DC: U.S. GPO, October 1986), p. 133, Table 16; and U.S. Department of Commerce, International Trade Administration, *United States Trade Performance in 1987* (Washington, DC: U.S. GPO, June 1988), p. 111, Table 16.

26. The NAS survey of businesses found that administrative costs had risen sharply since new auditing procedures associated with DLs had been instituted. Estimates of administrative costs borne by companies to conform with export control requirements vary widely. One estimate was of 10% of total sales, another estimate was of $1-$1.5 million yearly, and a third put it at "probably $10 million a year." See LeMunyon, interview, and not-for-attribution interviews with representatives of major U.S. electronics firms, Washington, DC, February-March 1988. See also National Academy of Sciences, *Balancing*, pp. 115-16, 246-47; Stephen E. Becker Esq. and Harold Paul Luks, "Corporate Compliance With the National Security Controls of the Export Administration Regulations," in *Balancing the National Interest*, Working Papers, ed. National Academy of Sciences (Washington, DC: National Academy Press, 1987), p. 38.

27. A representative of a major British computer manufacturer noted that de-Americanization is only a solution for some narrowly focused companies and is *not* considered if the choice is between forgoing the best technology and avoiding U.S. controls. See Alex McLoughlin, Head of Trade Relations, International Computers Limited, untitled address given at the *Strategic Export Controls Conference*, held at the Royal Institute of International Affairs, London, 19 November 1987, rpt. in *Conference Proceedings* (available from RIIA), p. 62. The auditing issue and the

threat of de-Americanization of foreign technology was addressed by several interviewees. See not-for-attribution interviews, representatives of a major U.S. computer exporter's British subsidiary, a major British computer firm, the British Foreign Office, and the Ost-Ausschuss der Deutschen Wirtschaft (Eastern Committee), London, 11, 29 November 1988 and 8 June 1989, Cologne, 6 March 1989. See also Henry R. Nau, "The West-West Dimensions of East-West Economic Relations," in *Selling the Rope to Hang Capitalism?*, eds. Charles M. Perry and Robert L. Pfaltzgraff, Jr. (London: Pergamon-Brassey's, 1987), p. 213; U.S. Department of Commerce, Bureau of Export Administration *Export Administration Annual Report FY 1987* (Washington, DC: U.S. GPO, November 1988), pp. 8-9; National Academy of Sciences, *Balancing*, pp. 234-35.

28.   National Academy of Sciences, *Balancing*, p. 13.

29.   The NAS warned of a "virtual breakdown" in the decontrol effort. Ibid.

30.   Figures from a 1988 GAO report, when combined with DOC figures for processed applications to all destinations for FY 1985-88, show a decrease in DOD reviews. For FY 1985-87, the percentages of DOD reviews, including Soviet and/or Eastern European and Free World destinations, were 4.8% (1985), 9.3% (1986), and 7.9% (1987). In FY 1981, the DOD reviewed approximately 5.7% of total applications for the Free World, the U.S.S.R., and Eastern Europe. See U.S. Congress, General Accounting Office, *Export Licensing: Number of Applications Reviewed by the Defense Department*, GAO/NSIAD-88-176FS (Washington, DC: U.S. GPO, May 1988), p. 3; U.S. Congress, General Accounting Office, *Export Control Regulation*, p. 7; and U.S. Congress, General Accounting Office, *Export Controls: Extent of DOD Influence on Licensing Decisions*, GAO/NSIAD-89-155 (Washington, DC: U.S. GPO, June 1989), p. 18, Table 2.5.

31.   By 1988, the DOD reviewed licenses for exports to only 8 Free World countries. Of the original 15, Spain had joined COCOM and Austria, Finland, Sweden, and Switzerland had "graduated" after satisfying the United States that their national control mechanisms had been upgraded. This illustrated the relative success of U.S. policy seeking to close avenues for diversions via European neutrals. The remaining countries are mostly on the Pacific Rim or are states subject to foreign policy controls including among others--South Africa, Iran, Iraq, Syria, and India. The recent sale of a supercomputer to India suggests that India may no longer be on the list. See U.S. Congress, General Accounting Office, *Export Licensing: Number*, p. 2; and U.S. Congress, General Accounting Office, *Export Licensing: Commerce-Defense Review of Applications to Certain Free World Nations*, GAO/NSIAD-86-169 (Washington, DC: U.S. GPO, September 1986), p. 10, footnote 4.

32.   The GAO concluded that for West-West license review, "DOD's input to the review of free world license applications is principally based on its interpretation of the information contained on the license application rather than on unique information in its possession. Its review brings a second opinion rather than a unique perspective to the licensing process." The DOC also reported that in the 2 years since DOD had been granted authority to review all West-West cases to selected destinations, in only one instance had the DOD provided additional

information not available to the DOC. Furthermore, during calendar year 1986, of 78 West-West cases the DOC had denied which the DOD had also reviewed, the DOD had recommended approval or approval with conditions for 46 cases. See U.S. Congress, General Accounting Office, *Export Controls: Extent*, pp. 3, 23, 25. See also U.S. Congress, General Accounting Office, *Export Licensing: Commerce-Defense Review*; U.S. Congress, General Accounting Office, *Export Licensing*, pp. 15-16; and Department of Commerce, "Response to Questions of Chairman Bonker," in U.S. Congress, House Subcommittee on International Economic Policy and Trade, *Omnibus Trade and Competitiveness Act of 1988 (Vol. II)*, hearings, 100th Congress, 1st session, 11-12 March 1987 (Washington, DC: U.S. GPO 1988), p. 35.

33. U.S. Department of Commerce, *Export Administration Annual Report FY 1987*, pp. 51-52; and Allan I. Mendelowitz, Associate Director, National Security and International Affairs Division, U.S. General Accounting Office, prepared statement, 11 March 1987, in U.S. Congress, House Subcommittee on International Economic Policy and Trade, *Omnibus Trade and Competitiveness Act of 1988 (Vol. II)*, hearings, 100th Congress, 1st session, 11-12 March 1987 (Washington, DC: U.S. GPO, 1988), pp. 118-19.

34. See U.S. Congress, General Accounting Office, *Export Controls: Need to Clarify Policy and Simplify Administration* (Washington, DC: U.S. GPO, 1 March 1979); and U.S. Congress, General Accounting Office, *Commerce's Assessment of the Foreign Availability of Controlled Items Can Be More Effective*, GAO/NSIAD-88-71 (Washington, DC: U.S. GPO, February 1988), p. 8.

35. U.S. Congress, General Accounting Office, *Commerce's Assessment*, p. 10, footnote 3, citing section 5(f)(4) of the EAA.

36. Similar problems were noted in a 1979 GAO report. In March 1988, a DOC official complained that the DOD continued to block OFA access to DOD scientists consulted for their expertise on foreign availability. Ibid., pp. 10, 14, 16-17, 19-20, 23; not-for-attribution interview, U.S. Department of Commerce, Washington, DC, 14 March 1988; and U.S. Congress, General Accounting Office, *Export Controls: Need to Clarify Policy and Simplify Administration*, pp. 28-29.

37. If the DOC asserted its authority, less time would be lost in dispute-resolution at the NSC level. The NSC is considered a graveyard where the DOD can suspend decision making, thereby slowing decontrol efforts. But given the DOD's statutory inferiority to the DOC, and despite its assertiveness in recent years, such delaying actions and intransigence by DOD officials can be viewed simply as a sign of *weakness* relative to DOC. See Walsh, interview; Pat Eveland, Administrative Assistant, office of Rep. Bill Frenzel, interview, Washington, DC, 2 June 1988; Ron Fitzsimmons, staff of Rep. Les AuCoin, interview, Washington, DC, 1 June 1988; Wayne Abernathy, Legislative Assistant, staff of Sen. Phil Gramm, interview, 27 May 1988 and Bill Reinsch, Chief Legislative Assistant to Sen. John Heinz, interview, Washington, DC, 19 May 1988.

An intangible and difficult-to-assess factor is how the personalities of bureaucratic players shape the interagency balance. Numerous interviewees and studies point to the dominant role of specific individuals at the DOD who have been able to block many reform initiatives and licenses owing to superior ability and knowledge of how to work the bureaucracy and influence the White House. One observer noted that during the Reagan administration DOD representatives would "literally go and bleed on the President's carpet" in order to block licenses they opposed. Another former DOC official, now representing industry interests, noted the ideologically driven character of DOD officials and described the Defense Technology Security Administration--the DOD's primary export control body--as "five engineers and 100 commissars." A sign that the balance between DOC and DOD may have shifted under President Bush is the unilateral DOC decision to decontrol certain PCs which Secretary of Defense Cheney vehemently opposed. However, it appears that Commerce Secretary Mosbacher's close relationship with Bush gave DOC enough interagency authority to overcome DOD protests. See Suzanne P. Tichenor, Director, International Trade Affairs, Cray Research, interview, Washington, DC, 2 May 1988; not-for-attribution interview, Washington, D.C., 18 April 1988; David Hoffman and Ann Devroy, "Cabinet Members Finding Many Roads Lead to Bush," *Washington Post*, 30 July 1989, section A, p. 1, columns 3-4; section A., p. 18, columns 1-2; and Peter Truell, "Bob Mosbacher Wields Rare Degree of Power For a Commerce Chief," *Wall Street Journal*, 1 September 1989, section A, p. 1, column 6.

38. U.S. Congress, Acts and Bills, *Omnibus Trade and Competitiveness Act of 1988*, Public Law 100-418, 23 August 1988 (Washington, DC: U.S. GPO, 1988), p. 102 Stat., 1356.

39. U.S. Department of Commerce, *Export Administration Annual Report FY 1987*, pp. 51-52 and Mendelowitz, statement, pp. 118-19.

40. A representative of a major U.S. computer firm praised the reduction in unilateral controls, confiding that while they still posed a burden the situation was much better than in the early 1980s; not-for-attribution interview, Washington, DC, 18 May 1988.

41. For example, the DOD is reportedly outflanking a more assertive DOC--and taking advantage of the State Department's relative analytical and bureaucratic weakness--by placing dual-use items on the Munitions List which should otherwise remain on the CCL; not-for-attribution interviews, representatives for a major U.S. electronics trade association and a major British computer firm, Washington, DC, 24 June 1988 and London, 11 November 1988, and Thornton, *A New Export Regime*, p. 39.

42. Reports of de-Americanization owing to U.S. controls go back at least a decade. See William A. Root, Director, Office of East-West Trade, Bureau of Economic and Business Affairs, Department of State, statement, in U.S. Congress, Senate Committee on Banking, Housing, and Urban Affairs, Subcommittee on International Finance, *U.S. Export Control Policy and Extension of the Export Administration Act*, Part III, hearing, 96th Congress, 1st session, 3 May 1979 (Washington, DC: U.S. GPO, 1979), p. 168.

43. See the discussion in William F. Finan, Perry D. Quick, and Karen M. Sandberg, *The U.S. Trade Position in High Technology: 1980-1986*, A Report for The Joint Economic Committee, U.S. Congress, October 1986 (photocopied).

44. National Academy of Sciences, *Balancing*, p. 119, Figure 5-1.

45. The 5 additional categories are guided missiles and spacecraft, ordinance and accessories, drugs and medicines, industrial and inorganic chemicals, and plastics and resins. See U.S. Department of Commerce, International Trade Administration, *United States Trade Performance in 1987*, p. 110, Table 15.

46. Ibid., pp. 10 and 118-19, Figure 5-1.

47. U.S. Department of Commerce, International Trade Administration, Capital Goods and International Construction Sector Group, *A Competitive Assessment of the U.S. Computer-Aided Design and Manufacturing Systems Industry* (Washington, DC: U.S. GPO, February 1987), pp. 29-30.

48. The 10 categories under the DOC-3 definition are guided missiles and spacecraft; communications equipment and electrical components; aircraft and parts; office, computing, and accounting machinery; ordinance and accessories; drugs and medicines; industrial and inorganic chemicals; professional and scientific instruments; engines, turbines, and parts; and plastics and resins.

49. The *de-minimus* liberalization's predicted effect was noted by Jim LeMunyon of the American Electronics Association and by a former DOC export control official; LeMunyon, interview; and not-for-attribution interview, Arlington, VA, 17 March 1988.

5

Assessment and Recommendations

Strategic export controls have been an important part of overall U.S. policy toward the U.S.S.R. and Eastern Europe for virtually the entire postwar period. While never entirely free of controversy, criticism of this practice has gradually grown as relative U.S. military and economic power has declined. During the embargo's early years, there was little concern for the costs--in terms of lost trade--of controls imposed on the United States. However, global postwar trends eventually eroded the U.S. military and economic dominance that undergirded the policy and perceptions governing the embargo. First, the economic recovery of the allies, along with the emergence of several other new and vibrant technology producers, inevitably reduced U.S. economic and technological superiority. In an increasingly competitive and interdependent world market, impediments to U.S. export performance--such as export controls--are intensely scrutinized and debated. A second factor complicating U.S. policy was the Soviet drive to match U.S. military capabilities. This buildup was facilitated by Soviet access to advanced technologies that are increasingly available globally. This trend threatens to undermine COCOM's capability to regulate East-West technology transfer and the West's qualitative weapons superiority. In light of these developments, U.S. policy is thought by some to be unrealistic and in need of reevaluation. U.S. policy has had to adapt to domestic and allied pressure to rationalize and relax controls. Complicating decision making are the tumultuous systemic changes unfolding in Eastern Europe and the former U.S.S.R., and the implications and challenges they pose for the future of export controls.

In this chapter an overall assessment and evaluation of the study's findings and conclusions are presented. Prescriptions are also offered.

SUMMARY OF PRINCIPAL FINDINGS AND ASSESSMENT
OF U.S. POLICY

U.S. high-technology export control policy remains controversial. Despite heated and sometimes exaggerated rhetoric, a long-term perspective suggests that the basic U.S. policy goal of delaying Soviet acquisition of dual-use high technologies has been successful at relatively small cost. This success has not been *costless*, however. It has strained relations with allies and discourages high-technology exports. However, in macroeconomic terms, these costs are generally marginal relative to GNP (see Table 26). At the microeconomic level, there is much anecdotal but very limited hard evidence that individual firms or industries suffer a loss of competitiveness and disproportionate sales losses. One possible exception is the analytic instruments industry (see Chapter 4), although even in this case the evidence is not conclusive since long-term industry or government studies are not available. More assessment and evaluation of the economic cost question follows. Furthermore, despite the embargo's and COCOM's apparent success, and because of the profound changes taking place in Eastern Europe, U.S. policy ought to adapt to changing circumstances and COCOM should not be dissolved. To argue otherwise is short-sighted and unrealistic because of the still uncertain outcome of these changes and the possibility that Russia will remain a formidable threat to U.S. regional and global interests--at least for the foreseeable future.

Two other pertinent observations about COCOM and persistent issues facing the multilateral export control regime are briefly outlined here and discussed in greater detail below. First, despite a relative decline in military and economic power, the United States continues to take the lead as the driving force in COCOM and is accepted as such by the allies. But leadership also means that the United States must set an example by showing willingness to bear the same burdens imposed by controls as the allies while being careful to pursue well-argued[1] and consistent policies that do not conflict with COCOM's objectives. As export control liberalization in the 1970s followed by the high-profile emphasis on tightening controls in the 1980s demonstrated, precedents once set become the basis for allied actions and shape allied as well as Soviet perceptions. Inconsistent U.S. policy undermines effective leadership. Thus, it is unsurprising that the allies questioned U.S. intentions and leadership in the early 1980s when Washington insisted on broadening the scope of high-technology controls while U.S. farmers profited from exports to the U.S.S.R. Nor is the U.S. case bolstered by acrimonious interagency disagreements over policy and reasonable reform proposals that suggest disarray and slow decision making in COCOM.

Second, given its leadership position, the United States must continue to adjust to the implications for national policy and for COCOM of the global spread of technology production and innovation. To allow control lists to become outdated or to adamantly oppose reasonable liberalization initiatives not only undermines the flexibility and consensus building that enables an informal body like COCOM to function, but also fosters cynicism, laxity, and distrust among members who see no possibility of controlling widely available technological commodities. While steps were taken during the 1980s to update and shorten lists and improve enforcement, sustaining this momentum could prove difficult. As in the 1970s, it is possible that because of the lists' irrelevance and flagging interest in maintaining multilateral controls, COCOM could again become moribund. The United States is in a delicate position since strategic controls are ineffective without allied cooperation. Furthermore, Washington must encourage discipline and solidarity within COCOM, yet may pay a diplomatic price in straining relations with allies. The allies, while sometimes disagreeing with the United States on East-West issues and expressing suspicion of occasionally heavy-handed U.S. rhetoric and policy initiatives in COCOM, have also shown flexibility and a willingness to go along with reasonable and well-argued U.S. initiatives. Most threats to allied consensus in COCOM have their genesis in instances where diverging U.S. and allied foreign policy interests spill over into the supposedly technical realm of strategic controls.

Washington's activist policies in COCOM during the 1980s have done much to revive the regime. This has been facilitated, despite sometimes undiplomatic rhetoric and policy disarray, by a combination of leverage, hard bargaining, and compromise, as outlined below.

COCOM and East-West Trade: Contending Views and Policies

In principle, COCOM functions as a forum for coordinating allied policies designed to deny the Russians militarily critical technology. While this is a strategic goal, COCOM has inevitably also served some foreign policy purposes. This follows from its legacy as a tangible manifestation of the postwar containment policy the United States implemented and has essentially followed to the present day. Furthermore, because East-West trade carries different weight in the national security and foreign policies of the United States and the principal COCOM allies, disagreement is probably inevitable. The question remains as to how much sustained friction is bearable. It does appear that previous contentious episodes were resolved or at least patched over, suggesting willingness to compromise among all members in order to sustain COCOM as an organization. U.S. policy implementation and COCOM leadership is also complicated by domestic and interagency divisions over the wisdom of East-West trade and the effects of the cyclical pattern of U.S.-Soviet relations. This is reflected in the politically charged character of foreign policy debate in the United States. The recent changes in Eastern Europe have rekindled these divisions. How the United States responds to these changes will affect, perhaps fundamentally, the future direction of COCOM policy.

Strategic control policy is inevitably influenced by evolving foreign policy conditions.[2] The evolution of the "China differential" from a virtual economic warfare policy during the early 1950s to the U.S.-sponsored liberalization thirty years later exemplifies this. Similarly, differentiating between Moscow and the Soviets' Eastern European satellites was also indicated by a relatively more liberal attitude regarding exports to, for example, Hungary and Romania. Furthermore, whether intentionally or unintentionally, U.S. actions in COCOM and domestically signal evolving U.S. intentions and perceptions to the embargo's targets and to Washington's allies.[3] For example, as detente bloomed in the early 1970s, the lack of U.S. attention to domestic and multilateral compliance and enforcement, along with a large number of U.S. exception requests in COCOM, signaled that improved East-West relations would be accompanied by eased trade restrictions. Such signals did not go unnoticed in Moscow and the COCOM capitals. As East-West relations deteriorated in the late 1970s and early 1980s, renewed emphasis on the strategic embargo reflected a new U.S. policy tack. National security and foreign policies again overlapped as relatively stricter COCOM controls were agreed to (at U.S. insistence) on exports to Poland and the U.S.S.R. With the lifting of martial law in Poland and withdrawal of Soviet troops from Afghanistan, the United States (at allied urging) lifted the "no exceptions" policy on exports to these countries. Washington also began to ease controls on exports to Eastern Europe, but not the U.S.S.R., as sweeping political liberalization promised further erosion of Soviet domination over the area.[4]

In general, the United States desires a broader scope for strategic controls and Washington has frequently imposed unilateral trade sanctions for foreign policy purposes. While agreeing on the necessity of some strategic controls, the allies advocate a relatively narrow strategic embargo of only clearly military technologies. For a variety of domestic political and economic reasons, and owing to geopolitical circumstances, the allies generally oppose using COCOM to implement negative trade sanctions for foreign policy purposes.[5] Sanctions are thought to have little effect and may even worsen conditions in Eastern Europe, causing domestic unrest and stifling evolving liberalization. But the allies also have been willing to change or relax COCOM policies to suit their own foreign policy goals. The unilateral ending of the initially restrictive "China differential" in the 1950s and periodic pressure on the United States to reduce the size of the dual-use list are examples. In addition, expanding East-West trade ties and the alleged laxness of France and the F.R.G. in enforcing controls during the 1970s and early 1980s occurred while Paris and Bonn pursued improved relations with Moscow and Eastern Europe. The United States, of course, had helped to foster export control relaxation through its own growing ties with Eastern Europe. And when Washington again changed course after 1979, the greater importance to the Europeans of stable East-West trade ties, grounded in foreign policy and economic security priorities, clashed with the U.S. policy that assumed trade and technology transfer were important aspects of globalized zero-sum competition with the U.S.S.R. For the Western Europeans, and the F.R.G. in particular, renewed U.S.-Soviet confrontation threatened the carefully nurtured web of political and economic relations between East and West. Trade and technology transfer is an important part of that policy. Given the friction generated in COCOM, Washington must unambiguously and very carefully explain its proposals to the other COCOM members in the future. Controversy over the P.R.C. liberalization and recent poorly received U.S. proposals to ease controls on certain technologies that the European allies believe are essential to the political and economic recovery of Eastern Europe underline the necessity for clearly elucidated proposals by Washington. There are also other forums, such as NATO and bilateral consultations, where broad foreign policy questions and initiatives can be discussed and negotiated. In principle, COCOM should be kept insulated from foreign policy pressures as much as possible and should remain principally a forum for technical discussions and decisions. This assumes that objective, purely technical discussion among experts is possible. But in the U.S. case at least, that itself can pose problems given the bureaucratic dynamics affecting U.S. policy, as discussed more fully below. In practice, foreign policy considerations inevitably intrude in COCOM, given East-West trade links relative importance as part of the allies' foreign, economic, and national security policies. Some controversy over the foreign policy consequences of COCOM policies is therefore probably inevitable.

     As suggested by the discussion in this section, and elaborated more fully in Chapter 2, unique historical, geopolitical, domestic political, and different foreign policy considerations undergird and influence U.S. and allied perceptions of East-West trade policy. To some extent, these factors form a largely immutable background to any discussion of the persistent challenges faced by the multilateral export control regime. Thus, the importance to the F.R.G. of rapid reunification with East Germany overrode potential problems posed by the transfer of industries and technology eastward. Bonn is also pressing for expanding trade and investment flows to the rest of Eastern Europe and the for Soviet republics in the belief that this will help prevent regional instability and bolster Gorbachev during a difficult transition period. The importance of cementing unification in the context of regional European harmony is also reflected in German insistence on fulfilling existing G.D.R.-Russian contract obligations after reunification. This raises the possibility of unrestricted exports and could be controversial in future COCOM meetings.[6] One of the peripheral consequences of Moscow's conciliatory policy toward German reunification and encouragement of reform in Eastern Europe is Bonn's, and to a lesser extent also Paris' and London's, reluctance to maintain what are perceived as the restrictive and outdated trade controls of the recent past. How well the United States and COCOM can meet this challenge will be a test of the organization's adaptiveness and of U.S. policy.

Despite periodic disagreements, U.S. success in revitalizing the strategic control effort has been achieved through leverage, compromises, and agreements within COCOM and between the U.S.-led COCOM and non-COCOM high-technology producers. Although disagreements in COCOM have sometimes been heated, the fact that no member has quit COCOM or has knowingly exported proscribed goods without COCOM approval (according to the late Commerce Secretary Baldrige)[7] testifies to its flexibility and to all members' essential agreement on basic goals. Yet several of the problems dealt with in COCOM during the 1970s and 1980s persist while the upheaval in Eastern Europe raises serious questions about COCOM's future.

The U.S. Effort to Revitalize the Embargo

A combination of leverage (arguably bordering on unilateralism), quiet persuasion, and compromise has characterized U.S. policy. Vocal criticism of allies by U.S. policymakers for blithely "selling the rope" to the Soviets complemented U.S. insistence on enforcing the extraterritorial provisions of U.S. export control regulations. Under these regulations, U.S.-origin goods, including those reexported from other COCOM countries, were subject to U.S. licensing and regulatory control even if incorporated in other foreign-manufactured items. Quiet government-to-government discussions on Soviet technology acquisitions, and growing disillusionment by the early 1980s among allied leaders with the results of East-West trade and the prospects for detente, helped Washington's cause. Although criticized for not presenting an adequate public case for extensive controls on dual-use technologies, the elevation of defense ministries and greater input from intelligence services in the licensing review and enforcement process in the U.K. and France suggest that Washington's alarm over Soviet bloc activities convinced allied leaders of the seriousness of the technology control issue. On balance, more military input in allied export control decision making is desirable, given the sophisticated technical features of some exports as well as their strategic potential. But despite the legacy of disillusionment with detente's shortcomings in the 1970s, it is possible that the perception of improving East-West relations could precipitously sway *political* leaderships in Western countries with possible unfavorable consequences for domestic strategic control efforts. Trade and foreign policy considerations might again become paramount, while strategic criteria might be deemphasized for political reasons. Relatively conservative leaders or, as in France, leaders who came to distrust Soviet motives, were amenable to U.S. warnings in the early 1980s. But as the political constellations inevitably change, new leaders could be more inclined to seek closer East-West links under popular pressure to eliminate vestiges of Europe's Cold War division. Opposition parties in the F.R.G. and Denmark, for example, urged sharp reductions in controls and for their governments to ignore COCOM restrictions.[8] It is also unclear whether the extraterritoriality issue has been resolved despite demonstrated desire on both sides to patch differences.

Faced with choosing between the huge U.S. market and the anemic Eastern European economies, and not wanting to forgo supplies of U.S.-origin technology despite reexport restrictions, European governments and companies grudgingly complied with U.S. regulations. The combination of incentive and disincentive was also evident in U.S. efforts to assuage allied concerns regarding the impact of reexport controls and the more blatant effects of extraterritoriality.[9] In the United States, concerns for potential U.S.-European friction over U.S. reexport authority once the 1992 single European market is established also played a role in this effort. For example, the 1988 Omnibus Trade Act did stipulate what amounted to a license-free zone in COCOM,--whereby no U.S. license would be required for exports from the United States to a COCOM member or for a reexport of U.S.-origin technology within the COCOM area. The act also stipulated that this privilege was contingent on each COCOM member's passing a DOC review of the member's export control mechanism. But while foreign analysts welcomed the prospect of a license-free COCOM export area, they remained skeptical of the results of the DOC review. Skepticism was warranted since by 1991, the United States still had not removed all licensing requirements, although substantial liberalization had been undertaken.[10] Additional evidence of U.S. efforts to blunt anger over extraterritoriality, and the implication that the allies cannot be trusted to enforce controls, is suggested by negotiated agreements governing auditing and use of U.S.-origin computers located in COCOM countries. After protests, the British, French, and West Germans agreed to compromises that either permitted local officials to accompany U.S. auditors and inspectors or, as in France, that accepted local auditor's inspections in lieu of U.S. personnel. Suggestive evidence of U.S. leverage came from the London representative of a major U.S. computer firm which noted that, while the U.K. protested auditing in principle, the British bowed to "economic realities" when businesses were authorized by the British government to make "corporate decisions" regarding whether to permit U.S. audits.[11]

Arguably, the United States exercised a degree of unilateralism in order to shake up the COCOM regime and complacent allies. While this appears to have been effective and contributed toward marshaling allied cooperation, such a course of action may not be available in the future should conditions again warrant a restrengthening of multilateral controls (admittedly a remote prospect at this time). This is possible given the growing number of high-technology producers outside the United States, since foreign firms could develop new sources of supply in order to avoid problems with U.S. regulations. Foreign governments might therefore be less inclined to compromise with Washington. Furthermore, as critical domestic reaction in the United States to proposals to sanction Toshiba for selling sensitive technology suggests, many U.S. business interests and the Executive agencies oppose comprehensive sanctions. This is due to the dependence of many U.S. high-technology manufacturers on foreign-sourced components and government concern that a cut-off of those sources might imperil critical defense-industrial production and weapons systems. In short, Washington could well do more damage to national security and economic competitiveness by acting unilaterally, given the high degree of interdependence characteristic of the international market. The costs of unilateralism are also likely to grow when and if the EC, currently the major market for U.S. high-technology exports, fully implements its long-delayed goal of a single market, adds new Eastern European members, and becomes a truly united and influential global economic and political power.

While the extraterritoriality issue has subsided, it is unclear whether these compromises will completely defuse potential clashes over U.S.

regulations that hinder operation of a barrier-free Europe after 1992. There are fundamentally different interpretations of international law and perceptions of sovereignty that must be resolved before the United States and its allies can finally settle disagreements over the extraterritoriality issue. One significant hurdle preventing limitation of the broad assertion of U.S. extraterritorial rights is the reluctance of U.S. courts to impede the Executive Branch's authority in national security matters. It is also arguable that in some instances, this authority is necessary to protect the national interest. The question remains as to where to draw the line in the exercise of that power.

A permanent solution, rather than tenuous, informal government-to-government understandings (as was the case in the U.K.) is desirable since the threat of U.S. reexport controls elicits deep anger and frustration among allied governments and foreign companies. The utility of reexport controls is also questionable since they are generally ignored by small foreign companies that often violate the embargo. According to the DOC, only about 10 percent of reexport requests are from the largest European companies while the remainder are from U.S.-controlled subsidiaries. The license-free zone provision in the 1988 Omnibus Trade Act is a partial solution but does not resolve the underlying legal issues. Additional complications could result from future EC expansion when Eastern European nations such as the G.D.R. (as part of a united Germany), Poland, and Hungary become members. Unquestionably, the strategic situation, East-West relations, and these countries' economic condition would have to improve significantly before such integration could become a reality. Currently, there is no EC representative at COCOM, although EC interests are no doubt taken into account by the European COCOM members. British Foreign Office officials with considerable experience in COCOM matters stressed that the EC Commission recognized the sensitive political issues bound up in export controls and that the commission would therefore not insist on a seat at COCOM. Individual EC members are in any case reluctant to cede authority for decisions, in an area considered vital to national security, to any supranational authority. Nor is it likely an EC and COCOM state would want to forgo the flexibility afforded by the current COCOM decision making structure and the veto right each member now enjoys. One possible solution for the problem of an expanded EC membership, and the conflict between controls and the goal of an unrestricted flow of goods within the EC, might be an EC-level licensing and/or monitoring and enforcement organization. Whether members would be willing to renounce sovereignty in this area remains an open question.[12]

In sum, there is some prospect for resolving the extraterritoriality issue because neither side wants to repeat the acrimony of the early 1980s and because Washington, although slow to do so and sometimes undercutting its position owing to interagency disagreements over policy, has recently shown flexibility on the question of streamlining controls and minimizing reexport controls. With shorter lists of truly critical items, fewer commodities would be subject to extraterritorial controls, extraterritoriality might be more palatable, and enforcement would be less daunting.

Washington has also exercised leverage against, and sought to strengthen controls and enforcement of exports from, non-COCOM high-technology producers. The tougher policy begun under Reagan was a distinct break from the past, when Washington avoided sanctions against embargo violators for fear of jeopardizing other foreign policy interests and joint programs. Again, as in the case of auditing, it is arguable that the *implicit* threat of a disruption of U.S. high-technology supplies, the closing off of the U.S. market, and lengthier U.S. processing of licenses for exports to and from these countries may have been persuasive.

But as a DOC official stressed, while this was implicit, in negotiations the United States preferred the explicit offer of liberalized technology transfers in exchange for improved domestic controls.[13] In effect, the so-called Third Country Initiative has expanded de facto COCOM-like controls by encouraging neutral European and several Pacific Rim producers to adopt national control mechanisms that are acceptable to the United States.[14] For countries that comply, Washington promises expedited license processing on a par with the relatively liberal licensing in effect for exports to the COCOM area.[15] Those states initially deemed too lax (Sweden, Austria, Switzerland, etc.) were placed on a special list whereby licenses for U.S. exports to these countries were given more scrutiny by the DOD and generally took longer to process. The "graduation" of several of these countries and their compliance with COCOM-like controls suggests that the U.S. initiative was relatively successful.[16] In East Asia, several of the Newly Industrializing Countries (NICs) continue to rely on the U.S. security umbrella, giving Washington additional leverage in securing agreements that are arguably in the national security interest of the NICs. But if in the future peaceful conditions prevail in Asia and in Eastern Europe, the NICs' export-driven economies can be expected to expand growing trade and investment links with current and former communist states. This will further complicate U.S. policy unless stable regional conditions and a permanent reduction in East-West tensions reduce the need for controls. Expanding COCOM membership to include advanced neutrals, as was suggested by a State Department official,[17] is infeasible given their jealously guarded neutrality and the possibility that COCOM would become unwieldy. In the future, however, increasing numbers of developing economies producing more sophisticated dual-use technology mean that continuing bilateral negotiations will be necessary. This implies that the State and Commerce Department's resources must remain adequate to track and sustain this effort. Furthermore, the United States must continue to urge the major COCOM allies to continue participating in this effort in order to share the burden. Shorter lists, including decontrol of less advanced technological commodities, will also ease the problem of non-COCOM sources since newly industrializing countries tend to be producers of relatively less sophisticated technologies.

Persistent Problems: List Streamlining and Globalized Technology Production

The list streamlining issue will continue to be critical as technology diffuses and non-COCOM states produce more advanced high-technology goods. As both the 1987 NAS study *Balancing the National Interest* and the 1988 National Research Council study *Global Trends in Computer Technology and Their Impact on Export Control* pointed out, controls over technological commodities that are or that rapidly become globally available are simply infeasible. To continue to insist on blanket controls on categories of widely available commodities not only overwhelms control mechanisms but devalues the entire multilateral effort.

Recognizing this and responding to allied criticism of the scope of controls, the United States agreed to "higher fences around fewer items" in 1988. In exchange for an allied commitment to bolster enforcement, the United States agreed to expeditious reduction of the dual-use list. However, in interviews in 1988-89, foreign interviewees expressed dissatisfaction with the pace of the decontrol effort, complaining of U.S. reluctance to speed up the process. Lists are still considered too long, although in 1990 Washington took steps to pare down the industrial list and to create a new "core list" of eight broad categories of particularly sensitive technologies. Despite these reforms, skepticism of U.S. sincerity and intentions may be revived, devaluing the strides made since 1988. On the other hand, the Farewell papers revealed that clandestine Soviet efforts had been most successful in Europe and continued evidence of poor allied enforcement does not foster U.S. confidence in the allies' willingness or ability to prevent illegal transfers.[18] Should streamlining falter, the rapid pace of global technological innovation threatens to make dual-use controls irrelevant, as was the case with the computer list during the 1970s. The allies would therefore be less willing to effectively maintain controls.[19]   Nor are the prospects for adequate allied cooperation very good if the strategic basis and foreign policy conditions for maintaining controls change and the United States refuses to adapt controls to new circumstances in Europe. Thus, the dual-use list's size cannot be analyzed in isolation from the rapid changes in Eastern Europe and the implications these changes have for allied foreign policy and economic interests. Reportedly, by early 1990, the United States stood alone in COCOM in opposing decontrol of certain items the allies felt were needed in Eastern Europe to revive stagnant economies.[20]   As U.S. officials acknowledge, the allies have little patience with cautious U.S. initiatives.[21]   For example, the Germans are pressing for relaxation of controls and this pressure can be expected to grow, since from Bonn's perspective bolstering the success of reform efforts in Poland, Hungary, and Czechoslovakia increases the prospects for peaceful change and maintaining regional stability. Political and economic stability is also imperative during the difficult reintegration of the two Germanys. Thus, any economic help that furthers reforms in those countries is important.[22]

While larger political and foreign policy questions are best dealt with in fora such as NATO, the relatively lower-profile and informal COCOM body should play an important secondary role. In COCOM, the United States can forge an allied consensus on strategic controls and technology transfer (closely coordinated with political and foreign policy decisions adopted in NATO and similar fora) that protects Western interests without alienating the West Germans or the other allies. COCOM's informality permits some give and take on issues such as streamlining where political and foreign policy considerations may clash with strategic and security priorities.

The list's size is a perennial problem. Increasingly, "technologies advance much faster than most bureaucratic processes."[23]   Part of the reason for U.S. intractability is interagency disagreement over what constitutes a strategically critical item. Agency experts disagree over highly technical questions concerning a system's performance parameters. This is one reason why the inevitable bureaucratic compromise agreed to among U.S. agencies and presented at COCOM is frequently more restrictive than other COCOM members' proposals.[24]   To circumvent this, there may be some merit in attempting, through high-level and closely coordinated action by the President and the Secretaries of Commerce, State, and Defense, to force list revisions in order to overcome bureaucratic cautiousness and opposition. This was done during the Reagan administration to rapidly implement liberalization of trade with China.[25]   However, in that case, political, foreign policy, and certain strategic benefits appeared to outweigh the danger of technology loss. High-level agreement on liberalization of trade with the former Soviet republics would be predicated upon similar circumstances that may not be duplicated in the short term. The conditions appear to be much more favorable in several Eastern European states. Furthermore, unless the United States is careful to fully explain its decontrol policy, suspicion of commercial motives behind the U.S. shift (however unlikely) could be raised, as happened in the wake of the P.R.C. decontrol. This is especially likely if the United States is seen to be blocking legitimate allied trade.

Reduction of the dual-use list's size should be a top priority for the U.S. government. Some items must not be decontrolled because of potential end use in military systems, but it should be possible to identify less critical items more rapidly. Questions over end use have plagued, and no doubt will continue to plague, policymakers, although technical redesign and on-site inspections offer some safeguards. For some products at least, end-use is less of a problem because simply acquiring end products piecemeal does not permit discovery or development of the know-how and technology (the keystone technologies) that go into designing and producing a high-quality finished product. This was the rationale behind the Bucy Report's recommendation for decontrolling end products while protecting keystone technologies. The increasing difficulty of reverse-engineering, as the miniaturization and sophistication of many chip-based technologies grows, further supports the rationale for decontrolling end products and, by extension, shortening control lists.

Technical complexities inevitably will remain a significant obstacle to full decontrol of some items as analysts debate the significance of technical parameters. In addition, a currently innocuous and uncontrolled technology could rapidly become militarily critical owing to unforeseen theoretical breakthroughs and unexpected innovations and adaptations which, when coupled with the innocuous technology, could necessitate its control. One solution would involve carefully integrating a product's life cycle into the domestic bureaucratic and COCOM evaluation process. As newer generations of the product emerge, and their viability is established, increasingly out dated products can either be reclassified under less restrictive controls or decontrolled altogether. Currently, there is provision in COCOM for a member to call for a review of a specific technology that may not be part of the one-quarter of the list undergoing yearly review. This provision should be utilized more frequently, or the current reviewing system should be replaced by a continuous review, as was the case up until the early 1980s. This would facilitate keeping the list current with global technological developments. In addition, a proposal for a proportional voting system in COCOM on issues such as list reduction, to facilitate decision making, has merit and has been discussed. But as a British Foreign Office official pointed out, the unanimity rule benefits not only the United States but other members as well and members would be leery of abandoning it.[26] Instead, the present exception policy, selected case-by-case reviews, and carefully evaluated liberalization on the pattern of the P.R.C. decontrol are probably the only realistic solutions. These measures do permit exports of otherwise controlled technology under certain circumstances. Given the changes in Eastern Europe, this flexibility is important. Delays while member governments evaluate and debate exports coming under these categories are inevitable and prudent in the case of particularly sensitive items. Also inevitable, given the present legal framework and conflicting bureaucratic interests and perceptions, is some degree of policy discord among the principal U.S. agencies. But if the U.S. position on streamlining and other COCOM issues is undermined by interagency discord, as was the case during the 1980s, the credibility of U.S. leadership and initiatives will be seriously compromised. Steps must be taken to reduce the adverse consequences of this friction.

In order to project balanced U.S. policy in COCOM, the State Department must be the principal representative of U.S. interests at COCOM and this role should be reinforced by Presidential backing. Only the Department of State represents a neutral view between the pro-trade orientation of the DOC and the DOD's defense and security interests. Currently, with a permanent DOD presence in Paris (but no permanent DOC representative), the allies perceive that U.S. policy is skewed and unrealistic given the changes in the U.S.S.R. and Eastern Europe. A more prominent role for the DOC would also send the wrong signal to the allies. However desirable depoliticized and purely technical COCOM deliberations are in theory, leaving negotiations up to technically qualified representatives would bias U.S. policy. Such expertise is drawn principally from the DOD and DOC (and other agencies as needed), and thus actual and perceived agency bias would undermine the U.S. negotiating position and enflame controversy among the COCOM allies. Therefore, a relatively neutral voice such as the State Department could best represent U.S. interests, although this again raises the question of foreign policy considerations overriding what would seem to be purely technical issues. It would appear that, on balance, the choice is among the lesser of evils, although the White House should also be careful to avoid politicizing East-West trade issues.

Only the State Department can balance contending interests and undertake the careful and low-profile negotiations with the allies that are essential if multilateral cooperation is to be effective. While the State Department should have the lead role in actual deliberations, DOC and

DOD input is also necessary and these agencies must still be consulted *prior* to COCOM meetings. Eliminating either or both agencies from planning would risk depriving the U.S. delegation of valuable expertise that the State Department does not possess. Such an effort would also be resisted by the President and by the DOC and DOD, since it would represent a diminution of Presidential discretion in conducting foreign policy and a reduction of bureaucratic clout. Furthermore, while the State Department traditionally has been assigned the lead in the COCOM delegation, the NAS criticized the State Department's inability to exercise that leadership and balance conflicting interests (owing to an assertive DOD presence). To bolster the State Department's influence, consideration should be given to maintaining a cadre of experienced COCOM and technology control specialists at the State Department (in the Bureau of Economic and Business Affairs, for example) so as to facilitate day-to-day relations with counterparts in other countries and to avoid bureaucratic discord at COCOM, which weakens U.S. policy.[27]

In this context, a reinforced role for the State Department at the NSC level is also warranted. Frequently, after a change in administration, new political appointees manning key posts with responsibilities, including export controls, can cause disruption of stable and coherent policy. As a result, swings in U.S. policy have often been criticized by the allies. A cadre of seasoned analysts at the State Department with responsibility for export control and East-West trade policy would help ensure policy continuity and a longer-term perspective effectively voiced in policymaking bodies such as a revived NSC-level Senior Interagency Group for Technology Transfer chaired by the State Department.[28]

Foreign interviewees stressed that the DOD's continuing intransigent position at COCOM caused delays, slowing the decontrol process, and confused the allies, who were not sure whether DOD representatives spoke for the government. Washington's influence is undermined when allies must interpret cacophonous and conflicting U.S. representatives from various government agencies.[29] While DOD input is necessary, it would be prudent to eliminate the DOD presence at regular COCOM meetings, although the DOD should still participate in the military body that advises COCOM. The DOD already contributes as a participant in U.S. interagency bodies which decide on exception requests and on decontrolling list items. Furthermore, the DOD can communicate analytical expertise and provide intelligence to other COCOM nations' defense ministries. This is an indirect means of influencing allies' COCOM policies and supplements limited intelligence and analytical capabilities in several COCOM states.

Washington has invested a great deal in revitalizing the COCOM regime and in coaxing sometimes reluctant allies to cooperate in the U.S. effort. This commitment and interviews with U.S. and European officials strongly suggest that all the allies agree on the necessity of maintaining some strategic controls and that COCOM is and will remain important for the United States and its allies. Although this commitment will be tested should comprehensive arms-control treaties or a significant and encompassing political agreement between East and West be reached, there would still be grounds for maintaining multilateral controls. For example, any future agreement slashing nuclear arsenals would be an important step in easing the East-West confrontation. But until significant conventional arms limits are also agreed to and fully implemented, there will be increasing emphasis on high-technology "smart" weapons to replace the reduced deterrent capacity of nuclear arms. Reliance on sophisticated conventional arms also means that research and development investments will need to be protected, already an implicit COCOM goal and one which was spelled out by the U.S. administration in the "guidance" issued to military commanders in February 1990. Even if a significant easing in East-West tensions leads to pullbacks and reduction of NATO and Commonwealth forces, U.S. military planners can be expected to seek the development and deployment of new sophisticated weapons and defensive systems to balance manpower cuts. This in turn means that the dual-use question would need continued monitoring in COCOM so that the West's qualitative superiority in conventional weapons is not lost.[30]

The uncertainties raised by the crumbling of Russian hegemony in Eastern Europe and the shaky condition of reformist regimes also suggest that COCOM's mission should not be ended prematurely. While it functions out of the public eye, COCOM remains important for U.S. and allied security interests, providing a useful structure for coordinating U.S. and allied policies in an informal setting. Some inevitable degree of disagreement is to be expected and divergent opinions and policies is both acceptable and sustainable. COCOM's flexibility is a strong asset during uncertain times. Yet the efficacy of strategic controls must be balanced against actual and potential costs. The benefits and costs are difficult to assess or quantify, however several observations suggest how well U.S. policy has served the national interest. They also suggest that, given adequate safeguards, there are grounds for cautiously liberalizing controls because the strategic threat from technology transfers is exaggerated.

HIGH TECHNOLOGY EXPORT CONTROL POLICY: STRATEGIC AND ECONOMIC EVALUATIONS

Covert and Illegal Acquisition and Protection of Strategic Technology

While increasingly warmer U.S.-Russian relations and spreading reform in Eastern Europe suggest otherwise, a cautious approach toward expanded East-West technology transfer is warranted in light of intelligence findings. Prior to the disintegration of the U.S.S.R., respected government, private sector, and academic analysts persuasively described the long-term Soviet effort to acquire Western dual-use technology. It is important to note, however, that a large part of this effort involved *covert* and *illegal* means of acquisition, including espionage, smuggling, and diversions. U.S. and German intelligence officials have recently warned that the Russians may actually increase clandestine acquisitions as relations improve and as Moscow increases its emphasis on technologically based industrial renewal.[31] There has also been heavy Soviet reliance on publicly available open-source documents. The existing export control structure is not designed to stop such efforts, although it does deter inattentive or unscrupulous exporters.

Staunching covert activities and diversions of otherwise legal exports implies that increased counterintelligence and enforcement efforts are needed. COCOM remains essential for coordinating allied counterintelligence and enforcement. The United States set an example by instituting Operation Exodus and strengthening Customs operations. The CIA also established a technology transfer committee to pool intelligence and the FBI bolstered its counterintelligence effort. Enforcement operations at the DOC were reorganized and separated from licensing operations. After U.S. urging, it appears that COCOM members and several non-COCOM exporters have implemented "higher walls" in an effort to enforce export controls. Allied enforcement efforts appear to have improved in the U.K. and France to the extent that military and intelligence expertise has greater input in these countries' control efforts. Initially, the response was less satisfactory elsewhere, although U.S. prodding allegedly speeded improvements in Japan and the F.R.G. COCOM served, and will continue to serve, as a needed forum for coordinating allied enforcement efforts given the myriad of sophisticated means, such as electronic data transmission, by which controls can be circumvented.[32]

U.S. officials admit that stopping high-technology smuggling is a daunting task. With relatively porous borders and limited resources, all possible avenues of leakage cannot be covered thoroughly. Furthermore, the heavier volume of European transborder and East-West trade and population flows inevitably heightens the risk of smuggling, diversions, and espionage.[33]   Adding to the problem is the very professionalism of "technobandits," the elusiveness of the contraband, and the proliferating and uncontrolled avenues for technology transfer.

There is no foolproof means of preventing illegal acquisition activities short of a radical change in covert Russian activities and, by extension, Russian national security policy. The United States can take some comfort in the fact that the Sovietss spent so much time and considerable resources on covert efforts, an effort which implies that legal avenues are effectively blocked by the export control regime. The Farewell intelligence corroborates this conclusion. But Washington should not permit the enforcement effort to rapidly deteriorate with a change in the international political situation, as occurred during the 1970s. Although U.S. officials stress that the lessons of the 1970s, when Soviet acquisition increased and export controls were allowed to stagnate, have not been forgotten and will not be repeated, any actual or perceived loosening on the part of the United States will encourage the allies to lower their vigilance. Therefore, a prudent policy would be for the United States and its allies to closely monitor KGB and related covert Russian technology transfer activities in the West over a period of years. Consistent signs of decreased covert activities and some indication that these activities would not be resumed might then be grounds for reevaluating enforcement and the scope of controls themselves.

One measure of the level of Soviet activity would be related to technology security in Eastern Europe. The traditionally close links between East European and Russian intelligence and military services are grounds for carefully examining preferential technology transfers to Eastern Europe. Although efforts to end these intelligence links reportedly are being initiated by the Czechoslovak government, it is possible that pro-Russian and communist sympathizers will retain a presence in several Eastern European governments (despite the communist parties' loss of legitimacy) and in other management positions. There are also long-standing economic ties with the former Soviet republics which could complicate end-use verification.[34] However, negotiations patterned after COCOM's Third Country Initiative have resulted in several noncommunist-dominated governments in Eastern Europe agreeing to observe reexport restrictions and on-site inspections in exchange for sorely-needed technology. Over time, initial concerns that inexperience and lack of manpower would weaken the Eastern European COCOM-approved export control systems should lessen, given U.S. and allied assistance and greater familiarity with the new controls.[35] Furthermore, large and influential communist parties have participated in several COCOM members' political systems for many years. Examples include the Italian and French communist parties, which from time-to-time since 1945 have had a considerable presence in national politics, with French communists briefly serving in minor cabinet posts during the early 1980s. Their presence has not notably undermined technology security and so it is not certain that this would necessarily happen in Eastern Europe.

Absolute certainty is not guaranteed, however. The P.R.C. liberalization represents a precedent with relevance for the situation in Eastern Europe. For example, although the P.R.C. is considered by the State Department and the CIA to be a secure destination for U.S.-origin technology, according to the National Research Council, emerging Chinese computing capabilities may mean a growing risk of diversion and technology losses.[36] Furthermore, recent Chinese arms and missile sales, and budding Chinese-Soviet rapprochement, raise the specter of possible leaks. Whether the threat of a cut-off of U.S. technology or military cooperation is a sufficient deterrent remains unclear.[37]   In Eastern Europe, as in the P.R.C., political considerations and long-term foreign policy goals may well outweigh the risk of the occasional diversion. In fact, it is arguable that the loss of a few end products, without the accompanying technical and production know-how, is of little consequence, as discussed below.

Efficacy of Soviet Technology Utilization

While the scale of the Soviet effort (actively assisted by Warsaw Pact intelligence agencies, according to the CIA and former senior Czech Defense Ministry official Jan Sejna) was formidable, its success was less clearcut. U.S. intelligence (see Chapter 3, Figure 1) and respected analysts such as former Air Force Secretary John McLucas concluded that the Soviets continued to lag behind technologically, despite the varied effectiveness and success of controls over the years, and the gap may have widened. Analysts with the National Research Council found that covert and passive (e.g., document analysis) acquisition, such as practiced by the Soviets, "had limited effectiveness" compared with overt and active (e.g., hands-on training) efforts.[38]

Simply acquiring a high-technology item does not guarantee incorporation into a military system. Given the pattern of Russian military R&D, the item must be adapted to Russian needs, often resulting in development of a Soviet version. This cautious practice suggests a desire not to become dependent on wholly Western sources which could be cut off. But there are costs associated with this strategy exacerbated by the uncertainty export controls inject into the highly centralized planning and production process.[39] Costs include delays while the new technology is adapted and the heightened risk that the Soviet "clone" will be technologically obsolete in comparison to dynamic Western developments. In addition, it is probable that when completed, it does not meet the highest performance parameters or cannot be utilized effectively since subcomponents may be outdated, faulty, or produced under less than ideal manufacturing conditions. For example, Soviet software development is hampered by underdeveloped programming environments, and obsolete telecommunications systems inhibit computer networking.[40] Finally, reliance on copying or reverse-engineering Western designs is becoming increasingly difficult and discourages "learning by doing," an essential ingredient in fostering the creativity of Western researchers and designers.[41]

It appears that controls have effectively *delayed* Soviet development of advanced, militarily critical, dual-use technology. This has been the basic goal of U.S. denial policy since the early 1950s, after a short period of economic warfare ended. Until the 1970s, the economic consequences of U.S. policy were largely discounted. This is no longer the case as U.S. economic and technological preeminence continue to erode in relative terms.

Economic Evaluation of Export Control Policy

For most of the postwar period, the cost of export controls in macroeconomic terms and in terms of losses suffered by individual U.S. firms was ignored in the interest of maintaining national security. This was not unreasonable given U.S. military and economic predominance and American leadership in many dual-use technologies. Even as its economic and/or technological edge slipped in relative terms, the United States continued to lead in maintaining the West's qualitative superiority over Soviet forces. However, while strategically and intuitively prudent, the denial policy eventually seemed to be undercut by the apparently serious loss of technological leadership and associated declines in the defense-industrial base. As the domestic consensus on East-West policy (including export controls) as well as postwar Executive Branch dominance in foreign affairs began to break down, the question of forgone trade by the United States grew more salient. This concern heightened as domestic and global structural economic changes coincided with and caused a *relative* decline in U.S. economic power and modest growth in exports. High-technology industries in particular, the most dynamic and important U.S. export sector, were thought to be unduly hampered by onerous controls. The old trade-off between security and welfare now appears to be much less favorable. As such, the reevaluation of the economic cost of controls echoes the much deeper reevaluation of the U.S. role as the West's principal military power, and of whether military strength has as much meaning today as it did in 1950.

For policymakers, balancing national security and economic interests in formulating and implementing export control policy has become an increasingly difficult task, particularly during the 1980s. Initially, postwar U.S. economic supremacy meant that the economic cost of controls could be and was largely ignored. But political pressure to enhance U.S. economic competitiveness and Congressional micromanagement of foreign policy, including export control policy, has increased in recent years. This trend was in part a reaction to an actual and perceived relative decline in U.S. military and economic power. While they were reluctant in the past to initiate mandated reforms (e.g., the delays in implementing foreign availability studies), the recent and grudging flexibility on the part of agencies in responding to domestic and Congressional pressures for liberalized controls reflect the differing clienteles, perceptions, and interests each side responds to. It also suggests that the bureaucratic "brake" balances sometimes hasty initiatives that might undermine national security. Given suggestive (albeit sketchy) evidence in Chapter 4 (and the Appendix) that the economic cost of controls has not been "overly excessive," some caution is reasonable, although recent events and long-term trends may profoundly change the strategic, foreign policy, domestic political, and economic considerations upon which existing policy rests. Careful and ongoing attention to the issues raised in this study is therefore warranted.

Precise definition of what constitutes "overly excessive" costs remains a judgmental exercise. At best, because precise historical data on costs per se are nonexistent, one must necessarily make inferences from the other limited economic data available. If, as is alleged, high-technology exporters are suffering grave and sustained sales and market share losses over several years owing to controls, *suggestive* evidence of such losses should be reflected in available trade data. Exports of high technology should be declining, for example. There is also supplementary evidence gleaned from examining bureaucratic and regulatory actions (license denial/approval rates, processing times, extent of DOD influence over licensing decisions, etc.). This examination can therefore serve as a means of testing several of the criticisms raised against the current system of controls. Synthesizing these sources, and incorporating the important views of industry representatives (whose firms are otherwise reluctant to publish proprietary data on the effects of controls), is then the basis for what can be no more than an estimate of the "excessiveness" of controls.

A precise, quantifiable measurement of costs remains elusive whether one examines costs at the macroeconomic level, at the sectoral level, or at the level of the individual firm. As Table 26 suggests, even given an inflated estimate of lost sales owing to controls, in order to account for yearly fluctuations, margin of error, and other exogenous variables, losses as a percentage of GNP remained under 0.8 percent for the surveyed period. Although losses had more than doubled between 1978 and 1987, the average rate of increase in losses appears to be very low (0.04%; see Table 27). In comparison, actual exports of high technology (see Table 26 for definition) as a percentage of GNP also nearly doubled from 1978 to 1987. As a percentage of GNP, actual exports of high technology rose an average of 0.1 percent yearly from 1978 to 1987 (Table 27). In other words, the average rate of increase of actual exports of high technology as a percentage of GNP was 150 percent higher than the average rate of increase in GNP losses (which was 0.04%). Furthermore, for 1985-87, actual exports as a percentage of GNP again began to grow at an average rate 200 percent higher than the rate of GNP losses for the same period. The fact that high-technology exports as a percentage of GNP have continued to grow at a faster average rate than has the rate of GNP loss, and that this average has increased in recent years, *suggests* that controls have at most a marginal macroeconomic impact.

Despite an apparently low impact at the macroeconomic level, macro-economic indices may hide serious sectoral or microeconomic costs suffered by entire high-technology industries and individual firms. Since high-technology industries are essential to the defense-industrial base, and because the brunt of controls falls on high-technology exporters, quantifiable measurement of the impact of controls is desirable.

The lack of systematic, comprehensive, and reliable microeconomic data--in particular, publicly available data from industrial sectors and individual firms which allege they suffer a competitive disadvantage owing to export controls--makes it very difficult to verify exporter claims of losses owing to controls. While considerable anecdotal evidence and some documented circumstantial evidence (such as letters from foreign firms warning of a shift in sourcing from U.S. firms to non-U.S. sources in order to avoid U.S. controls) are in the public record, the firms' cases are greatly diminished by the lack of quantifiable proof of lost sales. Such in-house studies have been undertaken, according to business people. Their concern over disclosing proprietary information is understandable, however without hard data demonstrably establishing a consistent pattern of losses owing to excessive controls, business claims must ultimately remain suspect. This is not to imply that most business people who lobby the government are not sincere. However, given the consistent lobbying for regulatory relief since the 1960s, the lack of documented quantified proof of damage in the public record, as well as business peoples' own admissions, one must conclude that exporters cannot or will not undertake to identify and release the relevant data. Lost markets and declining competitiveness may also be due to poor business planning and unaggressive export efforts on the part of U.S. firms who for so long enjoyed nearly uncontested market dominance. Trade barriers may also be a factor.

Assuming that the proprietary data question can be overcome, and that there is a desire and resources to do so on the part of members, it is recommended that industry associations undertake to monitor members' sales and to track instances where export controls had a negative impact on sales. Associations would presumably be able to draw upon the necessary resources and expertise to undertake this effort, an expense many smaller firms could not afford. Mere casebooks of individual examples, as are sometimes presented, are not adequate since a consistent and causal link between controls and losses must be established. This link must also be documented to the extent that proprietary interests allow and the studies necessarily must be carried out over a number of years. Surveys could also be undertaken of license processing times in order to verify whether members are being unduly disadvantaged vis-a-vis competitors. Such studies need not reveal confidential client or product information but merely consistently document processing patterns over an appropriate time period. Also possible are surveys of the effects of certain regulatory changes to determine whether regulations continue to be too restrictive or whether regulatory agencies are carrying out mandated changes. In conjunction with periodic GAO, DOC, and DOD studies recommended below, the private sector data would bolster the credibility of exporters' claims while contributing to a growing empirical foundation upon which to base more conclusive judgments regarding the economic impact of export controls.

If a convincing case can eventually be developed proving lost sales due specifically to export controls, there is a question of whether businesses should be recompensed to recoup lost revenues. Indeed, actually *proving* that a sale was lost due to controls *exclusive* of any other grounds is very difficult, as industry representatives readily admit.[42] Compensation is a thorny administrative and legal matter that also raises the related issue of whether judicial review is a practical and appropriate means of resolving conflicts between exporters and regulatory agencies.

Traditionally, the courts have held that the government has the right to regulate commerce that might be injurious to national security. This right derives from the very broad constitutionally derived powers and discretion the Executive Branch has with respect to foreign affairs and national defense, as recognized by the Supreme Court. In addition, administrative functions carried out under the EAA, except as specified, are exempt from the Federal Administrative Procedures Act.[43]   As a consequence, no judicial review of, for example, a negative licensing determination is permitted. While it is conceivable that Congress could mandate compensation to exporters who suffer from slow or inefficient regulatory action not in conformance with existing law, this could be challenged as an infringement on the President's constitutional duty to protect the nation. It is arguably this power that is ceded to the President and the agencies by Congress in the EAA, since the EAA directs the DOC and other designated agencies to carry out the law's provisions. Any requirement that affected exporters be permitted to seek legal redress and compensation could, in some instances, put the courts in the potential position of having to decide on the validity of national security policy, a violation of the separation of powers doctrine. Furthermore, sensitive intelligence materials and sources could be exposed in open court, a prospect which has already proved difficult to resolve in other cases. Litigation, appeals, lawyers' fees, and related costs could absorb considerable time and resources that many companies, particularly smaller ones, could not afford.

It is also uncertain whether any compensation that is won can entirely recompense potential revenue that the exporter could have expected from the forbidden or canceled sale. The sale, had it been consummated, could also have led to possibly substantial follow-on sales, including sales of spare parts, services, additional product lines, and other technology. Determining these amounts in calculating fair compensation would be a next to impossible task. Likewise, even if Congress simply mandated a schedule of fines to be imposed on an agency (or agencies) responsible for a lost sale, determining the correct fine amount would be difficult and require some independent body to recommend compensatory figures. The make-up of that body and the scope of its authority could be the subject of interminable legislative debate and wrangling among Congress, business interests, and Executive agencies. There would seem to be no other choice but the courts to settle such matters, with the attendant problems noted above.

Both political and economic costs and benefits result from strategic export control policy. Clearly, from a purely economic point of view, unilateral controls on certain technology exports to the former Soviet republics, while economic competitors freely sell the same technology, impose a negative cost. Arguably, the substantial reduction in unilateral controls since the early 1970s (see Appendix, Table 16) may have reduced the costs to U.S. exporters. But even when approximately thirty categories continue to be unilaterally controlled, as happened in 1988, U.S. exporters are disadvantaged. In effect, the United States surrenders any share of the Russian market and tells competitors to sell all they can to the Russians. But there are political benefits, although they may not be immediately evident since the embargo may only succeed in preventing future unacceptable behavior. First, to some extent this policy, in that it signals U.S. perceptions, intentions, and resolve to the Russians, benefits from the *appearance* of U.S. willingness and commitment to absorb some costs in order to achieve a desired policy goal. Accepting the associated burden conveys legitimacy to U.S. policy both in Russian and U.S. allies' eyes and enhances Washington's status as the protector of Western interests and leading advocate of an effective embargo.[44] It also signals that trade relations will not be isolated from other aspects of U.S.-Russian relations. Economic costs must also be weighed against the political benefit and legitimacy to be gained from taking the moral high ground and defending principle when the United States steadfastly refuses to sell sensitive technology--because of threatening Soviet actions--which others may have little or no compunction exporting. Finally, by simply selling any technology to the former Soviet republics, because of inability to convince other producers to control exports, the United States would put itself in the position of allowing other allies to dictate U.S. national security policy.

While not denying that there are some economic costs associated with strategic export controls, and recognizing the disproportionate burden placed on certain businesses by controls, the economic evaluation in this study *suggests* that these costs are less than feared, at least in the short term.[45] Success has not been achieved without some cost in terms of lost actual or potential exports, with the regulatory burden falling most heavily on smaller firms or on firms that are inexperienced and unfamiliar with export controls. The National Academy of Sciences found that small firms were 2.5 times as likely to be denied a license and that small-firm applications to Free World destinations took 25 percent longer on average to process than those from larger exporters.[46] Not only do larger firms have the resources and expertise to navigate the licensing process, but because many multinationals bulk-ship to off shore subsidiaries that have in-house controls on transfers as a condition for granting the parent a bulk license, there is more of a predisposition to view these end users as reliable. A license is therefore more readily granted to such firms, whereas a smaller firm that only intermittently ships to a variety of other independent end users must take additional time to obtain an individual validated license for each shipment.

Controls discourage some exports, although accurately measuring this loss is probably impossible without access to proprietary data. However, robust export growth in key high-technology sectors and commodities such as aircraft and computing as well as robots and CAD/CAM--products which are particularly subject to controls--also suggests that controls themselves have had little overall effect on these sectors (see Chapter 4 and Tables 17-18, 24-25). This conclusion is buttressed by an examination of licensing patterns over a number of years. A large percentage of licenses to the Free World and to the U.S.S.R. and Eastern Europe were approved. Licenses for exports to the COCOM area were virtually never rejected. There is also suggestive evidence (as shown in the Appendix, Table 17) that over the longer term, when U.S. high-technology controls were considered more restrictive than those of its allies, U.S. market shares did not decline enough to warrant casting suspicion on controls as the exclusive reason for the declines. In fact, for several of the most sensitive technologies, sales continued to be quite strong.

Analysis of licensing in terms of outright license denials, licenses returned without action (RWA), license processing time, and licensing efficiency suggests the relative burden of controls. Very few licenses are denied outright while RWAs remain low and appear to be declining. Both DOC and DOD processing efficiency did decline in the late 1970s and early 1980s while the volume of applications rose in tandem with burgeoning use of foreign policy controls, increased government emphasis on licensing, and wider business awareness of the law's requirements. However, by 1987, license processing times were markedly improved both overall and, significantly, also for exports to the Free World and COCOM areas where the bulk of U.S. exports are traded. Improved efficiency together with a sharp reduction in unilateral controls since 1972 (Appendix, Table 16) indicates that U.S. exporters are less disadvantaged than previously.

The relative inconclusiveness of the study's economic evaluation was expected, given the paucity of precise, long-term data available from private and government sources. More complete agency data and measurements are called for in order to improve upon government data and to provide data comparable to that gathered by the private sector, as recommended above. Congress should mandate that the DOC and other involved agencies carry out studies of the licensing process and regularly make public statistics specifically covering strategic export control licensing activity. Present information does not disaggregate strategic from other types of licensing; this should be done in the future. Breakdowns of activity for individual country destinations would also be helpful. Furthermore, the DOC and DOD should be required to publish timely findings indicating how regulatory changes, either mandated by Congress or instituted by the agency, have affected licensing in terms of volume, processing efficiency, and processing time. These findings should be published regularly and should compare expected trends with actual results. In particular, studies of licensing of high-technology products, including what percentage is covered by controls, should also be published. Adequate funding to conduct and publish these studies must, of course, be provided by Congress. Separately, or in conjunction with the agency studies, the General Accounting Office (GAO) should also be required to either regularly conduct and publish independent studies of licensing performance, or publish assessments of the agencies' reports. The GAO is respected for its impartiality, and its ongoing oversight would encourage agencies to comply with Congressional mandates. Regular GAO reports would keep Congress and the public informed on improvements or deficiencies in the export control effort.

If an adequate data base can be developed from these recommended studies, this will contribute to analysis of the long-term implications of controls for exporters and the defense-technology base. For example, correlation between regulatory liberalization or increased controls and export growth or losses over a period of time might be possible. Such an attempt was made in the NAS study *Balancing the National Interest*, but this was constrained to a specific category of items and a relatively short period of time because data were limited. A special dispensation from the privacy requirements of the Export Administration Act was also necessary. Under the proposed recommendations, no proprietary information need be revealed. Instead, statistics covering licensing of strategic exports under broad high-technology categories could be published. Even more detailed examination of narrower product categories might be feasible as long as confidentiality was maintained.

Given the suggestive evidence that most intra-COCOM licensing is unnecessary since virtually all applications to this area are approved, the government should carefully consider nearly complete decontrol of all intra-COCOM licensing. Only a few "crown jewels," where the United States either remains preeminent (e.g., certain software, according to the National Research Council) or shares a technological lead with another country or very few other countries (e.g., supercomputers), and which are acknowledged as particularly useful in designing and enhancing military systems, would still be controlled. While decontrol is the goal of the 1988 Omnibus Trade Act, the act stipulated that countries have adequate control mechanisms in place before decontrol is granted. This stipulation is prudent yet curious given the already high license approval rate and the compromises on auditing that the United States agreed to. A difficult balance must be maintained among trusting the allies, complying with decisions made in COCOM, and risking losses despite good-faith efforts on the part of the allies. There is the additional dilemma of what the repercussions might be from reinstatement of U.S. licensing should a COCOM ally fail to maintain adequate domestic controls. Successful implementation of safeguards in Eastern Europe could help ease concerns over diversions from the COCOM area via Eastern Europe to the former Soviet republics. A virtually license-free COCOM could thereby become a reality.

Some evidence for criticizing agency delays in licensing can be drawn from the data and GAO studies. It appears that criticism of the DOD's role in the licensing process is overstated, although the DOD has occasionally been unduly obstructive. The DOC, however, has not adequately exerted its statutory leadership role in the licensing process.

The Interagency Balance

While the DOD has been given increased authority to review West-West exports, the relatively small percentage of licenses DOD reviews as well as the relative unimportance, in trade terms, of the destinations DOD reviews suggest that any delays and economic costs caused by the DOD are at most marginal. Various Congressionally mandated reforms and administration compromises, including shorter processing deadlines, higher *de minimus* levels, foreign availability decontrols, and compromises on auditing, which attempted to balance what has been supposedly lost owing to an overly defense-oriented policy on controls, have had mixed success. Some interviewees such as Jim LeMunyon of the American Electronics Association did acknowledge relative improvements. Yet by 1989, the National Machine Tool Builders charged that the DOD was blocking technical changes in rules governing machine tools. And in 1990, the Electronics Industry Association complained that the DOD insisted on classifying certain commercial dual-use items under broad and restrictive Munitions List criteria because the State Department (which issues export licenses for items on the Munitions List) lacked adequate expertise to evaluate these items, thereby slowing the license processing. It is apparent that the DOD continues to demonstrate capability to deflect and neutralize the intended consequences of Congressional export control reform efforts. Despite this intransigence--or important check on technology losses, depending on one's perspective--the GAO has concluded that DOD influence on West-West licensing is minimal (see Chapter 4 and Table 15). This diminished influence compared with the recent past may be why the DOD has sought other avenues to slow licensing.[47]

There is evidence of large-scale but ineffective covert Russian effort to acquire U.S.-origin technology, and this ineffectiveness suggests that an expansion of the DOD's role in the export control licensing process is not warranted. Counterintelligence is best left to the FBI and CIA. But, as Henry Nau suggests, the strengthening of DOD processing and evaluation resources did spur sorely needed improvements in the DOC's own operations.[48] The DOD's expertise is an asset in gathering and analyzing intelligence on covert activities, utilization of technology in Soviet military systems, and in interagency deliberations over exports of particularly sensitive dual-use items or concerning control list reviews.

While there was a growing bureaucratic imbalance during the early 1980s in favor of the security-oriented DOD view, a strong DOD--or the *perception* of a strong DOD--has (perhaps unintentionally) served to bolster the administration's leverage. It demonstrates apparent U.S. seriousness on technology transfer issues to both COCOM allies and domestic and non-COCOM exporters. While there is a trade-off in terms of aggravating relations with the allies, negating effective presentation of coherent policy owing to heightened interagency bickering, and discouraging domestic exporters, the evidence suggests that the overall impact of the DOD is relatively slight. In this connection, it is warranted that the GAO continue to monitor the DOD in export controls. This should include periodic follow-up studies of the DOD's impact on both East-West and West-West licensing decisions. If, as seems to be the case, the DOD continues to add very little to West-West licensing determinations, the DOD's role should be reevaluated and downgraded, although it should not be eliminated entirely from the process. On the other hand, the political function of DOD review as a means of, in effect, threatening other countries deemed to be uncooperative with stricter U.S. export control policy cannot be ignored and appears to have some utility.

Controversy over the DOD's influence has not subsided and there are grounds for criticizing the department's intransigence. But the fact remains that *under present law*, the DOC is the lead agency in coordinating and implementing domestic export control policy while the State Department (under Sec. 5(k) of the EAA) is authorized to conduct multilateral negotiations. Therefore, the DOC must exert its power. Increased concern over flagging exports generally, loss of technological competitiveness, and an easing of U.S.-Russian tensions also suggest that the DOC may become more influential, although it has nowhere near the competence in national security issues as found in the State Department and DOD. Clear and explicit Presidential backing would further strengthen the DOC's hand while proposals that an entirely new agency be created to exclusively handle export controls and licensing are not warranted. Such an agency could become completely dominated by either pro or antitrade views, thereby upsetting the critical balance of views which now exists, however imperfectly, among the DOC, DOD, and State Department.

Evidence of future DOC and State Department deferral to a potentially aggressive and growing DOD presence on the bureaucratic map bears further watching. Partly, the interagency balance is a management decision and a function of the preferences and policies of the President and his top advisors and of the personalities of agency heads. This balance reflects the proper role of agencies as the implementors of Presidential desires and policies.[49] For example, as the Nixon and Ford administrations pursued detente, export controls were liberalized and export license processing and enforcement were relaxed. Under Carter (after about 1979) and Reagan (during his first term), controls were tightened and national security considerations increased in importance. A particularly conservative group of policymakers was appointed by Reagan to positions in the DOD where they, supported by like-minded elements in the CIA and on the NSC, effectively influenced export control policy and administration. Presidential backing is a powerful advantage in bureaucratic jousting when coupled with the expanded resources the DOD was provided. But as East-West tensions eased and priorities slowly shifted after 1985, the administration's preference for warmer U.S.-Soviet relations suggests that the bureaucratic balance was slowly restored with a relative deemphasis of export controls. The appointment of William Verity as Commerce Secretary, a strong advocate of expanded U.S.-Soviet trade, was one sign of this shift. Furthermore, the DOC increased its manpower and the creation of the Bureau of Export Administration in 1987 was a bureaucratic effort to match the DOD's Defense Technology Security Administration.[50]

By the late 1980s, interviews suggested a consensus that the DOC was approaching parity with the DOD in terms of expertise and resources, although a 1989 staff report for the House Committee on Science, Space, and Technology found that DOC licensing staff continues to have a significantly heavier workload than DOD staff. It is also difficult for the DOC to hire and retain qualified technical personnel. Heavy workloads and inadequate expertise cause licensing delays and, possibly, poor reviews which may jeopardize national security if a significant technology is inadvertently licensed for export. However, a very large percentage of applications reviewed by the DOC are routine and relatively low-technology goods and therefore undergo perfunctory screening. The workload issue is therefore overstated, although a shorter control list would also ease the problem. The prospect of losses owing to lack of qualified analysis is also overstated since most Russian acquisitions are via espionage and diversions. However, the staff report's recommendation that the National Bureau of Standards (NBS) be given lead authority in technical evaluation has merit and should be considered. Utilizing the NBS would enhance both the DOC's pool of expertise and it status as the lead export control agency.[51]

Strategic export control policy has been adapted during the postwar era to changing foreign policy conditions. Although the United States has advocated and generally carried out a tighter embargo against the U.S.S.R. and its allies, Washington's policy has changed, often belatedly in the allies' view but sometimes significantly, in line with evolving East-West relations and the cyclical pattern of the U.S.-Soviet relationship. In a period of historic change in Eastern Europe and the former Soviet Union, lingering Cold War rationales underlying the denial policy are under reevaluation. Further adaptation of the denial policy to evolving conditions should be considered in light of these changes.

GORBACHEV, YELTSIN, CHANGE IN EASTERN EUROPE, AND THE FUTURE OF EXPORT CONTROLS

The extraordinary political changes and social upheaval in Eastern Europe raise important questions regarding the future of COCOM and U.S. strategic export controls. Any reevaluation of U.S. export control policy is also inseparable from the state of the U.S.-Russian relationship and perceptions of the relative threat the former Soviet republics pose to U.S. interests. U.S.-Soviet and U.S.-Russian relations have been improving steadily since 1985 and many arms controls, regional, and human rights issues that for so long spilled over and constrained economic relations either are being or have a good possibility of being resolved. The changes in Eastern Europe and first Gorbachev's and now Yeltsin's reformist inclination hold out the promise of resolving fundamental conflicts originating in the earliest days of the Cold War. Because of this prospect, the geopolitical and intellectual foundations of postwar U.S. strategic export control policy are being challenged and may increasingly lose their relevance, requiring adaptation to radically changed circumstances.

At the same time, the purely military rationale for strategic export controls remains a function of the relative Russian military threat and Russian military capabilities. At present, with the initiation of Soviet troop pullbacks from parts of Eastern Europe, the increasing likelihood of complete Soviet withdrawal in the future, and the   disintegration of the

Warsaw Pact as a viable military organization, the immediate threat to Western Europe is receding according to U.S. military officials. However, favorable developments in Europe do not necessarily justify a quick and substantial relaxation of strategic controls given the implications of Gorbachev's and Yeltsin's economic policies for Russian military capabilities, as discussed more fully below.

Evaluation of Russian Policy and Intentions

While liberalization in Russia and the other former Soviet republics and the crumbling of Soviet hegemony over the Eastern European satellites are welcomed events among Western publics and leaders, in terms of protecting security interests any rush to greatly liberalize East-West strategic export controls would be imprudent, even foolhardy. Given the present uncertainty over Russia's and the other republics' domestic conditions and intentions, inevitable reminders of historic Soviet militancy and Russian nationalist aspirations, and the cyclical pattern of postwar U.S.-Soviet relations, a rapid deterioration in East-West relations and increased tensions is not inconceivable. Furthermore, high-technology trade does provide some leverage, although it is naive to overstate its efficacy as a lever, as was popular in the 1970s. Therefore, and only in concert with the allies, the trade carrot can encourage political and economic developments in reforming Eastern European states (in particular) and in Russia and the other republics in a desirable direction. An immediate and wide-ranging liberalization of controls would reduce the potential leverage high-technology trade offers.

The United States has stressed that strategic controls will not be loosened radically despite pleas from Moscow. Officials do not want a repeat of detente-era technology losses, and public opinion opposes expansion of trade in militarily related goods.[52] This hesitancy faces mounting political pressure, domestically and abroad, to encourage and bolster reforms in Eastern Europe and Russia through expanded trade. Advocates argue that there is a historic opportunity for conclusively ending Russian domination over most or perhaps all the Eastern European states and promoting viable, pluralist democracies. While they might not be allied militarily with the West, even a neutral status a la Finland during the Cold War would be a pivotal development in postwar Europe and a successful culmination to years of U.S. policy toward the area. Ultimately, in the wake of successful reforms, there is the promise of an end to Europe's division and even the possible reintegration of Russia and the other former Soviet republics into a web of political and economic relations eventually negating any latent expansionist interests.

Conversely, Yeltsin's overthrow, or the threat of complete political and social destabilization if reform efforts fail or are perceived as ineffective, could result in a conservative backlash and a reversion (by a new neo-communist or ultranationalist leadership) to a militant policy toward the West. This occurrence would strengthen calls in the West to curtail technology transfers, as happened in the wake of disappointments with detente during the 1970s. Both the CIA and the DOD continue to disagree over the likelihood of such a reversal.[53] Prior to the August 1992 coup attempt and the subsequent dissolution of the U.S.S.R., former CIA Director Webster deemed it unlikely that even a new and militant Soviet leadership will militarily threaten the West. Webster's successor, Robert Gates has called for redirecting CIA resources away from monitoring East-West trade and technology transfer, emphasizing instead the growing threat from global weapons proliferation and industrial espionage by U.S. economic competitors. This argument reveals an emerging recognition that the threat posed by the former Soviet republics is significantly diminished.[54] Defense Secretary Cheney and others inside and outside the defense community are less sanguine. Until a stronger consensus over the present Soviet regime's viability and future intentions is reached, from a strategic point of view a cautious skepticism is arguably the safest approach. Given new, unexpected circumstances, export control policy will not only be a function of political relations between Washington and Moscow but also a function of how U.S. policymakers perceive Soviet intentions in the context of historical experience and the evolution of events.[55]

While it is difficult to define actual Russian intentions with regard to East-West technology transfer, the outlines are discernible. It is clear that the former Soviet republics' and Eastern European economies have increasingly stagnated since the 1970s and that they appear unable to provide much more than a basic level of welfare for their citizens. The technological lag has affected military R&D and procurement with serious implications for Russian national security. Prior to the U.S.S.R.'s collapse, leading Soviet military figures (such as Marshal Ogarkov) recognized the serious implications rapid Western advances and lagging Soviet capabilities and productivity had for Soviet military R&D.[56] There is also evidence that basic measurements of health and welfare have eroded, suggesting that fundamental structural weaknesses are galvanizing frustrated citizens into protests against ossified authorities and social inequities.

To combat this mounting crisis, Gorbachev and then Yeltsin initiated ambitious plans to revitalize the Soviet-Russian economy with an infusion of Western know-how, stressing the importance of high technology as the cure for the sclerosis gripping the economy. This tactic is not new, the Russians and/or Soviets have traditionally relied on Western technology to overcome "backwardness" and perceived lags. But while certain reforms, such as legalizing joint ventures, have been initiated to implement the new policy, economists are very skeptical of the reforms' success unless the basic command-economy structure is scrapped in favor of something akin to a Western-style market mechanism.[57]

There was, moreover, a strong autarchic vein in Soviet economic theory and practice that meshed with the military's desire to maintain domestic self-sufficiency in defense industries and production. It will be difficult to wean the massive military-industrial complex built under the communists from its traditional pattern of production. It is also clear that, given sufficient time and resources, the Soviets could develop indigenous technology, and military technology in particular, to match Western systems. Despite serious economic dislocation, the skills and resources marshalled by the Soviets are still available to Russia and the other successor republics. Furthermore, there appears to be no desire to permit growing dependence on Western suppliers. Rather, Gorbachev's expressed intention was to expand indigenous Soviet production capabilities so as to increase exports of high-quality and competitive goods based on infusions of Western technology and managerial and organizational practices. Yeltsin and other republics' leaders have urged the West to invest in the former Soviet domains and for Western governments and international bodies to provide aid and trade credits and financial assistance. The military has had to accept cuts in funding as investments are channeled into the civilian sector. But the high-technology industries targeted for investment and Western aid and know-how, such as machine building, are also those that incorporate or manufacture dual-use technology and supply the military. Under Gorbachev, the Soviet military-industrial complex still enjoyed priority access to technology despite much-ballyhooed Soviet claims that a conversion of some defense factories to civilian production was taking place. Reportedly, weapons procurement absorbed about one-third of the Soviet machine-building sector's output.[58] While efforts at conversion have continued and accelerated under Yeltsin, many factories still produce weapons and other militarily-related goods as they did under the former system. Even if the military-industrial complex does succeed in converting to civilian production, a strengthened civilian sector could assist Russian military R&D and production in the future, whereas today the industrial base is antiquated and civilian industry is plagued by bottlenecks and inefficiency. During the late 1980s, CIA and Defense Intelligence Agency analysts concluded that Gorbachev negotiated a compromise with powerful military interests worried about declining productivity trends.[59]   The military acquiesced to a smaller budget and investment share while the civilian economy was resuscitated. In the long term, so the argument went, the military expected to benefit from a more modernized and efficient defense-industrial base and stimulation of domestic innovation and R&D.[60] Although economic conditions and performance have continued to deterio- rate under Yeltsin, assuming Western aid and investment--and eased technology controls--do help revive the Russian economy, then this could boost the modernization process significantly. Yeltsin plans a pared-down, more efficient Russian military which will still be the largest in Europe. In the future this smaller force could rely on high-technology weaponry developed and produced by a revived industry. Should renewed tensions or internal political instability bring about an anti-Western reaction or Yeltsin's ouster, the implications for U.S. and Western security would be troubling.

Aside from his domestic policy, Gorbachev engaged in a foreign policy that sought to create a breathing space and to lessen East-West tensions so that his domestic crises and reforms could be dealt with and implement- ed.[61]   A series of initiatives in arms control, human rights, and regional issues were inaugurated to defuse long-standing disagreements with the West.   Soviet troop pullbacks from Eastern Europe and cuts in defense spending were confirmed by the CIA and DOD, with CIA Director Webster and Defense Secretary Cheney acknowledging the decreased threat the dissolving Warsaw Pact now posed to NATO.[62]   These trends have continued under Yeltsin and the Warsaw Pact is now history.   Cheney, however, still warns of the threat from the massive Soviet military forces deployed in the U.S.S.R. proper.   In this context, under Gorbachev and Yeltsin, Kremlin support for reforms in Eastern Europe can also be seen not only as a means of encouraging an orderly transition from unpopular leadership cadres and preventing an explosion of social unrest but also as a means of eliminating conservative poles of opposition to Moscow's reformist agenda and easing a serious drain on Russian resources.   In addition, Moscow has confirmed that the era of steadfast Soviet domination over Eastern Europe, a domination justified by the Brezhnev Doctrine, is over. This was one of the conditions President Bush urged for improved relations.[63]

Prior to the attempted coup and his replacement by Yeltsin, one interpretation of Gorbachev's sincerity at least *implicitly* suggested that much Soviet foreign policy was a sham to lull the West into concessions ultimately strengthening an inherently aggressive Soviet state.   While acknowledging the potentially positive consequences of Gorbachev's efforts for U.S.-Soviet relations, analysts such as Richard Pipes, Fred Ikle, and Stephen Bryen were skeptical of Soviet tactics and the long-range outcome of the Soviet leader's efforts.[64] A differing interpretation was that Gorbachev was a skillful politician and hardnosed realist who had concluded that the severity of the Soviet crisis was profound. He perceived that the old policies were completely irrelevant and discredited and that major retrenchment was necessary to overcome mounting domestic challenges to the Soviet state's and Communist Party's legitimacy. Easing East-West tensions and resolving long-term U.S.-Soviet disagreements was therefore part of Gorbachev's policy. Much the same can be said about Yeltsin who must grapple with a host of challenges. These include a steadily declining economy, the entrenched anti-reformist bureaucratic holdovers from the old command system who thwart systemic change, mounting popular unrest over the pace and pain of reform, and various ethnic disturbances and centrifugal forces challenging his authority. As the dominant member of the shaky Commonwealth, any significant weakening or the collapse of Moscow's authority could result in political chaos and immense suffering for millions. Yeltsin's long-term political survival and the successful outcome of his initiatives are consequently in U.S. and Western interests assumptions which are at least implicit to advocates of assisting the Russian and the other former Soviet republics.[65] If true, this has implications for U.S. strategic export control policy.

Systemic Change in Eastern Europe and Recommendations for U.S. Policy

Economic containment may also become irrelevant as a result of the changes sweeping Eastern Europe and the former U.S.S.R. Geopolitically, the grounds for containment rested on a long-term goal of restraining Soviet expansionism, preventing Soviet domination over all of Europe, and forcing the U.S.S.R. to turn inward and mellow as domestic problems and diversions sapped historic global ambition. To an extent, this appears to be happening in that the Russian domestic crisis commands center stage in the Kremlin.

Whether export controls have contributed to the historic changes in the U.S.S.R. is an intriguing question and one which relates to the much larger issue of whether the U.S. postwar "grand strategy" of containment "won" the Cold War. Since the outcome of the changes in the U.S.S.R. is still in doubt, and only historical perspective can provide truly satisfactory answers, only a preliminary judgment regarding the effect of controls can be rendered.

Strategic controls and the denial policy were a component of containment as it emerged in the late 1940s and early 1950s. To the extent that containment has succeeded in forcing the emerging, apparently pragmatic and reform-minded Soviet leadership cadres who came of age politically during the postwar era to confront the U.S.S.R.'s structural deficiencies and long-simmering ethnic and social cleavages, then controls in some way also aided containment's success. To be sure, it is too simplistic to cite the economic embargo as the *principal* cause of the historic changes in the Soviet and communist world. The historical record must in any case remain open on the question of causation. However, it is arguable that by hindering (to some degree) transfers of technology, the patently inefficient Soviet economic system was forced to devote scarce human and capital resources to the development of dual-use technologies and related industries. Controls therefore revealed and exacerbated the inherently flawed allocation powers of a system that could succeed for a time at growth based on *quantitative* resources, but which failed as the developed market economies rapidly shifted to growth generated by higher efficiency *qualitative* advantages--the basis for a high-technology economy and society. The Soviet economy stagnated. Important civilian sectors of the economy became obsolescent and inefficient. Heavy investment in defense systems, including indigenous development of embargoed defense-related technologies, in order to match Western military advances, penalized Soviet consumers who endured a declining standard of living that by the 1980s was demonstrably lower than some of the Newly Industrializing Countries. The mounting dissatisfaction with these conditions and their alleviation continues to be a serious challenge to leaders of the former Soviet republics, since their very legitimacy is at stake. But in the case of Russia, Ukraine, and potentially, several other republics, economic cripples continue to be powerful military giants.

Although conventional arms negotiations and the Conference on Security and Cooperation in Europe promise to pave the way for establishment of a security regime and political settlement in Europe, U.S. policymakers must not grow complacent over the continent's long-term military balance. While Moscow tolerated electoral defeat or voluntary self-liquidation of communist leaderships and parties in Eastern Europe, Russia will probably draw the line where its vital security interests are involved. Moscow's historical interest in protecting the Russia's Western approaches would seem to rule out complete withdrawal of its troops from the entire area without adequate negotiated guarantees. However, negotiations for agreements on troop pullbacks are under way with several Eastern European states and pullbacks from Czechoslovakia and Hungary have been completed. Even if substantial or complete pullbacks occur, the Russia will remain the preeminent military power in Europe and therefore a *potential* threat to neighboring states. The United States must also bear in mind the fragility of Yeltsin's domestic position and the uncertain prospects of current and any future non communist-led governments in Eastern Europe. A conservative backlash (led by communists or perhaps non communists) and defeat of Yeltsin's and the other reform efforts in the former Soviet republics and in some of the Eastern European states is a possibility. And the chances could increase if several years of continuing economic stagnation and deteriorating social conditions kindle renewed public cynicism and discontent, conditions which are already evident. The poor results of Gorbachev's perestroika policy so far are indicative of the mammoth obstacles that must be overcome and the limited prospects for success.[66]

If history is any guide, even the development of a prosperous Soviet Union (the "fat Russian" scenario) as a consequence of expanded trade is no guarantee that global Russian ambitions would necessarily be subsumed by domestic prosperity and self-satisfaction.[67] An economically revived Russia could again become a global threat. The global U.S.-Russian rivalry might sharpen given the deep-seated distrust both sides have of the other's motives. High growth rates and relative improvement in the standard of living from the 1950s to 1970s did not discourage the U.S.S.R. from pursuing regional and global policies inimical to U.S. and Western interests. Therefore, controls should not be unduly liberalized as long as Russia and other former Soviet republics threaten vital U.S. and Western interests outside of Europe, continue to supply anti-Western states or organizations, or maintain a military force and defense-base out of proportion to "justifiable" defense needs.

All of these issues can be negotiated but, given their sensitivity, and even assuming goodwill on both sides, this process could well take years to complete. Renewed tensions between East and West resulting from a crackdown against reformers and/or friction over arms control and regional issues are therefore conceivable for at least the foreseeable future. A newly aggressive and nationalist policy by the Russians in Europe and globally must be accounted for even if, as seems likely, domestic contradictions remain unresolved. The implications for strategic controls and technology transfer of a reversal in present trends suggest that, given the uncertain pattern of events, no radical loosening of controls is warranted until such time as systemic reforms and military reductions in the U.S.S.R. can be regarded as permanent.[68]

Many in the United States and abroad argue that fears of Gorbachev's and the Eastern European reformists' failure and possible reemergence of East-West confrontation are bound to become self-fulfilling prophecies unless much more is done to assist these crisis-ridden and floundering economies.[69] Increased technology flows must be part of a larger scheme including financial and managerial assistance, outright aid, and efforts aimed at encouraging investment in Eastern Europe. Imports need not be leading-edge technology, which studies and experience show these economies have trouble absorbing. Instead, concrete improvements in welfare could be achieved through imports of relatively less sophisticated Western medical, light industrial, agricultural, and food processing and refrigeration technology and know-how. Assuming willingness to reform rigidified economies, basic managerial and organizational skills could be taught that eventually translate into improvements in the efficiency of the existing civilian industrial base in Eastern Europe and the former Soviet republics. This would help increase the supply of basic consumer goods, thereby enhancing the reformist regimes' legitimacy and giving inexperienced leaders, professional and/or managerial cadres, and the population as a whole a stake in continuing and supporting more progressive and open policies.

While it cannot be expected that U.S. trade with Eastern Europe and the former Soviet republics will grow rapidly in the short and medium term, the prospect and economic potential of eventually developing large, relatively untapped markets must be considered. Assuming no major downturn in East-West relations (as happened in the late 1970s), as well as a favorable investment climate in Eastern Europe and the former Soviet republics, U.S. firms should be competitive in several of the industries and related service sectors mentioned above. While strategic considerations must remain paramount, as global economic competition inevitably grows, and as the importance of foreign trade to U.S. economic growth, welfare, and security increases, policymakers must consider the benefits of future increased trade.[70]

Trade can also increase national security. For example, the economic dividends of trade, such as some portion of future profits from expanding sales, can be reinvested in R&D on new dual-use technologies. Growing demand in these markets *could* also help revitalize some struggling domestic high-technology exporters facing increasingly stiff foreign competition. Their export success would thereby help bolster the viability of a critical component of the defense-industrial base. The Soviets also have substantial reserves of key strategic minerals and other raw materials--resources which are, or which will eventually be, depleted in the United States. Trading technology for minerals would therefore have a strategic rationale. While the U.S. energy picture in terms of imports is better than that of Europe or Japan, rising consumption trends, declining domestic production, and growing dependence on oil from historically unstable areas such as the Middle East suggest that eventually negotiating for Russian and other republics' energy resources should be considered.   Exports of U.S. extraction know-how and technology to assist the former Soviet republics in efficiently recovering, processing, and transporting minerals and energy products for domestic uses and for export to the United States would therefore be mutually beneficial from both U.S. economic and national security perspectives.   An added plus, albeit a more distant outcome given the underdeveloped state of markets in the former Soviet republics and of U.S.-Russian and U.S.-Eastern European trade, is the potential benefit for easing macroeconomic problems such as the trade deficit, as is suggested in a recent Overseas Development Council study.[71]   How much these benefits outweigh the cost of maintaining and complying with remaining export controls is difficult to determine but, nonetheless, they are longer-term considerations.

The U.S. should not expect that the economic carrot will be particularly or immediately effective in influencing domestic change in the former Soviet repubics or in Russia's or the other republics' foreign policy.   But the indirect influence of expanded access to high technology and consumer goods could create conditions for the pluralization of former communist societies over the long term.   Differentiated and politicized interest groups, deriving political leverage from functional roles enhanced by technological progress, could become new poles for articulating interests.[72]   To take another example, increased use of personal computers (PCs) and access to printers could benefit opposition groups and further the exchange of information.[73]   Indirect evidence for this comes from Poland, where clandestine desktop publishing provided the Solidarity opposition with a means of communicating with the Polish people even as the regime sought to stifle Solidarity activities.   Greater access to PCs might also increase the power of the managerial, technocratic, and intellectual elite, thereby helping to balance the decrepit and entrenched party *apparatchiks* and strengthening these elites as a force lobbying for change and defending new thinking.[74]

Perhaps equally as important, successful investment in civilian production assisted by imports of non-strategic Western technology and know-how *could* encourage a sustained reduction in available factor inputs and investment allocation to the military and weapons production, although U.S. intelligence expects that if it happens this will only be evident over the longer term.[75]   According to John Hardt, reallocation to the civilian sector may already be part of the reason for the slowdown in the growth of Soviet defense expenditures since 1976.[76]   Yeltsin clearly has a stake in placating mounting consumer discontent and preventing environmental degradation, and his policy expands on half-hearted attempts begun in the 1960s designed to enhance the Soviet population's welfare. A policy of expanded but carefully screened and monitored nonstrategic technology transfers that can relatively quickly benefit Soviet consumers and enhance environmental safety would therefore seem to be in the U.S. interest.[77] The apparently poor condition of nuclear safety in the former Soviet republics and environmental pollution controls are also areas where cooperation between the West and the Commonwealth would yield mutual benefits.

End-use problems could be overcome by periodic monitoring of production facilities and assessment of their performance in meeting consumer needs. This appears to be acceptable to the former Soviet republics as evidenced by the safeguard conditions attached to the recent sale of advanced U.S. computers for upgrading nuclear plant safety. Future U.S. joint venture partners and possible U.S. government-backed loans (assuming current prohibitions are lifted) could require such oversight as a condition for sharing or financing imports of U.S.-origin technology. On-site inspections by Western personnel of installed high technology are reportedly acceptable to some Eastern European governments and were recently endorsed by the British House of Commons Trade and Industry Committee.[78] Such restrictions and careful down grading of otherwise sensitive technology were successful in protecting technology security in Eastern Europe and the U.S.S.R. during the 1960s-70s, according to R. J. Carrick, former British representative at COCOM. Down grading technology, known as technology transfer engineering, has also been endorsed by the DOD.[79] Presumably, inspections might be carried out by representatives of the Western company, by U.S. and allied government representatives, a combination of the two, or even U.N. personnel.[80] This has the added advantage of permitting export of relatively sophisticated items that would not necessarily have to be technically down graded to conform to national security limits, although that was successfully done in the past according to Carrick. Furthermore, the DOC believes various restrictions on spare parts and maintenance agreements tied to high-technology exports can be negotiated on a case-by-case basis. This was done in the cases of a recent sales of advanced U.S. civilian jetliners--incorporating sophisticated avionics--and jet engines to several Eastern European domestic airlines and the Soviets. Although cautious about this approach, DOD officials have not rejected it outright.[81] As an analyst at the West German Foreign Ministry pointed out, acceptance of on-site inspections would be a confidence-building measure boosting Western trust in the safety of legal technology transfers.[82] Any violation would be severely embarrassing to the host government, confronting it with the prospect of either losing access to technology imports in the shorter or longer term or having to accept down graded or inferior technology. There is also limited precedent for on-site inspections in the arms-control sphere.[83]   Whether the Russians would agree to inspections in key installations that supply both the civilian and military sectors is unknown, however permitting such inspections would be a test of Yeltsin's openness policy.   Furthermore, assuming inspections are allowed in principle, a probationary period might be required during which the Russian government and the purchasing company would be expected to follow the letter of agreement (including inspections and other restrictions) concerning the acquired technology.   Future sales would be contingent on performance during this (and possibly future) probations.

Die-hard opponents of technology sales to the former Soviet republics would not easily be placated despite this cautious approach. But given a track record of poor adaptation of Western technology and the likelihood that spares and Western maintenance expertise for critical components, which the Russians could not replace quickly (if at all), could be withdrawn in case of egregious violations, their objections seem less credible. Furthermore, even after a decade of liberalized technology transfers, by the early 1980s Soviet lags in several critical dual-use technologies were unchanged or had even grown and the civilian industrial base continued to erode.   Also indicative of the historic inability of the U.S.S.R. to fully absorb and utilize Western technology transfers is the relatively slower (even declining) rates of Soviet economic growth that coincided with trade liberalization during the 1970s.[84] In comparison, very high rates of growth were recorded during the 1950s and 1960s, when control lists were much longer. Barring unexpected, highly classified Russian development of a weapon representing a quantum leap in military technology derived from Western technology (a *very* unlikely possibility[85]), U.S. and allied intelligence agencies will keep abreast of Soviet evolutionary military developments and warn of diverted technology incorporated in Russian systems. The considerable gaps between acquisition, adaptation, incorporation, testing, and deployment of significant numbers of a system based on diverted dual-use technology means that Western analysts should have opportunities to warn of consequences for the military balance, as they did in the late 1970s and 1980s. Western governments can then take appropriate action placing pressure on the Russian government to own up to and cease its violations or endure a range of sanctions, including renewed technology transfer restrictions.

An added factor militating against the Russians' gaining undue advantage is the dynamic pace of technological innovation in the West, which is not likely to be matched at any time soon by the Russians even if innovative energies and managerial know-how are improved through expanded East-West contacts. Unless sweeping reforms are implemented, the stifling burden of decades of bureaucratic control and probable continuing lack of wider personal freedom and incentives to innovate (what Marshall Goldman calls the "systems gap"[86]) cannot be discounted as a powerful brake on creativity. Full implementation of requisite reforms endangers the regime's and entrenched interests' legitimacy and therefore is unlikely for the foreseeable future.[87] Indeed, dependence on Western technology may actually increase, despite conscious resistance on the part of the leadership, as appears to have been the pattern with computer and related technology. In addition, the extremely complex designs of new generations of semiconductor-driven technology appear to offer considerable protection against reverse-engineering of diverted goods not caught during inspections. Even if reverse-engineering is possible in certain instances and over a period of time, rapid technological developments in the West and short product life cycles suggest that a Soviet "clone" would be leapfrogged by the time it is thoroughly developed and utilized. Faster incorporation of leading-edge technologies into U.S. military systems would also maintain the U.S. edge over Russian advances.

A final argument for liberalizing controls, at least to some degree, relates to the established policy of differentiation between Eastern Europe and the former Soviet republics. If adequate safeguards and assurances can be negotiated, there would be an incentive for the Poles and Hungarians, for example, to protect technology imports from unauthorized use or diversions. Conservatives such as Richard Perle have recently expressed support for adequately safeguarded technology transfers to Eastern Europe for civilian purposes.[88] To the extent that differentiation and Most Favored Nation treatment have been successful in encouraging independence from Moscow, the added lure of expanded technology flows, contingent on successful and continuing reform efforts, could help to solidify these gains while bolstering strongly felt nationalist opposition to Russian domination. That in turn might further weaken any residual influence by domestic anti reformers and domination by Russia as Poland, Hungary, and other Eastern European states become more deeply enmeshed in expanding political and trade relations with the West. A two-track policy of relatively greater and lesser liberalization of controls vis-a-vis, respectively, Eastern Europe and the former Soviet republics (already practiced to a limited extent in COCOM during the early 1980s) could eventually have desirable effects on Russian behavior and reforms. To the extent that Yeltsin or his successors view the reforms in Eastern Europe as worthy of emulation (and this already is the case), and if the West's technology transfusion contributes to that success, the (it is hoped) moderate Western-style models that evolve in Eastern Europe could influence reformers in the former Soviet republics and bolster Yeltsin's and other moderate and pro-Western leaders' standing.[89] Increased exposure to Western-style affluence and cultural and political liberties could also have a demonstrable effect akin to the influence West German living standards had on the East German population. Over time, the former Soviet republics might follow the Eastern European lead, in the process becoming a more open society where interest in increasing integration into the global economy slowly replaces obsolete autarchic economic ideology, eases historic insecurity, and ends expansionist illusions. At some point, comprehensive strategic export controls directed against the U.S.S.R. might no longer be needed.

CONCLUSION

Strategic export controls on high technology are and will continue to be necessary for both the U.S. and COCOM allies for the foreseeable future. During a period of historic change in East-West relations posing fundamental challenges to the entire rationale underlying U.S. strategic policy and policy in Europe, the United States must not forsake its leadership role in the multilateral control effort. Nor must U.S. policymakers be slow to recognize how these powerful forces for change impact on U.S. strategic export control policy as well as their implications for prudent adaptation of that policy. While the outcome of the sudden changes in Eastern Europe and the apparent dissolution of Russian hegemony there is uncertain, there is now a unique prospect of reuniting Europe and protecting and enhancing the geopolitically vital U.S. interest in Western Europe's security and stable conditions in Eastern Europe.

Careful liberalization of controls on high technology, as part of a broad-range scheme to revitalize and reform stagnant economies in Eastern Europe, can pay political dividends and smooth the area's transition through an uncertain and difficult present. While protecting national security must still be the overriding concern, this study's strategic and economic evaluations suggest that U.S. policymakers enjoy some flexibility in tailoring policy to changing conditions. This flexibility is possible because the qualitative gap in dual-use technology between the U.S. and the former Soviet republics has not eroded and is widening, while the burden and costs of controls themselves are overstated and probably minimal.

Specifically, despite years of intensive Soviet efforts to acquire sensitive dual-use technology and the varying effectiveness and comprehensiveness of the U.S. and multilateral embargo, the Soviets continue to lag behind the United States in many dual-use technologies. To the extent that export controls, as an important component of postwar U.S. containment strategy, compounded inherent flaws in the Soviet economic system and forced the Kremlin to allocate scarce resources to the military sector at the expense of the civilian economy, then controls may be said to have had some role in influencing a new generation of postwar Soviet leaders toward addressing neglected economic and social problems. A generally acknowledged reason for the reformist drive and conciliatory foreign policy of Russia and the other former Soviet republics is the widening scope of the techno-economic gap vis-a-vis the West, exacerbated by a highly inefficient and deeply entrenched central planning system that stifled creative dynamism.

A more flexible U.S. policy, where controls are eased on many technologies (but clearly not on some nuclear know-how or conventional weapons) would not necessarily or immediately translate into an improvement in Russian military capabilities. Even if they were enhanced, this could take years while the crumbling civilian economy would also be vying for its share and U.S. capabilities also advanced. In addition, U.S. analysts have been prone to overestimate Russian capabilities as the "missile" and "bomber" gaps of yore attest to. Furthermore, having a capability is not necessarily threatening unless Russia and some or all the other former Soviet republics shifts political gears and again threatens U.S. and Western interests, a prospect the CIA now believes is unlikely. Even in that event, the West could reduce or freeze investment, trade, and technology transfers depending on the nature of the threat in order to punish Russian transgressions. This is particularly feasible in the short and medium term as Moscow scrambles for investments and technology and attempts to reform its sclerotic economy. Given his deteriorating domestic situation, it is unlikely that Yeltsin would risk his ties with the West. As was the case after the souring of detente in the 1970s, reimposition of tighter controls or braking trade and technology transfers would be sustainable by the West since most technology trade will continue to be between Western market economies for the foreseeable future. Because the nature of the modern global economy is increasingly one of ever-tighter interdependence, as time passes the stronger and more established Russian ties are with the Western economies, the more the welfare and economic cost of endangering or reversing those ties rises. In the longer term, there would seem to be decreasing prospects for Moscow to risk a reversal of the expected gains coming from its opening to the West, although such a reversal cannot be completely ruled out.

A collapsed Soviet empire, weak economic and technological capacity, and concrete signs of Soviet willingness to resolve long-standing political and foreign policy questions have created conditions for reevaluating U.S. policy. This is important since the United States must coordinate its policy with the COCOM allies, who are eager to respond to events and resolve Europe's division. COCOM provides a forum for allied discussions and the United States must be prepared to recognize legitimate allied interests. At the same time, there are also potential economic and national security benefits accruing to the United States from expanding trade in the wake of export control liberalization, at least over the longer term. For example, the United States and its COCOM allies share an interest in a politically and economically stable Eastern Europe and the avoidance of endemic civil conflict in the former Soviet republics that threatens to reverse reformist initiatives.

Over the longer term, political and economic reintegration of Eastern Europe and the former Soviet republics with the West might forge lasting interdependence and eliminate vestiges of ideological animosities. If this occurs, the crucial role strategic controls played in protecting and furthering U.S. interests will have been validated.

NOTES

1. Critics urge more coherent and detailed exposition by the United States of evidence linking rising defense expenditures to militarily critical technology transfers. The public might therefore be more sympathetic to the U.S. case. While CIA and DOD publications have made the case, these critics urge even more openness. This is a reasonable suggestion, although protection of intelligence sources is also a consideration and precludes some revelations. See Admiral Sir James Eberle, Director, Royal Institute of International Affairs and Terence Murphy, attorney, Murphy and Malone, comments at the *Strategic Export Controls Conference*, held at Royal Institute of International Affairs, London, 19 November 1987, rpt. in *Conference Proceedings* (available from RIIA), pp. 115-17; and Hugh Malim, Assistant Director, Barclays Bank, PLC, interview, London, 26 October 1988.

2. Henry R. Nau, "Export Controls and Free Trade: Squaring the Circle in COCOM," in *Controlling East-West Trade and Technology Transfer: Power, Politics, and Policies*, ed. Gary K. Bertsch (Durham, NC: Duke University Press, 1988), p. 401.

3. The significance of signaling through the use of embargoes and trade sanctions has been stressed by David Baldwin and others. See Philip Hanson, *Western Economic Statecraft in East-West Relations*, Chatham House Papers, no. 40 (London: Routledge and Kegan Paul, 1988), p. 18, citing David A. Baldwin, *Economic Statecraft* (Princeton, NJ: Princeton University Press, 1985) and Robert

E. Klitgaard, "Sending Signals," *Foreign Policy*, no. 32 (Fall 1978), pp. 103-06.

4. President Bush announced the lifting of the "no exceptions" policy toward the U.S.S.R. in May 1989. By early 1990, the United States announced it was willing to ease controls on exports to several Eastern European countries. See President Bush, "Proposals for a Free and Peaceful Europe," address at Rheingold-halle, Mainz, Federal Republic of Germany, 31 May 1989, rpt. in U.S. Department of State, Bureau of Public Affairs, *Current Policy*, no. 1179 (June 1989), p. 2; and Stuart Auerbach, "U.S. to Back High-Tech Sales Boost to East Bloc," *Washington Post*, 22 January 1990, section A, p. 13, columns 5-6; section A, p. 17, columns 1-2.

5. For example, Sir Brian Tovey, former Director-General of the U.K.'s Government Communications Headquarters, stressed that COCOM was never intended to punish Soviet wrongdoing or to force economic hardship on the U.S.S.R.; interview, London, 15 December 1988.

6. National Academy of Sciences, *Finding Common Ground: U.S. Export Controls in a Changed Global Environment* (Washington, D.C.: National Academy Press, 1991), pp. 44-45, 277.

7. Malcolm Baldrige, Secretary of Commerce, response to written questions of Sen. Gramm, in U.S. Congress, Senate Committee on Banking, Housing and Urban Affairs, Subcommittee on International Finance and Monetary Policy, *Export Controls*, hearings, 100th Congress, 1st session, 12, 17 March 1987 (Washington, DC: U.S. GPO, 1987), p. 174.

8. Uffe Gardel, "Handelen med ostlande skal liberaliseres [Trade With Eastern Europe Must be Liberalized]," *Berlingske Tidende* [Copenhagen], 9 March 1990, section 2, p. 12; "SPD for Drastic Shortening of Cocom List," *This Week in Germany*, 27 October 1989, p. 6; and Scott Otteman, "Gejdenson Said to be Considering EAA 'Sunset Provisions' to Spur Decontrol," *Inside U.S. Trade*, vol. 8, no. 13 (30 March 1990), p. 3.

9. It is possible that Washington used the prospect of greater nuclear cooperation as a reward or incentive to France for tightening export controls. Apparently, such subtle arm-twisting can be effective as a means of achieving low-profile success. This is inferred from Richard Ullman's research on covert U.S. assistance to the French nuclear weapons program. See Richard H. Ullman, "The Covert French Connection," *Foreign Policy*, no. 75 (Summer 1989), pp. 3-33.

10. A British Foreign Office analyst described the 1988 Omnibus Trade Act as evidence that the United States was attempting the most extensive liberalization among the COCOM states and he welcomed the effort as did a West German Foreign Ministry official. But other current and former British and West German officials were less sanguine about the pace of U.S. efforts; Nick Cooper, North American Trade Policy Section, Department of Trade and Industry, interview, London, 9 November 1988; Tovey, interview; and not-for-attribution interviews, Foreign and Commonwealth Office, London, 3 November 1988 and Ministry of Economics and Foreign Ministry, Bonn, 1 March 1989.

11. Not-for-attribution interview, London, 29 November 1988.

12. According to a British Foreign Office official, in the wake of the 1982 pipeline affair, the U.S. and U.K. reached an informal understanding setting up procedures to head off future U.S. extraterritorial assertions. While the agreement had held up fairly well, this official worried that a future U.S. administration would ignore its provisions or it would simply be forgotten and future conflicts could arise as a result. The official and his colleague also noted the EC Commission's reluctance to demand formal representation at COCOM. See not-for-attribution interview, Foreign and Commonwealth Office, London, 8 June 1989; and Jurgen Notzold and Hendrik Roodbeen, "The European Community and COCOM: The Exclusion of an Interested Party," in *After the Revolutions: East-West Trade and Technology Transfer in the 1990s*, eds. Gary K. Bertsch, Heinrich Vogel, and Jan Zielonka (Boulder, CO: Westview Press, 1991), pp. 119-39. For the figures on reexport requests, see Paul Freedenberg, Assistant Secretary for Trade Administration, Department of Commerce, testimony, 12 March 1987, in U.S. Congress, Senate Committee on Banking, Housing, and Urban Affairs, Subcommittee on International Finance and Monetary Policy, *Export Controls*, hearings, 100th Congress, 1st session, 12, 17 March 1987 (Washington, DC: U.S. GPO, 1987), p. 27.

13. William Root, former Director, Bureau of East-West Trade, Department of State, interview, Washington, DC, 8 March 1988; and not-for-attribution interview, Department of Commerce, 9 March 1988.

14. Negotiations began in late August 1989 between the United States and South Korea on drawing up a list of restricted items. See "Seoul Discusses Controls on Strategic Goods," *Financial Times* [U.S. edition], no. 30,933 (30 August 1989), p. 7, column 8.

15. Since many non-COCOM countries desire Western technology, the United States gains considerable leverage by granting or withholding this "privilege," according to the DOC's Paul Freedenberg. Another DOC official stressed that the threat of a technology cut-off was implicit but that instead of threats, "We say look at the benefits we offer you." See Paul Freedenberg, Under Secretary for Export Administration, Department of Commerce, remarks at a National Issues Forum on *U.S. Export Control Policy: Balancing National Security Issues and Global Competitiveness*, held at The Brookings Institution, Washington, DC, 9 June 1988 and not-for-attribution interviews, Departments of Commerce and State, Washington, DC, 9 March and 23 February 1988.

16. U.S. officials praised Austrian cooperation in curtailing diversions via Austria. See Joe Pichirallo, "Bloch Played Major Role on Technology-Export Issue in Austria," *Washington Post*, 27 August 1989, section A, p. 24, column 4; Stuart Auerbach, "Sweden Approves Strict New Controls On Export of High-Tech Products," *Washington Post*, 6 March 1986, section E, p. 2, columns 4-6; and Jan Stankovsky and Hendrik Roodbeen, "Export Controls Outside COCOM," in *After the Revolutions: East-West Trade and Technology Transfer in the 1990s*, eds. Gary K. Bertsch, Heinrich Vogel, and Jan Zielonka (Boulder, CO: Westview Press, 1991), pp. 71-91.

17. Not-for-attribution interview, Department of State, Bureau of Economic and Business Affairs, Washington, DC, 23 February 1988.

18. In 1989, German officials acknowledged that the F.R.G., Switzerland, and Austria had accounted for about 70% of COCOM violations over the last decade. See David Marsh, "Profiting From Perestroika," *Financial Times* [London], no. 30,787 (7 March 1989), p. 18, column 7; and Joseph Fitchett, "French Investigate Executive in Technology Leak to Russia," *International Herald Tribune*, 15 March 1989, p. 2, columns 1-6.

19. As Brian L. Crowe, Commercial Minister at the British Embassy noted, "Controls are like speed limits." If they are perceived as unreal, even responsible citizens will not respect them; comments at a National Issues Forum on *U.S. Export Control Policy: Balancing National Security Issues and Global Competitiveness*, held at The Brookings Institution, Washington, DC, 9 June 1988. Similar sentiments were expressed by other current and former policymakers. See Tovey, interview; Stewart Nunn, Director (Policy Unit) Export Controls, Department of Trade and Industry, interview, London, 9 November 1988; not-for-attribution interview, Ministry of Defence, London, 31 October 1988; not-for-attribution interviews, Ministry of Foreign Affairs, Bonn, 1, 3 March 1989; and Michael Mastanduno, "Technological Revolution and East-West Relations: Is There a Future for COCOM?", discussion paper prepared for the Aspen Institute Berlin East-West Study Group meeting on *East-West Economic, Technological, and Ecological Cooperation Within a "European House"*, Budapest, Hungary, 15-19 March 1989, p. 8.

20. Telecommunications and machine tools were particularly difficult commodities to reach agreement on, and disagreements between the United States and the allies slowed finalization of the new core list. See *Export Control News*, vol. 5, nos. 1-3 (25 January, 25 February, 26 March 1991) and Clyde H. Farnsworth, "U.S. Balks at Easing Technology-Export Curbs," *New York Times*, 1 March 1991, section C, p. 2, columns 1-4.

21. Auerbach quoting "a senior administration official," "U.S. to Back," section A, p. 17, column 1; David White, "CoCOM Rocked by the Crumbling Wall," *Financial Times* [U.S. edition], no. 31,018 (7 December 1989), p. 6, columns 1-5; and David Goodhard, "Bonn to Press for New Export Rules," *Financial Times* [U.S. edition], 31 January 1990, pp. 1, 16. One U.S. administration official conceded that "If we don't [compromise], we're going to have a major diplomatic row on our hands that will make the Siberian pipeline look like a Boy Scout jamboree." Quoted in Mark Frankel, et al., "High-Tech Tussle," *Newsweek* [European edition], 15 January 1990, p. 45.

22. Chancellor Kohl remarked that "We support political, economic and social change in states of the Warsaw Pact, not least because these changes naturally also affect the GDR. If reforms in Poland and Hungary founder, then the chances also fade for a change in the GDR." Quoted in Robert J. McCartney, "W. German Leader Urges Free Elections in East Germany," *Washington Post*, 22 October 1989, section A, p. 38, column 2.

23. National Research Council, *Global Trends in Computer Technology and Their Impact on Export Control* (Washington, DC: National Academy Press, 1988), p. 219.

24. A State Department official stressed the highly technical questions experts debated, noting that disagreements sometimes revolved around a question of microns either way. This meant that no agency came away with all it wanted and that policymakers who were not experts were forced to compromise based on sometimes, technically speaking, ambiguous choices. Lionel Olmer, a former senior DOC official, noted that different agencies view the question of military criticality differently. One view is that any item used in a U.S. weapons system is critical, regardless of whether the Russians consider it strategic. Given this view, the tendency is to propose additions that inflate the control list with items the Soviets may have no interest in. A British Defence Ministry official noted that limited resources preclude responsible ministries from devoting enough time to reassessing lists. Instead, they strive to be current on the latest technological developments since they pose potential dangers. See not-for-attribution interview, Department of State, Bureau of Economic and Business Affairs, Washington, DC, 23 February 1988; Lionel H. Olmer, attorney, Paul, Weiss, Rifkind, Wharton, and Garrison, testimony, 11 March 1987, in U.S. Congress, House Committee on Foreign Affairs, Subcommittee on International Economic Policy and Trade, *Omnibus Trade and Competitiveness act of 1988 (Vol. II)*, hearings, 100th Congress, 1st session, 11-12 March 1987 (Washington, DC: U.S. GPO, 1988), p. 84, and not-for-attribution interview, Ministry of Defence, London, 31 October 1988.

25. The former DOC official who described the high-level P.R.C. liberalization process insisted that only by such actions could the dual-use list be reduced. The P.R.C. Green Line decision was reached in "about 8 weeks," whereas many months or years usually pass before agency decisions or list changes of this magnitude are made; not-for-attribution interview, Arlington, VA, 17 March 1988.

26. Nunn, interview, and not-for-attribution interview, Foreign and Commonwealth Office, London, 8 June 1989. See also Eric Beston, Head, Overseas Trade Division 2, Branch 3, responsible for COCOM matters, Department of Trade and Industry, testimony, in U.K., House of Commons, Foreign Affairs committee, *Eastern Europe and the Soviet Union*, minutes of evidence, Session 1988-89, 25 January 1989 (London: HMSO, 1989), pp. 198-99; and William E. Whyman, *Strategic Export Controls: Responses to Changing Markets and Technology*, RIIA Discussion Papers, no. 6 (London: Royal Institute of International Affairs, 1988), p. 19.

27. According to the NAS: "It is also essential that State vigorously fulfill its traditional role of ensuring that the U.S. government speak with a single, coherent voice when dealing with foreign governments it is essential that State officials now play a more assertive leadership role in the U.S. CoCom delegation so as to create a balanced representation of U.S. economic and defense interests." National Academy of Sciences, *Balancing the National Interest*, Washington, DC: National Academy Press, 1987), p. 174.

A British Foreign Office official noted that the replacement of key U.S.

personnel, such as the State Department's long-time COCOM expert William Root, upset established and informal working relationships between the United States and the U.K., making informal resolution of problems more difficult. On the other hand, he acknowledged that a fragmented and bickering U.S. representation made it easier to lobby the administration by playing bureaucratic interests against each other; not-for-attribution interview, Foreign and Commonwealth Office, London, 8 June 1989.

28. Henry Nau advocates this; Nau, "Export Controls," p. 414.

29. Not-for-attribution interviews, Ministries of Defense and Foreign Affairs, Bonn, 2-3 March 1989.

30. Patrick E. Tyler, "New Pentagon 'Guidance' Cites Soviet Threat in Third World," *Washington Post*, 13 February 1990, section A, p. 1, columns 5-6; section A, p. 9, columns 1-6; and Lawrence Brady, Sanders Associates, former Assistant Secretary of Commerce for Export Administration, testimony, 17 March 1987, in U.S. Congress, Senate Committee on Banking, Housing, and Urban Affairs, Subcommittee on International Finance and Monetary Policy, *Export Controls*, hearings, 100th Congress, 1st session, 12, 17 March 1987 (Washington, DC: U.S. GPO, 1987), pp. 153-54.

31. Marsh, "Profiting," p. 18, column 7.

32. Given the small size of very sophisticated semiconductors, it is easy to avoid their being detected. Several interviewees expressed concern over the potential of electronic data transmittal as a means of circumventing controls. An analyst at the British Ministry of Defence confessed that he had no idea how such transfers via modems could be prevented. Apparently, COCOM had not yet tackled such questions. International computer networks are also vulnerable and "probably represent the fastest growing gap between development and decision in export control strategy," according to the National Research Council. Several years after the Reagan administration's initial efforts to increase COCOM awareness of covert technology losses, U.S. officials expressed dissatisfaction with allied enforcement efforts. In 1988, a State Department official reported that there were still COCOM countries where only two officers must screen 10,000 applications. The January 1988 agreement is designed to help rectify such problems. See not-for-attribution interviews, Ministry of Defence, London, 31 October 1988, and Department of State, Bureau of Economic and Business Affairs, Washington, DC, 23 February 1988. See also Richard Perle, Assistant Secretary for International Security Policy, Department of Defense, testimony, 1 March 1987, in U.S. Congress, House Committee on Foreign Affairs, Subcommittee on International Economic Policy and Trade, *Omnibus Trade and Competitiveness Act of 1988 (Vol. II)*, hearings, 100th Congress, 1st session, 11-12 March 1987 (Washington, DC: U.S. GPO, 1988), pp. 39-40; Richard Perle, "The Making of Security Policy: Reflections on the Reagan Years," address given at King's College, London, 8 June 1989; not-for-attribution conversation with a CIA analyst, June 1988 and National Research Council, *Global Trends*, p. 224.

Japan, Norway, and the F.R.G. increased enforcement activities in the wake of the heated controversies sparked in the United States by the Toshiba-Kongsberg scandal and disclosure that West German firms had sold equipment to Libya which was used in manufacturing chemical weapons. State Department officials stressed that Japanese government efforts were much improved in the wake of the 1987 Toshiba scandal.

33. A West German Foreign Ministry official admitted that the heavy trade volume and cross-border population flows made effective enforcement difficult. Numerous reports of East German espionage against West German military and industrial targets suggested the size of the counterintelligence problem facing authorities in the F.R.G. From a counterintelligence point of view, the massive influx of German refugees was worrying although it was politically impossible to stop or delay the flow; not-for-attribution interview, Ministry of Foreign Affairs, Bonn, 3 March 1989. See also Marsh, p. 18, column 7 and Philip Hanson, *Soviet Industrial Espionage: Some New Information*, RIIA Discussion Papers, no. 1 (London: Royal Institute of International Affairs, 1987), pp. 24-25.

34. The Czechoslovak interior minister was quoted as saying that President Havel would demand an end to Czech-KGB intelligence links when he visited Moscow at the beginning of February 1990. See Jim Hoagland, "Havel to Press for Troop Cuts," *Washington Post*, 21 January 1990, section A, p. 29, columns 2-4; section A, p. 31, columns 4-6. The assumption that any dual-use technology sold to Eastern Europe will eventually be obtained or examined by the Soviets was expressed by Talbot Lindstrom, Deputy Director, Defense Technology Security Administration. See Talbot Lindstrom, prepared statement, in U.S. Congress, House Committee on Foreign Affairs, Subcommittees on Europe and the Middle East and on International Economic Policy and Trade, *United States Trade Relations with Eastern Europe and Yugoslavia*, hearing, 100th Congress, 1st session, 28 October 1987 (Washington, DC: U.S. GPO, 1988), pp. 15-16.

35. Such talks were under way as of December 1989, according to Commerce Secretary Robert Mosbacher. By early summer 1991, Poland, Hungary, and Czechoslovakia had all been granted preferential treatment by COCOM after implementing domestic controls and enforcement mechanisms. The former G.D.R.'s proscribed status ended by July 1990 as German unification became a reality. The United States had been actively involved in advising Eastern European countries on establishing domestic export controls. In Poland, U.S. inspectors undertook inspections accompanied by Polish customs inspectors. See interview, *American Interest* [public affairs television program], Public Broadcasting Service, 9 December 1989; Heinrich Vogel, "East-West Trade and Technology Transfer Reconsidered," in *After the Revolutions: East-West Trade and Technology Transfer in the 1990s*, eds. Gary K. Bertsch, Heinrich Vogel, and Jan Zielonka (Boulder, CO: Westview Press, 1991), p. 181; Glennon J. Harrison and George Holliday, *Export Controls, 1990*, CRS Issue Brief, IB87122 (Washington, DC: Congressional Research Service, Library of Congress, 10 December 1990), p. CRS-7; "COCOM Recognizes Central European Progress on Safeguards," *Export Control News*, vol. 5, no. 1 (25 January 1991), pp. 4-5; "COCOM, US Take Final Steps on New Central Europe Export Policy," *Export Control News*, vol. 5, no. 3 (26 March 1991), pp. 9-10; and

Andrzej Rudka, Deputy Director, Foreign Trade Research Institute, Warsaw, former member of the Polish delegaton to the negotiations with the U.S. on implementing a safeguard export control system, presentation at the Center for East-West Trade Policy, University of Georgia, Athens, GA, 10 January 1991, author's notes.

36.   National Research Council, *Global Trends*, p. 232, footnote 1.

37.   While there is no evidence that U.S.-origin technology is being illegally sold as part of growing Chinese military sales, the possibility cannot be disregarded. In 1988, the State Department's Allan Wendt noted that in 1987, COCOM had called off discussions to further liberalize P.R.C. trade in the wake of the Chinese sale of silkworm missiles to Iran, but he stressed that this was part of an evolving process and that the talks would resume. The Farewell papers also suggest that the P.R.C. is a source for Soviet acquisitions. However, U.S. officials, and a former British intelligence official, stress that the Chinese are reliable and protect sensitive U.S. technology. See Allan Wendt, Senior Representative for Strategic Technology Policy, Department of State, remarks at a National Issues Forum on *U.S. Export Control Policy: Balancing National Security Issues and Global Competitiveness*, held at The Brookings Institution, Washington, DC, 9 June 1988; Lee Zinser, Economic Analyst, Office of East Asian Analysis, Central Intelligence Agency, testimony, 3 August 1987 in U.S. Congress, Joint Economic Committee, Subcommittee on National Security Economics, *Allocation of Resources in the Soviet Union and China- 1986*, hearings, 100th Congress, 1st session, 19 March, 3 August 1987 (Washington, DC: U.S. GPO, 1988), p. 225; Paul Freedenberg, Assistant Secretary for Trade Administration, Department of Commerce, prepared statement, 11 March 1987, in U.S. Congress, House Committee on Foreign Affairs, Subcommittee on International Economic Policy, and Trade, *Omnibus Trade and Competitiveness Act of 1988 (Vol. II)*, hearings, 100th Congress, 1st session, 11-12 March 1987 (Washington, DC: U.S. GPO, 1988), p. 19; Malcolm Baldrige, Secretary of Commerce, testimony, 12 March 1987, in U.S. Congress, Senate Committee on Banking, Housing, and Urban Affairs, Subcommittee on International Finance and Monetary Policy, *Export Controls*, hearings, 100th Congress, 1st session, 12, 17 March 1987 (Washington, DC: U.S. GPO, 1987), p. 39; not-for-attribution interview with a former DOC official who was closely involved with the P.R.C. liberalization, Arlington, VA, 17 March 1988; Tovey, interview and Hansen, *Soviet Industrial*, p. 13.

38.   Admiral Bobby R. Inman, Deputy Director, CIA, prepared statement, 11 May 1982, in U.S. Congress, Senate Committee on Governmental Affairs, Permanent Subcommittee on Investigations, *Transfer of United States High Technology to the Soviet Union and Soviet Bloc Nations*, hearings, 97th Congress, 2nd session, 4-6, 11-12 May 1982 (Washington, DC: U.S. GPO, 1982), pp. 577; George Lardner Jr., "CIA Director: E. European Spies at Work," *Washington Post*, 21 February 1990, section A, p. 15, column 1; Jan Sejna, "Soviet and East European Acquisition Efforts: An Inside View," in *Selling the Rope to Hang Capitalism?*, eds. Charles M. Perry and Robert L. Pfaltzgraff, Jr. (London: Pergamon-Brassey's, 1987), pp. 70-74; John McLucas, CEO, Questech Corp.,

member, National Academy of Sciences Panel on National Security Export Controls, remarks, 12 March 1987, in U.S. Congress, Senate Committee on Banking, Housing, and Urban Affairs, Subcommittee on International Finance and Monetary Policy, *Export Controls*, hearings, 100th Congress, 1st session, 12, 17 March 1987 (Washington, DC: U.S. GPO, 1987), p. 48 and National Research Council, *Global Trends*, p. 235.

39. Richard Perle notes the uncertainty factor as a cause of greater Soviet reliance on inferior and unreliable domestic output; Richard Perle, Assistant Secretary for International Security Policy, Department of Defense, testimony, 11 March 1987, in U.S. Congress, House Committee on Foreign Affairs, Subcommittee on International Economic Policy and Trade, *Omnibus Trade and Competitiveness Act of 1988 (Vol. II)*, hearings, 100th Congress, 1st session, 11-12 March 1987 (Washington, DC: U.S. GPO, 1988), p. 51.

40. The highly interrelated character of advanced equipment parts, technical data, maintenance, and operation know-how is disrupted and virtually impossible to replicate by means of illegal acquisition. See Edward Derwinski, Acting Under Secretary of State, statement, 12 March 1987, in U.S. Congress, Senate Committee on Banking, Housing, and Urban Affairs, Subcommittee on International Finance and Monetary Policy, *Export Controls*, hearings, 100th Congress, 1st session, 12, 17 March 1987 (Washington, DC: U.S. GPO, 1987), p. 70; and National Research Council, *Global Trends*, p. 242.

41. A recent study by the National Research Council questions the usefulness of reverse-engineering of supercomputers. Reliance of foreign technology is a shortcut and therefore helpful in overcoming immediate gaps in knowledge and designs. In the long term, however, the originality needed to explore the outer edges of technological innovation suffers and this is compounded by structural rigidities plaguing the Russian R&D system. See National Research Council, *Global Trends*, p. 40.

42. Duff, interview, and not-for-attribution interview, representative of a major U.S. computer/electronics firm, Washington, DC, 18 May 1988.

43. The discussion of the legal and constitutional basis for the Executive's discretion is derived from Robert Y. Stebbings, "Export Controls: Extraterritorial Conflict- The Dilemma of the Host Country Employee," *Case Western Reserve Journal of International Law*, vol. 19 (1987), pp. 319, 338-39.

44. Willingness to accept costs is a key to successful sanctions policy, according to David Baldwin. See, Hanson *Western Economic Statecraft*, p. 18.

45. The updated 1991 NAS study on export controls does not suggest any need to change this conclusion. See National Academy of Sciences, *Finding Common Ground*, pp. 18-25, 199-265.

46. National Academy of Sciences, *Balancing*, pp. 115-16.

47. Mack, letter, p. 2; and Joseph R. Creighton, Vice President and Senior Legal Advisor, Harris Corporation, "EIA Testimony Before the House Foreign Affairs Subcommittee on Arms Control, International Security and Science and International Economic Policy and Trade," 8 February 1990 (photocopied), pp. 4-7, 10,

13.

48. Nau, "Export Controls," p. 413.

49. This was emphasized by a former DOC export administration official; not-for-attribution interview, Arlington, VA, 17 March 1988.

50. This was the feeling of a Commerce official and was echoed by officials at State. Not-for-attribution interviews, Departments of Commerce and State, Washington, DC, 14 March and 23 February 1988.

51. Not-for-attribution interviews, Department of State, Bureau of Economic and Business Affairs, Washington, DC, 23 February 1988; Department of Commerce, Washington, DC, 14 March 1988; representative for a major computer manufacturer, Washington, DC, 18 May 1988; and U.S. Congress, House Committee on Science, Space, and Technology, *Export Controls, Competitiveness and International Cooperation: A Critical Review*, staff report, 101st Congress, 1st session, February 1989 (Washington, DC: U.S. GPO, 1989), pp. 15, 18.

52. Reportedly, the United States did not agree to loosen controls on high technology at the December 1989 Malta summit. A *Wall Street Journal*/NBC News Poll in early December, 1989 found that 77% of those polled *opposed* allowing "U.S. companies to sell high-technology products to the Soviet Union if they have potential military uses." See Peter Gumbel, "U.S. Strengthens Gorbachev's Position Ahead of New Round of Soviet Reforms," *Wall Street Journal*, 4 December 1989, section A, p. 2, column 2; not-for-attribution interview, Department of State, Bureau of Economic and Business Affairs, Washington, DC, 23 February 1988; and Michel McQueen, "Summit, Changes in East Bloc Leave Americans Hopeful but Skeptical About Soviets, Cold War," *Wall Street Journal*, 6 December 1989, section A, p. 16, columns 1-6.

53. Patrick E. Tyler, "Webster Sees No Revival of Soviet Threat," *Washington Post*, 2 March 1990, section A, p. 1, column 6; section A, p. 30, columns 1-4.

54. The Director of the Defense Intelligence Agency explicitly noted that in the wake of the collapse of the U.S.S.R., "the military capabilities of Russia and the successor states are in profound decline." Glennon J. Harrison and George Holliday, *Export Controls*, CRS Issue Brief, IB91064 (Washington, DC: Congressional Research Service, Library of Congress, 1 May 1992), p. CRS-4; David Silverberg, "White House Move To Abolish CoCoM Worries Pentagon," *Defense News*, vol. 7, no. 16 (20-26 April 1992), p. 1, columns 1-2; p. 28, columns 1-5; John Burgess and John Mintz, "CIA, FBI Chiefs Warn Panel Over Economic Espionage," *Washington Post*, 30 April 1992, section B, p. 11, columns 2-3; section B, p. 13, columns 1-3; and Stuart Auerbach, "U.S. Shifts, Agrees to Ease Fiber Optics Export Curb," *Washington Post*, section D, p. 10, columns 5-6; section D, p. 12, columns 3-4.

55. Daniel Yergin posits two poles, the Riga and Yalta axioms, around which U.S. policymakers' views of the U.S.S.R. clustered during the Cold War. Adherents of the Riga view did not believe the Soviets could be trusted because they are driven by an ideologically rooted and aggressive world view that is not amenable to normal negotiation between states. The Yalta adherents perceived that the

U.S.S.R.--even in its Marxist-Leninist guise--acts only as any other great power that seeks a reasonable status quo balance of power and is troubled by deep internal cleavages. These images could still influence policymakers' thinking about the intentions of Russia and the other former Soviet republics. See Daniel Yergin, *Shattered Peace: The Origins of the Cold War and the National Security State* (Boston, MA: Houghton Mifflin, 1977).

56. For example, Abraham Becker of the RAND Corp. cites the views of Marshal Ogarkov "who was concerned about the rapid obsolescence of weapons under the acceleration of the 'scientific-technical revolution'" which upset the Soviets' cautious, evolutionary approach to weapons development. See Abraham S. Becker, "Gorbachev's Defense-Economic Dilemma," in *Gorbachev's Economic Plans*, Volume 1, study papers, ed. U.S. Congress, Joint Economic Committee, 100th Congress, 1st session, 23 November 1987 (Washington, DC: U.S. GPO, 1987), p. 368.

57. Some Soviet economists, pessimistic about the poor results of Gorbachev's policy, advocated this. Andrei Anikin, U.S.S.R. Institute of Global Economy and International Relations, "The Economic Crisis in the Soviet Union and Implications for the West," address at the American University, Washington, DC, 2 November 1989. See also the critique in Harry Harding and Ed. A. Hewett, "Socialist Reforms and the World Economy," in *Restructuring American Foreign Policy*, ed. John D. Steinbruner (Washington, DC: The Brookings Institution, 1989), pp. 158-84.

58. Dr. Peter J. Sharfman, Program Manager, International Security and Commerce, Office of Technology Assessment, written statement, 9 June 1983, in U.S. Congress, House Committee on Armed Services, Technology Transfer Panel, *Technology Transfer*, hearings, 98th Congress, 1st session, 9, 21, 23 June, 13-14 July 1983 (Washington, DC: U.S. GPO, 1984), p. 16; National Research Council, *Global Trends*, p. 237; and Richard F. Kaufman, "Industrial Modernisation and Defense in the Soviet Union," in *The Soviet Economy: A New Course?*, ed. Reiner Weichhardt, NATO Colloquium, 1-3 April 1987 (Brussels: North Atlantic Treaty Organization, 1988), p. 254 citing Central Intelligence Agency, *The Soviet Weapons Industry: An Overview*, 1986.

59. Douglas MacEachin and Rear Adm. Robert Schmitt, "Gorbachev's Modernization Program: A Status Report," paper presented by the Central Intelligence Agency and Defense Intelligence Agency for submission to the Subcommittee on National Security Economics of the Joint Economic Committee, Congress of the United States, in U.S. Congress, Joint Economic Committee, Subcommittee on National Security Economics, *Allocation of Resources in the Soviet Union and China- 1986*, hearings, 100th Congress, 1st session, 19 March, 8 August 1987 (Washington, DC: U.S. GPO, 1988), p. 13.

60. Becker, "Gorbachev's Defense," pp. 378, 382, 384; Paul Cocks, Office of Soviet Analysis, CIA, "Soviet Science and Technology Strategy: Borrowing From the Defense Sector," in U.S. Congress, Joint Economic Committee, *Gorbachev's Economic Plans*, Volume 2, study papers, ed. U.S. Congress, Joint Economic

Committee, 100th Congress, 1st session, 23 November 1987 (Washington, DC: U.S. GPO, 1987), p. 160; Herbert Levine, professor of economics, codirector of the Lauder Institute of Management and International Studies, University of Pennsylvania, prepared statement, 27 April 1988, in U.S. Congress, House Committee on Foreign Affairs, *United States-Soviet Relations: 1988 (Volume I)*, hearings, 100th Congress, 2nd session, 2, 8, 25 February, 17, 28 March, 13, 20, 27 April 1988 (Washington, DC: U.S. GPO, 1988), pp. 562-63; Ronald F. Lehman, Assistant Secretary for International Security Policy, Department of Defense, prepared statement, 12 July 1988, in U.S. Congress, House Committee on Foreign Affairs, *United States-Soviet Relations: 1988 (Volume II)*, hearings, 100th Congress, 2nd session, 2, 8, 25 February, 17, 28 March, 13, 20, 27 April 1988 (Washington, DC: U.S. GPO, 1988), pp. 334-35; and Judith A. Thornton, *A New Export Regime For Information Technologies*, FPI Policy Briefs, no. 19 (Washington, DC: Johns Hopkins University School of International Service, November 1988), p. 1.

61. See Carol Rae Hansen, International Affairs Fellow, The Council on Foreign Relations Fellow, Johns Hopkins Foreign Policy Institute, prepared statement, 13 April 1988, in U.S. Congress, House Committee on Foreign Affairs, *United States-Soviet Relations: 1988 (Volume I)*, hearings, 100th Congress, 2nd session, 2, 8, 25 February, 17, 28 March, 13, 20, 27 April, 1988 (Washington, DC: U.S. GPO, 1988), p. 408.

62. Molly Moore and Patrick E. Tyler, "Administration Seeks Defense Spending Cut," *Washington Post*, 18 November 1989, section A, p. 1, columns 5-6; section A, p. 12, columns 1-3; and David Ignatius, "Yes, It's Real: How Gorby is Cutting the Soviet Threat," *Washington Post*, 5 November 1989, section C, p. 1, column 4; section C, p. 4, columns 1-5.

63. Georgy Shakhnazarov, Gorbachev's senior adviser on Eastern Europe, confirmed the repudiation of the Brezhnev Doctrine. See Michael Dobbs, "Soviet Chief Expected to Ask Patience," *Washington Post*, 1 November 1989, section A, p. 1, column 6, section A, p. 20, columns 5-6; and President Bush, "Change in the Soviet Union," address at Texas A&M University, 12 May 1989, rpt. in U.S. Department of State, Bureau of Public Affairs, *Current Policy*, no. 1175 (Washington, DC: U.S. GPO, 1989), p. 2.

64. As Pipes argues: "Despite its widely advertised new thinking, Soviet foreign policy's overriding goal so far appears unchanged: relentless pursuit of tactical and strategic advantages short of direct military confrontation in a struggle against Western political and economic interests." Prior to the Soviet Union's dissolution, Stephen D. Bryen, former director of DOD's Defense Technology Security Administration, warned that supporting Gorbachev's policy should not come at the expense of U.S. security. For Bryen, loosening technology flows to the U.S.S.R. was unwise, as it gave the U.S.S.R. the wherewithal to modernize its military. See Richard Pipes, "Paper Perestroika," *Policy Review*, no. 47 (Winter 1989), p. 14; Adam Meyerson, "The Ever-Present Danger," interview with Fred C. Ikle, *Policy Review*, no. 49 (Summer 1989), pp. 7-8; and Stephen D. Bryen, "It's Still Smart to Ban High Tech to Moscow," *International Herald Tribune*, 4-5 March 1989.

Similar skepticism was evidenced in the DOD's 1988 annual *Soviet Military Power* and by the State Department's Allen Wendt. See Sherry C. Rice, "Technology Management as an Alliance Issue: A Review of the Literature," *Washington Quarterly*, vol. 13, no. 1 (Winter 1990), pp. 221-22, quoting U.S. Department of Defense, *Soviet Military Power: An Assessment of the Threat* and Allan Wendt cited in *Wall Street Journal* in Rice, p. 222.

65. While they advocated help for Gorbachev, Senator Bill Bradley, Czechoslovakia's President Havel, and columnist Stephen S. Rosenfeld presented arguments which also support assisting Yeltsin. Sen. Bill Bradley, "We Can't Afford Not to Help East Europe," *Washington Post*, 22 March 1990, section A, p. 23, columns 2-4; "Text of [President Vaclav] Havel's Speech to Congress," *Washington Post*, 22 February 1990, section A, p. 28, column 2; and Stephen S. Rosenfeld, "Feeding Russia, Saving Gorbachev," *Washington Post*, 16 March 1990, section A, p. 23, columns 2-3.

66. Michael Dobbs, "In Yaroslavl, Perestroika Brings Only More Hardship," *Washington Post*, 7 November 1989, section A, p. 1, columns 1-2; section A, p. 20, columns 1-4; and Steve Crawshaw, "Sakharov Attacks Gorbachev Regime," *The Independent* [London], no. 841 (21 June 1989), p. 1, columns 3-4.

67. Peter Wiles of the London School of Economics points out that both increasingly prosperous Germany and Japan were quite expansionist during the late 19th and early 20th centuries. Trade and an opening to the West did not mellow their behavior. While suggestive, such historical analogies are at best speculative. The crackdown in China also suggests the tenuousness of arguments that economic reform will pluralize a closed society. See Peter Wiles, "Is an Anti-Soviet Embargo Desirable or Possible?" in *The Conduct of East-West Relations in the 1980s, Part II*, IISS Annual Conference Papers, *Adelphi Papers*, no. 190 (London: The International Institute for Strategic Studies, summer 1984), pp. 37-50.

68. U.S. concern over continuing Soviet activities in the Third World was a major focus of the "guidance" for the 1990s issued to commanders in February 1990. One senior Commerce official argued that realistically, given improving relations, *some* relaxation of controls will occur but that it would be 10 to 20 years before the Soviets could be trusted enough to warrant selling them top-of-the-line technology. See Patrick E. Tyler, "New Pentagon 'Guidance' Cites Soviet Threat in Third World," 13 February 1990, section A, p. 1, columns 5-6, section A, p. 9, columns 1-6; and Anstruther Davidson, Director, Office of Export Enforcement, Department of Commerce, interview, Washington, DC, 24 February 1988.

69. For example, see Heinrich Vogel, "The Gorbachev Challenge: To Help or Not to Help?" revised version of a paper presented to the conference on "The Western Community and the Gorbachev Challenge," organized by the Atlantic Association Luxembourg-Harvard in Luxembourg, 19-21 December 1988, pp. 7, 9.

70. A similar argument is made by John Hardt of the Congressional Research Service. See John P. Hardt, "Changing Perspectives Toward the Normalization of East-West Commerce," in *Controlling East-West Trade and Technology Transfer: Power, Politics, and Policies*, ed. Gary K. Bertsch (Durham, NC: Duke University

Press, 1988), pp. 354-55.

71. Hobart Rowen, "Large Trade Surpluses Possible With Soviet Union, China, India," *Washington Post*, 21 February 1990, section A, p. 8, columns 1-3.

72. However, the recent crackdown in China also suggests that economic liberalization and aspirations for social reforms are not necessarily complementary. The pluralizing effects of technological progress are noted in Victor Basiuk, "Soviet Systemic Change, Technology Transfer, and U.S.-Soviet Relations," in *Selling the Rope to Hang Capitalism?*, eds. Charles M. Perry and Robert L. Pfaltzgraff, Jr. (London: Pergamon-Brassey's, 1987), p. 97.

73. Thornton, *A New Export Regime*, p. 40; and Peter B. Nyren, Office of Soviet Analysis, CIA, "The Computer Literacy Program: Problems and Prospects," in U.S. Congress, Joint Economic Committee, *Gorbachev's Economic Plans*, Volume 2, study papers, 100th Congress, 1st session, 23 November 1987 (Washington, DC: U.S. GPO, 1987), p. 200.

74. A similar argument was made by William Root, former Director of State's Bureau of East-West Trade. A more pessimistic view is held by David Wellman who foresees a potential *enhancement* of the autocratic state mechanism, resulting in a kind of supercommunism, arising from the computerization of Soviet society. Root, interview; and David A. Wellman, *A Chip in the Curtain* (Washington, DC: National Defense University Press, 1989), pp. 135-50.

75. This is so since most weapons production up to at least 1990 can be met by existing plants and resources. See MacEachin and Schmitt, "Gorbachev's Modernization," pp. 45-46.

76. As noted in John P. Hardt, "Gorbachev's Domestic Economic Strategy and East-West Commercial Relations," in *Selling the Rope to Hang Capitalism?*, eds. Charles M. Perry and Robert L. Pfaltzgraff, Jr. (London: Pergamon-Brassey's, 1987), p. 41. See also Basiuk, "Soviet Systemic Change," pp. 102-03.

77. Certain technology would also assist the former Soviet republics in safeguarding their civilian nuclear energy program, a goal of interest to the West in light of the deficiencies revealed by the 1986 Chernobyl accident. See Richard L. Hudson, "Soviets Order Control Data Computers Amid Signs of Easing of Export Curbs," *Wall Street Journal*, 13 December 1989, section A, p. 3, columns 2-3.

78. See Stuart Auerbach, "Soviets Buy Advanced Computers," *Washington Post*, 22 August 1990, section F, p. 2, columns 4-6; Heinrich Vogel, "East-West Trade and Technology Transfer Reconsidered," in *After the Revolutions: East-West Trade and Technology Transfer in the 1990s*, eds. Gary K. Bertsch, Heinrich Vogel, and Jan Zielonka (Boulder, CO: Westview Press, 1991), p. 181; Lutz Maier, "Technologietransfer-Impuls für die Ost-West-Zusammenarbeit," *Messemagazin International* (Leipzig), Heft 2 (1988); and U.K. House of Commons, Trade and Industry Committee, *Trade With Eastern Europe*, Second Report, Session 1988-89, Report together with the Proceedings of the Committee, Minutes of Evidence taken in Sessions 1987-88 and 1988-89, and Appendices (London: HMSO, 26 January 1989), p. xvii; not-for-attribution interview with a British businessman who frequently travels to Eastern Europe, London, 2 December 1988; and not-for-

attribution interview, Bundesinstitut fur Ostwissenschaftliche und Internationale Studien, Cologne, 8 March 1989.

79. R. J. Carrick, *East-West Technology Transfer in Perspective*, Policy Papers in International Affairs, no. 9 (Berkeley, CA: Institute of International Affairs, 1978), p. 39; and Talbot S. Lindstrom, Deputy Undersecretary for International Programs and Technology, Department of Defense, testimony, in U.S. Congress, House Committee on Armed Services, Technology Transfer Panel, *Technology Transfer*, hearings, 98th Congress, 1st session, 9, 21, 23 June, 13-14 July 1983 (Washington, DC: U.S. GPO, 1984), p. 171.

80. One U.S. firm's proposals for safeguarding computers sold to the Soviets is described in Hudson, "Soviets Order Control Data Computers."

81. Lindstrom, in U.S. Congress, *United States Trade Relations*, pp. 43-45; and Stuart Auerbach, "GE to Sell Jet Engines to Soviets," *The Washington Post*, 29 March 1990, section C, p. 1, column 6; section C, p. 4, column 4.

82. Not-for-attribution interview, Ministry of Foreign Affairs, Bonn, 3 March 1989.

83. Moscow has agreed to inspections of destruction of intermediate-range missiles, on-site monitoring of nuclear tests, and the presence of foreign observers at previously off-limits space launches.

84. A point made by Carrick, *East-West*, p. 71.

85. As one scholar of the Soviet economic system puts it: "Quite often there can be no guarantee that even lavish R&D spending will generate a solution at all; by definition, inventions contain an element of unexpectedness, which means that no level of spending on a particular technical problem is an absolute guarantee that it will be solved."; Hanson, *Western Economic*, p. 11.

86. According to Goldman, the Russians are handicapped by a "systems gap"-- i.e., an ingrained structural and attitudinal characteristic which resists technologically driven efficiency gains. This gap is rooted in the command economy's discouragement of risk-taking and an emphasis on planned output based on an assumption of abundant inputs. New Western technology is often used inefficiently and badly serviced because familiarity with new tools, and associated work habits, which puts a premium of flexibility and adaptability, are not valued or rewarded. See Marshall I. Goldman, "Western Technology in the Soviet Union: What Happens to It?", in *Selling the Rope to Hang Capitalism?*, eds., Charles M. Perry and Robert L. Pfaltzgraff, Jr. (London: Pergamon-Brassey's, 1987), pp. 78-79.

87. The importance of incentives as a spark to domestic innovation, which is considered much more valuable than merely importing foreign know-how, and the associated problem of dependence is noted in Thane Gustafson, *Selling the Russians the Rope? Technology Policy and U.S. Export Controls*, prepared for the Defense Advanced Research Projects Agency (Santa Monica, CA: RAND Corp., April 1981), pp. 73, 77. Even if social and economic reforms did establish conditions favorable for sparking innovation, these conditions could take years to develop and the reforms themselves might cause the ideological underpinning and political base of the communist party to erode further. That would encourage the kind of domestic

change containment was originally designed to facilitate.

88. Perle quoted in Auerbach, "U.S. to Back," section A, p. 17, column 2.

89. See Zbigniew Brzezinski, "If Gorbachev Keeps Moving, America Should Help Out," *Washington Post*, 12 November 1989, section D, p. 1, columns 1-2; section D, p. 2, columns 1-5; and Charles Krauthamer, "Our Man Gorbachev," *Washington Post*, 8 December 1989, section A, p. 19, column 5.

Appendix: Tables

Table 1
DOC--License Processing: Western and Neutral Communist
Countries and People's Republic of China (P.R.C.)

YEAR	# PROCESSED APPLICATIONS	DENIALS	RWAs	BACKLOG
1975[1]	52,600	NA	NA	NA
1977[2]	50,737	348	NA	NA
10/78- 3/79[3]	32,044	25	2,844	NA
FY 1979[4]	NA	NA	NA	536
FY 1980[4]	66,566	80	6,660	2,214
FY 1981[5]	63,659	126	6,333	1,908
FY 1982[6]	69,554	297	9,037	4,330
FY 1983[7]	80,579	376	9,914	10,213
FY 1984[8]	112,355	360	15,343	8,683
FY 1985[9]	117,854	566	19,326	8,889
FY 1986[10]	112,079	442	14,690	5,829
FY 1987[11]	99,664	547	5,265	4,102

Sources:

1. U.S. Congress, Office of Technology Assessment, *Technology and East-West Trade* (Washington, DC: U.S. GPO, 1979), p. 140, Table 19.

2. Elmer B. Staats, Comptroller General of the United States, answer to question submitted by Senator Jake Garn, in U.S. Congress, Senate Committee on Banking, Housing, and Urban Affairs, *U.S. Export Control Policy and Extension of the Export Administration Act*, Part I, hearings, 96th Congress, 1st session, 5-6 March 1979

Sources: Table 1 (continued)
(Washington, DC: U.S. GPO, 1979), p. 21.

3. U.S. Department of Commerce, Industry and Trade Administration, *Export Administration Report*, 119th Report on U.S. Export Controls to the President and the Congress, October 1978-March 1979 (Washington, DC: U.S. GPO, no date), p. 3.

4. U.S. Department of Commerce, International Trade Administration, *Export Administration Annual Report FY 1980*, (Washington, DC: U.S. GPO, February 1981), p. 6.

5. U.S. Department of Commerce, International Trade Administration, *Export Administration Annual Report FY 1981* (Washington, DC: U.S. GPO, February 1982), p. 7.

6. U.S. Department of Commerce, International Trade Administration, *Export Administration Annual Report FY 1982* (Washington, DC: U.S. GPO, February 1983), p. 7.

7. U.S. Department of Commerce, International Trade Administration, *Export Administration Annual Report FY 1983* (Washington, DC: U.S. GPO, June, 1984), p. 10.

8. U.S. Department of Commerce, International Trade Administration, *Export Administration Annual Report FY 1984* (Washington, DC: U.S. GPO, November 1985), p. 12.

9. U.S. Department of Commerce, International Trade Administration, *Export Administration Annual Report FY 1985* (Washington, DC: U.S. GPO, November 1986), p. 15.

10. U.S. Department of Commerce, Bureau of Export Administration, *Export Administration Annual Report FY 1986* (Washington, DC: U.S. GPO, December 1987), p. 14.

11. United States, Department of Commerce, Bureau of Export Administration, *Export Administration Annual Report FY 1987* (Washington, DC: U.S. GPO, November 1988), p. 15.

Notes:

RWAs = Returned Without Action
NA = Not Available

Table 2

Denials/RWAs as Percentage of Total Processed Applications for Exports to Western and Neutral Communist Countries and P.R.C.

YEAR	# APPLICATIONS	% DENIALS	% RWAs	% COMBINED
1977	50,737	0.7	NA	NA
10/78- 3/79	32,044	0.1	8.8	8.9
FY 1980	66,566	0.1	10.0	10.1
FY 1981	63,659	0.1	9.9	10.0
FY 1982	69,554	0.4	12.9	13.3
FY 1983	80,579	0.4	12.3	12.7
FY 1984	112,355	0.3	13.5	13.8
FY 1985	117,854	0.4	16.3	16.7
FY 1986	112,079	0.3	13.1	13.4
FY 1987	99,664	0.5	5.2	5.7

Source: Derived from Table 1.

Table 3

DOC— License Processing: U.S.S.R. and Allies

YEAR	# PROCESSED APPLICATIONS	DENIALS	RWAs	DOC REVIEW	JOINT DOC/DOD REVIEW	OC REVIEW	BACKLOG
10/78- 3/79	3,686	86	588	2,370	941	375	NA
FY 1980	6,506	323	1,318	4,225	1,904	377	2,021
FY 1981	7,541	677	1,805	4,806	2,525	210	903
FY 1982	7,123	588	1,613	5,324	1,675	124	367
FY 1983	7,182	259	1,563	3,934	3,062	186	3,506
FY 1984	9,297	241	1,145	6,285	2,903	109	1,814
FY 1985	14,249	269	1,305	9,634	4,580	35	1,998
FY 1986	9,444	138	872	6,130	3,279	35	1,204
FY 1987	9,531	415	637	6,281	3,208	42	776

Source: See Table 1.

Note:

OC = (interagency) Operating Committee

Table 4
License Processing- U.S.S.R. and Allies

YEAR	% DOC REVIEW	%DOC/DOD/OC REVIEW	%DENIALS(1)	%RWAs(2)	(1) + (2)
10/78- 3/79	64.2	35.7	2.3	15.9	18.2
FY 1980	64.9	35.0	5.0	20.2	25.2
FY 1981	63.7	36.2	8.9	23.9	32.8
FY 1982	74.7	25.2	8.3	22.7	31.0
FY 1983	54.7	45.2	3.6	21.7	25.3
FY 1984	67.6	32.4	2.5	12.3	14.8
FY 1985	67.6	32.3	1.9	9.1	11.0
FY 1986	64.9	34.7	1.4	9.2	10.6
FY 1987	65.9	33.7	4.3	6.6	10.9

Source: See Table 1.

Table 5
Denials/RWAs as Percentage of Total Processed Applications to FW and U.S.S.R. and Allies

YEAR[1]	# TOTAL PROCESSED APPLICATIONS	%FW	%DENIALS FW	%RWAs FW	%U.S.S.R. AND ALLIES(1)	%DENIALS (1) c.2.0[2]	%RWAs (1)
1967 10/78-3/79	NA	NA	NA	NA	NA	NA	NA
	35,730	89.6	0.1	8.0	10.3	0.2	1.7
FY 1980	73,072	91.1	0.1	9.1	8.9	0.4	1.8
FY 1981	71,200	89.4	0.2	9.0	10.5	0.9	2.5
FY 1982	76,677	90.7	0.3	11.8	9.2	0.8	2.1
FY 1983	87,761	91.8	0.4	11.3	8.1	0.2	1.7
FY 1984	121,652	92.3	0.2	12.6	7.6	0.1	0.9
FY 1985	132,103	89.2	0.4	14.6	10.7	0.2	0.6
FY 1986	121,523	92.2	0.3	12.0	7.7	0.1	0.7
FY 1987	109,195	91.2	0.5	4.8	8.7	0.3	0.5

Sources: See Table 1.

Notes:

FW = Free World

c. = circa

1. Lawrence C. McQuade, Assistant Secretary for Domestic and International Business, Department of Commerce, statement, 27 June 1968, in U.S. Congress, Senate Committee on Banking and Currency, Subcommittee on International Finance, *East-West Trade*, Part I, hearings, 90th Congress, 2nd session, 4, 13, 27 June, 17, 24-25 July 1968 (Washington, DC: U.S. GPO, 1968), p. 223.

2. Denials only for applications to Eastern Europe

Table 6
Combined Denials/RWAs: FW and U.S.S.R. and Allies (% of Total Applications)

YEAR	COMBINED DENIALS/RWAs
1977[1]	0.6[2]
10/78- 3/79	10.0
FY 1980	11.4
FY 1981	12.6
FY 1982	15.0
FY 1983	13.6
FY 1984	13.8
FY 1985	15.8
FY 1986	13.1
FY 1987	6.1

Sources: Derived from Table 5.

1. Elmer B. Staats, Comptroller General of the United States, in U.S. Congress, Senate Committee on Banking, Housing, and Urban Affairs, *U.S. Export Control Policy and Extension of the Export Administration Act*, Part I, hearings, 96th Congress, 1st session, 5-6 March 1979 (Washington, DC: U.S. GPO, 1979), p. 21.

2. Denials only for all destinations.

Table 7
Licensing to COCOM, Australia, New Zealand: Denials as Percentage of Processed Applications to All Western and Neutral Communist Countries and P.R.C.

YEAR	#PROCESSED APPLICATIONS(1)	APPLICATIONS APPROVED(2)	DENIALS(3)	%DENIALS (1)	%DENIALS (2+3)
1979²	?	22,377	0	?	0
1980	66,566	?			
1981	63,659	?	6²	0.003³	
1982	69,554	?			
1983	80,579	26,341⁴	45⁴	0.06	0.1
1984	112,355	32,315⁴	74⁴	0.07	0.2
1985	117,854	32,500⁴	49⁴	0.04	0.1

Sources: See Table 1.

1. Rounded figures. Figures are rounded to either nearest onethousandth, onehundreth, or one tenth of one percent.
2. Total denials, 1980-1982, inclusive. U.S. Congress, General Accounting Office, *Export Control Regulation Could Be Reduced Without Affecting National Security*, GAO/ID-82-14 (Washington, DC: U.S. GPO, 26 May 1982), pp. 10, 12.
3. Percentage denials, 1980-1982, inclusive.
4. Rep. Les AuCoin, *Congressional Record*, vol. 133, no. 27 (24 February 1987), p. E 566, column 2. Australia and New Zealand are *not* mentioned.

Table 8
**Exports Controlled for National Security Reasons as Percentage of
Total Exports to Selected Geographic Areas**

GEOGRAPHIC AREA	TOTAL EXPORTS (RANK) $ MILLIONS	PERCENT OF TOTAL (RANK)
NORTH AMERICA	37,869.9 (3)	< 0.5 (9)
LATIN AMERICA	21,557.2 (4)	17.7 (5)
CARIBBEAN	3,842.0 (9)	4.9 (8)
EUROPE	54,925.4 (1)	19.0 (4)
AFRICA	7,811.5 (6)	22.4 (1)
MIDDLE EAST	11,827.2 (5)	14.6 (6)
ASIA	46,565.3 (2)	13.3 (7)
OCEANIA	4,781.4 (8)	22.2 (2)
COMMUNIST COUNTRIES	5,087.6 (7)	20.4 (3)
AVERAGE		13.4

Source: Derived from U.S. Congress, General Accounting Office, *U.S. Exports Subject to National Security Controls*, GAO/NSIAD-84-137 (Washington, DC: U.S. GPO, 15 June 1984).

Table 9
DOC--Overall License Processing Time--Days (% of Total Applications Taking Less Than/More Than X Number of Days to Process)

YEAR	5-15	≤20	<25	<30	>30	>90	>100
1968[1]	98**						
10-11/75[2]	85	90					
1/78[3]	73					3.3***	
1979	73[4]					c.3[5]	
4/81[6]				29	35	22	14*
1982[7]				80.4	14.7	0.02	0.004
3/82-3/83[8]				80.8			<2.5

YEAR	5-15	≤20	<25	<30	>30	>90	>100
1983[9]					80		
1984**		41.3[10]					
1985	75[11]**	80[10]**					c.0.5[12]
1986 1st qtr.: (DOC)[13]			74	80			c.0.5
(NAS)[13]				80			
mid-1987[14]	80						2

Sources:

1. Within 10 working days. Lawrence C. McQuade, Assistant Secretary for Domestic and International Business, Department of Commerce, statement, 27 June 1968, in United States, Congress, Senate, Committee on Banking and Currency, Subcommittee on International Finance, *East-West Trade*, Part I, hearings, 90th Congress, 2nd session, 4, 13 June, 17, 24-25 July 1968 (Washington, DC: U.S. GPO, 1968), p. 229.

2. Machinery and Allied Products Institute, *U.S. Technology and Export Controls* (no publisher, 1978), p. 35, citing Arthur Downey, Deputy Assistant Secretary of Commerce for East-West Trade, statement, in U.S. Congress, House Committee on International Relations, Subcommittee on International Trade and Commerce, *Export Licensing of Advanced Technology: A Review*, hearings, 94th Congress, 2nd session, 11, 15, 24, 30 March 1976 (Washington, DC: U.S. GPO, 1976), pp. 75-76.

3. Processed within 10 days or less. Juanita M. Kreps, Secretary of Commerce, statement, 5 March 1979, in U.S. Congress, Senate Committee on Banking, Housing, and Urban Affairs, *U.S. Export Control and Extension of the Export Administration Act*, Part I, hearings, 96th Congress, 1st session, 5-6 March 1979 (Washington, DC: U.S. GPO, 1979), p. 34.

4. Percentage processed in 10 days or less. Stanley J. Marcuss, Senior Deputy Assistant

Sources: Table 9 (continued)

Secretary for Industry and Trade, Department of Commerce, prepared statement, 7 March 1979, in U.S. Congress, House Committee on Foreign Affairs, Subcommittee on International Economic Policy and Trade, *Extension and Revision of the Export Administration Act of 1969*, Part I, hearings and markup, 96th Congress, 1st session, 15, 22 February, 7-8, 14-15, 21-22, 26-28 March, 3-4, 24-26 April 1979 (Washington, DC: U.S. GPO, 1979), p. 100.

5. Frank A. Weil, Assistant Secretary for Industry and Trade, Department of Commerce, statement, in U.S. Congress, Senate Committee on Banking, Housing, and Urban Affairs, Subcommittee on International Finance, *U.S. Export Control Policy and Extension of the Export Administration Act*, Part III, hearing, 96th Congress, 1st session, 3 May 1979 (Washington, DC: U.S. GPO, 1979), p. 31.

6. Paul T. O'Day, Acting Undersecretary for International Trade, Department of Commerce, prepared statement, 14 April 1981, in U.S. Congress, House Committee on Foreign Affairs, Subcommittee on International Economic Policy and Trade, *Export Administration Amendments Act of 1981*, hearings and markup, 97th Congress, 1st session, 26 March, 14, 18 April, 13 May 1981 (Washington, DC: U.S. GPO, 1981), p. 95.

7. Lionel H. Olmer, Under Secretary for International Trade, Department of Commerce, prepared statement, 1 March 1983, in U.S. Congress, House Committee on Foreign Affairs, Subcommittee on International Economic Policy and Trade, *Extension and Revision of the Export Administration Act of 1979*, hearings, 98th Congress, 1st session, 24 February, 1, 3, 8 March, 5, 12-14, 28-29 April, 2, 4-5, 18, 25-26 May 1983 (Washington, DC: U.S. GPO, 1986), p. 188.

8. Lionel H. Olmer, Under Secretary for International Trade Administration, Department of Commerce, testimony, 2 March 1983, in U.S. Congress, Senate Committee on Banking, Housing, and Urban Affairs, Subcommittee on International Finance and Monetary Policy, *Reauthorization of the Export Administration Act*, hearings, 98th Congress, 1st session, 2, 16 March, 14 April 1983 (Washington, DC: U.S. GPO, 1983), p. 194.

9. Ibid.

10. William T. Archey, Acting Assistant Secretary for Trade Administration, Department of Commerce, prepared statement, Appendix A, 10 October 1985, in U.S. Congress, House Committee on Foreign Affairs, Subcommittee on International Economic Policy and Trade, *Implementation of the Export Administrations Act of 1985*, hearings, 99th Congress, 1st session, 10 October, 6 November 1985 (Washington, DC: U.S. GPO, 1988), p. 33.

11. William T. Archey, Acting Assistant Secretary for Trade Administration, Department of Commerce, prepared statement, in U.S. Congress, House Committee on Foreign Relations, Subcommittee on International Economic Policy and Trade, *U.S. and Multilateral Export Controls*, hearing, 99th Congress, 1st session, 23 April 1985 (Washington, DC: U.S. GPO, 1987), p. 35.

12. George Holliday and Glennon J. Harrison, *Export Controls*, Issue Brief, Number IB87122, Congressional Research Service, Library of Congress, 15 April 1987, p. CRS-4.

13. The DOC definition of processing time "extends from the day receipt of a license application is recorded to the day of license issuance or other final action." However, the NAS points out that for a firm "the processing time extends from the mailing or delivering of an application to the receipt of a notice of action. This is a better measure of the system's performance because it governs the timing of transactions and shipments." National Academy of Sciences, *Balancing the National Interest* (Washington, DC: National Academy Press, 1987), pp. 235-36.

14. U.S. Department of Commerce, *Business America* (8 June 1987), p. 3.

Notes: Table 9

    DOC = Department of Commerce (claimed percentage processed)

    NAS = National Academy of Sciences (estimated actual percentage processed)

    * = More than 180 days to process.

    ** = Free World only.

    *** = 96.7% processed <90 days.

Table 10
Average License Processing Time (LPT) by DOC and DOD, in Days, to Selected Destinations

YEAR*	OVERALL DOC	OVERALL DOD	FREE WORLD DOC	FREE WORLD DOD	COCOM DOC	COCOM DOD	U.S.S.R. AND ALLIES DOC	U.S.S.R. AND ALLIES DOD
1-10/ 78[1]		29						
10-12/ 78[1]		12						
1981[2]						50		
1982[3]						30		
1983		52[4]						70[5]
1984			33[6]				110[7]	30[8]
			46[9]					
			<20[10]					
1985	30[11]	<20[12]	<20[13]		20[14]	17[4]	84[7]	15[15]
			15-35					
1985 1st qtr.			20[17]				82[17]	
1985 4th qtr.			22[18]					
1986	20[19]		16	<3-12[21]	6[22]		60[20]	
1986 CY[23]			18	5				
1986 1st qtr.			18[17]				68[18]	
1986 2nd qtr.	27[24·]	8[24]	21[24]	6[24]	13[24]	48[24]	74[25]	31[24]
1987	18[11]	15[26]	13[11]			5[11]	58[11]	
1987 1st qtr.					7			
1987 2nd qtr.	14[27]							
1988				2-7[28]	5[28]			10[29]

Sources:

1. Ellen L. Frost, Deputy Assistant Secretary for International Economic Affairs,

Sources: Table 10 (continued)

Department of Defense, prepared statement, 7 March 1979, in U.S. Congress, House Committee on Foreign Affairs, Subcommittee on International Economic Policy and Trade, *Extension and Revision of the Export Administration Act of 1969*, hearings and markup, 96th Congress, 1st session, 15, 22 February, 7-8, 14-15, 21-22, 26-28 March, 3-4, 24-26 April 1979 (Washington, DC: U.S. GPO, 1979), pp. 173-75.

2. Applications reviewed by DOD only for requests by COCOM allies. U.S. Department of Defense, *The Technology Security Program*, A Report to the 99th Congress, second session, 1986, p. 31.

3. Ibid.

4. Stephen D. Bryen, Deputy Under Secretary of Defense for Trade Security Policy, Department of Defense, prepared statement, 6 November 1985, in U.S. Congress, House Committee on Foreign Affairs, Subcommittee on International Economic Policy and Trade, *Implementation of the Export Administration Amendments Act of 1985*, hearings, 99th Congress, 1st session, 10 October, 6 November 1085 (Washington, DC: U.S. GPO, 1988), p. 89.

5. U.S. Department of Defense, *The Technology Security Program*, p. 28.

6. William Archey, DOC's Acting Assistant Secretary for Trade Administration, testified that average LPT had fallen to 20 days by the last quarter of FY 1984. Based on his testimony I have calculated an overall average for FY 1984 at 33 days. William T. Archey, prepared statement in U.S. Congress, House Committee on Foreign Affairs, Subcommittee on International Economic Policy and Trade, *U.S. and Multilateral Export Controls*, hearing, 99th Congress, 1st session, 23 April 1985 (Washington, DC: U.S. GPO, 1987), p. 32.

7. Average for quarters 1-4. William T. Archey, Acting Assistant Secretary for Trade Administration, Department of Commerce, prepared statement, Appendix A, 10 October 1985, in U.S. Congress, House Committee on Foreign Affairs, Subcommittee on International Economic Policy and Trade, *Implementation of the Export Administration Amendments Act of 1985*, hearings, 10 October, 6 November 1985, 99th Congress, 1st session (Washington, DC: U.S. GPO, 1988), p. 33.

8. U.S. Department of Defense, *The Technology Security Program*, p. 29.

9. Beginning of 1st quarter. Figure is for cases *not* requiring interagency review. U.S. Department of Commerce, International Trade Administration, *Export Administration Annual Report FY 1985* (Washington, DC: U.S. GPO, November 1986), p. 3.

10. Average LPT claimed by DOC at end of FY 1985. Ibid.

11. U.S. Department of Commerce, International Trade Administration, *Export Administration Annual Report* FY 1987 (Washington, DC: U.S. GPO, November 1988), p. 7.

12. For licenses reviewed by DOD only. United States, Department of Defense, *The Technology Security Program*, p. 69.

13. For cases *not* requiring interagency review. See U.S. Department of Commerce, *Export Administration Annual Report FY 1985*, p. 3.

14. Requests from COCOM members reviewed by DOD only. See U.S. Department of Defense, *The Technology Security Program*, p. 31.

15. Ibid., p. 29.

16. For the period January-May 1985. See Archey, in U.S. Congress, *U.S. and Multilateral Export Controls*, p. 35.

17. Paul Freedenberg, Assistant Secretary for Trade Administration, prepared statement, 17 April 1986, in U.S. Congress, House Committee on Foreign Affairs, Subcommittee on International Economic Policy and Trade, *Omnibus Trade Legislation (Vol. II)*, hearings, 99th

Sources: Table 10 (continued)
Congress, 2nd session, 10, 17 April 1986 (Washington, DC: U.S. GPO, 1987), p. 166.

18. Malcolm Baldrige, Secretary of Commerce, prepared statement, 19 March 1986, in U.S. Congress, House Committee on Foreign Affairs, Subcommittee on International Economic Policy and Trade, *Renewal of Foreign Policy Export Controls and the 1987 Budget for the International Trade Administration*, hearing, 99th Congress, 2nd session, 19 March 1986 (Washington, DC: U.S. GPO, 1988), p. 19.

19. Malcolm Baldrige, Secretary of Commerce, statement, 12 March 1987, in U.S. Congress, Senate Committee on Banking, Housing, and Urban Affairs, Subcommittee on International Finance and Monetary Policy, *Export Controls*, hearings, 100th Congress, 1st session, 12, 17 March 1987 (Washington, DC: U.S. GPO, 1987), p. 11.

20. U.S. Department of Commerce, International Trade Administration, *Export Administration Annual Report FY 1986* (Washington, DC: U.S. GPO, December 1987), p. 8.

21. U.S. Department of Defense, *The Technology Security Program*, p. 41.

22. U.S. Department of Commerce, International Trade Administration, *Export Administration Annual Report FY 1986*, p. 7.

23. Response to questions of Chairman Bonker Subcommittee on International Economic Policy and Trade, from U.S. Department of Commerce, in U.S. Congress, House Committee on Foreign Affairs, Subcommittee on International Economic Policy and Trade, *Omnibus Trade and Competitiveness Act of 1988 (Vol. II)*, hearings, 100th Congress, 1st session, 11-12 March 1987 (Washington, DC: U.S. GPO, 1988), p. 36.

24. For the period January 5- April 5, 1986. See National Academy of Sciences, *Balancing the National Interest* (Washington, DC: National Academy Press, 1987), Table C-6, p. 236.

25. Figure represents an average of the processing times for the 1st and 2nd quarters of FY 1986. See Freedenberg, statement, p. 166.

26. "About 15 days." Richard N. Perle, Assistant Secretary of Defense for International Security Policy, statement, 23 April 1987, in U.S. Congress, House Committee on Science, Space, and Technology, *National Academy of Sciences Report on International Technology Transfer*, hearings, 100th Congress, 1st session, 4 February, 23 April 1987 (Washington, DC: U.S. GPO, 1987), p. 89.

27. U.S. Department of Commerce, *Business America*, 8 June 1987, p. 3.

28. U.S. Congress, General Accounting Office, *Export Controls: Extent of DOD Influence on Licensing Decisions*, GAO/NSIAD-89-155 (Washington, DC: U.S. GPO, June 1989), p. 19.

29. Robert L. Mullen, Deputy Under Secretary, Trade Security Policy, Department of Defense, enclosure to a letter to Frank C. Conahan, Assistant Comptroller General, National Security and International Affairs Division, U.S. General Accounting Office, dated 1 May 1988, rpt. in Ibid., p. 48.

Notes:
    *Fiscal Year unless otherwise indicated.
    $<$ = within
    CY = Calendar Year

Table 11
Comparison of LPT (in Days): U.S., CANADA, U.K., FRANCE,
F.R.G., 1987-88

	U.S.	CANADA	U.K.	FRANCE[1]	F.R.G.	JAPAN
OVERALL WESTERN EUROPE/	14				1[2]/4[3]	
JAPAN/COCOM	5	MINIMAL				
WEST/FW	13		5	c.14		2-3[4]
EAST/ U.S.S.R.+ ALLIES	58	42-56		c.21		

Sources: See Table 10. Unless otherwise noted: William A. Root, Solveig B. Spielmann, and Felice A. Kaden, "A Study of Foreign Export Control Systems," in *Balancing the National Interest*, Working Papers, ed. National Academy of Sciences (Washington, DC: National Academy Press, 1987), Appendix A, pp. 235-41.

Notes:

1. Immediate issuance for overcoverage because of use of tariff numbers; otherwise times are as indicated.

2. If adequately documented.

3. Not-for-attribution interview, U.S. Department of Commerce, Washington, DC, 14 March 1988.

4. National Academy of Sciences, *Balancing the National Interest* (Washington, DC: National Academy Press, 1987), p. 113.

Table 12
DOC Backlog: Processing Efficiency for FW (1) and U.S.S.R.
and Allies (2)

YEAR	# PROCESSED APPLICATIONS (1) AND (2)	BACKLOG (1)+(2)	OF WHICH: %(1)	OF WHICH: %(2)
FY 1979	NA	1593	NA	NA
FY 1980	73,072	4235	52.2	47.7
FY 1981	71,200	2811	78.7	32.1
FY 1982	76,677	4697	92.2	7.8
FY 1983	87,761	13,773	74.1	25.5
FY 1984	121,652	10,497	82.7	17.2
FY 1985	132,103	10,887	81.6	18.3
FY 1986	121,523	7096	82.2	16.9
FY 1987	109,195	4878	84.0	15.9

Sources: See Tables 1, 3.

Table 13
Distribution Licenses (DLs): License Processing Time (LPT) in Days,
Number Active/New DLs, Number of DL Audits

FY	AVE. LPT	NO. ACTIVE DLs	NO. NEW DLs	NO. DL AUDITS
1978[1]	NA	253	43	0[2]
1979[1]	NA	324	71	0[2]
1980[1]	NA	421	97	0[2]
1981[1]	NA	530	109	0[2]
1982[1]	NA	625	95	0[2]
1983[1]	NA	701	76	0[2]
1984[1]	200	780	79	18
1985[1]	120	702[3]	66	51
1986[1]	60-90	630[3]	23[4]	88
1987[5]	c.75	555	NA	122

Sources:

1. U.S. Department of Commerce, Bureau of Export Administration, *Export Administration Annual Report FY 1986* (Washington, DC: U.S. GPO, December 1987), pp. 4-5, 14.

2. Henry R. Nau, "The West-West Dimensions of East-West Economic Relations," in *Selling the Rope to Hang Capitalism?*, eds. Charles M. Perry and Robert L. Pfaltzgraff, Jr. (London: Pergamon-Brassey's, 1987), p. 213.

3. Some companies have elected not to continue under the DL program as a result of the new regulations. See U.S. Department of Commerce, Bureau of Export Administration, *Export Administration Annual Report FY 1986* (Washington, DC: U.S. GPO, December 1987), p. 14, Table 1-2.

4. As a result of prelicense consultations, only 36 applications for DLs were submitted. See Ibid.

5. U.S. Department of Commerce, Bureau of Export Administration, *Export Administration Annual Report FY 1987* (Washington, DC: U.S. GPO, November 1988), pp. 8-9.

Table 14
DOD--Overall License Processing Time--Days (% of Total Applications Taking Less Than/More Than X Number of Days to Process)

YEAR/DAYS	<2	<5	<7	<30	<60	≥61
7/75-1/76[1]		68		90		
1-10/78[2]			c.40	72		
10/78-3/79[2]			c.50	98		
10/79-4/81[3]				68	87	13
1982 qtrs. 1+2[4]				c.10		
1982 qtrs. 3+4[4]				42		
1983				42[5]	88[6]	<12[6]
1987[7]	56					

Sources:

1. Roger E. Shields, Deputy Assistant Secretary, International Economic Affairs, Department of Defense, prepared statement, in U.S. Congress, House Committee on International Relations, Subcommittee on International Trade and Commerce, *Export Licensing of Advanced Technology: A Review*, hearings, 94th Congress, 2nd session, 11, 15, 24, 30 March 1976 (Washington, DC: U.S. GPO, 1976), pp. 89-93.

2. William J. Perry, Undersecretary of Defense for Research and Engineering, "The Department of Defense Statement on the Department of Defense Export Control Policy," 5 March 1979, in U.S. Congress, Senate Committee on Banking, Housing, and Urban Affairs, *U.S. Export Control Policy and Extension of the Export Administration Act*, part I, hearings, 96th Congress, 1st session, 5-6 March 1979 (Washington, DC: U.S. GPO, 1979), pp. 132, 135.

3. Oles Lomacky, Director of Technology Trade, Office of the Undersecretary for Research and Engineering, Department of Defense, prepared statement, 14 April 1981, in U.S. Congress, House Committee on Foreign Affairs, Subcommittee on International Economic Policy and Trade, *Export Administration Amendments Act of 1981*, hearings and markup, 97th Congress, 1st session, 26 March, 14, 28 April, 13 May 1981 (Washington, DC: U.S. GPO, 1981), p. 127, Figure 4.

4. Richard Perle, Assistant Secretary for International Security Policy, Department of Defense, prepared statement, 1 March 1983, in U.S. Congress, House Committee on Foreign

Sources: Table 14 (continued)

Affairs, Subcommittee on International Economic Policy and Trade, *Extension and Revision of the Export Administration Act of 1979*, hearings, 98th Congress, 1st session, 24 February, 1, 3, 8 March, 5, 12-14, 28-29 April, 2, 4-5, 18, 25-26 May 1983 (Washington, DC: U.S. GPO, ?), p. 200.

5. Richard Perle, Assistant Secretary of Defense, testimony, 2 March 1983, in U.S. Congress, Senate Committee on Banking, Housing, and Urban Affairs, Subcommittee on International Finance and Monetary Policy, *Reauthorization of the Export Administration Act*, hearings, 98th Congress, 1st session, 2, 16 March, 14 April 1983 (Washington, DC: U.S. GPO, 1983), p. 194.

6. Talbot S. Lindstrom, Deputy Under Secretary for International Programs and Technology, Department of Defense, prepared statement, in U.S. Congress, House Committee on Armed Services, Technology Transfer Panel, *Technology Transfer*, hearings, 98th Congress, 1st session, 9, 21, 23 June, 13-14 July 1983 (Washington, DC: U.S. GPO, 1984), p. 162.

7. Richard Perle, Assistant Secretary of Defense for International Security Policy, Department of Defense, testimony, 12 March 1987, in U.S. Congress, Senate Committee on Banking, Housing, and Urban Affairs, Subcommittee on International Finance and Monetary Policy, *Export Controls*, hearings, 100th Congress, 1st session, 12, 17 March 1987 (Washington, DC: U.S. GPO, 1987), p. 80.

Table 15
Disposition of Defense Recommendations to Approve or Deny
License Applications, 1-12 April 1985

		%COMMERCE LICENSING ACTIONS		
DOD REC	#APPLICATIONS	APPROVED	DENIED	RWA
APPROVE	611 (91.0%)	78.0	1.2	19.3
DENY	60 (8.9%)	65.0	5.0	28.3
TOTAL	671	77.6	1.4	20.1

Disposition of Defense Recommendations to Approve or Deny
License Applications, June 1987-June 1988

		%COMMERCE LICENSING ACTIONS		
DOD REC	#APPLICATIONS	APPROVED	DENIED	RWA
APPROVE	3,563 (34%)	93	0.5	5
APPROVE WITH				
CONDITIONS	5,278 (51%)	93	0.9	5
DENY	840 (8%)	13	40.0	46
TOTAL[1]	10,380	83	4.0	13

Sources: For period 1-12 April 1985, derived from U.S. Congress, General Accounting Office, *Export Licensing: Commerce-Defense Review of Applications to Certain Free World Nations*, GAO/NSIAD-86-169 (Washington, DC: U.S. GPO, September 1986), p. 15, Table 2.1. For period June 1987-June 1988, derived from U.S. Congress, General Accounting Office, *Export Controls: Extent of DOD Influence on Licensing Decisions*, GAO/NSIAD-89-155 (Washington, DC: U.S. GPO, June 1989), p. 21, Table 3.1.

Notes:
    DOD REC = DOD Recommendation
    1. Since some DOD Recommendations have been deleted, sum in TOTAL column will not equal sum in first vertical column.

Table 16
Unilateral Controls

YEAR	CATEGORIES	ITEMS ELIMINATED
1972[1]	461	NA
1978[2]	84	NA
1979[3]	38	NA
1980-81[4]		1
1982[4]	28-30	1
1984[5]	29	NA
1986[6]	28	0
1987[7]	27	NA
1988[8]	c.30	NA

Sources:

1. William J. Long, "The Executive, Congress, and Interest Groups in U.S. Export Control Policy: The National Organization of Power," in *Controlling East-West Trade and Technology Transfer: Power, Politics, and Policies,* ed. Gary K. Bertsch (Durham, NC: Duke University Press, 1988), p. 44, footnote 44, citing Senate, S. Rept. 890, 92d Cong., 2d sess., 1972, p. 3.

2. John R. McIntyre and Richard T. Cupitt, "East-West Strategic Trade Control: Crumbling Consensus?" *Survey: A Journal of East and West Studies,* vol. 25, no. 2 (Spring 1980), pp. 90-91, footnote 22, citing "Interview with Mr. Charles Swanson, former head of the Operations division of the Office of Export Administration, Department of Commerce, in Dec. 1978."

3. U.S. Congress, General Accounting Office, *Perspectives on Trade and International Payments,* ID-79-11A (Washington, DC: U.S. GPO, 10 October 1979), p. 25.

4. U.S. Congress, General Accounting Office, *Export Control Regulation Could Be Reduced Without Affecting National Security,* GAO/ID-82-14 (Washington, DC: U.S. GPO, 26 May 1982), pp. 2, 5.

5. Harold Paul Luks, "U.S. National Security Export Controls: Legislative and Regulatory Proposals," in *Balancing the National Interest,* Working Papers, ed. National Academy of Sciences (Washington, DC: National Academy Press, 1987), p. 114, citing U.S. Department of Commerce, *Export Administration Annual Report FY 1984* (Washington, DC: GPO, 1985), pp. 145-54.

6. U.S. Department of Commerce, Bureau of Export Administration, *Export Administration Annual Report FY 1986* (Washington, DC: U.S. GPO, December 1987), pp. 165-72.

7. Lew Allen, Jr., Director, Jet Propulsion Laboratory, Chairman, National Academy of Sciences Panel on National Security Export Controls, statement, 12 March 1987, in U.S. Congress, Senate Committee on Banking, Housing, and Urban Affairs, Subcommittee on International Finance and Monetary Policy, *Export Controls,* hearings, 100th Congress, 1st session, 12, 17 March 1987 (Washington, DC: U.S. GPO, 1987), p. 43.

8. Paul Freedenberg, Under Secretary for Trade Administration, Depart

Sources: Table 16 (continued)

ment of Commerce, comments at a National Issues Forum on *U.S. Export Control Policy: Balancing National Security Issues and Global Competitiveness*, held at The Brookings Institution, Washington, DC, 9 June 1988.

Table 17
Average U.S. Share of Selected Total High-Technology
Commodity Exports, 1965-82 (in Percent)

| | COMMODITY CATEGORY | | | | | AVERAGE | AVERAGE |
PERIOD	1	2	3	4	5	1-5	1-5+OTHER
1965-70	21.2	55.9	31.9	25.1	26.9	32.2	28.6
1971-76	18.4	61.4	30.0	21.3	24.0	31.0	25.5
1977-82	17.8	51.8	33.8	20.1	24.1	29.5	24.7

Source: Derived from Victoria L. Hatter, *U.S. High Technology Trade and Competitiveness*, International Trade Administration, U.S. Department of Commerce (Washington, DC: U.S. GPO, February 1985), pp. 44 and 73, Table V.39. Note: From 1982-1988, the U.S. trade position in high technology declined and market shares in many commodity categories eroded. Much of this decline is attributable to numerous factors including unfavorable exchange rates and global structural shifts.

Commodity Category key:
   1 = Communications equipment and electronic components
   2 = Aircraft and parts
   3 = Office, computing, and accounting machines
   4 = Professional and scientific instruments
   5 = Engines, turbines, and parts

Notes:
   AVERAGE 1-5+OTHER = Average of categories 1-5 by year group
   AVERAGE 1-5+OTHER = Average of U.S. share of high-technology commodity exports, 1965-82, by year group. Includes average share of categories 1-5 plus share of 5 additional high-technology commodity export categories.

Table 18

Average Value of Selected U.S. High Technology Commodity Exports, 1965-87 (in Thousands of Dollars)

PERIOD	COMMODITY CATEGORY					AVERAGE 1-5
	1	2	3	4	5	
1965-70	1,092,955	2,175,944	893,673	1,059,635	504,381	1,145,318
1971-76	2,749,252	5,473,846	2,342,688	2,448,597	1,322,889	2,867,454
1977-82	7,157,577	12,055,863	7,167,335	6,019,254	3,273,361	7,134,678
1983-87	14,582,200	17,023,000	15,504,200	7,539,200	3,031,600	10,559,133

Sources: For 1965-82, derived from Victoria L. Hatter, *U.S. High Technology Trade and Competitiveness*, International Trade Administration, U.S. Department of Commerce (Washington, DC: U.S. GPO, February 1985), pp. 44 and 80, Table V.53. For 1983-87, see U.S. Department of Commerce, International Trade Administration, *United States Trade: Performance in 1985 and Outlook* (Washington, DC: U.S. GPO, October 1986), p. 132, Table 15; and U.S. Department of Commerce, International Trade Administration, *United States Trade Performance in 1987* (Washington, DC: U.S. GPO, June 1988), p. 110, Table 15.

Key: See Table 17.

Table 19

Percentage Increase/Decrease in Average Value of Selected U.S. High Technology Commodity Exports, 1965-87 (in Percent)

	COMMODITY CATEGORY					AVERAGE
PERIOD	1	2	3	4	5	1-5
1965-70 TO 1971-76	151.5	151.6	162.1	131.0	162.2	150.3
1971-76 TO 1977-82	160.3	120.2	206.0	145.8	147.4	148.8
1977-82 TO 1983-87	103.7	41.2	116.3	25.2	-7.3	47.9

Sources, Key, and Note: See Tables 17, 18.

Table 20
Percentage Change in Value of Selected U.S. High-Technology Commodity Exports to Selected Regions, 1980-87 (Figures Rounded)

REGION	80-81	81-82	82-83	83-84	84-85	85-86	86-87	AVERAGE 80-87
WORLD	10.4	-3.7	3.5	8.8	4.4	5.9	15.9	6.4
DEVELOPED COUNTRIES	11.2	-6.9	8.3	10.8	4.1	9.2	14.8	8.1
E.C. 10/12	2.5	-6.5	4.8	13.4	2.5	11.4	16.2	6.3
P.R.C.	24.3	-23.3	2.6	26.2	107.6	-25.0	12.0	17.7

Sources: U.S. Department of Commerce, International Trade Administration, *United States Trade: Performance in 1985 and Outlook* (Washington, DC: U.S. GPO, October 1986), p. 133, Table 16; and U.S. Department of Commerce, International Trade Administration, *United States Trade Performance in 1987* (Washington, DC: U.S. GPO, June 1988), p 110, Table 15.

Notes:
For a definition of U.S. high-technology exports see U.S. Department of Commerce, "DOC-3 definition."
E.C.10/12 = European Community of 10/12 members
AVERAGE 80-87 = Average for 1980-87

Table 21
Percentage Change in Value of Selected U.S. High-
Technology Commodity Exports to World, 1980-87
(Rounded Figures)

| COMMODITY | YEARS | | | | | | | AVERAGE |
CATEGORY	80-81	81-82	82-83	83-84	84-85	85-86	86-87	80-87
1	15.3	-20.1	3.6	-10.1	32.0	4.5	12.3	5.3
2	19.4	4.0	23.9	29.6	6.5	4.8	23.8	16.0
3	9.2	4.6	10.3	24.1	2.2	5.9	18.8	10.7
4	2.8	5.1	15.8	25.7	-17.2	15.7	25.7	10.5
5	23.9	3.1	-3.3	6.1	3.5	0.8	10.2	6.3
6	15.0	7.8	1.7	4.3	6.3	5.5	14.9	7.9
7	8.3	-4.4	1.1	14.8	-7.2	2.9	19.5	5.0
8	12.9	-11.3	-7.5	26.0	6.0	2.9	9.1	5.4
9	16.3	-3.4	-1.0	24.3	-7.1	6.7	17.7	7.6

Sources: U.S. Department of Commerce, International Trade Administration, *1984 U.S. Foreign Trade Highlights* (Washington, DC: U.S. GPO, March 1985), no pagination; and United States, Department of Commerce, International Trade Administration, *1987 U.S. Foreign Trade Highlights* (Washington, DC: U.S. GPO, May 1988), p. A-061.

Commodity Categories Key:
  1 = Aircraft, spacecraft, and associated equipment
  2 = Parts for office machines and automatic data processing machines
  3 = Automatic data processing machines
  4 = Electronic components and parts
  5 = Measuring, checking, etc., instruments
  6 = Telecommunications equipment
  7 = Electrical machinery and apparatus
  8 = Specialized industrial machinery
  9 = Electrical apparatus, current carrying, etc.

Note:
AVERAGE 80-87 = Average for 1980-87.

Table 22
Percentage Change in Value of Selected U.S. High-Technology
Commodity Exports to Western Europe, 1980-87
(Rounded Figures)

COMMODITY CATEGORY	YEARS							AVERAGE 80-87
	80-81	81-82	82-83	83-84	84-85	85-86	86-87	
1	0.1	0.5	10.9	19.6	-4.3	10.6	19.4	8.1
2	13.5	2.1	19.1	26.0	3.3	9.4	19.6	13.2
3	4.9	-34.2	24.9	-18.5	36.0	16.2	15.1	6.3
4	16.0	3.4	-3.8	7.7	2.7	3.8	7.9	5.3
5	-19.4	-3.8	5.1	43.1	-4.6	-0.1	17.4	37.7
6	9.7	0.7	-5.0	0.1	8.8	0.1	10.3	3.5
7	-3.6	-4.3	-0.6	9.1	-10.4	2.2	16.0	1.2
8	-0.8	-9.3	-3.1	29.0	15.7	-0.3	4.5	5.1
9	-1.9	-2.7	-1.1	27.2	-1.4	12.7	23.0	7.9

Sources: U.S. Department of Commerce, International Trade Administration, *1984 U.S. Foreign Trade Highlights* (Washington, DC: U.S. GPO, March 1985), no pagination; and U.S. Department of Commerce, International Trade Administration, *1987 U.S. Foreign Trade Highlights* (Washington, DC: U.S. GPO, May 1988), p. A-076.

Notes: See Table 21.

Table 23
Percentage Change in Trade Balance With Western Europe in U.S.
Computer Equipment and Parts ($ Millions)

YEAR	1980	1981	1982	1983	1984	1985	AVERAGE 80-85
BALANCE	4,154	4,400	4,447	5,014	5,833	5,242	
%CHANGE		5.9	1.0	12.7	16.3	-10.1	5.2

Source: Derived from U.S. Department of Commerce, International Trade Administration, Office of Computers and Business Equipment Science and Electronics, *A Competitive Assessment of the U.S. Microcomputer Industry: Business/Professional Systems* (Washington, DC: U.S. GPO, August 1986), p. 69.

Note:
AVERAGE 80-85 = Average 1980-85

Table 24
U.S. Exports of Robots, 1979-83

YEAR	QUANTITY (UNITS)	VALUE (1,000 DOLLARS)	AVERAGE UNIT VALUE (1,000 DOLLARS)
1979	173	8,909	51.5
1980	340	20,766	61.1
1981	413	23,309	56.4
1982	428	20,322	47.5
1983	631	33,738	53.5
%CHANGE 1979-83	264.7	278.7	

Source: Derived from U.S. Department of Commerce, International Trade Administration, Capital Goods and International Construction Sector Group, *A Competitive Assessment of the U.S. Robotics Industry* (Washington, DC: U.S. GPO, March 1987), p. 21.

Table 25
Growth of U.S. CAD/CAM Exports, 1977-88 ($ Million)

ITEM	1977	1980	1983	1988[1]	AVERAGE
U.S. EXPORTS CAD/CAM SYSTS.	18	243	480	1600	
% CHANGE 1977-88		1,250.0	97.5	233.3	526.9
%TOTAL REVENUES GENERATED IN INTERNATIONAL MARKETS	15	22	28	30	

Source: Derived from U.S. Department of Commerce, International Trade Administration, Capital Goods and International Construction Sector Group, *A Competitive Assessment of the U.S. Computer-Aided Design and Manufacturing Systems Industry* (Washington, DC: U.S. GPO, February 1987), p. 29.
   1. Projected

Table 26
Projected Gross National Product (GNP) Loss as Percent of
GNP, 1978-87 (Millions of Dollars Except Billions of
Dollars for "GNP" Column) (Figures Rounded)

YEAR	ACTUAL EXPORTS	PROJECTED EXPORTS	GNP LOSS	GNP	LOSS AS % OF GNP
1978	34,839	40,378	11,078	3,115.2	0.3
1979	43,524	50,444	13,840	3,192.4	0.4
1980	54,712	63,411	17,398	3,187.1	0.6
1981	60,390	69,992	19,204	3,248.8	0.5
1982	58,112	67,351	18,479	3,166.0	0.5
1983	60,158	69,723	19,130	3,279.1	0.5
1984	65,510	75,926	20,832	3,501.4	0.6
1985	68,425	79,305	21,759	3,618.7	0.6
1986	72,517	84,047	23,060	3,721.7	0.6
1987	84,071	97,438	26,735	3,847.0	0.7

Notes and Sources: Total lost West-West and West-East export sales estimated by the NAS to be $7.3 billion for 1985, equivalent to about 10.6% of the total value of high technology exports (DOC-3 definition) for 1985. Derived from National Academy of Sciences, *Balancing the National Interest* (Washington, DC: National Academy Press, 1987), p. 266, Table D-3.

Actual Exports: Figures from U.S. Department of Commerce, International Trade Administration, *United States Trade Performance in 1987* (Washington, DC: U.S. GPO, June 1988), p. 109, Table 14 (DOC-3 definition).

Projected Exports: Calculated by assuming that the 1985 NAS figure for lost West-West and West-East sales was 50% too low. Under the revised calculation, lost export sales represented about 15.9% of the total value of high technology exports during 1985.

GNP Loss: Based on a multiplier of 2, times the difference between Projected Exports and Actual Exports. The multiplier is from National Academy of Sciences, *Balancing the National Interest*, p. 272.

GNP: Figures from U.S. President, *Economic Report of the President* (Washington, DC: U.S. GPO, 1989), p. 310, Table B-2.

Table 27
Change in Actual Exports as Percent of Gross National Product
(GNP) Compared With Change in Loss of GNP as Percent of GNP

YEAR	ACTUAL EXPORTS AS % OF GNP	% RATE OF CHANGE	LOSS AS % OF GNP	% RATE OF CHANGE
1978	1.1		0.3	
1979	1.3	0.2	0.4	0.1
1980	1.7	0.4	0.6	0.2
1981	1.8	0.1	0.5	-0.1
1982	1.8	0	0.5	0
1983	1.8	0	0.5	0
1984	1.8	0	0.6	0.1
1985	1.8	0	0.6	0
1986	2.0	0.2	0.6	0
1987	2.1	0.1	0.7	0.1
AVERAGE GROWTH RATE 1978-1987		0.1		0.04

Source: Derived from Table 26.

References

BOOKS, REPORTS, ESSAYS, ARTICLES, THESES

Abbott, Kenneth W. "Defining the Extraterritorial Reach of American Export Controls: Congress as Catalyst." *Cornell International Law Journal* 17 (Winter 1984): 79-158.

Adler-Karlsson, Gunnar. *Western Economic Warfare, 1947-1967.* Stockholm: Almqvist and Wiksell, 1968.

Aeppel, Timothy. "The Evolution of Multilateral Export Controls: A Critical Study of the COCOM Regime." *The Fletcher Forum* 9 (Winter 1985): 105-24.

American Electronics Association. *Case Study Report American Electronics Association Export Control Task Force*, 12 March 1987.

Association of American Universities. *National Security Controls and University Research: Information for Investigators and Administrators.* Prepared by the Association of American Universities for the Department of Defense-University Forum. Washington, DC: Association of American Universities, June 1987.

Basiuk, Victor. "Soviet Systemic Change, Technology Transfer, and U.S.-Soviet Relations." In *Selling the Rope to Hang Capitalism?*, eds. Charles M. Perry and Robert L. Pfaltzgraff, Jr., 88-109. London: Pergamon-Brassey's, 1987.

Becker, Stephen E., Esq., and Harold Paul Luks. "Corporate Compliance With the National Security Controls of the Export Administration Regulations." In *Balancing the National Interest*, Working Papers, ed. National Academy of Sciences, 22-59. Washington, DC: National Academy Press, 1987.

Benson, Sumner. "Overcoming Complacency." *Society* 23 (July/August 1986): 12-15.

__. "United States Policy on Strategic Trade With the Soviet Bloc." In *Economic*

Relations With the Soviet Union, ed. Angela E. Stent, 99-123. Boulder, CO: Westview Press, 1985.

Berlack, Evan R., Cecil Hunt, and Terence Roche Murphy. *Coping With U.S. Export Controls 1986*. Practising Law Institute, 1986.

Bertsch, Gary K. "American Politics and Trade With the U.S.S.R." In *Trade, Technology, and Soviet-American Relations*, ed. Bruce Parrott, 243-82. Bloomington, IN: Indiana University Press, 1985.

__. "Introduction." In *Controlling East-West Trade and Technology Transfer: Power, Politics, and Policies*, ed. Gary K. Bertsch, 1-24. Durham, NC: Duke University Press, 1988.

__. "U.S. Export Controls." *Journal of World Trade Law* 15 (1981): 67-82. Reprinted as a shortened version in *National Security and Technology Transfer*, eds. Gary K. Bertsch and John R. McIntyre, 126-39. Westview Special Studies in National Security and Defense Policy. Boulder, CO: Westview Press, 1983.

__. "U.S.-Soviet Trade: The Question of Leverage." *Survey* 25 (Spring 1980). Reprinted in *National Security and Technology Transfer*, eds. Gary K. Bertsch and John R. McIntyre, 64-76. Westview Special Studies in National Security and Defense Policy. Boulder, CO: Westview Press, 1983.

Bertsch, Gary K., and Steven Elliott. "Controlling East-West Trade in Britain: Power, Politics, and Policy." In *Controlling East-West Trade and Technology Transfer: Power, Politics, and Policies*, ed. Gary K. Bertsch, 204-38. Durham, NC: Duke University Press, 1988.

Bertsch, Gary K., and Steve Elliott-Gower. "U.S. COCOM Policy: From Paranoia to Perestroika?" In *After the Revolutions: East-West Trade and Technology Transfer in the 1990s*, eds. Gary K. Bertsch, Heinrich Vogel, and Jan Zielonka, 15-31. Boulder, CO: Westview Press, 1991.

Bertsch, Gary K., and John R. McIntyre. "The Western Alliance and East-West Trade: In Pursuit of an Integrated Strategy." In *The Politics of East-West Trade*, ed. Gordon B. Smith, 209-35. Westview Special Studies in International Relations. Boulder, CO: Westview Press, 1984.

__, eds. *National Security and Technology Transfer*. Westview Special Studies in National Security and Defense Policy. Boulder, CO: Westview Press, 1983.

Bryen, Stephen. "Technology Transfer and National Security: Finding the Proper Balance." In *Selling the Rope to Hang Capitalism?*, eds. Charles M. Perry and Robert L. Pfaltzgraff, Jr., 10-15. London: Pergamon-Brassey's, 1987.

Bryon, Paige, Scott Sullivan, and Steve Pastore. "Capitalists and Commissars." *Policy Review* 22 (Fall 1982): 19-54.

Buchan, David. "Technology Transfer to the Soviet Bloc." *Washington Quarterly* 7 (Fall 1984): 130-35.

__. "Western Security and Economic Strategy Towards the East." *Adelphi Papers*, no. 192. London: International Institute for Strategic Studies, 1984.

Bucy, J. Fred. "Technology Transfer and East-West Trade: A Reappraisal." *International Security* 5 (Winter 1980): 132-51. Reprinted in *National Security and Technology Transfer*, eds. Gary K. Bertsch and John R. McIntyre, 198-216.

Westview Special Studies in National Security and Defense Policy. Boulder, CO: Westview Press, 1983.

Cahill, Kevin. *Trade Wars: The High-Technology Scandal of the 1980s.* London: W. H. Allen, 1986.

Carrick, R. J. *East-West Technology Transfer in Perspective.* Policy Papers in International Affairs, no. 9. Berkeley, CA: Institute of International Studies, 1978.

"Commerce Formally Delays Decision on License-Free High Technology Sales." *Inside U.S. Trade*, 2 December 1988, 7-9.

Cooper, Julian. "Western Technology and the Soviet Defense Industry." In *Trade, Technology, and Soviet-American Relations*, ed. Bruce Parrott, 169-202. Bloomington, IN: Indiana University Press, 1985.

Corson, Dale R. "Scientific Communication and National Security." In *National Security Controls and University Research: Selected Readings*, ed. David A. Wilson, 3-12. Prepared by the Association of American Universities for the Department of Defense-University Forum. Washington, DC: Association of American Universities, 1987.

Costick, Miles M. "Soviet Military Posture and Strategic Trade." In *From Weakness to Strength*, ed. W. Scott Thompson, 189-213. San Francisco: Institute for Contemporary Studies, 1980.

Crawford, Beverly, and Stefanie Lenway. "Decision Modes and International Regime Change: Western Collaboration and East-West Trade." *World Politics* 37 (April 1985): 375-402.

Dankert, Pieter. "Europe Together, America Apart." *Foreign Policy* 53 (Winter 1983-84): 18-33.

Dean, Jonathan. "How to Lose Germany." *Foreign Policy* 55 (Summer 1984): 54-72.

de Borchgrave, Arnaud, and Michael Ledeen. "Selling Russia the Rope." *New Republic*, 13 December 1980, 13-16.

Derian, Jean-Claude. "France." In "A Delicate Balance: Scientific Communication vs. National Security," eds. Mitchel B. Wallerstein and Stephen B. Gould, 46-48. *Issues in Science and Technology* 4 (Fall 1987).

Dickson, David. "Soviet High-Tech Spying Detailed in France." *Science* 228 (19 April 1985): 306.

Dobson, Alan P. "The Kennedy Administration and Economic Warfare Against Communism." *International Affairs* [London] 64 (Autumn 1988): 599-616.

Donaghue, Hugh. "A Business Perspective on Export Controls." In *Selling the Rope to Hang Capitalism?*, eds. Charles M. Perry and Robert L. Pfaltzgraff, Jr., 186-91. London: Pergamon-Brassey's, 1987.

Feldman, Jan. "Trade Policy and Foreign Policy." *Washington Quarterly* 8 (Winter 1985): 65-76.

Ferguson, Charles H. "High Technology Life Cycles, Export Controls, and International Markets." In *Balancing the National Interest*, Working Papers, ed. National Academy of Sciences, 60-86. Washington, DC: National Academy

Press, 1987.

Flamm, Kenneth, and Thomas L. McNaugher. "Rationalizing Technology Investments." In *Restructuring American Foreign Policy*, ed. John D. Steinbruner, 119-57. Washington, DC: The Brookings Institution, 1989.

Frankel, Mark, et al. "High-Tech Tussle." *Newsweek* [European edition], 15 January 1990, 44-45.

Fritsch-Bournazel, Renata. "France." In *Economic Warfare or Detente?*, eds. Reinhard Rode and Hanns D. Jacobsen, 128-40. International Perspectives on Security Series, no. 1. Boulder, CO: Westview Press, 1985.

Gallagher, Robert T. "Europeans Try to Trade High Tech For Soviet Natural Gas." *Electronics* 58 (15 July 1985): 38-9.

Gershman, Carl. "Selling Them the Rope: Business and the Soviets." *Commentary* 51 (April 1979): 35-45.

Gladwell, Malcolm. "A National Interest in Global Markets." *Insight* [magazine supplement to *Washington Times*], 29 June 1987, 9-14.

Goldman, Marshall I. "Western Technology in the Soviet Union: What Happens to It?" In *Selling the Rope to Hang Capitalism?*, eds. Charles M. Perry and Robert L. Pfaltzgraff, Jr., 75-80. London: Pergamon-Brassey's, 1987.

Goodman, Seymour, E. "High-Speed Computers of the Soviet Union." *Computer*, September 1988.

__. "Technology Transfer and the Development of the Soviet Computer Industry." In *Trade, Technology, and Soviet-American Relations*, ed. Bruce Parrott, 117-40. Bloomington, IN: Indiana University Press, 1985.

Gordon, Lincoln. *Eroding Empire*. Washington, DC: The Brookings Institution, 1987.

__. "Interests and Policies in Eastern Europe: The View from Washington." In *Eroding Empire*, ed. Lincoln Gordon, 67-128. Washington, DC: The Brookings Institution, 1987.

Gordon, James K. "Three Agencies Will Cooperate To Cut Export License Delays." *Aviation Week and Space Technology* 122 (6 May 1985): 104-06, 111.

__. "Export Controls Hampering Sale of U.S. High Technology Products," *Aviation Week and Space Technology*, 15 December 1986, p. 88.

Gould, Stephen B. "The Role of Foreign Nationals in U.S. Science and Engineering." In *Balancing the National Interest*, Working Papers, ed. National Academy of Sciences, 4-21. Washington, DC: National Academy Press, 1987.

Gray, James A. "Machine Tools: Exporting for Survival." In *Common Sense in U.S.-Soviet Trade*, eds. Margaret Chapman and Carl Marcy, 133-38. Washington, DC: American Committee on East-West Accord, August 1983.

Greenstein, Ruth L. "Federal Contractors and Grantees: What Are Your First Amendment Rights?" *Jurimetrics Journal* 24 (Spring 1984). Reprinted in *National Security Controls and University Research: Selected Readings*, ed. David A. Wilson, 73-84. Prepared by the Association of American Universities for the Department of Defense-University Forum. Washington, DC: Association of American Universities, 1987.

___. "National Security Controls on Scientific Information." *Jurimetrics Journal* 23 (Fall 1982): 50-58.

Griessebach, G.A. "East-West Trade: A European Perspective." In *The Politics of East-West Trade*, ed. Gordon B. Smith, 237-45. Westview Special Studies in International Relations. Boulder, CO: Westview Press, 1984.

Guillaume, Jean-Marie. "A European View of East-West Trade in the 1980s." In *Economic Relations with the USSR*, ed. Abraham S. Becker, 135-54. Lexington, MA: D.C. Heath and Company, 1983.

Gustafson, Thane. *Selling the Russians the Rope? Soviet Technology Policy and U.S. Export Controls*. Prepared for the Defense Advanced Research Projects Agency. Santa Monica, CA: RAND Corp., April 1981.

Haagsma, Auke. "Export Controls and the Single European Market." *Europe* 274 (March 1988): 16-17.

Hanson, Philip. *Soviet Industrial Espionage: Some New Information*. RIIA Discussion Papers, no. 1. London: Royal Institute of International Affairs, 1987.

___. *Western Economic Statecraft in East-West Relations*. Chatham House Papers, no. 40. London: Routledge and Kegan Paul, 1988.

Harding, Harry, and Ed. A. Hewett. "Socialist Reforms and the World Economy." In *Restructuring American Foreign Policy*, ed. John D. Steinbruner, 158-84. Washington, DC: The Brookings Institution, 1989.

Hardt, John P. "Changing Perspectives Toward the Normalization of East-West Commerce." In *Controlling East-West Trade and Technology Transfer: Power, Politics, and Policies*, ed. Gary K. Bertsch, 347-68. Durham, NC: Duke University Press, 1988.

___. "Gorbachev's Domestic Economic Strategy and East-West Commercial Relations." In *Selling the Rope to Hang Capitalism?*, eds. Charles M. Perry and Robert L. Pfaltzgraff, Jr., 25-59. London: Pergamon-Brassey's, 1987.

Harrison, Michael M. *The Reluctant Ally*. Baltimore, MD: Johns Hopkins Press, 1981.

Hassner, Pierre. "Recurrent Stresses, Resilient Structures." In *The Atlantic Alliance and Its Critics*, eds. Robert W. Tucker and Linda Wrigley, 61-128. New York: Praeger, 1983.

___. "The View from Paris." In *Eroding Empire*, ed. Lincoln Gordon, 188-231. Washington, DC: The Brookings Institution, 1987.

Hebditch, David, and Nick Anning. "Soviet Sting Sours." *Datamation* 31 (15 June 1985): 34-44.

Hein, Werner. "Economic Embargoes and Individual Rights Under German Law." *Law and Policy in International Business* 15 (1983): 401-23.

"High-tech Trade Caught in Red Tape." *New Scientist* 111 (24 July 1986): 21.

Hill, John D. "Controlling East-West Trade: The U.S. Vs Western Europe." MA thesis, American University, 1986.

Hill, Malcolm R. "East-West Technology Transfer: The British Experience." *Review of Socialist Law* 4 (1988): 331-61.

Hirschhorn, Eric. *Controls on Exports*. Law and Practice of United States

Regulation of International Trade, ed. Charles R. Johnston, Jr., no. 9. New York: Oceana Publications, Inc., June 1987.

Hoffmann, Stanley. "Gaullism By Any Other Name." *Foreign Policy* 57 (Winter 1984-85): 38-57.

Hunnings, Neville March. "Legal Aspects of Technology Transfer to Eastern Europe and the Soviet Union." In *Technology Transfer and East-West Relations*, ed. Mark E. Schaffer, 146-69. London: Croom Helm, 1985.

Huntington, Samuel P. "Trade, Technology, and Leverage: Economic Diplomacy." *Foreign Policy* 32 (Fall 1978): 63-80.

Jacobsen, Hanns-D. "East-West Trade and Export Controls: The West German Perspective." In *Controlling East-West Trade and Technology Transfer: Power, Politics, and Policies*, ed. Gary K. Bertsch, 159-82. Durham, NC: Duke University Press, 1988.

___. *Security Implications of Inner-German Economic Relations*. Woodrow Wilson International Center for Scholars, International Security Studies Program. Working Papers, no. 77. Washington, DC: 27 August 1986.

___. "The Special Case of Inter-German Relations." In *Economic Warfare or Detente?*, eds. Reinhard Rode and Hanns D. Jacobsen, 120-27. International Perspectives on Security Series, no. 1. Boulder, CO: Westview Press, 1985.

Joffe, Josef. "The View From Bonn: The Tacit Alliance." In *Eroding Empire*, ed. Lincoln Gordon, 129-87. Washington, DC: The Brookings Institution, 1987.

Joyce, Christopher. "Technology Transfer Through the Iron Curtain." *New Scientist* 111 (14 August 1986): 39-42.

Kaufman, Richard F. "Industrial Modernisation and Defense in the Soviet Union." In *The Soviet Economy: A New Course?*, NATO Colloquium, 1-3 April 1987, ed.Reiner Weichhardt, 247-61. Brussels: North Atlantic Treaty Organization, 1988.

Kiep, Walther Leisler. "The New Deutschlandpolitik." *Foreign Affairs* 63 (Winter 1984-85): 316-29.

Kiser, John W. "How the Arms Race Really Helps Moscow." *Foreign Policy* 60 (Fall 1985): 40-51.

Klitgaard, Robert E. "Sending Signals." *Foreign Policy* 32 (Fall 1978): 103-06.

Kuchment, Mark. "Active Technology Transfer and the Development of Soviet Microelectronics." In *Selling the Rope to Hang Capitalism?*, eds. Charles M. Perry and Robert L. Pfaltzgraff, Jr., 60-69. London: Pergamon-Brassey's, 1987.

Labbe, Marie-Helene. "Controlling East-West Trade in France." In *Controlling East-West Trade and Technology Transfer: Power, Politics, and Policies*, ed. Gary K. Bertsch, 183-203. Durham, NC: Duke University Press, 1988.

Lam, Margaret J. "Restrictions on Technology Transfer Among Academic Researchers: Will Recent Changes in the Export Control System Make a Difference?" *Journal of College and University Law* 13 (Winter 1986): 311-34.

Lamb, John. "US and Britain Tangle over Supercomputers." *New Scientist* 110 (29 May 1986): 18.

Langenberg, Donald L. "Secret Knowledge and Open Inquiry." *Society* 2 (July-

August 1986): 9-12.

Lebedoff, Geric, and Caroline Raievski. "A French Perspective on the United States Ban on the Soviet Gas Pipeline Equipment." *Texas International Law Journal* 18 (Summer 1983): 483-507.

Lellouche, Pierre. "Does NATO Have a Future?" In *The Atlantic Alliance and Its Critics*, eds. Robert W. Tucker and Linda Wrigley, 129-54. New York: Praeger, 1983.

Lindstrom, Talbot S. "Devising Fair and Effective Technology-Export Controls." *Defense Management Journal* 21 (First Quarter, 1985): 2-7.

Long, Janice R. "Scientific Freedom: Focus of National Security Controls Shifting." *Chemical and Engineering News* 63 (1 July 1985): 7-11.

Long, William J. "The Executive, Congress, and Interest Groups in U.S. Export Control Policy: The National Organization of Power." In *Controlling East-West Trade and Technology Transfer: Power, Politics, and Policies*, ed. Gary K. Bertsch, 27-62. Durham, NC: Duke University Press, 1988.

Lord Saint Brides. "Foreign Policy of Socialist France." *Orbis* 26 (Spring 1982): 35-47.

Lowe, A. V. *Extraterritorial Jurisdiction: An Annotated Collection of Legal Materials*. Cambridge, U.K.: Grotius Publications Limited, 1983.

Luks, Harold Paul. "U.S. National Security Export Controls: Legislative and Regulatory Proposals." In *Balancing the National Interest*, Working Papers, ed. National Academy of Sciences, 87-135. Washington, DC: National Academy Press, 1987.

Macdonald, Stuart. "Haemorrhage and Tourniquet: U.S. Export Controls and Industrial Espionage in High Technology." Paper presented to the Ninth International Economic History Congress held in Berne, Switzerland, August 1986.

__. "United States Export Controls and High Technology Information." Paper presented at the Royal Institute of International Affairs, London, 6 February 1987.

Machinery and Allied Products Institute. *U.S. Technology and Export Controls*. 1978.

Maier, Lutz. "Technologietransfer-Impuls fur die Ost-West-Zusammenarbeit." [Technology transfer--impulse for East-West Cooperation]. *Messemagazin International* (Leipzig), Heft 2 (1988).

Majak, R. Roger. "U.S. Export Controls: The Limits of Practicality." In *Selling the Rope to Hang Capitalism?*, eds. Charles M. Perry and Robert L. Pfaltzgraff, Jr., 172-77. London, Pergamon-Brassey's, 1987.

Mann, Paul. "Commerce Dept. Will Strengthen Monitoring of Computer Exports." *Aviation Week and Space Technology* 122 (21 January 1985): 108-09.

Marcus, Daniel. "Soviet Pipeline Sanctions: The President's Authority to Impose Extraterritorial Controls." *Law and Policy in International Business* 15 (1983): 1163-67.

Marquis, Harold L. "Export of Technology." *California Western Law Review* 20 (Spring 1984): 391-414.

Mastanduno, Michael. "Strategies of Economic Containment: U.S. Trade Relations With the Soviet Union." *World Politics* 37 (July 1985): 503-31.

___. "Technological Revolution and East-West Relations: Is There a Future for COCOM?" Discussion paper presented for the Aspen Institute Berlin East-West Study Group meeting on *East-West Economic, Technological, and Ecological Cooperation Within a "European House"* held at Budapest, Hungary, 15-19 March 1989.

McIlvaine, William B., Jr. "Reaction of the Private Sector to U.S. Foreign Trade Policies Towards the Soviet Union and Eastern Europe." In *The Politics of East-West Trade*, ed. Gordon B. Smith, 199-208. Westview Special Studies in International Relations. Boulder, CO: Westview Press, 1984.

McIntyre, John R. "The Distribution of Power and the Interagency Politics of Licensing East-West High Technology Trade." In *Controlling East-West Trade and Technology Transfer: Power, Politics, and Policies*, ed. Gary K. Bertsch, 97-133. Durham, NC: Duke University Press, 1988.

McIntyre, John R., and Richard T. Cupitt. "East-West Strategic Trade Control: Crumbling Consensus?" *Survey: A Journal of East and West Studies* 25 (Spring 1980): 81-108.

Merciai, Patrizio. "The Euro-Siberian Gas Pipeline Dispute- A Compelling Case For the Adaptation of Jurisdictional Codes of Conduct." *Maryland Journal of International Law and Trade* 8 (Spring-Summer 1984): 1-52.

Meyerson, Adam. "The Ever-Present Danger." *Policy Review* 49 (Summer 1989): 7-12.

Miller, Mark E. "The Role of Western Technology in Soviet Strategy." *Orbis* 22 (Fall 1978): 539-68.

Moisi, Dominique. "Mitterrand's Foreign Policy: The Limits of Continuity." *Foreign Affairs* 60 (Winter 1981-82): 347-57.

Moreton, Edwina. "The View From London." In *Eroding Empire*, ed. Lincoln Gordon, 232-68. Washington, DC: The Brookings Institution, 1987.

National Academy of Sciences. *Balancing the National Interest*. Washington, DC: National Academy Press, 1987.

___. *Finding Common Ground: U.S. Export Controls in a Changed Global Environment*. Washington, DC: National Academy Press, 1991.

___. *Scientific Communication and National Security: A Report Prepared by the Panel on Scientific Communication and National Security*. Washington, DC: National Academy Press, 1982.

National Research Council. *Global Trends in Computer Technology and Their Impact on Export Control*. Washington, DC: National Academy Press, 1988.

Nau, Henry R. "Export Controls and Free Trade: Squaring the Circle in COCOM." In *Controlling East-West Trade and Technology Transfer: Power, Politics, and Policies*, ed. Gary K. Bertsch, 390-416. Durham, NC: Duke University Press, 1988.

___. "Trade and Deterrence." *The National Interest* 7 (Spring 1987): 48-60.

___. "The West-West Dimensions of East-West Economic Relations." In *Selling the*

Rope to Hang Capitalism?, eds. Charles M. Perry and Robert L. Pfaltzgraff, Jr., 204-15. London: Pergamon-Brassey's, 1987.

Nollen, Stanley D. "The Case of John Brown Engineering and the Soviet Gas Pipeline." In *Export Controls*, ed. Michael R. Czinkota, 111-42. New York: Praeger, 1984.

Notzold, Jurgen, and Hendrik Roodbeen. "The European Community and COCOM: The Exclusion of an Interested Party." In *After the Revolutions: East-West Trade and Technology Transfer in the 1990s*, eds. Gary K. Bertsch, Heinrich Vogel, and Jan Zielonka, 119-39. Boulder, CO: Westview Press, 1991.

Olmer, Lionel. "National Security Export Controls in the Reagan Administration." In *Selling the Rope to Hang Capitalism?*, eds. Charles M. Perry and Robert L. Pfaltzgraff, Jr., 155-59. London: Pergamon-Brassey's, 1987.

Otteman, Scott. "Gejdenson Said to be Considering EAA 'Sunset Provision' to Spur Decontrol." *Inside U.S. Trade* 8 (30 March 1990): 3.

Parker, Phillip A. "The Challenge of Industrial Espionage." In *Selling the Rope to Hang Capitalism?*, eds. Charles M. Perry and Robert L. Pfaltzgraff, Jr., 178-81. London: Pergamon-Brassey's, 1987.

Pattison, Joseph E. "Extraterritorial Enforcement of the Export Administration Act." In *Export Controls*, ed. Michael R. Czinkota, 87-102. New York. Praeger, 1984.

Perle, Richard N. "The Strategic Impact of Technology Transfers." In *Selling the Rope to Hang Capitalism?*, eds. Charles M. Perry and Robert L. Pfaltzgraff, Jr., 3-9. London: Pergamon-Brassey's, 1987.

___. "The Strategic Implications of West-East Technology Transfer." In *The Conduct of East-West Relations in the 1980s, Part II*, IISS Annual Conference Papers. *Adelphi Papers*, no. 190. London: The International Institute for Strategic Studies, Summer 1984: 20-27.

Perry, Charles M., and Robert L. Pfaltzgraff, Jr. "West-West Technology Transfer: Implications for U.S. Policy." In *Selling the Rope to Hang Capitalism?*, eds. Charles M. Perry and Robert L. Pfaltzgraff, Jr., 219-34. London: Pergamon-Brassey's, 1987.

Pipes, Richard. "Paper Perestroika." *Policy Review* 47 (Winter 1989): 14-20.

Prestowitz, Jr., Clyde V. *Trading Places: How We Allowed Japan to Take the Lead*. New York: Basic Books, Inc., 1988.

Price, Robert. "COCOM After 35 Years: Reaffirmation or Reorganization?" In *Selling the Rope to Hang Capitalism?*, eds. Charles M. Perry and Robert L. Pfaltzgraff, Jr., 195-200. London: Pergamon-Brassey's, 1987.

Quigley, Kevin F. F., and William J. Long. "Export Controls: Moving Beyond Economic Containment." *World Policy Journal* (Winter 1990): 165-87.

Rice, Sherry C. "Technology Management as an Alliance Issue: A Review of the Literature." *Washington Quarterly* 13 (Winter 1990): 219-35.

Root, William A. "COCOM: An Appraisal of Objectives and Needed Reforms." In *Controlling East-West Trade and Technology Transfer: Power, Politics, and Policies*, ed. Gary K. Bertsch, 417-41. Durham, NC: Duke University Press,

1988.

___. "Trade Controls That Work." *Foreign Policy* 56 (Fall 1984): 61-80.

Root, William A., Solvieg B. Spielmann, and Felice A. Kaden. "A Study of Foreign Export Control Systems." In *Balancing the National Interest*, Working Papers, ed. National Academy of Sciences, 206-48. Washington, DC: National Academy Press, 1987.

Rosenthal, Douglas E., and William M. Knighton. *National Laws and International Commerce: The Problem of Extraterritoriality*. Chatham House Papers, no. 17. London: Routledge and Kegan Paul, 1982.

Royal Institute of International Affairs. *Conference Proceedings of the Strategic Export Controls Conference*, held in London, 19 November 1987. Available from RIIA.

Schneider, William, Jr. "Technology Transfers and U.S. Foreign Policy: Challenges and Opportunities." In *Selling the Rope to Hang Capitalism?*, eds. Charles M. Perry and Robert L. Pfaltzgraff, Jr., 83-87. London: Pergamon-Brassey's, 1987.

Schweigler, Gebhard. "The Domestic Setting of West German Foreign Policy." In *The Soviet Problem in American- German Relations*, eds. Uwe Nerlich and James A. Thomson, 21-62. New York: Crane Russak, 1985.

Sejna, Jan. "Soviet and East European Acquisition Efforts: An Inside View." In *Selling the Rope to Hang Capitalism?*, eds. Charles M. Perry and Robert L. Pfaltzgraff, Jr., 70-74. London: Pergamon-Brassey's, 1987.

Shattuck, John, and Muriel Morisey Spence. *Government Information Controls: Implications for Scholarship, Science and Technology*. Washington, DC: Association of American Universities, March 1988.

Sloan, Stanley R. *NATO's Future*. Washington, DC: National Defense University Press, 1985.

Smith, Gordon B. "Controlling East-West Trade in Japan." In *Controlling East-West Trade and Technology Transfer: Power, Politics, and Policies*, ed. Gary K. Bertsch, 137-58. Durham, NC: Duke University Press, 1988.

___. "The Politics of East-West Trade." In *The Politics of East- West Trade*, ed. Gordon B. Smith, 1-32. Westview Special Studies in International Relations. Boulder, CO: Westview Press, 1984.

Spero, Joan Edelman. *The Politics of International Economic Relations*. 2nd ed. New York: St. Martin's Press, 1981.

Stankovsky, Jan, and Hendrik Roodbeen. "Export Controls Outside COCOM." In *After the Revolutions: East-West Trade and Technology Transfer in the 1990s*, eds. Gary K. Bertsch, Heinrich Vogel, and Jan Zielonka, 71-91. Boulder, CO: Westview Press, 1991.

Stebbings, Robert Y. "Export Controls: Extraterritorial Conflict- The Dilemma of the Host Country Employee." *Case Western Reserve Journal of International Law* 19 (1987): 303-41.

Stent, Angela E. "East-West Economic Relations and the Western Alliance." In *Trade, Technology, and Soviet-American Relations*, ed. Bruce Parrott, 283-323.

Bloomington, IN: Indiana University Press, 1985.

__. "East-West Trade and Technology Transfer: The West's Search for Consensus." *The World Today* 40 (November 1984): 452-62.

__. *From Embargo to Ostpolitik.* Cambridge, U.K.: Cambridge University Press, 1981.

Sundelius, Bengt, ed. *The Neutral Democracies and the New Cold War.* Boulder, CO: Westview Press, 1987.

Sutton, Antony C. *Western Technology and Soviet Economic Development.* 3 vols. Stanford, CA: Hoover Institution Press, 1968-73.

__. *National Suicide: Military Aid to the Soviet Union.* New Rochelle, NY: Arlington House, 1973.

Thornton, Judith A. *A New Export Regime For Information Technologies.* Foreign Policy Institute, Johns Hopkins University, Foreign Policy Briefs, no. 19. Washington, DC: Johns Hopkins Foreign Policy Institute, November 1988.

Treverton, Gregory. "West Germany and the Soviet Union." In *Western Approaches to the Soviet Union,* ed. Michael Mandelbaum, 1-23. New York: Council on Foreign Relations, 1988.

Trewhitt, Henry, et al. "Bush's Bold Bid to Rescue NATO." *U.S. News and World Report* 106 (12 June 1989): 26-29.

Ullman, Richard H. "The Covert French Connection." *Foreign Policy* 75 (Summer 1989): 3-33.

Van Cook, Arthur F. "Checks on Technology Transfer: The Defense Stakes Are High." *Defense Management Journal* 21 (Fall Quarter 1985): 9-15.

Vogel, Heinrich. "East-West Trade and Technology Transfer Reconsidered." In *After the Revolutions: East-West Trade and Technology Transfer in the 1990s,* eds. Gary K. Bertsch, Heinrich Vogel, and Jan Zielonka, 171-85. Boulder, CO: Westview Press, 1991.

__. "The Gorbachev Challenge: To help or Not to Help?" Revised version of a paper presented to the conference on "The Western Community and the Gorbachev Challenge." Organized by the Atlantic Association Luxembourg-Harvard held in Luxembourg, 19-21 December 1988.

__. "Western Security and the Eastern Bloc Economy." *Washington Quarterly* 7 (Spring 1984): 42-50.

von Nordheim, Manfred. "Technology Transfer and Alliance Relations: A West German Perspective." In *Selling the Rope to Hang Capitalism?,* eds. Charles M. Perry and Robert L. Pfaltzgraff, Jr., 201-03. London: Pergamon-Brassey's, 1987.

Vorona, Jack. "Technology Transfer and Soviet Military R&D." In *Selling the Rope to Hang Capitalism?,* eds. Charles M. Perry and Robert L. Pfaltzgraff, Jr., 16-22. London: Pergamon-Brassey's, 1987.

Walkinsky, Louis J. "Coherent Defense Strategy: The Case for Economic Denial." *Foreign Affairs* 61 (Winter 1982-83): 271-92.

Wallerstein, Michael B. "Scientific Communication and National Security in 1984." *Science* 224 (4 May 1984): 460-66.

Wallerstein, Michael B., and Stephen B. Gould. "A Delicate Balance: Scientific Communication vs. National Security." *Issues in Science and Technology* 4 (Fall 1987): 42-46.

Wellman, David A. *A Chip in the Curtain.* Washington, DC: National Defense University Press, 1989.

Whyman, William E. *Strategic Export Controls: Responses to Changing Markets and Technology.* RIIA Discussion Papers, no. 6. London: The Royal Institute of International Affairs, 1988.

Wilczynski, J. "Strategic Embargo in Perspective." *Soviet Studies* 19 (July 1967): 74-86.

Wildhaber, Luzius. "The Continental Experience." In *Extra-territorial Application of Laws and Responses Thereto*, ed. Cecil J. Olmstead, 63-69. Oxford: International Law Association and ESC Publishing Limited, 1984.

Wiles, Peter. "Is an Anti-Soviet Embargo Desirable or Possible?" In *The Conduct of East West Relations in the 1980s, Part II.* IISS Annual Conference Papers. *Adelphi Papers*, no. 190. London: The International Institute for Strategic Studies (Summer 1984): 37-50.

Willis, F. Roy. *The French Paradox.* Stanford, CA: Hoover Institution Press, 1982.

Wilson, David A. "Federal Control of Information in Academic Science." *Jurimetrics Journal* 27 (Spring 1987). Reprinted in *National Security Controls and University Research: Selected Readings*, ed. David A. Wilson, 105-16. Prepared by the Association of American Universities for the Department of Defense-University Forum. Washington, DC: Association of American Universities, 1987.

__. "National Security Control of Technological Information." *Jurimetrics Journal* 25 (Winter 1985). Reprinted in *National Security Controls and University Research: Selected Readings*, ed. David A. Wilson, 85-103. Prepared by the Association of American Universities for the Department of Defense-University Forum. Washington, DC: Association of American Universities, 1987.

Woodward, Patricia L. "Commerce Simplifies Export Licensing." *Business America*, 8 June 1987, 2-10.

Woolcock, Stephen. "Great Britain." In *Economic Warfare or Detente?*, eds. Reinhard Rode and Hanns D. Jacobsen, 141-56. International Perspectives on Security Series, no. 1. Boulder, CO: Westview Press, 1985.

__. "Western Policies on East-West Trade and Technology." In *Technology Transfer and East-West Relations*, ed. Mark E. Schaffer, 188-207. London: Croom Helm, 1985.

Yergin, Angela Stent. "East-West Technology Transfer: European Perspectives." *The Washington Papers* 8 (1980).

Yergin, Daniel. *Shattered Peace: The Origins of the Cold War and the National Security State.* Boston, MA: Houghton Mifflin, 1977.

Young, Leo. "Commentary: The Control of Government-Sponsored Technical Information." *Science, Technology, and Human Values* 10 (Spring 1985): 82-86.

Zeigler, Ann. "The Siberian Pipeline Dispute and the Export Administration Act: What's Left of Extraterritorial Limits and the Act of State Doctrine?" *Houston Journal of International Law* 6 (Autumn 1983): 63-91.

INTERVIEWS, PUBLIC ADDRESSES, CONFERENCE COMMENTARY, CORRESPONDENCE

Abernathy, Wayne. Legislative Assistant, staff of Senator Phil Gramm. Interview by author, 27 May 1988, Washington, DC. Author's notes.

Beran, J. Managing Director, Berox Machine Tool Company, Inc. Interview by author, 8 November 1988, London. Author's notes.

Bertnolli, Edward C. Vice President, Professional Activities, U.S. Activities Board, Institute of Electrical and Electronics Engineers, Washington, DC, letter to Senator Patrick Leahy, Chairman, Senate Subcommittee on Technology and the Law, Washington, DC, 18 April 1988. Photocopied.

Bonker, Representative Don. Comments at a National Issues Forum on *U.S. Export Control Policy: Balancing National Security Issues and Global Competitiveness* held at The Brookings Institution, Washington, DC, 9 June 1988. Author's notes.

Bonsignore, Michael. "Balancing Competitiveness and National Security Issues: A View From American Business." Address at a National Issues Forum on *U.S. Export Control Policy: Balancing National Security Issues and Global Competitiveness* held at The Brookings Institution, Washington, DC, 9 June 1988. Author's notes.

Bush, President George. "Change in the Soviet Union." Address at Texas A&M University, 12 May 1989. Reprinted in U.S. Department of State, Bureau of Public Affairs, *Current Policy*, no. 1175. Washington, DC: U.S. GPO, 1989.

___. "Proposals for a Free and Peaceful Europe." Address at Rheingoldhalle, Mainz, Federal Republic of Germany, 31 May 1989. Reprinted in U.S. Department of State, Bureau of Public Affairs, *Current Policy*, no. 1179 (June 1989).

Carlucci, Frank. Deputy Secretary of Defense, Washington, DC, letter to William D. Carey, Executive Officer and Publisher, *Science*, no date. Reprinted in "Scientific Exchanges and U.S. National Security." *Science* 215 (8 January 1982): 140-41.

Cooper, Nick. North America Trade Policy Section, Department of Trade and Industry. Interview by author, 9 November 1988. London. Author's notes.

Copeland, John. Director, Export Administration, Motorola, Inc. Interview by author, 25 February 1988. Washington, DC. Author's notes.

Creighton, Joseph R. Vice President and Senior Legal Advisor, Harris Corporation. "EIA Testimony Before the House Foreign Affairs Subcommittee on Arms Control, International Security and Science and International Economic Policy and Trade." Washington, DC, 8 February 1990. Photocopied.

Crowe, Brian L. Commercial Minister, British Embassy. Comments at a National

Issues Forum on *U.S. Export Control Policy: Balancing National Security Issues and Global Competitiveness* held at The Brookings Institution, Washington, DC, 9 June 1988. Author's notes.

Davidson, Anstruther. Director, Office of Export Enforcement, International Trade Administration, U.S. Department of Commerce. Interview by author, 24 February 1988, Washington, DC. Author's notes.

Drucker, Jerome. Manager, Corporate Export/Trade, Digital Equipment Corp. Interview by author, 4 May 1988, Washington, DC. Author's notes.

Duff, Mike. Scientific Apparatus Makers Association. Telephone interview by author, 5 April 1990, Washington, DC. Author's notes.

Eberle, Admiral Sir James. Comments at a half-day discussion with major corporate funders of the Institute on *The Future of East-West Relations* held at the Royal Institute of International Affairs, London, 17 April 1989. Author's notes.

Eveland, Pat. Administrative Assistant, Office of Representative Bill Frenzel. Interview by author, 2 June 1988, Washington, DC. Author's notes.

Fitzsimmons, Ron. Staff of Representative Les AuCoin. Interview by author, 1 June 1988, Washington, DC. Author's notes.

Flax, Dr. Alexander. "Policies for Control of the Export of Technology: Do They Benefit American Security Interests?" Address at the American University, Washington, DC, 10 November 1987.

Franklin, Michael. Department of Trade and Industry. Interview by author, 9 November 1988, London. Author's notes.

Freedenberg, Paul. Comments at a National Issues Forum on *U.S. Export Control Policy: Balancing National Security Issues and Global Competitiveness*, held at The Brookings Institution, Washington, DC, 9 June 1988. Author's notes.

Garn, Senator Jake. Interviewed on *MacNeil-Lehrer Newshour*. Public Broadcasting Service, 28 October 1987. Author's notes.

Goate, Peter. Economist, Department of Trade and Industry. Interview by author, 9 November 1988, London. Author's notes.

Gruenberg, Martin. Staff Director, Subcommittee on International Finance and Monetary Policy, Senate Banking Committee. Interview by author, 23 May 1988, Washington, DC. Author's notes.

Hesseltine, Michael, MP. "A Strategy For Europe." Address at the Royal Institute of International Affairs, London, 23 November 1988. Author's notes.

Hirschhorn, Eric. Executive Secretary, Industry Coalition on Technology Transfer. Interview by author, 18 April 1988, Washington, DC. Author's notes.

Judd, Arden. Dresser Industries. Interview by author, 27 April 1988, Washington, DC. Author's notes.

LeMunyon, Jim. Senior Manager, Government Relations, American Electronics Association. Interview by author, 11 May 1988, Washington, DC. Author's notes.

Luc, Ambassador Robert. "The Foreign Policies of Francois Mitterrand." Address at the University of California at Santa Barbara, Santa Barbara, CA, 8 February 1983.

Mack, James H. Public Affairs Director, National Machine Tool Builders

Association, Washington, DC, letter to Representative Helen D. Bentley, Washington, DC, 21 September 1989. Photocopied.

Malim, Hugh. Assistant Director, Barclays Bank, PLC. Interview by author, 26 October 1988, London. Author's notes.

Mates, Michael, MP. Chairman, Commons Select Committee on Defence, London, to the author, London, 10 February 1989. Author's personal correspondence.

Mendelowitz, Allen. Comments at a National Issues Forum on *U.S. Export Control Policy: Balancing National Security Issues and Global Competitiveness*, held at The Brookings Institution, Washington, DC, 9 June 1988. Author's notes.

Mosbacher, Robert. Secretary of Commerce. Interview on *American Interest* [public affairs television program]. Public Broadcasting Service, 9 December 1989. Author's notes.

Nunn, Stewart. Director, Security Export Controls (Policy Unit), Branch 3, Overseas Trade Division 2, Department of Trade and Industry. Interview by author, 9 November 1988, London. Author's notes.

Park, Robert L. Director, Office of Public Affairs, American Physical Society. Interview by author, 28 June 1988, Washington, DC. Author's notes.

__. "Comments Prepared for the Export Control Policy Forum on Technical Data Export Controls," 11 February 1988. Photocopied.

Perle, Richard N. "The Making of Security Policy: Reflections on the Reagan Years." Address at King's College, London, 8 June 1989. Author's notes.

Reinsch, Bill. Chief Legislative Assistant to Senator John Heinz. Interview by author, 19 May 1988. Washington, DC. Author's notes.

Relyea, Harold C. Government Division, Congressional Research Service, Library of Congress. Interview by author, 24 June 1988, Washington, DC. Author's notes.

Reigle, Jr., Senator Don, et al. Washington, DC. Letter to President George Bush, Washington, DC, 9 February 1990. Photocopied.

Root, William A. Former Director, Bureau of East-West Trade, Department of State. Interview by author, 8 March 1988, Washington, DC. Author's notes.

Rudka, Andrzej. Deputy Director, Foreign Trade Research Institute, Warsaw. Presentation at the Center for East-West Trade Policy, University of Georgia, 10 January 1991. Athens, GA. Author's notes.

Runkle, Deborah. American Association for the Advancement of Science. Interview by author, 13 July 1988, Washington, DC. Author's notes.

Schneider, William, Jr. "East-West Relations and Technology Transfer." Address delivered by Michael B. Marks, Senior Policy Adviser for Under Secretary for Security Assistance, Science, and Technology Schneider before the Federal Bar Association in Newton, MA, 29 March 1984. Reprinted in *Department of State Bulletin* 84 (August 1984): 68-71.

Schopflen, George. "Hungary's Crisis: Change, Collapse or Reform." Address at the Royal Institute of International Affairs, London, 15 February 1989. Photocopied.

Shannon, Kevin. Electronic Industries Association, Washington, DC. Telephone interview by author, 5 April 1990. Author's notes.

Shultz, George. "Vienna Meeting: Commitment, Cooperation, and the Challenge of Compliance." Address at the closing session of the Conference on Security and Cooperation in Europe (CSCE), Vienna, 17 January 1989, rpt. in U.S. Department of State, *Current Policy* 1145 (January 1989).

Suttle, Tom. Institute For Electrical and Electronic Engineers, Inc. Interview by author, 6 July 1988. Washington, DC. Author's notes.

Tichenor, Suzanne P. Director, International Trade Affairs, Cray Research. Interview by author, 2 May 1988. Washington, DC. Author's notes.

Tovey, Sir Brian. "COCOM Restrictions, Extraterritoriality Claims and Their Impact on the Information Technology Industry." Unpublished address. Photocopied.

__. Defence and Political Adviser, Plessey Electronic Systems Limited, former Director-General, Government Communications Headquarters. Interview by author, 15 December 1988. London. Author's notes.

Urban, Ann. Computer and Business Equipment Manufacturer's Association, Washington, DC. Telephone interview by author, 13 April 1990. Author's notes.

Wallerstein, Mitchel B. Associate Executive Director, Office of International Affairs, National Research Council. Interview by author, 22 July 1988, Washington, DC. Author's notes.

Walsh, John. Minority Staff Economist, Senate Committee on Banking, Housing, and Urban Affairs, Subcommittee on International Finance and Monetary Policy. Interview by author, 7 June 1988. Washington, DC. Author's notes.

Wendt, Allen. Comments at a National Issues Forum on *U.S. Export Control Policy: Balancing National Security Issues and Global Competitiveness*, held at The Brookings Institution, Washington, DC, 9 June 1988. Author's notes.

__. "U.S. Stance Toward the Soviet Union on Trade and Technology." Address before the Houston Club, Houston, Texas, 27 October 1988, rpt. in U.S. Department of State, *Current Policy*, 1128 (November 1988).

Willenbrach, F. Karl. "Role of Professional Communications in U.S. Technological Progress." Address at the AAAS/IEEE Congressional Seminar "Information Controls and Technological Competitiveness," Washington, DC, 30 January 1986. Photocopied.

Not-for-attribution interview by author, 2 March 1989. Advisor on security affairs, Social Democratic Party. Bundeshaus, Bonn. Author's notes.

Not-for-attribution conversation with author, June 1988. CIA analyst. Washington, DC. Author's notes.

Not-for-attribution interview by author, 3 November 1988. Foreign and Commonwealth Office, London. Author's notes.

Not-for-attribution interview by author, 8 June 1989. Foreign and Commonwealth Office, London. Author's notes.

Not-for-attribution interviews by author, 1, 3 March 1989. Foreign Ministry, Bonn. Author's notes.

Not-for-attribution interview by author, 31 October 1988. Ministry of Defence, London. Author's notes.

Not-for-attribution interview by author, 2 March 1989. Ministry of Defense, Bonn.

Author's notes.

Not-for-attribution interview by author, 1 March 1989. Ministry of Economics, Bonn. Author's notes.

Not-for-attribution interview by author, 2 February 1988. U.S. Department of Commerce, Washington, DC. Author's notes.

Not-for-attribution interview by author, 9 March 1988. U.S. Department of Commerce, Washington, DC. Author's notes.

Not-for-attribution interview by author, 14 March 1988. U.S. Department of Commerce, Washington, DC. Author's notes.

Not-for-attribution interview by author, 23 February 1988. U.S. Department of State, Bureau of Economic and Business Affairs, Washington, DC. Author's notes.

Not-for-attribution interview by author, 31 January 1989. West German government official, London. Author's notes.

Not-for-attribution interview by author, 8 March 1989. Bundesinstitut fur Ostwissenschaftliche und Internationale Studien, Cologne. Author's notes.

Not-for-attribution interview by author, 17 October 1988. East European Trade Council, London. Author's notes.

Not-for-attribution interview by author, 24 June 1988. Electronics association representative, Washington, DC. Author's notes.

Not-for-attribution interview by author, 18 April 1988. Industry association representative, Washington, DC. Author's notes.

Not-for-attribution interview by author, 6 March 1989. Ost-Ausschuss der Deutschen Wirtschaft [Eastern Committee], Cologne. Author's notes.

Not-for-attribution interview by author, 11 November 1988. Representative of a major British computer firm, London. Author's notes.

Not-for-attribution interview by author, 29 November 1988. Representative of a major U.S. electronics subsidiary, London. Author's notes.

Not-for-attribution interview by author, 18 May 1988. Representative of a U.S. computer firm, Washington, DC. Author's notes.

Not-for-attribution interview by author, 17 March 1988. Representative of a U.S. electronics firm, Arlington, VA. Author's notes.

Not-for-attribution interview by author, 2 December 1988. Representative of a U.S. office machines subsidiary, London. Author's notes.

Not-for-attribution interview by author, 24 June 1988. Representative of a U.S. electronics trade association, Washington, DC. Author's notes.

Not-for-attribution interview by author, 14 April 1988. U.S. Chamber of Commerce, Washington, DC. Author's notes.

Not-for-attribution telephone interview by author. Senior Manager [name unknown], Government Relations, American Electronics Association, Washington, DC. 5 April 1990. Author's notes.

GOVERNMENT DOCUMENTS, OFFICIAL REPORTS

Ahearn, Raymond, and Ronald O'Rourke. *Toshiba-Kongsberg Technology Diversion: Issues For Congress.* U.S. Library of Congress, Congressional Research Service, Issue Brief no. IB87184. Washington, DC, 9 October 1987.

Bundesrepublik Deutschland. Statistisches Bundesamt. *Warenverkehr mit der Deutschen Democratischen Republik und Berlin (Ost)*, Fachserie 6, Reihe 6 (Jahreshefte und Monatshaft Dezember 1987). Weisbaden, Federal Republic of Germany: Statistisches Bundesamt, 1988.

Congressional Information Service, Inc. *Annual Abstracts.* Washington, DC: Congressional Information Service, Inc.

__. *Annual Index.* Washington, DC: Congressional Information Service, Inc.

__. *CIS/Index* (Index, Abstracts). Washington, DC: Congressional Information Service, Inc.

__. *Four Year Cumulative Index.* Washington, DC: Congressional Information Service, Inc.

Drammen [Norway] Police Department. *Report. Investigation of the Transfer of Technology from Kongsberg Vaapenfabrik to the Soviet Union*, 14 October 1987. Photocopy.

European Parliament. *Resolution Adopted 21.2.86 on Technology Transfer*, PE 103.484. Photocopied.

Finan, William F., Perry D. Quick, and Karen M. Sandberg. *The U.S. Trade Position in High Technology: 1980-1986.* A Report for The Joint Economic Committee, United States Congress, October 1986. Photocopied.

Gould, Stephen B. "National Security Controls on Technology: In Search of a Consensus." In *U.S. Export Control Policy and Competitiveness*, eds. John P. Hardt and Jean F. Boone, 125-31. U.S. Library of Congress. Congressional Research Service. No. 87-388S, 30 April 1987.

Hardt, John P and Jean F. Boone, eds. *U.S. Export Control Policy and Competitiveness.* Congressional Research Service Report No. 87-388 S. Washington, DC: Congressional Research Service, 30 April 1987.

__. *U.S.-U.S.S.R. Commercial Relations: Issues in East-West Trade.* Congressional Research Service, U.S. Library of Congress, Issue Brief, no. IB86020. Washington, DC: U.S. GPO, 24 March 1987.

Harrison, Glennon J., ed. *East-West Trade and the Congress.* Proceedings of a CRS Seminar. U.S. Library of Congress, Congressional Research Service, CRS Report for Congress no. 90-529E. Washington, DC, 15 November 1990.

Harrison, Glennon J., and George Holliday. *Export Controls.* U.S. Library of Congress, Congressional Research Service, Issue Brief no. IB91064. Washington, DC, 1 May 1992.

__. *Export Controls, 1990.* U.S. Library of Congress, Congressional Research Service, Issue Brief no. IB87122. Washington, DC, 10 December 1990.

Hatter, Victoria L. *U.S. High Technology Trade and Competitiveness*, International Trade Administration. U.S. Department of Commerce. Washington, DC: U.S.

GPO, February 1985.

Holliday, George, and Glennon J. Harrison. *Export Controls*. U.S. Library of Congress, Congressional Research Service, Issue Brief no. IB87122, 15 April 1987.

International Monetary Fund. *Direction of Trade Statistics Yearbook 1987.* Washington, DC: International Monetary Fund, 1987.

__. *Direction of Trade Statistics.*

Jackson, Senator Henry M. "Technology Transfer Policy- The High Stakes." *Congressional Record*, vol. 128, no. 12 (11 February 1982), S769-73.

Mastanduno, Michael. "CoCOM and the Special Responsibilities of the U.S." In *U.S. Export Control Policy and Competitiveness*, eds. John P. Hardt and Jean F. Boone, 111-22. U.S. Library of Congress, Congressional Research Service, no. 87-388S, 30 April 1987.

Metten, Alman. "Report Drawn Up on Behalf of the Committee on Energy, Research and Technology on Technology Transfer." European Parliament, *Report*, no. A 2-99/85 (30 September 1985).

Pregelj, Vladimir N. *U.S. Commercial Relations With Communist Countries: Chronology of Significant Actions Since World War II, and Their Present Status.* U.S. Library of Congress, Congressional Research Service, Report no. 84-67 E. Washington, DC, 30 March 1984.

Relyea, Harold C. *National Security Controls and Scientific Information.* U.S. Library of Congress, Congressional Research Service, Issue Brief no. IB82083, 17 June 1986.

Root, William A. "COCOM- A Unified System." In *U.S. Export Control Policy and Competitiveness*, eds. John P. Hardt and Jean F. Boone, 91-110. U.S. Library of Congress, Congressional Research Service, no. 87-388S, 30 April 1987.

Systems Security Steering Group. "National Policy on Protection of Sensitive, But Unclassified Information in Federal Government Telecommunications and Automated Information Systems," 29 October 1986. Photocopied.

U.K. *Parliamentary Debates* (Commons).

U.K. Parliament. House of Commons. Foreign Affairs Committee. *Eastern Europe and the Soviet Union.* Session 1988-89. Minutes of evidence. London: HMSO, 25 January 1989.

__. *UK-Soviet Relations.* Session 1984-85. Second Report, Vol. II. Session 1985-86. Minutes of Evidence and Appendices. London: HMSO, 26 March 1986.

U.K. Parliament. House of Commons. Trade and Industry Committee. *Trade With China.* Third Special Report, Vol. II. Session 1984-85. Minutes of Evidence and Appendices. London: HMSO, 11 July 1985.

__. *Trade with Eastern Europe.* Second Report. Session 1988-89. London: HMSO, 26 January 1989.

U.S. Central Intelligence Agency. *Soviet Acquisition of Western Technology*, April 1982. Photocopied.

U.S. Congress. Acts and Bills. *Omnibus Trade and Competitiveness Act of 1988.*

Public Law 100-418, 23 August 1988. Washington, DC: U.S. GPO, 1988.

U.S. Congress. General Accounting Office. *Commerce's Assessment of the Foreign Availability of Controlled Items Can Be More Effective.* GAO/NSIAD-88-71. Washington, DC: U.S. GPO, February 1988.

__. *Export Control Regulation Could Be Reduced Without Affecting National Security.* GAO/ID-82-14. Washington, DC: U.S. GPO, 26 May 1982.

__. *Export Controls: Extent of DOD Influence on Licensing Decisions.* GAO/NSIAD-89-155. Washington, DC: U.S. GPO, June 1989.

__. *Export Controls: Need to Clarify Policy and Simplify Administration.* Washington, DC: U.S. GPO, 1 March 1979.

__. *Export Licensing: Commerce-Defense Review of Applications to Certain Free World Nations.* GAO/NSIAD-86-169. Washington, DC: U.S. GPO, September 1986.

__. *Export Licensing: Number of Applications Reviewed by the Defense Department.* GAO/NSIAD-88-176FS. Washington, DC: U.S. GPO, May 1988.

__. *Exports Subject to National Security Controls.* GAO/NSIAD-84-137. Washington, DC: U.S. GPO, 15 June 1984.

__. *The Government's Role in East-West Trade - Problems and Issues.* Summary Statement of Report to the Congress by the Comptroller General of the United States. ID-76-13A. Washington, DC: U.S. GPO, 4 February 1976.

__. *Perspectives on Trade and International Payments*, ID-79-11A. Washington, DC: U.S. GPO, 10 October 1979.

U.S. Congress. House. Committee on Armed Services. Technology Transfer Panel. *Technology Transfer.* Hearings. 98th Congress, 1st session, 9, 21, 23 June, 13-14 July 1983. Washington, DC: U.S. GPO, 1984.

U.S. Congress. House. Committee on Energy and Commerce. Subcommittee on Commerce, Transportation, and Tourism. *U.S. Trade Relations With the Soviet Union.* Hearing. 99th Congress, 2nd session, 25 June 1986. Washington, DC: U.S. GPO, 1986.

U.S. Congress. House. Committee on Foreign Affairs. *U.S. Foreign Policy and the East-West Confrontation.* Historical Series. Selected Executive Session Hearings of the Committee, 1951-56, Volume XIV. Washington, DC, 1980.

U.S. Congress. House. Committee on Foreign Affairs. Subcommittee on Europe and the Middle East. *United States-Soviet Relations: 1988 (Volume I).* Hearings. 100th Congress, 2nd session, 2, 8, 25 February, 17, 28 March, 13, 20, 27 April 1988. Washington, DC: U.S. GPO, 1988.

__. *United States-Soviet Relations: 1988 (Volume II).* Hearings. 100th Congress, 2nd session, 5, 11-12 May, 27, 29 June, and 12, 14 July 1988. Washington, DC: U.S. GPO, 1988.

U.S. Congress. House. Committee on Foreign Affairs. Subcommittees on Europe and the Middle East and on International Economic Policy and Trade. *United States Trade Relations with Eastern Europe and Yugoslavia.* Hearing. 100th Congress, 1st session, 28 October 1987. Washington, DC: U.S. GPO, 1988.

__. *United States-Soviet Trade Relations.* Hearings. 100th Congress, 1st session,

14 July and 22 September 1987. Washington, DC: U.S. GPO, 1988.

U.S. Congress. House. Committee on Foreign Affairs. Subcommittee on International Economic Policy and Trade. *Export Administration Amendments Act of 1981*. Hearings and markup. 97th Congress, 1st session, 26 March, 14, 28 April, 13 May 1981. Washington, DC: U.S. GPO, 1981.

__. *Extension and Revision of the Export Administration Act of 1969*. Part I. Hearings and markup. 96th Congress, 1st session, 15, 22 February, 7-8, 14-15, 21-22, 26-28 March, 3-4, 24-26 April 1979. Washington, DC: U.S. GPO, 1979.

__. *Extension and Revision of the Export Administration Act of 1979*. Hearings. 98th Congress, 1st session, 24 February, 1, 3, 8 March, 5, 12-14, 28-29 April, 2, 4-5, 18, 25-26 May 1983. Washington, DC: U.S. GPO, 1986.

__. *Implementation of the Export Administrations Act of 1985*. Hearings. 99th Congress, 1st session, 10 October, 6 November 1985. Washington, DC: U.S. GPO, 1988.

__. *Omnibus Trade and Competitiveness Act of 1988 (Vol. II)*. Hearings. 100th Congress, 1st session, 11-12 March 1987. Washington, DC: U.S. GPO, 1988.

__. *Omnibus Trade Legislation (Vol. II)*. Hearings. 99th Congress, 2nd session, 10, 17 April 1986. Washington, DC: U.S. GPO, 1987.

U.S. Congress. House. Committee on Foreign Relations, Subcommittee on International Economic Policy and Trade. *U.S. and Multilateral Export Controls*. Hearing. 99th Congress, 1st session, 23 April 1985. Washington, DC: U.S. GPO, 1987.

U.S. Congress. House. Committee on International Relations, Subcommittee on International Trade and Commerce. *Export Licensing of Advanced Technology: A Review*. Hearings. 94th Congress, 2nd session, 11, 15, 24, 30 March 1976. Washington, DC: U.S. GPO, 1976.

U.S. Congress. House. Committee on Science and Technology, Subcommittees on Science, Research and Technology and on Investigations and Oversight. *Scientific Communications and National Security*. Hearing. 98th Congress, 2nd session, 24 May 1984. Washington, DC: U.S. GPO, 1984.

U.S. Congress. House. Committee on Science, Space, and Technology. *Export Controls, Competitiveness and International Cooperation: A Critical Review*. A Summary and Analysis of Hearings on the National Academy of Sciences Report on National Security Export Controls. Staff report. 101st Congress. 1st session, February 1989. Washington, DC: U.S. GPO, 1989.

__. *National Academy of Sciences Report on International Technology Transfer*. Hearings. 100th Congress, 1st session, 4 February, 23 April 1987. Washington, DC: U.S. GPO, 1987.

U.S. Congress. House. Committee on Science, Space, and Technology, Subcommittee on International Scientific Cooperation. *Sharing Foreign Technology: Should We Pick Their Brains?*. Hearing. 100th Congress, 2nd session, 27 April 1988. Washington, DC: U.S. GPO, 1989.

U.S. Congress. House and Senate. Committees on Foreign Affairs and Foreign Relations. *Legislation on Foreign Relations Through 1985*. Volume 2.

Washington, DC: U.S. GPO, June 1986.

U.S. Congress. Joint Economic Committee. *East European Economic Assessment: Part I- Country Studies, 1980.* 97th Congress, 1st session, 27 February 1981. Washington, DC: U.S. GPO, 1981.

U.S. Congress. Joint Economic Committee. *East European Economies: Slow Growth in the 1980s. Volume I. Economic Performance and Policy.* Selected papers. 99th Congress, 1st session, 28 October 1985. Washington, DC: U.S. GPO, 1985.

__. *East-West Technology Transfer: A Congressional Dialogue With the Reagan Administration.* 98th Congress, 2nd session, 19 December 1984. Washington, DC: U.S. GPO, 1984.

__. *Gorbachev's Economic Plans.* Volume 1. Study Papers. 100th Congress, 1st session, 23 November 1987. Washington, DC: U.S. GPO, 1987.

__. *Gorbachev's Economic Plans.* Volume 2. Study Papers. 100th Congress, 1st session, 23 November 1987. Washington, DC: U.S. GPO, November 1987.

U.S. Congress. Joint Economic Committee. Subcommittee on National Security Economics. *Allocation of Resources in the Soviet Union and China-1986.* Hearings. 100th Congress, 1st session, 19 March and 3 August 1987. Washington, DC: U.S. GPO, 1988.

U.S. Congress. Joint Economic Committee. Subcommittee on Trade, Productivity, and Economic Growth. *Prospects for Improved American-Soviet Trade.* Hearing. 99th Congress, 1st session, 9 October 1985. Washington, DC: U.S. GPO, 1986.

U.S. Congress. Office of Technology Assessment. *Holding the Edge: Maintaining the Defense Technology Base.* OTA-ISC-420. Washington, DC: U.S. GPO, April 1989.

__. *Science, Technology, and the First Amendment.* OTA-CIT-369. Washington, DC: U.S. GPO, January 1988.

__. *Technology and East-West Trade.* Washington, DC: U.S. GPO, 1979.

__. *Technology and East-West Trade: An Update.* Washington, DC: U.S. GPO, 1983.

U.S. Congress. Senate. Committee on Banking and Currency. Subcommittee on International Finance. *East-West Trade.* Part I. Hearings, 90th Congress, 2nd session, 4, 13, 27 June, 17, 24-25 July 1968. Washington, DC: U.S. GPO, 1968.

U.S. Congress. Senate. Committee on Banking, Housing, and Urban Affairs. *Enforcement of the Export Control Enforcement Act.* Hearing. 98th Congress, 2nd session, 2 April 1984. Washington, DC: U.S. GPO, 1984.

__. *Proposed Trans-Siberian Natural Gas Pipeline.* Hearing. 97th Congress, 1st session, 12 November 1981. Washington, DC: U.S. GPO, 1982.

__. *U.S. Export Control Policy and Extension of the Export Administration Act.* Part I. Hearings, 96th Congress, 1st session, 5-6 March 1979. Washington, DC: U.S. GPO, 1979.

U.S. Congress. Senate. Committee on Banking, Housing, and Urban Affairs, Subcommittee on International Finance. *U.S. Export Control Policy and*

Extension of the Export Administration Act. Part III. Hearing, 96th Congress, 1st session, 3 May 1979. Washington, DC: U.S. GPO, 1979.

U.S. Congress. Senate. Committee on Banking, Housing, and Urban Affairs. Subcommittee on International Finance and Monetary Policy. *East-West Trade and Technology Transfer.* Hearing. 97th Congress, 2nd session, 14 April 1982. Washington, DC: U.S. GPO, 1982.

__. *Export Controls.* Hearings. 100th Congress, 1st session, 12, 17 March 1987. Washington, DC: U.S. GPO, 1987.

__. *Reauthorization of the Export Administration Act.* Hearings. 98th Congress, 1st session, 2, 16 March, 14 April 1983. Washington, DC: U.S. GPO, 1983.

__. *Toshiba-Kongsberg Diversion Case.* Hearing. 100th Congress, 1st session, 17 June 1987. Washington, DC: U.S. GPO, 1987.

U.S. Congress. Senate. Committee on Foreign Relations and Library of Congress, Congressional Research Service. *The Premises of East-West Commercial Relations.* Workshop. 97th Congress, 2nd session, 14-15 December 1982. Washington, DC: U.S. GPO, 1983.

U.S. Congress. Senate. Committee on Foreign Relations. Subcommittee on International Economic Policy. *Soviet-European Gas Pipeline.* Hearing. 97th Congress, 2nd session, 3 March 1982. Washington, DC: U.S. GPO, 1982.

U.S. Congress. Senate. Committee on Governmental Affairs. Permanent Subcommittee on Investigations. *Transfer of Technology.* Hearings. 98th Congress, 2nd session, 2-3, 11-12 April 1984. Washington, DC: U.S. GPO, 1984.

__. *Transfer of United States High Technology to the Soviet Union and Soviet Bloc Nations.* Hearings. 97th Congress, 2nd session, 4-6, 11-12 May 1982. Washington, DC: U.S. GPO, 1982.

U.S. Congress. Senate. Committee on the Judiciary. Subcommittee to Investigate the Administration of the Internal Security Act and Other Internal Security Laws. *Export of Strategic Materials to the U.S.S.R. and Other Soviet Bloc Countries.* 87th Congress, 1st session, part 1, 23 October 1961. Washington, DC: U.S. GPO, 1961.

U.S. Department of Commerce. *Business America.* 8 June 1987.

U.S. Department of Commerce. Bureau of the Census. *U.S. Exports Schedule E Commodity by Country.* FT 410/ November 1988. Washington, DC: U.S. GPO, 1989.

U.S. Department of Commerce. Bureau of Export Administration. *Export Administration Annual Report FY 1986.* Washington, DC: U.S. GPO, December 1987.

__. *Export Administration Annual Report FY 1987.* Washington, DC: U.S. GPO, November 1988.

U.S. Department of Commerce. Industry and Trade Administration. *Export Administration Report.* 119th Report on U.S. Export Controls to the President and the Congress, October 1978-March 1979. Washington, DC: U.S. GPO, no date.

U.S. Department of Commerce. International Trade Administration. *Commerce Enforcement of U.S. Export Controls: The Challenge and the Response.* Revised ed., September 1986.

___. *Export Administration Annual Report FY 1980.* Washington, DC: U.S. GPO, February 1981.

___. *Export Administration Annual Report FY 1981.* Washington, DC: U.S. GPO, February 1982.

___. *Export Administration Annual Report FY 1982.* Washington, DC: U.S. GPO, February 1983.

___. *Export Administration Annual Report FY 1983.* Washington, DC: U.S. GPO, June 1984.

___. *Export Administration Annual Report FY 1984.* Washington, DC: U.S. GPO, November 1985.

___. *Export Administration Annual Report FY 1985.* Washington, DC: U.S. GPO, November 1986.

___. *1984 U.S. Foreign Trade Highlights.* Washington, DC: U.S. GPO, March 1985.

___. *1987 U.S. Foreign Trade Highlights.* Washington, DC: U.S. GPO, May 1988.

___. *United States Trade: Performance in 1985 and Outlook.* Washington, DC: U.S. GPO, October 1986.

___. *United States Trade Performance in 1987.* Washington, DC: U.S. GPO, June 1988.

U.S. Department of Commerce. International Trade Administration. Capital Goods and International Construction Sector Group. *A Competitive Assessment of the U.S. Computer-Aided Design and Manufacturing Systems Industry.* Washington, DC: U.S. GPO, February 1987.

U.S. Department of Commerce. International Trade Administration. Capital Goods and International Construction Sector Group. *A Competitive Assessment of the U.S. Robotics Industry.* Washington, DC: U.S. GPO, March 1987.

U.S. Department of Commerce. International Trade Administration. Office of Computers and Business Equipment Science and Electronics. *A Competitive Assessment of the U.S. Microcomputer Industry: Business/Professional Systems.* Washington, DC: U.S. GPO, August 1986.

U.S. Department of Defense. *Soviet Acquisition of Militarily Significant Western Technology: An Update.* Intelligence Community White Paper, September 1985.

___. *Soviet Military Power 1986.* 5th ed. Washington, DC: U.S. GPO, March 1986.

U.S. Department of Defense. Department of the Air Force. *Current News.* Special edition, *Technology Security.*

U.S. Department of Defense. Director of Defense Research and Engineering. *An Analysis of Export Control of U.S. Technology- A DOD Perspective.* A Report of the Defense Science Board Task Force on Export of U.S. Technology. No publisher, 4 February 1976.

U.S. Department of Defense. Office of the Under Secretary of Defense Acquisition.

The Militarily Critical Technologies List. Washington, DC, October 1986. Unclassified version.

U.S. Department of Defense. Office of the Under Secretary of Defense for Policy. *Assessing the Effect of Technology Transfer on U.S./Western Security.* No publisher, February 1985.

U.S. Department of Defense. Secretary of Defense. *The Technology Security Program, A Report to the 99th Congress, Second Session,* 1986.

__. *The Technology Transfer Control Program.* A Report to the 98th Congress, 2nd session, February 1984.

U.S. Department of State. *Intelligence Collection in the USSR Chamber of Commerce and Industry.* No publisher, no date.

__. *The 1958 Revision of East-West Trade Controls.* Twelfth Report to Congress. Mutual Defense Assistance Control Act of 1951. Washington, DC: U.S. GPO, April 1959.

__. *Problems of Economic Defense.* Second Report to Congress. Administrator, Mutual Defense Assistance Control Act of 1951. Washington, DC: U.S. GPO, January 1953.

__. "Results of the Senior Political Meeting on Strengthening the Coordinating Committee on Multilateral Export Controls (COCOM)." Press release, 29 January 1988.

U.S. Department of State. Foreign Operations Administration. *The Revision of Strategic Trade Controls.* Fifth Report to Congress. Mutual Defense Control Act of 1951. Washington, DC: U.S. GPO, 1954.

U.S. Department of State. International Cooperation Administration. *The Strategic Trade Control System 1948-56.* Ninth Report to Congress. Mutual Defense Assistance Control Act of 1951. Washington, DC: U.S. GPO, 1957.

U.S. International Trade Commission. *Tariff Schedules of the United States Annotated (1983).* USITC Publication 1317.

U.S. President. *Economic Report of the President.* Washington, DC: U.S. GPO, 1989.

NEWSPAPERS, NEWSLETTERS

Berlingske Tidende [Copenhagen]
Export Control News
Financial Times [London]
Financial Times [U.S. edition]
The Guardian [Manchester]
The Independent [London]
International Herald Tribune
The New York Times
The Sunday Times [London]
This Week in Germany

The Times [London]
Wall Street Journal
The Washington Post
The Washington Post National Weekly Edition

Index

ABOUT THE AUTHOR

Douglas E. McDaniel is an analyst with the Inspector General's Office of the U.S. Department of State. He earned his Ph.D. at The American University.